W9-AVG-333

Publications of the Committee on
Taxation, Resources and Economic Development

4

Proceedings of a Symposium Sponsored by the

Committee on Taxation, Resources and
Economic Development (TRED)

At the University of Wisconsin—Milwaukee, 1966

Other TRED Publications

1 *Extractive Resources and Taxation* ✓
    MASON GAFFNEY, EDITOR

2 *Property Taxation—USA*
    RICHARD W. LINDHOLM, EDITOR

3 *The Property Tax and Its Administration* ✓
    ARTHUR D. LYNN, JR., EDITOR

Land and Building Taxes

▲▲▲ *Their Effect on Economic Development*

EDITED BY
ARTHUR P. BECKER

The University of Wisconsin Press

Madison, Milwaukee, and London

1969

Published by
The University of Wisconsin Press
Box 1379, Madison, Wisconsin 53701

The University of Wisconsin Press, Ltd.
27–29 Whitfield Street, London, W.1

Printed in the United States of America by
Kingsport Press, Inc., Kingsport, Tennessee

SBN 299–05460–8; LC 70–84951

CONTRIBUTORS

Arthur P. Becker, Professor of Economics, University of Wisconsin— Milwaukee

Richard M. Bird, Associate Professor of Economics, Institute for the Quantitative Analysis of Social and Economic Policy, University of Toronto

L. L. Ecker-Racz, Assistant Director, Advisory Commission on Intergovernmental Relations

Ernest A. Engelbert, Professor of Political Science, University of California, Los Angeles

Arthur L. Grey, Jr., Chairman and Professor of Urban Planning, College of Architecture and Urban Planning, University of Washington

James Heilbrun, Assistant Professor of Economics, Columbia University

Albert T. Henley, Jones, Griswold & Henley, Attorneys-at-Law, San Jose, California

Daniel M. Holland, Professor of Finance, Alfred P. Sloan School of Management, Massachusetts Institute of Technology

Max Neutze, Senior Fellow in Charge, Urban Research Unit, The Australian National University

William G. Rhoads, Chief of Public Finance, Economic Mission of the United States in the Republic of Colombia, Agency for International Development

J. A. Stockfisch, Senior Research Associate, Member Research Council, Institute for Defense Analyses

John Strasma, Associate Professor of Economics and Director of the Chile Project, Land Tenure Center, University of Wisconsin

A. M. Woodruff, Chancellor, University of Hartford

Preface

While there seems to be general agreement that the property tax plays a significant role in economic development, there is far less agreement on the nature and importance of that role. Concern has been rising as to whether the property tax (and especially the real estate tax) acts as a possible deterrent to continued progress in economic development in general and to urban development in particular. Lack of knowledge about the property tax in the face of this rising concern has prompted the Committee on Taxation, Resources and Economic Development to direct and encourage scholarly attention to the problem.

The primary purpose of the present volume is to help fill this scholarly gap by inquiring into the nature and operation of the components of the real estate tax and how they are related to economic development. Experts in the dual disciplines of the property tax and economic development have shared in the inquiry, and their contributions have been brought together in this volume.

Part I presents a theoretical analysis of taxes on land and buildings and of their broad effect on economic development. Various micro and macro aspects of these taxes are considered in terms of their general impact on the economy. Next, their impact on certain economic problems of development is examined. Taxes on land and building values are analyzed in terms of their effect on the maintenance and rehabilitation of housing, urban renewal, metropolitan growth and planning, and investment in multiple-family housing.

Part II consists of five case studies which attempt to relate the economic development of various countries to their taxes on land and buildings. Political, economic, and social realities that influence the course of economic development in various states and countries often require the adoption of tax institutions considerably removed from what one might regard as ideal. Nevertheless, the different approaches to taxing land and building values in each country are interesting and often instructive.

This book is based primarily on papers delivered at or stimulated by the conference, "The Property Tax and Economic Development," which

vii

took place on the campus of the University of Wisconsin—Milwaukee, during 13–15 June 1966. The chapters by Ernest A. Engelbert, Albert T. Henley, and Arthur L. Grey, Jr., are based on unpublished papers delivered at earlier conferences, but were included in this volume because they strengthen and complement the other chapters. They have been brought up to date where it was found necessary to do so and have also been integrated with the other papers. John Strasma was in Chile at the time of the conference and therefore was unable to present his paper in person. It fit so well with the others, however, that it was included in Part II.

ARTHUR P. BECKER

Milwaukee, Wisconsin
February 1969

Acknowledgments

The Committee on Taxation, Resources and Economic Development (TRED) is an association of academic economists whose purpose is to stimulate research, writing, and discussion in the important but neglected field of natural resource taxation and in the relation of this taxation to such other concerns of economists as the allocation and utilization of resources, economic development, income distribution, and employment.

The committee sponsored the conference at which these papers were presented. Much is owed to the members—Arthur P. Becker (Chairman), Professor of Economics, University of Wisconsin—Milwaukee; Paul E. Alyea, Emeritus Professor of Finance, University of Alabama; Karl Falk, Professor of Economics, Fresno State College; Mason Gaffney, Professor of Economics, University of Wisconsin—Milwaukee; Harold M. Groves, Professor of Economics, University of Wisconsin; Daniel M. Holland, Professor of Finance, Massachusetts Institute of Technology; Richard W. Lindholm, Dean, School of Business Administration, University of Oregon; Arthur D. Lynn, Jr., Professor of Economics and Associate Dean of Faculties, Ohio State University; Carl McGuire, Chairman, Department of Economics, University of Colorado; and William S. Vickrey, Professor of Economics, Faculty of Political Science, Columbia University —for their common concern in the problems of taxing natural resources.

The interest and financial support of the Robert Schalkenbach Foundation in the activities of TRED are appreciated. For their steadfast support special thanks are due Albert Pleydell, president, Violetta Peterson, executive secretary, and to the directors of the foundation.

I wish to acknowledge the rare talents of Weld Carter, executive secretary of the Committee on Taxation, Resources and Economic Development. His understanding of the taxation of natural resources is exceeded only by his sensitive regard for the scholarly mind. His counsel to the committee and the editor of this book has been inspired, as well as helpful. Special appreciation is also given to Mrs. Faye Levner for her able assistance in clarifying passages, improving style, preparing figures, and typing much of the final manuscript, and to Milton R. Hoffman for his preparation of the index. Most of all I wish to express my appreciation to the contributors of this book, whose creative efforts have it possible.

Contents

Part I. Theoretical Aspects of Taxing Land and Buildings

Introduction   3

1 *Principles of Taxing Land and Buildings for
   Economic Development*   11
   ARTHUR P. BECKER

2 *The Influence of the Property Tax on Investment
   and Employment*   49
   J. A. STOCKFISCH

3 *Reforming the Real Estate Tax to Encourage Housing
   Maintenance and Rehabilitation*   63
   JAMES HEILBRUN

4 *Urban Renewal and Land Value Taxation*   81
   ARTHUR L. GREY, JR.

5 *The Political Aspects of Real Estate Taxation in Relation to
   Metropolitan Growth and Planning*   97
   ERNEST A. ENGELBERT

6 *Property Taxation and Multiple-Family Housing*   115
   MAX NEUTZE

Part II. Land and Building Taxes: Five Case Studies

Introduction   131

7 *Land Value Taxation by California Irrigation Districts*   137
   ALBERT T. HENLEY

8 *Property Taxes and Land-Use Patterns in
   Australia and New Zealand*   147
   A. M. WOODRUFF AND L. L. ECKER-RACZ

xi

9   *Property Taxation in Chile*   187
     JOHN STRASMA

10   *The Valorization Tax in Colombia: An Example for
     Other Developing Countries?*   201
     WILLIAM G. RHOADS AND RICHARD M. BIRD

11   *A Study of Land Taxation in Jamaica*   239
     DANIEL M. HOLLAND

     Conclusion   287

     Index   299

Tables

1.1	The Capitalization Effect of Taxing Land Values	35
2.1	Derivation of Asset Earnings, 1956–1966	50
2.2	Net National Product, Estimated Property Earnings, and Major Asset-Earnings Taxes, 1956–1966	51
2.3	National Wealth, by Type of Physical Assets and by Sector, 1956	52
2.4	Effective Property Tax Rates, by Major Types of Assets, 1956	55
8.1	Per Capita Governmental Receipts and Expenditures, Fiscal Year 1963	149
8.2	Local-Government Revenues in Australia, 1959–1960	150
8.3	Federal, State, and Local Tax Collections in Australia and the United States, Fiscal Year 1963	151
8.4	Local-Government Revenues in New Zealand, Fiscal Year 1963	151
8.5	Rates of Australian Commonwealth Land Tax	154
8.6	Commonwealth of Australia Land Tax Revenues, 1939–1963	156
8.7	Rates of Selected Australian State Land Taxes, 1963	157
8.8	New Zealand Land Tax Rates, 1963	158
8.9	Definitions of Unimproved Capital Value and Assessed Annual Value for Rating Purposes in the Australian States and New Zealand	159
8.10	Bases for Local Rating in Australia, 1962	168
8.11	New Zealand Local-Government Tax Systems, Fiscal Year 1964	170
8.12	Bases of Rating for Water Supply and Sewerage Purposes in Australia, Fiscal Year 1964	171
9.1	Composition of Chilean Fiscal Revenues, 1966	189
10.1	Use of Municipal Valorization Taxes, by Department, 1963	214
10.2	Importance of Municipal Valorization Tax, 1959–1963	215
10.3	Medellín: The Importance of Valorization Taxes, 1956–1966	216
10.4	Bogotá: The Importance of Valorization Taxes, 1959–1965	217
10.5	Municipal Tax Revenues Per Capita, 1963	217
11.1	Unimproved Land Valuations in Seven Parishes	254
11.2	Number, Value, and Rates of Taxation on Unimproved Land Value for Properties in St. Catherine Parish as of 1959	260
11.3	Examples of Valuations and Tax Liabilities on Old and New Bases for a Few Particular Properties	261

Figures

1.1	The Supply of Urban Land	19
1.2	The Effect of Taxing Buildings (Improvements) on Building Investment	29
1.3	The Effect on the Money and Commodity Markets of Taxing Land Values	37
1.4	The Effect on the Money and Commodity Markets of the Ad Valorem Tax on Buildings	40
1.5	The Effect on the Money and Commodity Markets of Eliminating the Ad Valorem Tax on Buildings	41
1.6	The Effect on the Money and Commodity Markets of Taxing Land Values and Eliminating the Tax on Buildings	43
1.7	The Effect on Aggregate Supply and Demand of Taxing Land and Untaxing Buildings	44
3.1	Equilibrium of the House-Operating Firm	69
3.2	Diagram of a Rental-Housing Market (Schematic)	70
11.1	Rates of Unimproved Land Value Taxation, St. Catherine Parish	259

PART I

Theoretical Aspects of Taxing
Land and Buildings

INTRODUCTION

Since World War II, economic growth and development have been elevated to the status of major economic goals and have attracted universal interest. Nations that enjoy advanced economic development want a more rapid growth to achieve a still higher level of living and sometimes to improve their relative position or to give proof of the superiority of their economic institutions. The greatest rivalry is that of Communist and non-Communist nations, but even within each of these blocks serious rivalries exist. Less well-developed countries simply want, at least for the time being, to experience as rapidly as possible sufficient economic development so as to be able to achieve minimum standards of health, comfort, and dignity for their people.

The rapidity and pattern of a country's economic growth or development depend upon the size, organization, and character of its productive resources, including improvements in the quantity and quality of factors of production and the manner in which they are put to work. Factors of production consist of the size and performance of labor in the work force, the amount of land and other national resources and their suitability and availability in meeting productivity requirements, and the quantity and productivity of such needed capital goods as tools, equipment, machinery, and buildings. Improvements in the manner of utilizing factors of production also have great bearing on economic development. Such improvements include technological advances, increases in specialization and the scale of production, and reallocations of resources or transformations of the economy.

The pattern and speed of a country's economic development is determined in large measure by its institutions. These institutions constitute the organization that in turn determines the availability, quality, and efficiency of its resources, including incentive to work, save, and invest. Public financial institutions (taxes, expenditures, and debt arrangements) are among the most influential institutions in terms of the economic role that the citizens of a country will play. Among various taxes the property tax is one of the oldest surviving taxes in the United States and other countries.

Support seems to be growing for the view that urban development, low- and middle-income housing, and even industrial development may be inhibited by the property tax. In a number of states and local govern-

3

ments as well as foreign countries, this view has already caused the passage of measures that usually reduce the property tax on a temporary or partial basis. It is assumed that such property tax concessions will hasten urban redevelopment, provide more low- and middle-income housing, and also spur industrial development.

The granting of property tax concessions and the underlying assumption that this will promote economic development raise, however, some very fundamental theoretical questions about the property tax. Foremost among these questions is whether the tax in its entirety (that is, on land, improvements, and tangible personalty) inhibits economic development. A tax abatement or subsidy that applies to land and improvements (and possibly tangible personalty) assumes, at least implicitly, that the taxes on each type of property are equally deterrents to economic development. But is this true? Does the property tax on land and improvements really have the same effect on incentive, profitability, investment opportunities, cost of land, and so on? Or are the effects different? If they are different, why? Furthermore, if the effects are different, what changes are indicated in the policy of granting equal tax abatements to all components of the property tax? These are some of the questions that Arthur P. Becker faces in Chapter 1. The first portion of his examination stays primarily within the scope and uses the tools of micro-economic analysis. In the final section of Chapter 1 Becker examines systematically the ad valorem tax on land and buildings in terms of the essential aspects of macro-economic analysis. His conclusions are summarized at the end of the chapter.

In Chapter 2 J. A. Stockfisch analyzes the influence of the property tax on investment and employment and the general interdependence of the parts of the economic system. With respect to the latter, he examines the effect of the property tax variations of different classes of property on efficiency, resource distribution, and prices of various economic activities. In this connection he presents the concept of "price-reallocation effect." A key question in his analysis is what happens to investment returns in less heavily taxed activities as well as in those more heavily taxed. Only when this question is answered, according to Stockfisch, is it possible to determine ultimately the effect of the tax on investment and employment in the economy as a whole.

Stockfisch believes that the reality of tax burdens and their income effect must be better accounted for than is presently done by the doctrine of forward shifting of taxes. It is inadequate to emphasize, as this doctrine does, that in the long run consumers will bear taxes. Not only do investors in more heavily taxed industries suffer, but investors in less heavily taxed industries do also. The price-reallocation effect causes resources to leave or avoid heavily taxed industries and move into nontaxed or less heavily taxed industries to increase their output. The result is not only lower prices for consumers of the products of less heavily taxed industries, but also lower earnings for investors in those industries. Some theorists say, moreover, that if taxes are shifted forward by inflation they produce no adverse effect upon investment and employment.

Once the effects of asset-earnings taxes on net earnings of assets are established, by applying either the investment theories of J. M. Keynes or the neoclassicists, it is possible to determine the effects on marginal efficiency of capital, investment, liquidity and time preference, interest rates, consumption, and national income. Applying Keynesian theory, Stockfisch shows that the American property tax reduces the marginal efficiency of investment (capital) from 10 percent to 8.5 percent. This reduction includes the tax on land as well as on buildings (and other improvements) and on personal property. Unfortunately, aggregate data on the land component of the property tax are not available and therefore the true burden of the property tax cannot be accounted for accurately in its influence on marginal efficiency of investment. In view of the fact that the value of aggregate improvements is several times land values, however, Stockfisch's use of aggregate property tax data as though they referred exclusively to nonland property is entirely defensible.

With the property tax lowering the marginal efficiency of investment, the level of investment spending will fall and, through the multiplier process, so will consumption spending and total income. According to Stockfisch, property taxes produce a similar effect on investment when analyzed according to the neoclassical theory of interest and investment, which relies in part on the time-preference theory. Essentially, it maintains that a tax which lowers the rate of return on investment will induce individuals to save and invest less.

Still another approach in analyzing the effect of the tax is that based on Frank H. Knight's "productivity" theory of interest. Here the elasticity of consumer demand plays a central role in determining the effect of the tax on the rate of return and investment spending. According to this theory, new taxes that reduce net asset earnings on the margin of new investment will increase the price of future dollars and discourage investment. The elasticity of demand for future dollars will determine the extent to which investment will be discouraged. The property tax, therefore, may affect investment incentive either adversely or favorably, depending upon the degree of elasticity in investment preference. Further effects may be felt upon the rate of return, depending upon the shape of the supply curve for future dollars.

Lastly, Stockfisch analyzes the effects of asset-earnings taxes on the value of assets via the capitalization process. He concludes that if all assets are taxed more or less, only those assets with excess tax burdens will find their taxes capitalized to produce lower asset values. This would seem to be the case in the short run if the supplies of various assets were equally inelastic. In the long run, however, the difference in the elasticity of supply of land and buildings should reduce the initial capitalization of the tax on buildings.

Whereas Becker and Stockfisch are concerned with general micro and macro aspects of taxes on land and buildings, the other contributors examine the effects of land and building taxes on such current problems as housing, urban renewal, and metropolitan growth and planning. These problems are found in all countries, both developed and underdeveloped, although their institutional frameworks may differ widely. The analyses presented require, however, the assumption of a money economy that is essentially oriented toward the market and with an educational level high enough to allow the administrative feasibility of taxing land, buildings, or both.

Despite the fact that in some countries (the United States, for example), the tax on land and buildings may be so high that it absorbs 16 to 20 percent of gross housing rent, no careful study has been made heretofore of the relationship of various real estate taxes, including the traditional American levy on assessed values, to the maintenance of housing quality. Yet, an important aspect of economic development is the maintenance of housing quality. In his effort to fill this gap, James Heilbrun systematically analyzes a variety of land and building taxes in terms of their effect on the three elements of housing quality. He first selects for study five varieties of property taxes, of which all but that based on net income have been or are now employed in many parts of the world. They are: (1) an ad valorem tax on assessed site value; (2) an ad valorem tax on the assessed value of site and improvements combined (the traditional American levy); (3) a proportional tax on the actual (not the assessed) gross rent of site and improvements combined; (4) a tax on the net income of site and improvements combined; and (5) any of the above combined with a tax abatement to encourage maintenance and rehabilitation.

Heilbrun further observes that housing quality depends upon the following three elements: (1) the original cost of building the structure and subsequent investment in remodeling, if any (expenditures that establish the layout and spaciousness of the apartment units and determine the kind and extent of equipment they contain); (2) the level of quality at which structure and equipment are maintained; and (3) the level of operating outlays that the owner applies to the given structure, which in turn determines the quality and extent of operating services he can offer.

After establishing this analytical framework, Heilbrun makes a comparative analysis of the effect of the five kinds of property taxes on the three elements in the quality of housing and finds only the tax on land values to be without harmful effects of any sort on housing quality.

Heilbrun is concerned, however, whether the yield of taxing land values would be sufficient to replace the revenue lost by untaxing buildings. He feels that the yield might be adequate only if tax rates were raised to confiscatory levels. If taxes on land values were raised only modestly in order to avoid the charge of inequity, the stimulus to construction might not be significant, considering the magnitude of the housing-quality problem. Nevertheless, he is willing to risk the inequity charge to a degree because he recommends the Pittsburgh type of graded tax in which the municipal tax rate on building values is only one half of that on land values. An alternative tax-policy recommendation might be a tax abatement to encourage housing rehabilitation and perhaps new construction. A third possibility would be some combination of the two (the graded tax and tax abatement).

Economic development as it applies to older urban areas has come to be called "urban renewal." It refers to three specific kinds of activities: (1) clearance and redevelopment, with a new building or other improvements; (2) rehabilitation, reconditioning, or remodeling; and (3) conservation (which includes redecorating and minor repairs). Since 1954 federal-local governmental activities in urban renewal have involved major efforts across the land. Even the friendliest observer of this direct government-action program will concede that it is not equal to the task of fighting urban decay and that other forces need to be put into the battle.

In Chapter 4 Arthur L. Grey, Jr., examines the taxing of land values in terms of achieving various urban renewal objectives, including not only the three mentioned above but also (4) the recovery of value in the area outside of project boundaries, and (5) the provision of open space. He feels that tax reform cannot be overstated as a means of accomplishing the objectives of urban renewal. Furthermore, Grey recognizes that the neutrality and efficiency of taxing land values would provide a strong stimulus in achieving the objectives of urban renewal except that of providing open spaces. Moreover, he stresses the importance of land value taxation for urban renewal because it operates to accomplish its objectives within the market system.

As to the provision of open spaces, it appears that land value taxation is ambivalent. On the one hand it may make it more costly to provide much open space in central areas where location values are generally high. On the other hand, much more space will be available for public purposes on the urban fringe without going out too far. The present property tax seems to encourage a limited amount of open space close in and a great deal of open space at a considerable distance from the downtown area.

While taxing land values can do much for urban renewal, Grey does not feel that the present federal-local program can be abandoned. He takes the view that both the land value tax and governmental activities will work together for a more effective urban renewal and that these policies should be pursued simultaneously.

Grey recognizes that land values are very suitable for taxation because they are socially created values and constitute a surplus return. He sees, however, both the land value tax and capital gains tax as important devices whereby surplus returns may be reached. While a land value tax might best tap land surpluses, he feels that nonland surpluses might best be reached through income tax reform, particularly in regard to capital gains and depreciation.

One of the greatest obstacles to rational and economical urban development is the local political fragmentation of metropolitan areas. The economic and social disorganization of metropolitan communities that results from multiple uncoordinated local governments is well known. Because the taxing of land and buildings either uniformly or differentially has a profound influence in the shaping of urban development, it is not surprising that the municipalities of a metropolis employ tax policies in carrying on their rivalry. The political-ethical requirements that taxes should not discriminate and that they must be used for a public purpose do not provide sufficient restraints to prevent the growth of metropolitan problems (caused by unwise property tax policies) that might have been avoided.

In Chapter 5 Ernest A. Engelbert observes that urban development is shaped by (1) property taxation; (2) planning and zoning; and (3) the location of public improvements, including highways. He devotes particular attention to the ways in which the real estate tax and its practice among metropolitan municipalities contribute to their collective problems.

Engelbert shows that taxpayers hold different views as to the proper role of the property tax and that these views depend upon where (in which municipality of the metropolis) the taxpayer resides, works, or holds property. Differences in viewpoints arise also between property owners and tenants. Attitudes of taxpayers also vary as to the desirability of certain types of land use. Taxpayers of a given municipality often have similar economic roles and stakes and tend to develop common viewpoints with respect to tax policy. These municipalities with their often conflicting viewpoints compete with one another to enlarge their economic base or financial advantage or to achieve their land use objectives, frequently at the expense of other municipalities.

To further its objectives a municipality utilizes a variety of financial, political, and administrative strategies. Financial strategies include various assessment practices, property classifications, exemptions, rate limits, and so on. To tell of the consequences of applying these strategies is to recite many of today's well-known urban woes: economic inefficiency and waste in land use, unbalanced urban growth and development, property tax inequities, local fiscal crises and dependency, and metropolitan fragmentation. It is interesting how much agreement can be found as to the undesirability of these consequences (except for fragmentation) by the very taxpayers who support the strategic means that produce these consequences.

In order to reduce and perhaps minimize these bad effects, the horizons of property tax policy may well be broadened. Engelbert makes several recommendations to that end. He would (1) establish a single assessment district for an entire metropolitan area and give the taxing units within the area uniform taxing power; (2) abandon state limitations on local property tax rates; and (3) emphasize the taxation of land values rather than building values. Engelbert underscores the urgency of action to alleviate problems of metropolitan development and other economic problems, for the very survival of locally controlled government is at stake.

It is generally agreed that land and building taxes have a profound effect on speculation, economic development, and housing in general. However, the possible effect of these taxes on the kind of housing, specifically multiple-family or single-family units, has received little attention. Another interesting question rarely examined is the effect that land and building taxes may have on the location of multiple-family housing; whether economic forces produced by tax policy favor multiple-family construction either in the central city or suburbs. A third neglected problem is the effect of land and building taxes on land distribution.

It is common knowledge that urbanization of sufficient magnitude and density leads eventually to the construction of multiple-family housing facilities. While multiple-family apartments are being constructed initially in several of the "new towns," this procedure is at variance with the stage of urban economic development when multiple-family apartments are constructed in most cities. Ordinarily, very little of this housing is built in the early stages of the urbanization process.

In Chapter 6 Max Neutze seeks a plausible explanation for this phenomenon. He finds the answer in the fact that multiple-family housing carries excessive investment risks because of its extreme sensitivity to possible changes in land use and the uncertainty of what the future trends in the development of the urban area will be. Accordingly, investment in single-family housing is favored because it represents the minimum loss alternative. After an urban area is well developed, the risks arising out of probable changes in land use and housing demands are far less, and the time is right for investment in multiple-family housing. In fact, it probably becomes the earliest available and safest land use in the process of redevelopment. Moreover, direct accessibility is no longer the all-important criterion for a suitable site for multiple-family housing. Indirect accessibility may be sufficient if combined with locational advantages of convenience (as for shopping) or amenities (such as nearness to open spaces).

Neutze believes that taxing land (site) values discourages speculation to a minor extent where real estate is purchased for the purpose of redevelopment. The extent to which it is discouraged depends upon the net cost of demolition, which raises slightly the cost of redevelopment compared with building on vacant land. To the new owner who acquires land after the tax is imposed, taxing land values does not increase the total cost of holding vacant land. The cost of the land to the speculator is reduced by the capitalized value of the tax. The tax on the value of land also reduces the attractiveness of land as an investment asset to persons with a low opportunity cost of capital, and increases it to those whose opportunity cost is higher. This would tend to redistribute land from the wealthy to the less wealthy. It would also discourage those large-scale developments that hope to benefit from increases in site values.

According to Neutze, the taxing of land values probably would reduce the attractiveness of large-scale developments, both single and multiple family (which would be relatively less attractive) in urban fringe growth (suburban) areas. Decreasing the attractiveness of investment in land and the discouraging of land speculation would encourage redevelopment in central urban rather than suburban areas and would also concentrate apartment development in the central areas of cities.

Neutze concludes that taxing buildings reduces both high-density development and the total volume of investment in buildings. Taxing buildings also reduces concentration in central cities because suburban land-users substitute lower-than-cost communication, transportation, and utility services for housing land that would permit closer linkages with their other activities. Each of these effects of taxing buildings tends to reduce investment in and construction of apartments more than single-family housing. Moreover, investment and construction of apartments in or near the central city are penalized most of all with a tax on buildings.

Taken as a whole, therefore, the chapters in Part I draw upon logic and deduction to determine the probable consequences on economic development of the ad valorem tax on land and buildings. Both micro- and macroeconomic analytical techniques are applied in order to determine general effects, and the effects of the tax on special problems, including aggregate investment, housing maintenance and rehabilitation, urban renewal, multiple-family housing, speculation and investment in land, and intra-metropolitan rivalry also are considered.

1 Principles of Taxing Land and Buildings for Economic Development

 ARTHUR P. BECKER

The general property tax continues to play the dominant role in local-government tax revenues despite a decline in its relative importance in total state and local tax revenues. Since local governments depend so heavily upon the property tax, it is important that the tax be improved in all possible ways, administratively and substantively. Administrative objectives and methods for improving the property tax have commanded a great deal of scholarly attention over the years. Less attention has been given to the substantive aspects of the general property tax.

Perhaps administrative improvements have been emphasized because they are easier to understand, have generated somewhat less controversy, and have proved easier to adopt than substantive changes. The substantive aspects of the property tax are far more difficult to grapple with, and some basic issues have failed to produce any agreement among economists. One of these issues is whether the real estate tax should be viewed as a whole or as separable into its components of land and buildings.[1] A related question is whether land can or should be valued separately from buildings. Still another issue is whether the incidence of the tax is on the landowner, building owner, or occupier (tenant) and the degree of this incidence under a variety of conditions. After their search for answers to these questions, such outstanding economists as Alfred Marshall, N. G. Pierson, F. Y. Edgeworth, Edwin R. A. Seligman, and Harry Gunnison Brown have drawn varied and often opposite conclusions.[2] The lack of consensus—based perhaps largely

1. Unless otherwise indicated, the terms "buildings" and "improvements" will be used interchangeably in this chapter for convenience. As a matter of fact, "improvements" is more inclusive than "buildings."

2. See Herbert A. Simon, "The Incidence of a Tax on Urban Real Property," *Quarterly Journal of Economics,* 57, no. 3 (May 1943): 398–420; reprinted in *Readings in the Economics of Taxation,* ed. Richard A. Musgrave and Carl S. Shoup (Homewood, Ill.: Richard D. Irwin), pp. 416–435.

11

upon different assumptions, acknowledged or unacknowledged—may have left the last two generations of economists confused and led them to believe that any further efforts along such lines would be fruitless.

Whatever the reason may be, "orthodox" economists generally have avoided concerning themselves with certain substantive aspects of the general property tax in the last half century. Any effort that may be made now to reopen discussion of the substantive issues of the property tax may be criticized for several reasons, but not for being premature. It is time, therefore, that we examine the theoretical criticisms of the general property tax, especially those dealing with substantive issues seldom emphasized, but which may be of vital importance in evaluating tax policy. First, a few observations about the theoretical criticisms of the general property tax and an examination of the complex economic effects of the tax will be made. Then attention will be turned to land value taxation as an alternative to the general property tax and its effect on incentive, investment, value of land, and price or rental values of urban land facilities examined. After investigating these micro-economic questions pertaining to taxing land more heavily and untaxing buildings, a short exploration of the macro-economic aspects of such a tax policy will be undertaken.

Theoretical Criticisms

Theoretical criticism of the general property tax has generally taken three forms. One criticism is directed at the double taxation arising out of taxing both intangibles as well as other objects of property. The validity of this criticism has been broadly recognized and has led to the widespread exemption of intangibles from the general property tax and the replacement of lost revenues with some other tax (usually on income or sales) and grants to local governments. Another major theoretical criticism is that the general property tax does not conform to ability to pay, but is instead regressive in terms of the owner's income. This has led to homestead exemptions in Florida, Georgia, Hawaii, Louisiana, Mississippi, and Oklahoma. The many disadvantages that accompany the homestead exemption, however, have cautioned other states from adopting this modification in the property tax. Several other alternatives have been proposed to answer the regressivity charge. One of the more promising proposals, a real estate tax credit for low-income persons, has already been enacted in Wisconsin, where a credit is granted toward the state income tax for persons over sixty-five.

A third theoretical criticism that has been used against the property tax is that it has a depressing effect on incentive and productivity. Perhaps

the most significant property tax change made in response to this criticism
is the complete exemption of tangible personal property in Delaware, Hawaii, New Jersey, New York, and Pennsylvania,[3] and the partial or complete exemption of tangible agricultural personal property in many states.[4]
These modifications have proceeded with uncertainty and hesitation and
do not furnish a simple and clear guide to property tax reform that would
provide added incentive and productivity. In this chapter I will examine
primarily the criticism that the property tax inhibits incentive and productivity and will look for a simple and clear guide, if it can be found, to property tax reform.

A remarkable aspect of these theoretical criticisms is that they have not
led very many scholars to recommend substantive improvements in the
general property tax. Critics have, instead, prescribed a search for other
sources of revenues. As shall be discussed shortly, these adverse arguments
may have been based upon the assumption that the components of the
general property tax base are governed by the same conditions of supply
and that their taxation on an ad valorem basis produces the same effect on
prices, supply, and incentive. This assumption is incorrect, at least in the
long run, and any theoretical criticism based upon it is most vulnerable.
The recognition that economic rent was to be found in other factors of
production as well as land, may have played a large role in this assumption,
and may have led many economists to conclude too quickly that there was
after all (notwithstanding what David Ricardo has said on the subject) no
essential difference between land and the other factors of production.
Although economic rent may be found in all factors of production, substantive and normative differences remain. Normally, temporary or quasi-
rents of some durables and labor arise out of a short-run inelasticity of
supply, whereas the supply of land both in the short and long run is sufficiently inelastic to produce continuous economic rents.[5] Moreover, the supply of land, unlike that of durable goods and labor, is physically different [6]

3. It may be pointed out here that by far the greater portion of tangible personal
property on the tax rolls is business assets and the exemption of this property from
the property tax is often of great help in increasing business profitability and expansion. Taxing nonbusiness personal property has been found generally unenforceable
and little revenue is lost by exempting it from the property tax.

4. See Harvey Shapiro, "Assessment and Taxation of Tangible Personal Property
on Farms," *National Tax Journal*, 18, no. 1 (March 1965) : 30.

5. See Alfred Marshall, *Principles of Economics,* 8th ed. (London: Macmillan and
Co., 1938), p. 421 ; and Joan Robinson, *Economics of Imperfect Competition* (London: Macmillan and Co., 1933), chap. 8.

6. That is, the essential physical characteristic of land, its three-dimensional surface space on the earth.

because it is given, fixed, and indestructible and economically different because it has no cost.

The indiscriminate application of the theoretical criticisms of the general property tax to property as an indivisible whole (ignoring its different effects on the components of the tax base) cannot be defended on a scholarly basis. Yet this thinking is not uncommon even among economists. Perhaps the "uniformity rule" [7] engraved in the statutes and constitutions of the states has persuaded critics that a more refined approach to the general property tax would be without immediate practical value. Institutional obstacles to policy, however, have seldom deterred economists from analyzing other problems, nor should they here.

If one separates taxable general property into land and nonland components, two interesting historical trends can be discerned. The first shows that most of the property value exempted over the years consists of nonland property. Both administrative and theoretical arguments have induced the long and steady stream of exemptions to the general property tax. Assuming that the most common exemptions reflect the weakest links of the general property tax, it is noteworthy that personal property has been more susceptible to exemption from the general property tax base than has real estate. Such exemptions have proceeded by legal action as well as by administrative default.[8]

Another interesting trend is the dramatic reduction in relative land values compared with total property values. The trend can be placed in perspective by recalling that the general property tax was instituted throughout the nation when property consisted almost exclusively of land. The value of land remained of relatively greater magnitude than the value of nonland property until sometime between World War I and World War II. The great change occurred between 1922 and 1956, when land values as a percentage of total property values in the United States had declined from 60.8 percent to 36.0 percent.[9] The fact that the rising criticism of the general property tax has coincided with this nation-wide change in the composition of property values raises the possibility of a causal relationship, although proof cannot be furnished easily.

It is an interesting historical fact that the property tax was instituted when it was primarily a land tax. Objections to the property tax grew during the nineteenth century as the tax weighed more heavily on rapidly

7. See Harold M. Groves, *Financing Government*, 5th ed. (New York: Holt, 1958), p. 54.

8. Frederick L. Bird, *The General Property Tax: Findings of the 1957 Census of Governments* (Chicago: Public Administration Service, 1960), p. 3.

9. Joseph S. Keiper, Ernest Kurnow, and Clifford D. Clark, *Theory and Measurement of Rent* (Philadelphia, Pa.: Chilton Company, 1961), p. 156.

growing stocks of nonland property.[10] Subsequently, most of the substantive reform in the general property tax has occurred in eliminating or reducing the burden of taxing nonland property. This sequence of events may not have been entirely accidental. The following section provides one explanation of this reaction.

Economic Effects of Taxing
Land, Buildings, and Personalty

Let us examine briefly the components of the general property tax base. They fall into four primary types—land, improvements, tangible personalty, and intangible personalty—which differ from each other in basic physical characteristics. Intangible personalty is eliminated from consideration because the great bulk of taxable property values is found in land, improvements, and tangible personalty. As we have seen, there is a widespread exemption of intangibles for administrative and theoretical reasons. The vast majority of intangibles do not lend themselves to the ad valorem property tax in a free society for the simple reason that compiling a reasonably complete tax roll of intangibles has proved excessively difficult. Moreover, since the real estate and tangible personal property tax is based upon gross rather than net value, the taxation of many intangibles involves the double taxation of other taxable property. The reasons for not taxing intangible personal property are regarded here as sufficient grounds for the complete exemption of this class of property. These arguments, however, carry less or no weight with the other three classes of property. The tax, therefore, will have to be evaluated on these classes of property in other terms.

Differentiation in Terms of Origin

Leaving intangible personal property aside, it is essential to distinguish the other components of the property tax base from each other in terms of

10. Probable reasons for the reversal in the relative total values of land and improvements include: (1) The transportation revolution of the twentieth century, based primarily on the motor vehicle and vast network of roads and highways, greatly increased the supply of adequately accessible land. This has reduced the cost of friction and, in turn, reduced the economic rent of land and its capital (and market) values. (2) The increased needs and costs of other factors of production in the modern economy has reduced the net economic rents of land and its capital (and market) values. (3) The increase in excise, sales, and income taxes has made further inroads upon the economic rent of land and its capital (and market) values. (4) The vast increase in the stock of producer durables as well as buildings for manufacturing, commercial, and residential use.

their origin or source of quantity and quality of supply.[11] The quantitative supply of land has been determined by nature as a gift to man. In addition, many qualitative characteristics of land, such as soil conditions, contour, gradient, elevation, and level of the water table, have been similarly determined by nature, at least originally.[12] The quality of land as reflected in its value for urban use is also dependent upon the amount and type of public capital improvements, including streets, street lighting, water utilities, sewers, and schools. In a larger sense, it is the general presence of an urban population and its many activities that endows urban land with locational or site value.[13] On the other hand, the quantity and quality of improvements and tangible personalty spring from specific human effort applied to create each unit of nonland property.[14]

The origin of the basic classes of property carries a vital significance for equity considerations of the ad valorem property tax. If one holds the view that the worker should enjoy the full fruit of his efforts insofar as it is possible, then the taxation of land values should be given a high priority over the taxation of values of improvements and tangible personalty.[15] Inasmuch as land values are caused by the bounty of nature, public capital, and the presence, work, and investment of people other than the landowner, it

11. This analysis follows the Marshallian supply-demand theory of value. The characteristic under present consideration deals, however, only with the supply side of the analysis, and assumes that any differences in demand for land, improvements, or tangible personalty will not invalidate the significance of the differences cited in supply.

12. To avoid confusion I will call the value resulting from these qualities of land its natural, original, or inherent value. Such natural values can be contrasted with the "public values" which Alfred Marshall states are that part of "inherent value" (annual) that can be traced to action (work and outlay) of men. Note here that Marshall uses "original value" and "inherent value" to include "public value," whereas in my usage these terms are exclusive of each other. For further discussion of these concepts, see Marshall's *Principles of Economics,* pp. 433–434. See also his *Memorandum by Professor Alfred Marshall on the Classification and Incidence of Imperial and Local Taxes* (London: Royal Commission on Local Taxation, 1899), p. 115; which is also found in his *Official Papers* (London: Macmillan and Co., 1926), pp. 327–364.

13. In discussing urban land values, Marshall states that "it is obvious that the greater part of situation value is public value."—Marshall, *Principles of Economics,* p. 442.

14. According to Marshall, ibid., p. 433, "that part [of the value of land] which can be traced to work and outlay by its individual holder may be called its 'private' value." For a discussion of the distinction between improvements and unimproved land value, see A. C. Pigou, *A Study in Public Finance,* 4th rev. ed. (London: Macmillan and Co., 1962), p. 151.

15. Similar high-priority taxation might also be accorded to inheritances, windfall gains, and perhaps gifts.

seems particularly appropriate to tax these indivisible values and thereby return them to urban populations via their local governments.

The Need for Economic Inducements

Land also differs economically from improvements and tangible personalty because these two require economic inducements for their production. Since urban land, considered in terms of its most essential characteristic as three-dimensional space, is a gift of nature, no economic inducement or compensation is required to bring it into existence. Objection to this view might arise on the grounds that improvements to a site are necessary to make it usable. While most capital improvements merge into the land itself, the fact remains that the essential characteristic of urban land, space, is not and cannot be created by means of improvements to the land and requires no economic inducement to appear. Moreover, inducements are not required to maintain the supply of land, since nature has already provided for this by endowing land with the quality of indestructibility. Such improvements to the land as leveling or filling may be permanent because they merge with the land and become a characteristic of it. The life of most improvements on the land as well as all tangible personalty are temporary, however, even though they are called "durable goods," for the ravages of use and the elements will in time destroy and ultimately convert them into the materials of land itself. Consequently, they require not only initial economic inducements to bring them into being, but also repeated economic inducements to insure their maintenance and ultimate replacement when it becomes necessary.

The need of economic inducements for man-made goods (improvements and tangible personalty) and the lack of this need for land is the key to the behavior of the ad valorem general property tax as applied to the components of the tax. The supply of land, by virtue of its indestructibility, cannot be reduced by taxing land value. Also, with an increase in the ad valorem property tax, supplies of improvements and those items of tangible property that are classed as durable goods will not be reduced sufficiently in the short run to establish a new equilibrium. In the long run, however, as improvements and tangible personalty wear out, replacement will be at less than 100 percent or of lesser quality until a new equilibrium is established.[16] A decrease in the ad valorem property tax would tend to in-

16. An increase in the property tax on improvements and tangible property will force marginal operations into the submarginal category. Submarginal property will be used in the short run (even though earnings on property investment are reduced below the level of "necessary profits") as long as income covers actual outlays. Once

crease the quantity and/or quality of improvements and tangible personalty in response to the greater economic inducement provided in the tax
reduction.

Let us pause for a moment to examine the supply of land. We have already seen that land can neither be created nor destroyed. The indestructible quality of land, which Ricardo stressed, has led the majority of economists to regard the supply of land as fixed. The total supply of land has
been described as perfectly inelastic and would be represented graphically
by a supply curve drawn perfectly vertical to the axis measuring the amount
of land. The supply of urban land is not perfectly inelastic, however, since
it is the complement of rural land and its proportion of total land can and
has been expanding at the expense of rural land.

Economists generally agree that in the short run the total supply of urban
land in a metropolitan area is inelastic. It is the long-run concept that has
produced some disagreements. Perhaps the difficulty lies in the assumptions
made about the demand for urban land. If a growing demand for land is
assumed, the elasticity of supply will be found to be quite different than if
the demand were assumed to be falling. Yet both assumptions are necessary to get a complete picture of the supply of urban land. A fluctuating
growth and decline in demand for urban land produce a ratchet effect on
the supply of land. (See Figure 1.1.) Let us see why this is so.

If a rising demand for urban land due to a growing population and
economic base of an urban area is assumed, the price of land will rise.
Physical, technical, and legal problems will permit a very small response
immediately and only a little more in the short run, which will reflect a
price inelasticity in the first stages of the price rise (AB in Figure 1.1). If
the higher price remains steady or increases further for a long enough
period, however, it will be possible to convert fringe farm land into urban
land and to build vertically on land already in urban use. Thus, the long-
run supply of urban land is elastic in the face of a price rise (AC), assuming no political or physical barriers.

Now if the demand for urban land declines in an urban area because of
a population loss, weakening of its economic base, higher taxes, or interest,
the price of land will fall. The response (in terms of the supply of urban
land) to this price fall will be negligible at first (CD) and slow and small
over a protracted period of time (CE). Thus, a decrease in the supply of

---

costs rise to a level above income, however, improvements and tangible personalty
will no longer be used, nor will they be replaced. They will also not be replaced even
though inadequate profits continue to the very end of the property's life. Land will
not be put to the same income use with a replacement structure unless the investment
promises "necessary profits" on what might be earned on an alternative ownership
investment with similar risk.

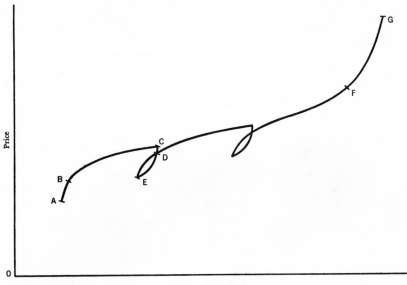

Price

Amount of urban land

AB = short-run response to rising demand.
AC = long-run response to rising demand.
CD = short-run response to falling demand.
CE = long-run response to falling demand.
FG = long-run response to rising or falling demand where rural fringe is unavailable or is a poor substitute because of zoning, inaccessibility, and so on.

Figure 1.1. The Supply of Urban Land

urban land will be inelastic in the short run and only a little less so in the long run. Rural land uses are not a practical alternative for most urban land, except perhaps for some unimproved urban-fringe land. Urban-fringe land already improved with buildings and public capital improvements will not be converted to rural use without the lapse of many years, maybe not in the lifetime of the present generation. The time elapsed will be longer than the average remaining life of private and public buildings on urban land in general because urban-fringe land usually holds the newest private buildings and public capital improvements. When these buildings or public installations eventually wear out, however, the failure to replace them or to build vertically to the same extent as before and the conversion of the land to rural use would indicate some reduction in the supply of urban land.

Over the long run, then, the supply of urban land tends to be inelastic with a price decline and elastic with a price rise. In a central city ringed with suburbs or a rural fringe assessed on the basis of agricultural uses, the supply of surface urban land (although the supply of vertically used space can still be increased) is most nearly inelastic in the long run with a price rise as well as with a price fall (*FG* in Figure 1.1). No more urban land can be added horizontally to the city with a price rise; with a decline in the price of urban land, little if any land in the central city will be converted to rural use as long as the suburbs of the central city continue to exist. Any long-run change in the supply of land can come about solely by means of more or less vertical building.[17]

Cost-Value Relationships

A third basic economic difference between the components of the general property tax base relates to the relationship between the value (or price) and cost of each component. The value (or price) of most land bears no relation whatsoever to the cost of bringing it into existence and little or no relation even to bringing it into a given use, except at the moment of time that it is brought into use. A simple illustration can make this point clear.

Assuming that the decision to convert land into a new use is not premature, the basic costs involved will be those of site improvements. Assuming further that necessary site improvements merge with the land itself, these and other privately borne costs must be covered in the selling price of the land.[18] Additional supplies of urban land are provided to the point where marginal cost equals marginal revenue. In the meantime, however, the price of land brought into urban use in previous years will rise with the growth of population.[19] Current prices of such land will bear no relationship to the original costs of urban land development, even if those costs are adjusted for changes in purchasing power. Indeed, the value of some land previously brought into urban use may rise far above original urban land development costs, exceeding what might be expected from a general growth in the demand for urban land.[20] The reason for this phenomenon

17. Of course, if the demand for urban land is not limited to the central city, available rural land on the suburban fringe may be brought into suburban use as an acceptable substitute for additional central-city land. The degree of substitutability, however, will be determined by the location, accessibility, suburban public services, and other characteristics of the new urban land.

18. The cost of site improvements may be no more than one-third to one-half of marginal cost or revenue. Additional costs include those of purchasing the raw land, taxes, and interest on capital used to purchase land and finance site improvements as well as to pay taxes.

19. Even assuming no changes in the quality or per capita quantity of transportation facilities that are used, the price will still rise.

20. Profound changes in transportation during the twentieth century, such as the widespread use of the motor vehicle and the building of improved roads, have altered

lies in the locational heterogeneity of land as well as in the locational preferences of an increasing population.[21]

The value of improvements and tangible personalty, however, will be governed in the long run by their marginal costs of production.[22] A sudden rise in demand may create a condition of temporary shortage in the supply of improvements. Their prices may rise above costs and provide their owners with "quasi-rents." [23] The latter will then provide an incentive to increase the production of improvements. Increasing the stocks of improvements will drive their prices down to the point where they equal their marginal cost of construction. The price-cost relationship for durable tangible personalty, such as machinery and equipment, will be similar to that of improvements, although the length of the long-run time period and the price-cost differential may be somewhat less. The price of nondurables will be even less likely to rise above their marginal costs and for shorter periods of time, unless attended by monopolistic conditions of supply.

The ad valorem property tax on land values is generally regarded as non-shiftable.[24] This view is based on the assumption that landowners by and large are charging what the traffic will bear before the imposition of the tax.[25] Taxes can be shifted only with a reduction in the supply of the taxed object, and, since the supply of urban land cannot be reduced except over a considerable time period, land rentals cannot be raised because of the tax. The latter, however, reduces that portion of the economic rent of the land retained by owners which in turn, *ceteris paribus*, causes the market

the framework of locational preferences. In many urban areas rapid suburbanization has tended to depress central-city land values. The same cost-price analysis holds true, however, even though a change in relative price levels of land has occurred between the central and outlying portions of urbanized areas.

21. The marginal cost of an addition to a product may influence the price of the total output only if all its units are homogeneous and are traded under conditions of perfect competition. Urban land, however, is not only heterogeneous, but also traded in an extremely imperfect market.

22. Competitive conditions and the availability of supplies of factors of production to permit the construction of improvements and production of tangible personalty are assumed.

23. Marshall, *Principles of Economics*, pp. 431–432. An improvement or tangible personalty that is unique in terms of historical significance, artistic merit, musical quality, etc., combined with an increased demand, will produce a rent for as long as the improvement or personalty or the demand for them will last. This kind of rent or value, in terms of longevity, would probably fall somewhere between quasi-rents and rents attributable to land.

24. See Pigou, *Study in Public Finance*, p. 147 ; Marshall, *Principles of Economics*, pp. 794–804 ; Groves, *Financing Government*, pp. 142–145.

25. Landlords may charge less if they lack economic motivation, are ignorant of their opportunity costs, or if governmental intervention (such as rent controls) prevents them from availing themselves of their opportunity costs.

value of the land to decline. The extent of the decline would tend to equal the capitalized value of the tax, and therefore it is said that a tax on land values is capitalized, not shifted.

The effect of an ad valorem tax on the value of improvements to land and other durable goods *in the short run* will tend to be similar to the effect on land.[26] The durable nature of improvements and of much personalty assures that despite the imposition of the tax, no immediate change will occur in the physical supply. The tax, however, will force the annual costs of marginal improvements above their revenue with the consequence that they will not be replaced when they wear out or when their variable costs exceed their revenues. The reduction in supplies of improvements and personalty will continue to the point where the rentals of remaining supplies rise sufficiently to reimburse their owners for the ad valorem taxes (and the $MC = MR$ equilibrium is again restored).

Differentiation in Terms of Level of Use

A fourth economic characteristic whereby land can be differentiated from improvements and personalty relates to flexibility in the level of use. Land is capable of being used at levels of almost an infinite range. The actual level of use is set by economic and other social rather than physical determinants. The level of use of improvements and personalty, however, is established by the physical capacity for which they were built. Occasionally, the level of use can be raised somewhat by modifying the improvement or personalty, but only within limits, if at all.

The ad valorem tax on a plot of land with a given value will induce the owner to put his land to a higher level of use if possible in order to provide additional income to cover the ad valorem tax. The highest possible use will minimize the burden of the tax to the owner since the tax does not rise with the level of use. Therefore, the tax might be regarded as a penalty for placing land in a low level of use and an incentive for placing it in the highest use. Conversely, a reduction in the ad valorem tax on land values would remove this incentive for keeping land in as high a level of use as that in which it presently finds itself.

The ad valorem tax on the value of improvements and personalty, however, constitutes a large part of the cost of these factors of production along with interest and maintenance. An increase in the tax would increase the carrying cost of these capital goods.[27] If a site is already being utilized to

26. Walter A. Morton, *Housing Taxation* (Madison, Wis.: The University of Wisconsin Press, 1955), pp. 110–115.

27. The expression "capital goods" is employed here as an alternative to "improvements and personalty." It includes "man-made goods intended for further production" of future streams of income or utility.

capacity (assuming no tax on improvements) or to the point of maximum profitability (assuming present taxes on improvements), the introduction (or increase) of a tax on the value of improvements will not permit an increase in output to offset the tax (or tax increase). If the owner is just breaking even, the additional fixed charge will cut into necessary profits or make it impossible to meet interest payments. Eventually, some improvements and personalty will not be replaced when they wear out or become obsolete. In exceptional cases, if the tax were to exceed capital costs, the owner might be forced to sell or destroy the improvements and personalty even before they were worn out or obsolete.

In the long run the tax acts as a penalty for maintaining the present level of improvements and personalty and as an incentive to replace them (at the appropriate time) with investments of lesser value since the tax burden would be reduced accordingly. Similarly, an increase in the application of capital goods to land would increase the tax paid by the owner. The tax may therefore be regarded as a penalty for putting land to its highest use by investing capital in the land up to its capacity. Conversely, a reduction in the ad valorem tax on improvements and personalty would provide an incentive for investing more heavily in these capital goods to the extent that nontax factors permit.[28]

According to the foregoing analysis, the long-run effect of the property tax on land values is fundamentally different, in fact usually the opposite, of that on the values of improvements and personalty. The real estate tax therefore should really be viewed as a combination of property taxes that produce conflicting, yet simultaneous, results among its components. It is quite inaccurate to refer to "the effect" of the property tax in general as though it contained but one item in its base. Moreover, references to the real estate tax generally fit the description of the tax on improvement values, although that is not specified. This error is in part understandable; two-thirds or more of the property tax base in urban areas consists of nonland assessment values. A careful evaluation of the property tax, however, cannot be based upon such an extreme oversimplification of the nature of the tax.

An initial consideration of "the effect" of the property tax may lead one to believe that it is entirely reasonable to ascertain a general composite effect. While such an analysis may have some value for certain purposes, it actually is misleading for understanding property tax reform proposals because the ratio of the assessed land values to nonland values is nowhere uniform, either geographically or in terms of land use, even in a given city. Differing ratios produce differing composite effects. The effects of the tax on various parcels of real estate cannot be compared unless their land-to-

28. Ralph Turvey, *The Economics of Real Property* (London: George Allen and Unwin, 1957), pp. 87–92.

nonland ratios are similar. Even where this similarity prevails, the more ordinary obstacles of differing assessment ratios [29] and tax rates cast a cloud on the validity of comparisons. As a rule, the real estate tax affects each piece of real estate uniquely and to a different degree.

Micro-Economic Aspects of Taxing Land and Untaxing Buildings

Having analyzed the economic effects of taxing the various types of tangible property, we can now proceed to describe and understand the economic effects of increasing the tax on land values and eliminating the tax on building values. Several assumptions, however, must be made in order to avoid misunderstanding and to keep the analysis within bounds. First, this type of land value tax is one in which the annual property tax levy on total land values would be increased only to compensate for the removal of the property tax on real estate improvements. The land value tax would become a substitute for the ad valorem real estate tax in the present tax structure. The establishment and operation of this kind of land value tax will be regarded (in this chapter) as constituting land value taxation. This assumption does not include an increase in the tax levy on land values to allow for the elimination of the personal property tax or for the substitution of any other tax.

A second assumption is that landowners will be charging lessees what the traffic will bear. It is assumed that owners will recognize and demand the full opportunity costs for their land and that their efforts will not be thwarted by rent controls. Thirdly, it is assumed that the supply of building factors is relatively elastic and that average costs will not rise appreciably as increased building occurs. A related assumption is that additional building funds are available and that interest rates will remain unchanged.

Four Effects on Economic Development

Perhaps the most important consequence of converting the real estate tax into a land value tax in urban areas will be a sizable stimulus in the economic development and use of land, both extensive and intensive.[30] There

29. This is the ratio of the assessed value of a taxable item of property to its market or full value.

30. Extensive development of urban sites requires that the vacant or idle sites be put to some beneficial use. This ordinarily implies construction of a building or other structure, although cultivated green spaces may be included. A site may be idle rather than vacant if the structure on it is not in use or if the site is fenced off from use and view. Intensive development would include modification of the existing structure or replacement with an entirely new structure in order to produce the potential net income of the site.

are four incentives that will help bring about such increased development: the capitalization, holding-cost, fixed-cost, and unburdening effects. The first three explain why increasing the ad valorem tax on land can be expected to increase investment in improvements, the fourth why reducing the tax on improvements is necessary to increase investment in improvements.

The capitalization effect of taxing land values reduces the financial obstacles in the acquisition of land by a would-be developer. The benefit arises out of the fact that an additional tax burden on land values is capitalized into lower land values and prices. A higher annual cost in the form of taxes is traded for a lower (annual and capital) market value and cost of land. Thus, any tax on land values remains neutral as to the total cost of land acquisition.

One might view the capitalization effect of taxing land as a conversion of part of the capital (or annual) market value of land to the annual tax. It is a significant advantage for many, and perhaps most, investors to face lower financial hurdles in land acquisition. The benefit would be the equivalent of an automatic perpetual loan to the developer for purposes of land acquisition in the amount of the capitalized value of the land tax.

Investment funds previously intended for land acquisition can now be turned to the purchase of a larger site or, more probably, invested in improvements on a larger scale. The high cost of land acquisition for development and redevelopment has become a serious problem in urban America even where credit is relatively abundant. The advantage of land value taxation would seem to hold special importance for underdeveloped countries where available credit for land acquisition and development is in very short supply.

Unfortunately, the capitalization effect will not be clearly visible on many sites in the tax model suggested at the beginning of this section. The reason lies in the workings of the fixed-cost and unburdening effects, which will be discussed presently. These will operate to increase the value of land while simultaneously the capitalization and holding-cost effects will operate to lower its value. The relative strength of these effects pulling in opposite directions will determine the actual value of a given parcel of land. The capitalization and holding-cost effects will have the upper hand on poorly located land. The fixed-cost and unburdening effects, however, will win out over the capitalization and holding-cost effects on land that is strategically located or in great demand for nonlocational reasons.

The capitalization effect would be clearly visible if the tax on land values tax burden on improvements. The capitalization effect would also be were increased beyond the model's assumption that the tax burden on land values is increased more than an amount equal to the reduction of the

clearly visible if a land surtax were levied in addition to the present property tax.

The holding-cost effect of taxing land in the land value tax model will increase costs to an owner holding a site that is vacant or in a lower than average level of use if it is already improved (with some structure).[31] The effect has two dimensions, a maximizing insistence or tendency and a time persistence.[32] The magnitude of the holding-cost effect on a landlord will depend upon the difference between the potential and actual economic development of his site. The correlation between the size of the holding cost and those sites with the highest unused potential is ideal for stimulating growth because it puts the greatest economic pressure for development where the opportunities for private and public benefits are the greatest. Thus, the maximizing insistence aspect of taxing land values refers to the fact that the strongest forces for economic development are induced on sites with the largest increase in taxes, which are the very sites offering the highest capacity for improvement. The effect produces a tendency to raise the levels of use and net income of land to offset the higher tax. But, since the size of the tax differs among sites according to development potential, as each landowner attempts to offset his higher taxes by making additional improvements, resources will be allocated among the sites in such a way as to maximize aggregate land income.

The real estate tax on land values in the United States is characterized at present by its time persistence, that is, by the annually recurring liability that it imposes upon the owner regardless of whether he uses property or the extent to which he uses it. This characteristic helps hasten the development of idle land and tends to keep structures in use rather than idleness.[33] If the tax on land values were to be increased, perhaps by replacing the real estate tax with a land value tax, the time-persistence burden would become more acute for owners of vacant or underdeveloped land than under the present real estate tax, and the holding-cost effect would be enhanced.

The owner of a site is confronted with two choices if he wishes to avoid the holding cost of idle or underused land. One course of action is for him

31. "Lower than average" means a ratio of improvements value to land value for an owner that is less than the ratio of the municipality's total taxable value of improvements to its total taxable land value. It should be noted that in the illustration the level of improvement refers to that prevailing in the local taxing units whose rates apply against the real estate in question.

32. The time-persistence aspect of the holding-cost effect means that the *total* tax burden accumulates with the passage of time.

33. This type of property tax can be contrasted with that system of property taxes (as found in England, for example) in which taxes are imposed only if property is in actual use, and in accordance with the actual or imputed income it produces.

to sell his land (which will also permit him to escape the time-persistence burden). His other choice is to put the site to a level of use sufficiently high to offset the burden. An idle structure may be put to use once again (if no higher use is possible) or used nearer to capacity. The structure may lend itself to an alteration that can raise the intensity or capacity (or both) of the same use or provide an entirely new and more profitable use. As an alternative, the site may be redeveloped completely by replacing the present structure with one that will put the site to its highest and best use.

The holding-cost effect of taxing land values tends to cause land values to fall. Land with a low development potential, present or future, will find its values depressed as owners try to sell to avoid the higher cost of holding the land. Thereupon the benefits of the capitalization effect will ensue. If, however, land has a good development potential, its value may not fall but may even rise, because the holding-cost effect is more than offset by the fixed-cost and unburdening effects (see the following). With such land the owner can minimize his holding costs by putting the land to a higher use as promptly as possible.

The fixed-cost effect of land value taxation refers to the fact that the amount of the land value tax bears no relation to the extent of development of any given site (which is true even of the *land component* of the ad valorem real estate tax). Instead, the amount of the tax is based upon the value of a given site, which depends upon its advantages and disadvantages of location and exposure. The increase in the tax on land values when the tax change is introduced will be determined only by land values and not by the use of land. Moreover, if land is developed by marginal increments, total tax costs on land values will not rise. Instead, the average tax costs per unit of improvement [34] will decrease with an increase of investment in improvements. (Decreasing average tax costs will be experienced as land use [output] increases, because the fixed total tax cost will be spread over a larger number of improvement units.) The owner will be strongly encouraged to develop his land to its capacity with the knowledge that his tax liability will remain fixed regardless of the level of use to which the site is put and that the tax cost per unit of improvement will decline with an increase in the number of units in the improvement.

The fourth incentive for increased economic development of urban land is due to the unburdening effect, which refers to the elimination of the property tax obligation from the value of improvements. This effect places the land value tax in marked contrast to the real estate tax in which the

---

34. A unit of improvement may be regarded in any number of ways; for example, it may be an apartment unit in a multiapartment building, a square foot of residential, office, or factory space, or perhaps some dollar amount of investment in improvements ($1,000, $5,000, or $10,000).

tax on improvements is directly related to the value of improvements. The dampening effect that the real estate tax has on site development and redevelopment is commonly recognized and lamented. While the land value tax will increase the tax burden on land values, the simultaneous removal of the tax burden on the value of existing improvements will cause a net reduction in taxes to owners of land with a higher than average ratio of improvements value to land value. Urban redevelopment will be stimulated because tax liabilities will not be increased as would be the case under the real estate tax. The construction of higher quality and more spacious buildings will be encouraged because they will incur no more tax costs than if buildings were shabby and cramped. Owners will remodel their buildings more freely knowing that the fruit of their efforts will not be rewarded with an additional tax burden. The land value tax per thousand dollars of investment in improvements will be reduced more and more as investments in improvements rise.

The fixed-cost and unburdening effects combined result in (1) an increase in the profitability of adding increments of improvements, and (2) an increase in the capacity of urban land to absorb profitably investment capital in improvements. Both economic benefits will provide a considerable incentive to develop land to a higher level. Moreover, the holding-cost effect will, as we have noted above, provide incentive for earlier development, as well as for a higher level of development.

It can be shown graphically how eliminating the property tax on improvements will increase the amount of building investment on a given site. Let us assume that building and maintenance costs remain unaffected as building investment increases and that the demand for building facilities is unaffected by the tax change. Curve A in Figure 1.2 represents potential average returns on the site, exclusive of maintenance costs and taxes other than real estate taxes, as various amounts of investment are applied.

OI represents the going rate of interest on investments in improvements appropriate to this site. The property tax rate on full value of the improvements is represented by IN. Investments in improvements on this site will be determined at the point where the sum of the interest and tax rates equals the net marginal rate of revenue (D). Thus, assuming the rate of interest to be OI, and the rate of taxation to be IN, the most profitable building investment outlay would be OK. Area $OIGK$ would represent the interest on the building investment, $INDG$ the property taxes on improvements, and $NSUD$ the annual value of the site inclusive of the property tax on the site value.

If the tax on improvements $(INDG)$ is removed, the optimal investment outlay on improvement will increase from OK to $OP;$ that is, to the point where the rate of marginal net revenues equals the rate of interest (H). The potential annual value of the site rises to $IVJH,$ out of which,

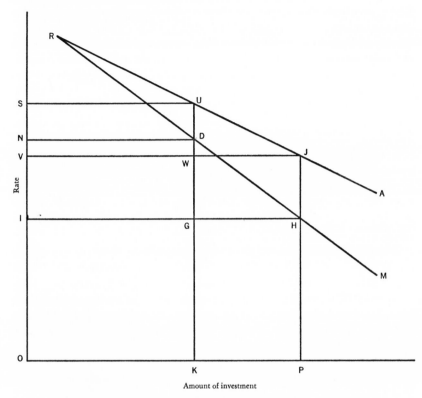

RA = potential average revenue on site, net of maintenance costs, and non-real-estate taxes.

RM = marginal net revenue on site, net of maintenance costs, and non-real-estate taxes.

OK = amount of investment in improvements under real estate tax.

OIGK = interest on OK.
INDG = property tax on improvements (OK).
NSUD = annual value or return to site with a tax on improvements.

OP = amount of investment in improvements if untaxed.

OIHP = interest on OP.
IVJH = annual value or return to site without a tax on improvements.

Figure 1.2. The Effect of Taxing Buildings (Improvements) on Building Investment

however, the land value tax must be paid. The actual land value tax may be any part or all of *IVJH*. The amount of investment outlay on improvements is unaffected by the size of the land value tax, which is independent of the marginal net return curve *M*.

The conversion of the real estate tax to a land value tax will therefore tend to bring about an increase in investment outlays for improvements. This increase will cause a rise in both quantity and quality of construction and building facilities. The market price and rentals of real estate will fall. In Figure 1.2 we see how the rates of average net return will fall from *OS* to *OV* as investment outlay increases on the site. The same effect will be extended to all sites in the urban municipality. As the stock of dwellings, offices, and other structures is expanded, there will be a fall in market prices and rentals of urban land facilities of a given quality or the availability of a higher quality of urban land facilities at lower market prices and rentals.

Effects on Aggregate Value and the Average Price of Land

It is frequently claimed that land value taxation will provide an additional advantage for economic development through a reduction in the price of land. This conclusion arises out of a variety of assumptions. One person may assume the continued existence of the property tax on improvements and personal property. Another may not assume the present property tax and may instead apply (in his mind) the land value tax as a new ad valorem tax on land values alone. Yet another, while assuming the reality and dynamics of replacing the property tax with the land value tax, is influenced unduly by what happens to the value of vacant nonmarketable land rather than all urban land in a community. While land value taxation will reduce the value of land in all the cited instances, it will probably increase land values in the aggregate if the introduction of land value taxation is synchronized with the abandonment of the tax on improvements, both immediately and in the long run (assuming no general decline in urban income, population, or rise in interest rates).

The key to understanding what is likely to happen to land income and its market value if a land value tax were adopted in place of the present real estate tax lies in the unburdening effect. Removing the ad valorem tax from improvements will immediately raise the economic rent (from *NSUD* to *ISUG* in Figure 1.2). Furthermore, it will (by lowering the marginal cost, expressed as a percentage of investment, from *ON* to *OI*) immediately increase (1) the profitability of adding improvements, and (2) the capacity of land to absorb profitably investments in improvements.

For purposes of simplifying this analysis it will be assumed that all land and improvements on each parcel of real estate are held by the same ownership interest. It will be further assumed that the owner of each piece of real estate will apply the gain in the unburdening of improvements to offset the further burdening of land. It follows, then, that immediately after adopting land value taxation the effect on the net *actual* economic rent remaining to landowners in the aggregate remains unchanged compared with what it was under the real estate tax.[35] Accord-

35. For a literary treatment of the same conclusion, see Turvey, *Economics of Real Property*, p. 87.

ingly, the market value of land based on capitalized net land income should also remain unchanged. The forces of increased profitability and capacity on many sites will, however, raise their market value even more.

One might properly raise the question as to who would actually claim the increase in the economic rent that would arise with the removal of the ad valorem tax on improvements. This temporary increase might be regarded either as a quasi-rent attributable to improvements or as an offset to the higher tax on land. Where land and improvements are already owned by the same person it does not matter. Separate ownership of land and improvements, however, would present some practical problems where rental and tax agreements in leaseholds did not take into account the tax changeover. When the time arrives for the renegotiation of land leases, the relative bargaining positions of the building owner and landlord will determine the division or appropriation of the tax savings on improvements.

Once the property tax is removed from improvements, land becomes a warrant that gives the holders the opportunity for making a larger amount of profitable investment in improvements in addition to the increase in economic rent. This, and the guarantee that in the future the use of the land can be changed to one that will take the fullest advantage of not taxing improvements, will create a potential economic rent on well-located urban land that is higher than the short- or long-run economic rents (after removal of taxes on improvements) arising out of the present use. The market value should reflect the capitalized value of this higher potential economic rent.[36]

The question of how the tax savings on improvements is claimed is answered when old buildings are replaced by new ones. In the leasing or purchase of vacant land this short-run problem does not arise at all. The income or capital value of land in all of these cases will reflect its increased profitability and capacity to receive profitable investment. Investment in improvements will increase to the point where the rate of marginal net revenues equals the rate of interest. Increasing improvements over time will place the initial rise in economic rent or quasi-rent (due to removing the tax on improvements) on a solid footing; it will be sustained even under competitive conditions.

The long-run increase in economic rent will be based upon using the land more intensely even though the average revenue per dollar of investment in improvements drops. Whether the economic rent in the long run is greater or smaller than the initially enlarged economic rent ($IVJH \gtrless ISUG$) will depend upon the elasticity of the average revenue curve (A). If the elasticity of the average revenue curve is greater than unity, the

36. Turvey, ibid., p. 92, arrives at the same conclusion.

economic rent will rise in the long run. With an elasticity less than unity, the economic rent will fall. But even in the latter case the economic rent in the long run will be larger than what it was when improvements were taxed.

Effect on a Given Site

The actual immediate increase in economic rent (net of taxes) depends upon how close the present use is to the site's highest and best use, which will produce the most potential economic rent. In other words, the largest tax reduction will go to siteowners whose building-to-land-value ratios are highest. Land value taxes will be less than former real estate taxes for all owners of sites that are improved more than average. The resulting actual increase in net income (after land value taxes) of these landowners will tend to raise the market value of their land. In fact, the price will tend to rise even higher in order to reflect the present value of the highest net potential incomes that those sites are capable of producing, although this potential may not be realized until land use succession occurs.

In the case of a site with an average improvement (in terms of its building-to-land-value ratio), the amount of the tax will not change, and it might be concluded that, since the owner's net income remains the same, the value of his site will not change. Such a conclusion, however, overlooks the fact that the value of land tends to reflect the net potential income-producing ability of a site rather than its actual net income, unless the latter already is at its maximum. Since a change to a land value tax will increase the income-producing potential of land, its value will rise even if the actual tax burden remains the same. For the same reason, the value of land will rise for many sites with less than average improvements even though the changeover may increase taxes. Poorly developed and vacant land will decrease in price where the holding-cost effect is greater than the increase in income-producing potential. Land with a high income potential, even though poorly developed or vacant, will tend to increase in value. This, however, will increase the assessed value of the land and the holding-cost effect of its taxation and will hasten development or sale of the land by the owner.

Efficiency of Resource Allocation

The bulk of this chapter has dealt with the economists' concern for efficiency or neutrality in taxation and with how the uniform taxation of buildings and land under the property tax compares with the taxation of land alone. According to the principle of efficiency or neutrality, a tax is neutral or most efficient if it will "place the least burden on whoever is to be taxed. Taxes should accomplish their assigned objective but beyond this, they should not interfere with the functioning of the market system. There should be no excess burden that can be avoided. Unintended interference with the market mechanism may result in an excess burden that should be avoided." [37] The efficiency of taxing land values compared with taxing improvements and personal property can be explained in several ways.

Neutrality and efficiency are guaranteed by the fixity of supply of urban land. Taxing the economic rent of land cannot reduce the supply of sites and interfere with the market, whereas taxing improvements increases their costs (from *OI* to *ON* in Figure 1.2). This creates a burden greater than taxing land values and reduces the possibility of investment in improvements (from *OP* to *OK*).

Neutrality is also guaranteed because a land value tax is a lump-sum charge. A lump-sum tax produces the holding-cost and the fixed-cost effects that we have already described. A land value tax is neutral also in terms of its land use—a derivative of the fixed-cost effect. The tax will in no way influence the use to which the landowner will place his land among high-return land uses. In other words, the highest and best use will not be partial to the one requiring the most or the least investment on land. Taxing improvements is, however, partial to uses with a lower total return and those favoring a low investment in improvements and personalty. The property tax on improvements and personalty, in comparison with the tax on land, is quite inefficient and unneutral.

If landowners were planning to produce the highest economic rent on their land, the imposition of a land value tax would in no way alter the owners' decision to carry out their plans for land use. If, however, an ad valorem tax on improvements and personalty were to be levied, landowners would be obliged to reduce the scale of their investment in nonland property and perhaps even change the intended purpose of land use to one requiring a lower investment. This influence on investment scale and land use contrasts the inefficiency and unneutrality of taxing nonland property compared with taxing land.

The capitalization effect of taxing land values has been discussed in terms of its influence on the amount of investment in improvements. It will also produce a substantial gain in efficiency in the allocation of resources. Capital for land acquisition is not always readily available even in the United States. Credit for this purpose is rarely given directly or overtly by most financial institutions. Private sources must usually be sought out for land purchases. While persons may qualify in every other way to develop land to a higher use, they may be frustrated in their efforts

---

37. Richard A. Musgrave, *The Theory of Public Finance* (New York: McGraw-Hill, 1959), p. 141.

because of the lack of funds for land acquisition. This advantage of land value taxation to facilitate the transference of land to active developers is perhaps even more urgent in underdeveloped countries.

The reduction in land prices will exert a downward pressure on the rate of interest. The demand for loanable funds to acquire land titles will drop along with the need. This may be imperceptible in the real world with its innumerable determinants of interest rates. Moreover, the unburdening effect of removing nonland property from the property tax roles and replacing the real estate tax with a land value tax, will increase the demand for loanable funds and create a counter pressure on interest rates, causing them to rise. At least, the lowering of land prices will exert some tempering effect on rising interest rates induced by taxing land values. More is said on this subject later in the chapter.

The recognition of possible surplus income in all factors of production has led many economists to look upon the individual income tax as the best way to capture part of this surplus. It cannot, however, achieve the unique efficiency of the land value tax. While individual net income may include various factor surpluses, the latter are very difficult to identify and separate from necessary income for tax purposes.[38] Secondly, some surplus income is temporary, yet there is no way to identify such surplus and relieve income from taxation when the surplus disappears. Also, the danger of cutting into costs is great even in terms of labor, for the marginal utility of money is not the same for all workers. The danger of cutting into capital costs is almost unavoidable, since the amount of the individual's capital investment is generally ignored and income from capital is erroneously assumed to be identical with the cost of labor. On the other hand, land surplus can be identified, separated, and taxed by means of the land value tax. This is a rare combination in the tax pursuit of surplus returns to factors of production and is least likely to violate the requirements of neutrality and efficiency.

Comparative Tax Yields

Unless the taxing of land values can be demonstrated to have a revenue-producing capacity at least equal to that of the real estate tax, any shift of the latter to the former would have to be limited. Fortunately, land values do have an adequate fiscal capacity for such a shift, and value to spare. The economic rent of land would tend to rise, as noted before, for two reasons: (1) in the short run by an indeterminate amount because of the unburdening of nonland property, and (2) in the long run (which could be immediately for vacant land and land that is in a transition of use) be-

38. Ibid., p. 158.

cause of the increased profitability and capacity for investment in land. Because of the increased investment profitability and capacity of the land, its economic rent and surplus taxpaying capacity will grow in the long run for an entire urban area or municipality. This cannot be guaranteed, however, for an urban area or municipality that suffers locational disadvantages, which cannot be overcome otherwise, in maintaining its population and economic base.

It has often been remarked that if land value tax rates became too high the tax base would be destroyed. That, however, is impossible, no matter how high the tax rate is set. (See Table 1.1.) A rate set at the largest

Table 1.1—The Capitalization Effect of Taxing Land Values [a]

Tax rate (percentage of assessed value)	Interest rate plus tax rate	Tax	Owner's share of economic rent	Capitalized (market) value after tax
0%	6%	$ 0	$1,200.00	$20,000.00
1	7	171.43	1,028.57	17,142.86
2	8	300.00	900.00	15,000.00
3	9	400.00	800.00	13,333.33
4	10	480.00	720.00	12,000.00
5	11	545.45	654.55	10,909.09
6	12	600.00	600.00	10,000.00
18	24	900.00	300.00	5,000.00
24	30	960.00	240.00	4,000.00
30	36	1,000.00	200.00	3,333.33
44	50	1,056.00	144.00	2,400.00
50	56	1,071.43	128.57	2,142.86
66	72	1,100.00	100.00	1,666.66
84	90	1,120.00	80.00	1,333.33
94	100	1,128.00	72.00	1,200.00
100	106	1,132.07	67.93	1,132.07
1,000	1,006	1,192.84	7.16	119.28

[a] This table illustrates the mathematical relationships of various ad valorem tax rates to the capitalized (market) value of land income. It assumes a full annual economic rent of land (before any tax) of $1,200 and an interest (and capitalization) rate of 6 percent. The relationship between ad valorem tax rates and the capitalized (market) value of land income can be stated mathematically as follows: Let $t =$ the tax rate as a percentage of assessed value (column 1), $i =$ the interest and capitalization rate, $E =$ the full annual economic rent of land before any tax ($1,200), and $L =$ the capitalized (or market) value of land. The tax on land $= tL$, or $E\, t/(i+t)$ (column 3). The owners share of the economic rent after tax $= E - tL$, or $E\, i/(i+t)$ (column 4).

$$L = \frac{Ei/(i + t)}{i},$$

which can be reduced to $E/(i+t)$ (column 5).

number conceivable will do no better than yield a tax that approaches the economic rent of the land. The tax, however, will still fall short of the economic rent. Therefore, advocates of taxing the full economic rent of land have suggested that the tax base be shifted from the market value of land to economic rent itself. Then all economic rent might be captured with a rate of 100 percent, and presumably taxpayers would be more cooperative and better able to understand the tax than if a tax rate of, for example, 1000 percent were levied on the market value. On the other hand, the market value rate base has many comparative advantages, not the least of which is strategic if the portion of economic rent to be taxed is not too high. For example, a policy of capturing 50 percent of the economic rent of land may generate less objection with a 12 percent tax rate on the market value of land (see Table 1.1) than with a 50 percent tax rate on the economic rent of land.

Macro-Economic Aspects of Taxing Land and Untaxing Buildings

The Effects of Taxing Land

Taxing land values produces an assortment of macro-economic influences besides that of increasing investment.[39] They include changes in liquidity preference, the transactions demand for money, and the marginal efficiency of capital and interest rates. Subsequently, there will be a tendency for changes in employment, national income, and the general price level.

The holding-cost effect will raise liquidity preference since owners must set aside larger amounts of cash every year to pay higher taxes. The capitalization effect, however, will lower the demand for money, inasmuch as the aggregate quantity of funds that need to be accumulated for land acquisitions will fall. Converting the capital value of land into an annual tax is, as we have seen, equivalent to the granting of a perpetual loan automatically to land buyers. Therefore, the transactions demand for money is reduced with a reduction in land prices and the increase in credit equivalent. Similarly, liquidity preference is reduced because the demand for money as a store of value for future investment and speculation falls with lower land prices.

The temporary increase in land transactions is highly likely. Some persons will desire to purchase land for development, while some owners will wish to sell land to avoid further holding costs. The transactions demand for money for current purchases will rise as well as liquidity preference to make possible future transactions.

39. For purposes of this analysis one might assume that a new and separate tax on land values alone is added to prevailing property taxes.

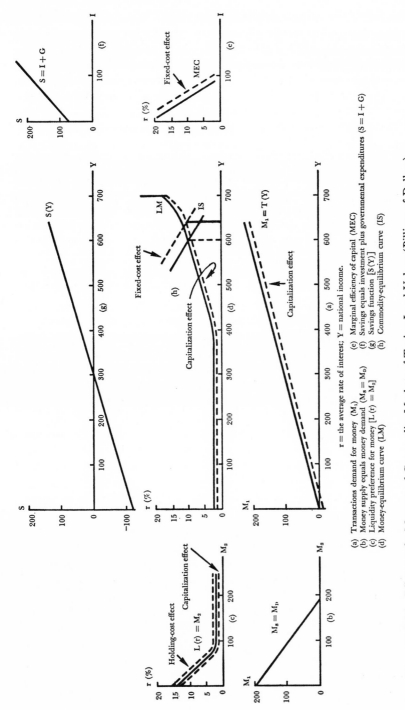

Figure 1.3. The Effect on the Money and Commodity Markets of Taxing Land Values (Billions of Dollars)

r = the average rate of interest; Y = national income.

(a) Transactions demand for money (M_1).
(b) Money supply equals money demand ($M_s = M_D$).
(c) Liquidity preference for money [$L(r) = M_2$].
(d) Money-equilibrium curve (LM).
(e) Marginal efficiency of capital (MEC)
(f) Savings equals investment plus governmental expenditures (S = I + G)
(g) Savings function [$S(Y)$]
(h) Commodity-equilibrium curve (IS)

By reducing the transactions demand for money (ignoring the temporary increase), additional sums of money are available for investment in securities. The increased demand for securities drives up their prices and forces down their yield and interest rates. The lower transactions demand for money tends to establish equilibrium in the money market at a lower level of interest rates. (See Figure 1.3.)

The capitalization effect does not seem to disturb the equilibrium of the commodity market. The conversion of the capital value of land into an annual tax is similar in effect to an increase in investment equal to the capitalized value of the tax, and therefore can be regarded as a shift (upwards) in the marginal efficiency of capital at prevailing interest rates. But the automatic creation of an equivalent of invested loanable funds can hardly be imagined without the automatic creation of the equivalent of savings. Thus, one can regard the savings function to have increased, which would then cancel out the effect of any increase in the marginal efficiency of capital induced by the capitalization effect.

The fixed-cost effect of taxing land values, however, will raise the marginal efficiency of capital, without any apparent offsetting influence, inasmuch as larger investments at prevailing interest rates can be made without added marginal tax costs. As investments increase, average land tax costs will fall. This will shift the commodity-equilibrium (savings-investment) curve so that equilibrium in planned savings and investment is established at higher interest rates or higher levels of national income.[40] It is conjectural, although probable, that the shift of the commodity-equilibrium curve will be of greater magnitude than that of the money-equilibrium curve. The effects of the shifting of both curves to the right will combine so as to maintain stability (or produce a slight rise) in interest rates and increase national output and income. (See Figure 1.3.)

The Effects of Taxing and Untaxing Buildings [41]

The ad valorem tax on buildings and other improvements is a burden more or less proportional to the amount of investment. The marginal efficiency of capital will decrease as additional increments of investment have

40. National income may increase by an amount equal to the product of the increase in investment and the multiplier. The higher national income will in turn produce higher transactions and speculative demand for money and perhaps a larger supply of money. This analysis, however, is limited essentially to initial effects.

41. In analyzing only the effect of taxing buildings, one might assume that a new and separate tax on buildings is added to prevailing property taxes. Conversely, in analyzing only the effect of untaxing buildings, one might assume a modification in the property tax so as to exempt buildings and leave the tax burden on the land unchanged.

to bear the tax cost plus interest rates. Assuming no change in the savings function or governmental expenditures, the commodity-equilibrium (savings-investment) curve will shift downward so that equilibrium in planned savings and investment is established at lower interest rates or lower levels of national income.

Liquidity needs will rise in order to prepare for paying the tax on improvements. Investment in buildings will fall with the imposition of the tax and decrease the transactions demand for money for current investments and liquidity preference for money for future investments. The combined effects of the shifts in the money- and commodity-equilibrium curves will be that of lowering the interest rates and a probable decrease in national output and income. (See Figure 1.4.)

Eliminating the ad valorem tax on buildings and other improvements will, as expected, produce the opposite effect; that is, it will increase the marginal efficiency of capital and induce more investment at prevailing interest rates. The commodity-equilibrium curve will shift upward and to the right so that planned savings and investment are in equilibrium at higher interest rates or higher levels of national income.

Liquidity needs for paying the tax itself on improvements would be eliminated along with the tax. Investment in buildings, however, will rise in response to the removal of the ad valorem tax on them. In order to carry out a larger program of investment the transaction demand for money for current investments will increase, as will also the liquidity preference for money for future investments. The combined effects of the shifts in the money- and commodity-equilibrium markets will be that of raising the interest rates and an increase in the national output and income, which may rise by an amount equal to the increase in investments times the multiplier. (See Figure 1.5.)

The Combined Effects of Taxing Land and Untaxing Buildings

We may now consider the probable macro-economic effects of eliminating the ad valorem tax on buildings and placing this added tax burden on land values. The effect on the demand for money will be considered first.

Liquidity needs of landowners to pay higher land taxes will be largely, if not completely, offset by the lower liquidity needs resulting from eliminating the tax on buildings. Liquidity preference would seem to remain unchanged insofar as providing for taxes is concerned. The reduction in liquidity preference caused by the capitalization effect on land prices, however, would seem to be more than offset by the increased storing of money for future investments in improvements. The reduced transactions demand

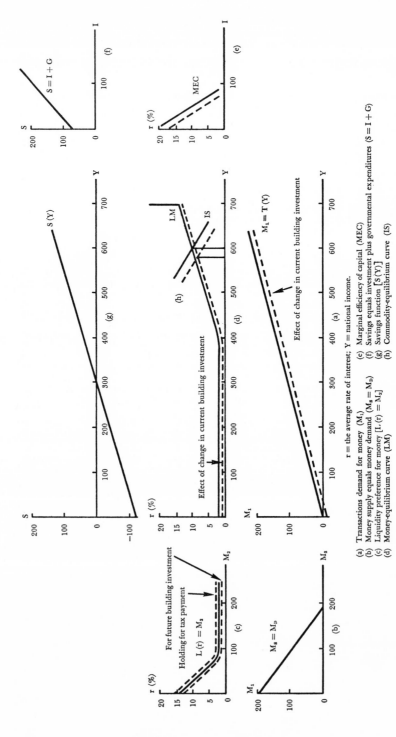

Figure 1.4. The Effect on the Money and Commodity Markets of the Ad Valorem Tax on Buildings (Billions of Dollars)

r = the average rate of interest; Y = national income.

(a) Transactions demand for money (M_t)
(b) Money supply equals money demand ($M_s = M_D$)
(c) Liquidity preference for money [$L(r) = M_2$]
(d) Money-equilibrium curve (LM)

(e) Marginal efficiency of capital (MEC)
(f) Savings equals investment plus governmental expenditures ($S = I + G$)
(g) Savings function [$S(Y)$]
(h) Commodity-equilibrium curve (IS)

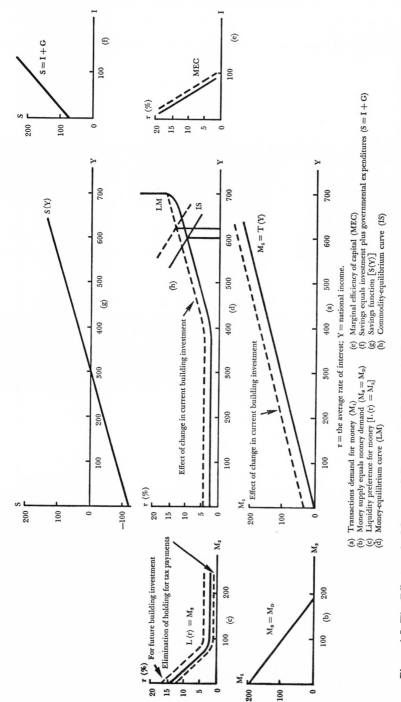

Figure 1.5. The Effect on the Money and Commodity Markets of Eliminating the Ad Valorem Tax on Buildings (Billions of Dollars)

r = the average rate of interest; Y = national income.

(a) Transactions demand for money (M_1)
(b) Money supply equals money demand $(M_s = M_D)$
(c) Liquidity preference for money $[L(r) = M_2]$
(d) Money-equilibrium curve (LM)
(e) Marginal efficiency of capital (MEC)
(f) Savings equals investment plus governmental expenditures $(S = I + G)$
(g) Savings function $[S(Y)]$
(h) Commodity-equilibrium curve (IS)

for money for land purchased caused by the capitalization effect on land prices will be more than offset by an increase in the transactions demand for money for increased investments in improvements as well as increased land acquisition. In addition, the transactions demand for money will increase in the short run because of the capitalization of land (into higher) prices caused by the untaxing of land.

It is likely, then, that the unburdening of taxes on improvements will induce sufficient investments to raise the money-equilibrium curve more than enough to offset the (lowering) effect induced by increasing taxes on land by an equal amount. This view is based on the strong probability that the increased demand for building investment funds will exceed the decline in the demand for funds for land acquisition. The view seems entirely reasonable considering the powerful new profit incentives for increased investments in buildings. Moreover, the unburdening effect of untaxing land will increase the price of land. The increased number of acquisitions may increase the total volume of money needed despite a fall in land prices over the long run.

As to the effect on the commodity-equilibrium curve (IS), the fixed-cost effect of taxing land values as well as the unburdening effect of untaxing buildings will both raise the marginal efficiency of capital and increase investments in buildings. Both tax changes will reinforce one another in shifting the commodity-equilibrium curve to the right and result in a higher national output and income equal to the total increase in investment times the multiplier. Interest rates will also rise. (See Figure 1.6.)

Aggregate Supply and Demand

The combined effect of increasing the tax on land values and decreasing or eliminating the tax on buildings will be that of producing a larger aggregate demand. That is to say, the aggregate demand for goods and services will rise and the national product and income will be greater at various possible price levels. The actual price level and national product, of course, will be in equilibrium only where aggregate supply intersects aggregate demand.

Since the supply of land is fixed, the aggregate supply of land cannot change. Now if taxes on improvements were imposed, the supply curve would shift upwards and to the left. The initial change might be modest but over the long run the supply curve would shift, showing combinations of higher prices and lower supplies, by an amount equal to the tax. The effect would be similar to an increase in excise or sales taxes.

On the other hand, if taxes on improvements were removed, the supply curve would shift downward and to the right (in the long run). The im-

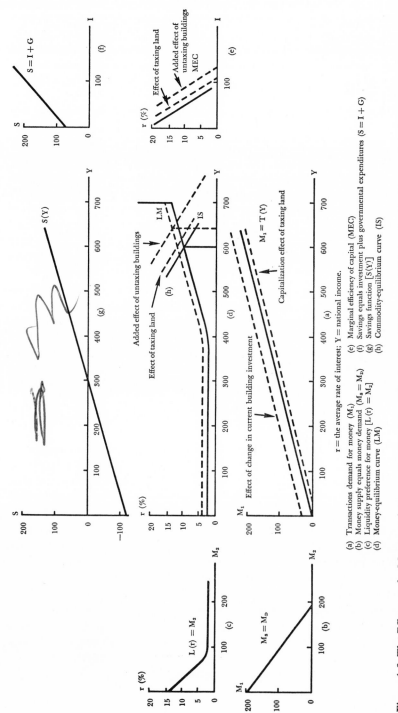

r = the average rate of interest; Y = national income.

(a) Transactions demand for money (M_1)
(b) Money supply equals money demand $(M_s = M_D)$
(c) Liquidity preference for money $[L(r) = M_2]$
(d) Money-equilibrium curve (LM)
(e) Marginal efficiency of capital (MEC)
(f) Savings equals investment plus governmental expenditures $(S = I + G)$
(g) Savings function $[S(Y)]$
(h) Commodity-equilibrium curve (IS)

Figure 1.6. The Effect on the Money and Commodity Markets of Taxing Land Values and Eliminating the Tax on Buildings (Billions of Dollars)

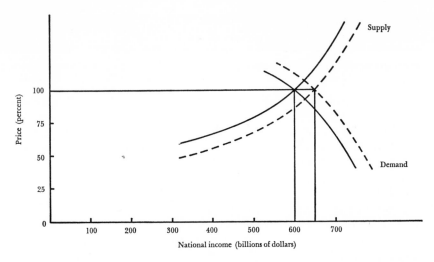

Figure 1.7. The Effect on Aggregate Supply and Demand of Taxing Land and
Untaxing Buildings

mediate change would be of limited scope; within a year, however, building and remodeling momentum would lower prices of building facilities
as their volume expanded. Expansion in the supply of consumer goods
would also occur as the multiplier effect was felt. The product of the
reduction in prices and increased supply of facilities should equal the
amount of taxes eliminated from improvements. The shifts in aggregate
supply and demand would combine to increase national output and income and to resist any increase in prices. (See Figure 1.7.)

Conclusions

Micro-Economic Effects

The effect of the general property tax is complex and involves forces
pushing in opposite directions. These opposite forces result from the
taxation of land as well as of man-made property. The primary differentiation between these two categories of property lies in their origin or
source of supply, quantitatively and qualitatively. Secondary differences
(arising from the primary) show contrasts in the need for economic
inducements to increase or maintain supplies, cost-value relationships, and
flexibility in the level of use to which property can be placed.

Much theoretical criticism of the general property tax is indiscriminate and has led to the conclusion that its effect is uniformly harmful and undesirable. An examination of the components of the general property tax shows, however, that the property tax affects land quite differently from man-made property, largely because it is governed by different conditions of supply. Many if not all of the harmful and undesirable economic effects of the general property tax can be attributed to the application of the tax to man-made property. Among these undesirable effects are the penalty of higher taxes following the improvement of urban land, the reduction of incentives to invest in land improvements, and the consequent hindering of economic growth. Taxing land values, however, produces a reverse effect and stimulates the investment in and improvement of land, thereby accelerating economic growth.

Converting the uniform real estate tax into a land value tax would provide an immediate stimulus for the economic development and use of urban land. This is based on the assumption that no legal or social obstacles stand in the path of landowners seeking the full opportunity cost of their land and that the supply of building factors is reasonably elastic. The spur to economic development results from four effects that a changeover to land value taxation releases: the capitalization, holding-cost, fixed-cost, and unburdening effects. Singly or in combination, these effects will exert a force to increase substantially the investment in improvements over a period of time without needing or having the benefit of an increase in demand for private urban land facilities. A larger quantity of facilities will be supplied at a lower price or higher quality.

The effect of converting a uniform real estate tax into a land value tax will probably cause an increase in the aggregate value of urban land involved, all other things being equal. Even though it may not cause an immediate change in the net actual economic rent of land, the new opportunities of increased investment and earnings will raise expectations that will be capitalized into higher land values. The value of land will rise most for urban land favored with locational advantages and whose potential use is faced with an elastic demand. In other words, the value of land tends to reflect the present value of its net potential income-producing ability, even though the land is poorly developed or vacant.

The outstanding virtue of the land value tax is its neutrality or efficiency; it will not interfere with the functioning of the market system. The tax will not reduce the supply of urban sites. Neither will it rise if land is put to a different or higher kind or intensity of use, nor will it force the land into a lower use if it is already in its highest and best use.

The advantage of neutrality in taxing land values would seem to justify consideration for giving the tax a special place in the tax structure. As a tax on surplus, the land value tax has the practical advantage of being easily administrable. The surplus income (economic rent) of land is relatively easy to identify and separate from the income of capital and labor. The yield of a land value tax will ordinarily be more than enough to exempt improvements from local urban taxes. The size of the tax rate will depend basically upon the trends in the population and economic base of the urban tax unit. In high property tax localities in the United States, the tax rate on land values may have to rise perhaps two to five times the present property tax rates. The key question is how the taxpayer will react to such unusual tax rates on land in exchange for the benefits of taxing land as well as not taxing improvements.

Macro-Economic Effects

The taxing of land values produces short- and long-run effects on the economic system as a whole, including aggregate investment, national income, and interest rates, as well as the general price level. The macro-economic influence of the tax follows the operation of the capitalization, holding-cost, and fixed-cost effects of the tax. In summarizing here I will consider the major short- and long-run effects.

An increase in the tax on land values will bring a short-run flurry of land sales and acquisitions that will raise the transactions demand for money temporarily. Over the long run, however, the capitalization effect will lower the transactions demand for money below its original level. The money-equilibrium curve will fall, which is to say that equilibrium in the money market will be achieved at lower interest rates.

The fixed-cost effect of increasing taxes on land values will raise the marginal efficiency of capital and raise the commodity-equilibrium curve so that planned savings will equal planned investment at higher interest rates and higher levels of national income. This shift in the commodity-equilibrium curve will probably more than offset the shift (in the opposite direction) of the money-equilibrium curve and create pressures for higher interest rates and an increase in national output and income.

The untaxing of building values will raise the marginal efficiency of capital and raise the commodity-equilibrium curve, thus reinforcing the effect of increasing taxes on land. A rise in building investments will raise the transactions demand for money in both the short and long run. This will reinforce the short-run increase in the transactions demand for money caused by increasing the tax on land values, and in the long run more than offset the reduction in the transactions demand for money for land acquisition. The net result of the combined shifts in the money- and commodity-equilibrium curves will be to raise national output and national income, as well as interest rates.

In terms of prices and national income the combined effect of increasing taxes on land values and untaxing building values is to raise aggregate demand in the economy. Because of the multiplier effect, the rise in the overall demand for goods and services will be several times the increase in building investment. An increase in building investment, on the other hand, will increase national output (building facilities and consumer goods)—also in accordance with the multiplier effect. Since aggregate supply and demand both will reinforce one another to increase employment, national output, and national income, there will be no tendency to increase price levels unless full employment is reached.

2 The Influence of the Property Tax on Investment and Employment

 J. A. STOCKFISCH

An Overview

About 25 percent of the net national product generated in the American economy is attributable to nonhuman productive agencies, the remaining 75 percent to labor. Table 2.1 presents a derivation of this estimate, based on the national income and product accounts, for the years 1956 through 1966. "Nonhuman productive agencies" may be described as "things"— such as land, structures, machinery and equipment, inventory, and combinations of these items—as contrasted with people. They are often termed "wealth," or "property," but these terms must be carefully defined if they are exclusively to encompass all nonhuman productive agencies. Here, for example, "wealth" denotes the market value of nonhuman agencies, which is derived from a capitalization or valuation process; "property" denotes rights and obligations between individuals and, strictly speaking, is a legal conception. As such, the property concept may not be confined to relationships treating physical agencies—as exemplified by such special monopoly privileges as patents and copyrights, liquor licenses, taxicab medallions, and so forth. The term "asset earnings" will be used to describe profits, rent (imputed and explicit), and interest, which have their origin in the productivity of nonhuman, physical resources.

According to the estimates in Table 2.1, asset earnings were about $80 billion in 1957 and $150 billion in 1966. The state obtained about 35 percent of asset earnings by means of property and corporate income taxes. Table 2.2 shows the derivation of these estimates, in terms of state and federal corporate income taxes, and property taxes. It can be seen from Table 2.2 that the impact of the property tax upon asset earnings has increased relative to corporate taxation during the 1960's.

Another way to view asset-earnings taxes is to relate them to wealth, when wealth denotes the value of physical assets. Table 2.3 shows selected

Table 2.1—Derivation of Asset Earnings, 1956–1966 [a]

	1956	1957	1958	1959	1960	1961	1962	1963	1964	1965	1966
Net national product	384,768	405,326	405,941	441,742	459,608	473,830	505,521	537,902	576,330	623,958	697,782
Employee compensation	242,502	255,499	257,142	278,528	293,648	302,086	322,878	341,004	365,720	393,932	435,719
Property earnings											
Corporate profits	41,990	41,669	37,155	47,192	44,453	43,768	46,997	58,933	66,276	74,898	82,196
Rental income	10,913	11,891	12,208	11,902	12,110	12,075	11,976	17,139	17,963	18,951	19,374
Net interest	11,716	13,427	14,827	16,384	18,050	20,027	22,036	13,838	15,794	17,917	20,163
Property taxes [b]	12,147	13,378	14,520	15,441	16,886	18,372	19,868	21,097	22,522	24,087	25,392
Total property earnings	76,766	80,365	78,710	90,919	91,499	94,242	100,877	111,007	122,555	135,853	147,125
Total earnings of employee compensation and property earnings [c]	319,268	335,864	335,852	369,447	385,147	396,328	423,755	452,011	488,275	529,785	582,844
Property earnings as percentage of total	24.0	23.9	23.4	24.6	23.8	23.8	23.8	24.5	25.0	25.6	25.2

ᵃ All figures are in terms of millions of dollars.

ᵇ These are the property and vehicle license taxes identified as "business" taxes and classified as an element of "indirect" business taxes in the national accounting scheme. They do not include an element of property taxes (specifically personal property taxes and vehicle license taxes) imposed on individuals which in the national accounting framework are classified as "personal" taxes. In 1966, these taxes were nearly $2 billion.

ᶜ The remainder of net national product claimed by nonfarm and farm proprietors (which the national accounts do not identify in terms of labor and nonlabor earnings) and the nonproperty tax elements of "indirect taxes"—specifically sales and excise taxes.

Source: *Survey of Current Business*, 41, no. 7 (July 1961): 6–7, 17; 43, no. 7 (July 1963): 12, 23; 47, no. 7 (July 1967): 16, 25.

Table 2.2—Net National Product, Estimated Property Earnings, and Major Asset-Earnings Taxes, 1956–1966 [a]

Year	Net national product	Estimated asset earnings [b]	Corporate taxes			Property taxes [c]			Total asset-earnings taxes	Asset taxes as percentage of asset earnings	Property taxes as percentage of asset taxes
			Federal	State	Total	Real and business	Motor vehicle licenses	Total			
1956	385,200	96,300	20,195	1,032	21,227	11,393	754	12,147	33,374	34.7	36.4
1957	404,000	101,000	19,916	1,006	20,922	12,614	764	13,378	34,300	34.0	39.0
1958	408,400	102,100	17,657	989	18,646	13,764	756	14,520	33,166	32.5	43.8
1959	442,300	110,500	21,948	1,204	23,152	14,681	760	15,441	38,593	34.9	40.0
1960	460,300	115,100	20,967	1,285	22,252	16,069	793	16,886	39,138	34.0	43.1
1961	474,900	118,700	20,685	1,329	22,014	17,561	811	18,372	40,386	34.0	45.5
1962	510,400	127,600	20,769	1,400	22,169	19,045	823	19,868	42,037	32.9	47.3
1963	537,900	134,500	24,640	1,684	26,324	20,226	871	21,097	47,439	35.3	44.5
1964	575,700	143,900	26,440	1,905	28,345	21,623	929	22,552	50,897	35.0	44.3
1965	621,600	155,400	29,305	2,053	31,358	23,099	988	24,087	55,445	35.7	43.4
1966	676,400	169,100	32,276	2,270	34,546	24,304	1,088	25,392	59,938	35.4	42.4

[a] All figures are in terms of billions of dollars.

[b] 25 percent of net national product.

[c] These taxes are the "business" portion of property and motor vehicle license taxes, as shown in source below. They do not include personal property and vehicle license taxes paid by individuals, which are classified as "personal" taxes in the national accounts.

Source: Survey of Current Business, 41, no. 7 (July 1961) : 16–17; 43, no. 7 (July 1963) : 22–23 ; 47, no. 7 (July 1967) : 24–25.

Table 2.3—National Wealth, by Type of Physical Assets and by Sector, 1956 [a]

Type of Asset	Total	Nonfarm households	Nonprofit organizations
Structures			
Residential	375.4	315.5	
Private nonresidential	215.3		22.3
Public civilian	145.7		
Producer durables			
Private	172.4		1.7
Public	5.1		
Livestock	11.1		
Inventories	108.4		
Consumer durables	163.3	149.3	
Land			
Agricultural	74.0		
Residential	55.5	47.2	
Nonresidential	71.3	24.4	6.4
Forests	14.7		
Subsoil	20.0		
Public	39.7		
Monetary metals	26.4	1.3	
Net foreign assets	17.8	4.1	
Military assets	84.3		
Total	1,600.4	541.8	30.4
Total government	319.6		
Total private	1,280.8		

[a] All figures are in terms of billions of dollars.

Source: Raymond W. Goldsmith, *The National Wealth of the United States* (Princeton, N.J.: Princeton University Press, 1962), Tables A-5, A-35—A-45, pp. 117, 177–194.

Agriculture	Unincorporated business	Corporations	State and local government	Federal government
18.5	15.8	20.0	5.1	.5
15.8	21.9	155.3		
			113.4	32.3
17.6	24.3	128.8		
			4.3	.8
11.1				
4.3	16.5	80.5	.2	6.9
14.0				
74.0				
	3.9	4.4		
	11.4	29.1		
	3.7	11.0		
	2.0	18.0		
			26.3	13.4
.2	.2	.2		24.5
		6.1		7.6
				84.3
155.5	99.7	453.4	149.3	170.3

characteristics of United States wealth for the end of the year 1956, by sector and by major types of assets. Total privately owned wealth was $1,280 billion. The following broad relationships found in Table 2.3 may be noted:

	Wealth (billions)	Taxes (billions)	Effective ad valorem tax rate
Corporate assets	$ 453.4	$21.23 (corporate only)	4.7%
Corporate and noncorporate earning assets [a]	1,095.6	12.15 (property)	1.1

[a] Total of $1,280.6 billion as shown in Table 2.3, less the value of privately owned monetary metals, net foreign assets owned by households, property of nonprofit organizations, and consumer durables. All but the last item are not purposefully taxed; consumer durables are taxed, but the property tax yields discussed above are those imposed on "business." Personal property and vehicle license taxes imposed on individuals are treated as personal taxes in the national accounting scheme. In 1956, these totaled $868 million.

These calculations indicate that the effective property tax rate for 1956, expressed as a rate of return on the value of assets, averaged 1.1 percent. The corporation tax (federal and state combined) is necessarily confined to the corporate sector and as such imposed a 4.7 percent ad valorem tax rate on corporate assets. If corporate-owned assets also bear their pro-rata share of the property tax, the overall ad valorem tax rate in the corporate sector was 5.8 percent.

These tax rates based on highly aggregated data conceal important differences between types of assets and various industries. Dick Netzer, using Raymond W. Goldsmith's wealth data and special tabulations of the data from a census of governments done for his study treating property taxes, provides further refinement of these aggregates. Table 2.4 presents these findings as related to property taxes.

In general, the United States property tax system bears least heavily on farming assets and most heavily on those of public utilities. Nonfarm (mainly urban) housing bears a heavy property tax burden. Manufacturing assets, as a broad aggregate, appear less heavily taxed than assets in other nonfarm activities due to the treatment of personal property. A large portion of manufacturing assets are machinery and inventory, which causes them to be classified as personal property. In New York and Pennsylvania (both large industrial states), personal property is not taxed. In other states industrial personal property is treated gently by tax assessors (either through statute or administrative practices) in order

Table 2.4—Effective Property Tax Rates, by Major Types of Assets, 1956

	Asset value (millions)	Property tax payments (millions)	Effective property tax rate
Nonfarm housing	$406,780	$5,195	1.28%
Agriculture	149,117	1,164	.78
Total nonfarm business	503,286	5,544	1.10
Selected utilities and transport	118,158	1,541	1.30
Manufacturing	161,814	1,620	1.00
Other	189,314	2,383	1.07

Source: Dick Netzer, *Economics of the Property Tax* (Washington, D.C.: The Brookings Institution, 1966), pp. 20, 28–29. Asset-value data are primarily from Goldsmith, *National Wealth*; property tax data are from the special census of governments undertaken for Netzer's study (cited above) and encompass fiscal years ending in 1956–1957. The latter magnitudes are not identical to the national income account magnitudes presented in Tables 2.1–2.2 above, which treat calendar years.

to create an environment favorable to the retention or attraction of industry. Effective property taxes on industrial activities, therefore, can vary markedly as between industries and location.[1]

The American system of asset-earnings taxation is thus characterized by significant unneutralities, both between the corporate and noncorporate sectors and within these sectors as well due to operational features of both the property and corporate tax systems.[2] Such unneutralities exact a toll in terms of economic efficiency,[3] a loss which is to be lamented.[4]

1. For further discussion of the property tax treatment of manufacturing activity, as between states, see J. A. Stockfisch, *A Study of California's Treatment of Manufacturing Industry* (Sacramento, Calif.: State of California, Printing Division, 1961), pp. 26–32.

2. The unneutral features of the corporate tax system include percentage depletion, the deductibility of interest (which tends to favor "debt-intensive" activities), the investment credit (whch tends to operate against inventory and structure-intensive industries), and no small amount of administrative capriciousness in the treatment of depreciation and the expensing of capital outlays.

3. See Arnold Harberger, "Efficiency Effects of Taxes on Income From Capital," in *Effects of Corporate Income Tax,* ed. Marian Krzyzaniak (Detroit, Mich.: Wayne State University Press, 1966), pp. 107–117, for an analysis of the adverse efficiency effects of the asset-earnings tax system.

4. There is no evidence, however, that indicates that either the corporate tax system or the property tax is any worse (or better) on this score than the federal personal income tax system with its complex of built-in excise subsidies that take the form of deductions, credits, exclusions, and exemptions. Particularly unhappy in the personal income tax is the treatment of physical asset earnings whereby undistributed

But tax inequalities between sectors, activities, or classes of assets tend to equalize by the operation of the price system through a "price-reallocation effect." Resources leave or avoid the heavily taxed activities (housing, for example, in the case of a property tax system which hits housing harder than other lines of investment) until the after-tax returns equal those obtainable in the less heavily taxed activities. This reallocation of resources also lowers returns in the less heavily taxed activities. To the extent that such a diffusion and equilibrating process operates in the economy, the combined impact of property and corporate taxes lowers the earnings of and the rate of return obtainable from investment by about 35 percent. Thus, if the average and marginal rate of return on investment is 10 percent (before taxes), corporate and property taxes reduce the rate of return to about 6.5 percent. The property tax system is currently responsible for 1.5 points of this reduction.[5]

---

corporate profits avoid personal taxation, to be converted into capital gains that may or may not be taxed at lower capital gains tax rates. It is the treatment of asset earnings under the personal income tax that provides any justification for the corporate tax, unless one accepts the notion that the corporation is a self-contained entity as contrasted with the stockholders who own it. But if one really believed in the entity concept, one should advocate that the corporation be subjected to the personal income tax.

One might rationalize the corporate tax on the ground that it is a way of subjecting property earnings (as contrasted with labor earnings) to heavier taxation, and that it is ethically desirable to tax property earnings more than labor earnings. The ethical position turns on a variety of pros and cons that need not be discussed here. If it is a social objective to tax property earnings more than labor earnings, the candid (or honest) way to do it is to subject property earnings to a special schedule of rates under the personal income tax.

5. These estimates are roughly supported by the 1956 estimate of asset earnings (as shown in Table 2.2 above) and their relationship to the Goldsmith (Raymond W. Goldsmith, *The National Wealth of the United States* [Princeton, N.J.: Princeton University Press, 1962], Tables A-5, A-35—A-45) wealth estimates for 1956. In that year, "earning assets" were $1,095.6 billion (excluding consumer durables, and selected other items) and "asset earnings" were $96 billion—an 8.7 percent average rate of return.

The estimate of the overall rate of return, however, should not be pushed too hard. The 8.7 percent rate of return is probably low due to both an underestimation of asset earnings and an overestimation of the value of the capital stock. On the earnings side, profits may be understated because depreciation is overstated due to tax incentives. Large elements of research and development outlays (including mineral exploration) undertaken by private firms are expensed rather than capitalized, which further understates profits. There is reason to believe that the "rental income of persons" shown in the national accounts is understated because of a conservative method by which the imputed rent for owner-occupied dwellings is estimated.

The wealth statistics also suffer from methodological difficulties. Estimates of wealth in "current dollars" are derived by using price indexes to inflate historical

A Methodological Digression

There are two approaches (or models) that may be used to analyze and evaluate the property tax. One approach is to examine a particular tax within the framework of the partial equilibrium demand and supply apparatus, to determine the extent to which the tax is "borne" by producers or consumers. Within this framework, to the extent that the supply schedule for the product or service is elastic, the tax is "borne by consumers" through a higher price of the taxed item. The remainder of the tax sticks to the specialized resources employed in the industry. It is from the application of this approach that many students assert that the property tax is borne by consumers.[6]

An alternative approach to the analysis of property taxes (or any other tax) is to ask what effect taxes have upon money resource earnings. In the absence of so-called "indirect" taxes, including property taxes, the value of the net national product would be entirely exhausted by income claims on the part of the owners of physical resources. The existence of such taxes, however, causes resource earnings and earnings rates to be lower than they would be if there were no taxes. It is the impact of taxes upon earnings rates that must be treated in order to answer the question of whether a tax affects investment and employment. Such an analysis necessitates an abandonment of the partial, one-at-a-time analysis of a particular tax. A price-theory model that explicitly recognizes the general interdependence that characterizes the pricing system, as contrasted with one that focuses only on a single industry, must be employed.

This position asserts that the notion that consumers "bear" taxes is either incomplete, misleading, or leads to a theoretical blind alley. Although a tax, because of its partial nature, may cause the price of a particular product to be higher than it would be if there were no tax (and thus burden some consumers), it has this effect precisely because it induces resources to leave or avoid the industry upon which the initially heavy burden is imposed. The resource displacement forces down earnings rates in nontaxed or less heavily taxed activities, as well as in the taxed activity. The "consumer-burden" doctrine is incomplete if it

---

accounting series. Most price indexes treating assets (especially construction indexes) rely heavily on input prices. For this reason, their use will cause old assets to be valued too high. Finally, only limited account is taken of the possibility that old assets should be valued downward by the availability of new equipment that embodies a more efficient technology.

6. See, for example, Dick Netzer, *Economics of the Property Tax* (Washington, D.C.: The Brookings Institution, 1966), pp. 33–36, for a recent exposition of this method.

ignores this impact of lower earnings rates. But as soon as account is taken of lower earnings rates in both taxed and especially nontaxed activities, the prices of nontaxed items must be lower. Some consumers experience benefits. For this reason, the orthodox theory is misleading.

A newer version of the orthodox theory is to assert that taxes are "shifted forward" to consumers through higher prices by some combination of industrial (and labor union) price fixing and either inflationary monetary or fiscal policies or both.[7] Under such assumptions or circumstances, no one as a vendor of productive services experiences an effect upon earnings rates. Hence, the tax should have no impact on investment, since rates of return are unchanged. Nor should a "forward-shifted" tax affect employment adversely since its imposition results in no reductions in the money demand for labor. It is because of conclusions like these that the doctrine of forward shifting of taxes constitutes a theoretical blind alley.[8]

At a minimum, the notion that property taxes (or any other taxes) are shifted forward in such a manner would seem to eliminate any concern that taxes per se can affect investment and employment; or for that matter, that they affect anything other than the general price level. But I do not think that taxes can be dismissed so casually. Taxes are coercive financial devices. They take dollars from people. Resource owners attain and earn fewer dollars because taxes exist. This income effect reduces earnings rates and rates of return on investment. Such are the reasons for the format of the overview in the first section of this chapter.

The Investment Incentive Effects of Asset-Earnings Taxes

If one accepts the view that asset-earnings taxes reduce the net earnings of assets in the aggregate (either because the tax is general or through a shifting-diffusion process), that effect will lower the rate of return, or the marginal efficiency of investment relevant to private investors. For

7. A notable exposition of this approach has been applied to the corporate income tax by Marian Krzyzaniak and Richard A. Musgrave in *The Shifting of the Corporation Income Tax* (Baltimore, Md.: The Johns Hopkins Press, 1963).

8. An attempt can be made to preserve the "forward-shifting" doctrine by asserting that individuals experience a reduction in real income as a result of the taxing-spending process, or because the government extracts some portion of total output for meeting its ends. But then the analysis must shift to the appraisal of spending programs. Taxes cease to have any effect as taxes. Perhaps the substantive force in the modern version of the forward-shifting theory is that any constraining fiscal act (like a tax) can be offset by expansionary fiscal acts (like creating and spending money).

example, if the marginal efficiency of investment is 10 percent (as suggested by the data in the above section), the American property tax system reduces the rate of return upon which private investors focus to 8.5 percent. It is through this rate of return effect that one can examine the investment consequences of the property tax. At this point, the analysis is one of applying a model (or theory) of investment to the analysis of the tax.

Several competing theories of investment behavior exist in economic literature. A popular one is that espoused by J. M. Keynes, who argued that the level of investment is determined by the relationship between the marginal efficiency of investment and the interest rate.[9] The interest rate is determined by the state of liquidity preference and the stock of money. If a tax lowers net asset earnings and through its announcement effect signals that the earnings of new assets will also be reduced, the tax lowers the marginal efficiency of investment. Given the interest rate, the level of investment spending falls. Through the multiplier process, consumption spending and total income fall.

As total income falls, the lower spending level will require less cash for transactions purposes. The release of cash can reduce the interest rate slightly and partially offset the tax's initial effect on investment spending. This latter offsetting effect, however, will only operate in the event that the interest rate is not already at a low level dictated by the "floor" (which is caused by a highly elastic portion of the liquidity-preference function).

A tax that lowers the rate of return on new investment will lead to an adverse impact on investment spending on the basis of a time-preference theory of interest. The application of this type of theory to asset taxation would run as follows: individuals achieve an equilibrium between current and future consumption. The interest rate is the "price" that reflects the terms on which individuals are willing to forego present consumption in preference to saving and investing. If a tax lowers the rate of return on investment, individuals will save and invest less. The supply of capital goods falls. The marginal productivity of capital goods will rise so as to increase the before-tax rate of return, which will restore or partially restore for asset-owners the same rate of return that they would enjoy if there were no tax. Like the Keynesian investment theory, the neoclassical theory of investment and interest—which draws either in whole or in part upon time preference as a determinant of the interest rate—asserts that the reduction in the rate of return on investment that

9. J. M. Keynes, *The General Theory of Employment, Interest, and Money* (New York: Harcourt, Brace and World, 1936), pp. 135–146, 165–174.

is caused by taxes will reduce the incentive to invest. Devoid of the modern nomenclature, these conclusions (and the underlying behavior propositions upon which they are based) are identical to the classical offerings of Ricardo and Mill when they addressed the subject of "profit" taxation.

One may take an approach to the theory of interest and investment that differs from that of either the Keynesian theory or the neoclassical theory. This alternative is suggested by the work of Frank H. Knight.[10] This approach is essentially a "productivity" theory of interest. The interest rate is determined on the margin of new investment. "The" interest rate is simply the rate of return over cost of producing new assets. It is helpful in this framework to conceptualize the rate of return as an expression of the cost of obtaining future net income flow. For example, if the rate of return is 10 percent, the cost of obtaining a future flow of one dollar of annual net income is ten dollars. If the rate of return is 20 percent, the price of a one-dollar annual flow is five dollars.

Within this framework a tax that reduces net asset earnings on the margin of new investment will increase the price of future dollars. In terms of the theory of consumer demand one can assert that if the price of future dollars increases, people will buy fewer of them. The theory of investment and the question of investment incentive, however, actually purport to treat the question of how much people *spend* in order to obtain future net income. The demand elasticity for future dollars is thus the critical factor. If demand is inelastic, an increase in the price of future dollars will cause people to spend more on new assets—that is, the tax that reduces the rate of return on investment will increase investment incentive. If the demand is of unitary elasticity, investment spending will remain unchanged. If it is elastic, investment spending will fall. Whether the property tax affects investment incentive adversely or favorably is thus a matter of "taste."

The Capitalization Effects of Asset-Earnings Taxes

To the extent that a tax that lowers the rate of return on investment does reduce or increase investment spending, it can have further effects upon the rate of return. And from these effects it is possible that capitalization effects will occur. These effects depend upon the shape of the supply curve for future dollars, or the marginal efficiency of investment function. Let us elaborate.

10. See Frank H. Knight, "The Quantity of Capital and the Rate of Interest, I," *Journal of Political Economy*, 44 (August 1936) : 433–463.

Initially, the tax reduces the net rate of return (and the capitalization rate) relevant for the decision-making of private investors. If the supply curve for future dollars is a horizontal line, the rate of return will fall by the same proportions that the tax initially reduces the capitalization rate. Let it also be assumed that the tax does not discriminate between the earnings of old versus new assets.[11] The earnings of old assets and the capitalization rate would fall by equal proportions. There would be no effect on the value of a capital stock. If the level of investment spending should change, however, and if the supply schedule for producing new assets is not a horizontal line, the capitalization rate will change by unequal proportions relative to the initial reduction in asset earnings. Should the tax increase investment incentive (which means that people spend more on future dollars) and if capital goods are produced under increasing cost, the capitalization rate will not fall by a proportion equal to the initial proportional impact of the tax on asset earnings. The capitalization rate will be relatively lower. The reduced earnings of existing assets will be capitalized by a relatively lower capitalization rate, and the value of the capital stock will rise. This is simply another way of saying that if the tax (or any other force) causes increasing costs in the capital goods industry, old assets will be appropriately valued upward to reflect those new and higher costs. Conversely, should the capital-goods industry reduce its output because of an adverse effect on investment incentive, the rate of return or capitalization rate will not fall by as great a proportion as do the net earnings of old assets. In this case the lower earnings of existing assets will be capitalized by a rate which is relatively higher than the after-tax earnings, and the value of the capital stock will fall.

These possible effects of general or diffused asset-earnings taxes upon the capitalization rate should be explicitly recognized when discussing such questions as whether a tax on land is capitalized. It is a part of orthodox tax theory to assert that a tax on land or vacant lots is capitalized, that the value of land will fall, and that its entire future burden therefore is borne by the owner at the time of the tax. But if land is subjected to taxes equal to what all assets bear (including new assets), no tax capitalization of the land tax will occur. Indeed, if land is taxed at

11. The idea of discriminating between the earnings of old assets and newly created assets is not far fetched. There have been two notable occasions of it during the recent past. In 1954, accelerated depreciation was introduced into the federal income tax; in 1962, the investment credit. Neither benefit could be applied to old assets. The effect was to permit new asset-owners to enjoy lower tax rates than could old asset-owners and to inflict capital losses on the owners of old assets. (For an account of the impact of the 1954 act on the inventories of used machinery dealers, see the *Wall Street Journal,* 16 November 1954.) It has never been made clear what grievance the government had against the owners of old assets.

a lower rate than all assets, its value will rise. The traditional or classical tax-capitalization doctrine is correct. However, it is only the "excess" tax burden that land may bear relative to all assets that will be capitalized in the fashion suggested by the traditional theory.

Conclusions

The effects of property taxes on investment and employment is a controversial issue. The controversy has its roots in the fundamental differences between alternative theories of capital, interest, and investment. The conclusions reached depend on the theory of investor behavior implicitly or explicitly accepted and applied to the analysis of asset taxation. In its most fundamental sense, the issue turns upon the shapes of the supply (cost) function for net future income and, especially, the demand function for net future income. As such, the issue is a priori indeterminate. One may only observe, however, that investment spending has held up remarkably well in the United States despite high levels of asset-earnings taxes during the past twenty-five years. This may have been because the demand for future dollars is inelastic or because the cost of producing future dollars may have fallen due to technological improvement, or both.

It should be recognized, however, that any asset-earnings tax, as well as any other tax (such as the personal income tax) will reduce people's money income. This reduction in money income occurs, however, only if the tax is not "shifted forward." With the consequential reduction in money income, individuals and business firms will therefore have less money to spend. For this reason they will buy fewer assets. This phenomenon essentially constitutes a leftward shift in the demand curve for new assets. It will operate to offset a positive investment incentive effect or to accentuate an adverse investment incentive effect. For this reason alone, therefore, a reduction of asset taxes will increase investment spending and over a longer period will increase capital accumulation, total output, and wages.

Little or a great deal can be said about the effects of property taxes on employment. Depending on one's predilection regarding the theory of investment, one can make assertions about the level of total spending. If it is also asserted that unique or specific levels of total spending are necessary to attain or sustain full employment, then the usual assertions about whether an asset-earnings-tax change will increase or reduce employment or increase the price level can be made.

3 *Reforming the Real Estate Tax to Encourage Housing Maintenance and Rehabilitation*

JAMES HEILBRUN

Introduction

Since the early 1950's urban-housing policy in the United States has increasingly emphasized the conservation and rehabilitation of existing buildings. Bulldozer methods have been widely criticized as unnecessarily destructive of both physical and social structures. Consequently, those interested in raising housing standards have tried to develop less drastic and more selective methods. Although new construction is still considered indispensable, a good deal of attention is now paid to the problem of maintaining quality in the standing stock. The following two questions will therefore be examined in this chapter: Does the traditional American real estate tax have unfavorable effects on the quality of existing housing? Would alternative ways of taxing real estate be preferable?

Since the urban housing problem is largely within the rental sector, analysis is limited to the effects of taxes on rental housing. Moreover, the present yield of the real estate tax is taken as a datum. I do not propose to investigate the question of whether the federal-state-local tax system as a whole is or is not neutral in its approach to real estate or rental housing and other economic activities. That is, of course, an important and interesting subject.[1] Here, however, I wish to investigate the narrower question of whether the real estate tax at its present level of yield could be reformed to the advantage of housing quality. By holding yield constant,

NOTE: For a fuller discussion of many of these issues see my longer study, *Real Estate Taxes and Urban Housing* (New York: Columbia University Press, 1966). I wish to thank the participants in the TRED conference and especially Professor Carl S. Shoup for his comments on an earlier draft of this chapter which led me to clarify or revise several points.

1. It has most recently been analyzed by Dick Netzer in *Economics of the Property Tax* (Washington, D.C.: The Brookings Institution, 1966), pp. 26–31, 67–74.

I am able to focus on the relative merits of the several varieties of the real estate tax itself without entering into the larger question of comparing real estate levies in general to other kinds of taxes.

Because local real estate taxes absorb something on the order of 16 to 20 percent of gross housing rent, it seems likely that they have significant effects on the condition of existing rental structures, but the matter has received no systematic treatment in related literature. Occasionally, one finds a statement to the effect that this or that variety of real estate tax would be more favorable to the maintenance of housing quality than is the traditional American levy on assessed value. Unless such statements are based on a systematic analysis of the way in which the rental-housing firm and industry operate, however, they remain unconvincing. The housing market, including the rental-housing sector, has been analyzed fruitfully in works by Chester Rapkin, Louis Winnick, and David M. Blank, by William G. Grigsby, and by others.[2] The house-operating firm, however, has received scant attention. Thus, my first task must be to outline a theory of the house-operating firm and of the rental-housing industry to provide a foundation for tax analysis.

A Theory of the Rental-Housing Firm

The quality of service offered is one of the variables that the owner of a rental structure can manipulate in attempting to maximize his return. This quality depends upon three elements:

1. The original cost of building the structure and subsequent investment in remodeling, if any. These expenditures establish the layout and spaciousness of the apartment units and determine the kind and extent of equipment they contain.
2. The level of quality at which structure and equipment are maintained.
3. The level of operating outlays that the owner applies to the given

2. See Chester Rapkin, Louis Winnick, and David M. Blank, *Housing Market Analysis* (Washington, D.C.: Housing and Home Finance Agency, 1953) ; and William G. Grigsby, *Housing Markets and Public Policy* (Philadelphia, Pa.: University of Pennsylvania Press, 1963). Lionel Needleman's *The Economics of Housing* (London: Staples Press, 1965), came to the author's attention after this study was completed. Important unpublished works are Sherman J. Maisel, "An Approach to the Problems of Analysing Housing Demand" (Ph.D. diss., Harvard University, 1948) ; and Wallace F. Smith, "An Outline Theory of the Housing Market, with Special Reference to Low-Income Housing and Urban Renewal" (Ph.D. diss., University of Washington, 1958).

structure and that determines the quality and extent of operating services he can offer.

Two other factors that have important effects on housing quality when broadly defined are:

1. The social characteristics of tenants. The quality of service afforded in a given apartment is affected by the character of the other tenants in the building.
2. Influence of the neighborhood. The quality of service afforded in a given building is affected by the quality of the neighborhood as an environment.

While no attempt has been made to incorporate either of these factors systematically, I believe that their omission does not affect the qualitative conclusions of the study.

The owner of a rental-housing property can vary the quality of service he offers by varying his outlays on structure, maintenance, or operation. At the same time, expenditures by consumers in the form of rent paid provide a market evaluation of the services provided. In general, the higher the quality of housing service offered the higher the rent consumers will pay. Depending upon the problem at hand, the output of service in a given building can therefore be measured either by the annual cost of factor inputs or the annual gross rent receipts. Of course, rent and cost are acceptable units of account for intertemporal comparisons only if we abstract from cyclical and secular changes in prices.

The rental-housing industry in a large city can be described as a case of monopolistic competition among a large group of sellers. The product is differentiated by quality, location, layout, rooms per unit, and the like. In general, the number of sellers is large enough and the largest firm is small enough in relation to the size of the whole market so that the effects of one firm's decisions on the others can be safely ignored, and it can be assumed that each building owner behaves as an atomistic competitor. The supply of space offered by the industry takes the form of a distribution of space by rent level per room, with the higher-quality units commanding the higher rents. Within this rent-quality distribution and constrained only by housing codes, the building owner can "move" his building either up or down, depending upon possibilities for profit indicated by the market. He accomplishes such a move by remodeling, by varying his outays for maintenance or operation, or by some combination of these three.[3]

In fact, these three matters are interdependent and decisions concern-

3. The possibility of "moving" buildings was apparently first pointed out by Herbert W. Robinson in *The Economics of Building* (London: P. S. King, 1939), p. 83.

ing them must be made simultaneously. For analytical purposes, however, I will examine them separately. Consider first the problem of choosing the optimum level of operating outlay. Assuming that the owner has already made any desirable changes by remodeling and has found the optimum maintenance policy, what level of operating outlays will be most profitable? Operating outlays cover such items of expense as fuel, janitorial and other labor services, painting (insofar as it is the owner's responsibility), repairs to structure and equipment, and administrative expenses. Within a considerable range these expenses are variable. Although housing, health, and sanitary codes establish certain minimum standards, the landlord may try to provide more (or, often, less) than the required level of service. For example, cleanliness in public areas and the speed with which minor repairs are attended to both depend upon the level of janitorial expense the owner is willing to undertake. Certain operating expenses are built into the structure, so to speak, but there remains a significant margin for variation. We all know what is meant by a well-run or badly-run building.

In fact, what I am suggesting is that in the short run a building can be regarded as a piece of fixed equipment to which the owner applies inputs in the form of operating outlays in order to obtain the output of housing services for which the tenant pays rent. The supply of such inputs is highly elastic since the owner will provide services as long as tenants are willing to pay at least their cost.

Moreover, I believe it is a reasonable hypothesis that for each type of property there is a more or less known best order in which services should be provided, proceeding from the most to the least profitable. (Such an hypothesis is supported by inference in numerous statements in property-management literature.[4]) For example, if a service costs $200 a month to provide and will enable the owner to enjoy a $300-a-month increase in gross rent, he will provide the service. He will undertake all such services until he reaches one that does not at least pay for itself. To choose a far-fetched example, it does not pay to provide a doorman in a building

4. Consider, for example, the following explanation of how to prepare a "plan for operation and service" of a rental property: "The successful operation of an income property depends a lot on the quality of service rendered *in* the building. . . . When the manager prepares his program for the year, he must decide exactly how the building is going to be operated and how far he can go beyond bare necessity in offering those special services which may increase tenant satisfaction and thus have tangible influence on the maintenance of gross income. . . . He considers each possibility in relation to the effect it may have on securing tenants and keeping them happy . . . he tries to come out with the best possible combinations."—H. G. Atkinson and L. E. Frailey, *Fundamentals of Real Estate Practice* (Englewood Cliffs, N.J.: Prentice-Hall, 1946), pp. 192–193.

catering to low-income groups, even though that service would increase the security of tenants; the poor are unwilling to pay the cost of the additional security. Owners are well aware of which services pay and which do not. They push service output to the point at which marginal revenue equals marginal cost.

Next consider how the owner can vary his outlays for maintaining the quality of structure and equipment. I refer here not to ordinary repairs, which are an operating outlay, but to replacement of worn-out structure and equipment. The dividing line between repairs and replacement is not logically clear in an entity as complex as an apartment building, but let us assume that a conventional dividing line can be drawn.

Replacement must also be distinguished from remodeling. In discussing replacement, layout and equipment are held constant. Suppose that the owner is committed to his present layout and to the retention of all existing types of equipment. The question reduces to one of how often an old item, such as a plumbing fixture, should be replaced by a new one.

Since much equipment and many parts of a structure deteriorate gradually over time, the more frequently they are replaced, at least up to a certain point, the better the average level of service rendered in the building will be and the higher the rent the tenants will be willing to pay. Instead of speaking of individual parts separately, we could, indeed, generalize by saying that the shorter the average period of replacement in a given building, the higher the quality of housing service rendered and the higher the attainable level of gross rent.

The owner regards each expenditure for replacement of structure or equipment as an act of investment that must compete with other possible uses of capital. He will undertake replacement whenever he expects the rate of return on such an outlay to exceed the opportunity cost of the necessary funds. The expected rate of return will, of course, be dependent upon the expected increment to future gross rent attributable to the act of replacement. This increment will be the difference between the series of annual gross rents the building would yield if replacement were undertaken and the series of smaller annual gross rents it would yield without replacement.[5]

A given piece of equipment will be kept in use not until it is thoroughly

5. The analysis of replacement decisions in this paragraph follows closely the argument of Smith, "Outline Theory," chap. 6, and differs considerably from the approach used in my earlier study, *Real Estate Taxes and Urban Housing* (New York: Columbia University Press, 1966), pp. 32–35, and in the first draft of this chapter. I am indebted to participants in the TRED conference discussion for persuading me to revise my analysis of this matter and of the effects of taxes on replacement decisions that follows from it in the second half of the chapter.

"worn-out" and ceases to yield *any* service, but only until the annual value of the service it renders has fallen far enough so that replacing it will produce a rise in gross rent sufficient to make the necessary investment in replacement profitable. Those who wish to obtain high-quality housing service must be willing to pay a high-enough absolute rent premium for new as compared to old equipment so as to make frequent replacement investment profitable to the owner. Tenants who do not seek high quality will not be willing to pay as large a premium for "newness." Owners of buildings catering to such tenants will find that replacement becomes profitable only after a longer period has elapsed. Thus, the average period of replacement in such buildings will be longer than in buildings serving the high-rent, high-quality segment of the market.

Of course, replacement policy and operating policy are interdependent; any change in the average period of replacement is likely to be accompanied by a change in the level of operating outlays as the owner "moves" his building into a new rent-quality class.

Finally, consider the possibility of moving a building by remodeling. Remodeling takes place when interior layouts are changed or additional equipment is installed. Like replacement, it involves an investment decision of the conventional variety. Remodeling requires the commitment of additional capital. The return on past investment in the building is not relevant. What matters is the expected return on the added funds. The owner will remodel if he expects the return on the additional funds he invests to exceed the opportunity cost of his capital. It is hardly necessary to add that remodeling is likely to result in a change in operating and replacement policy as well.

The argument so far can be summed up with the help of a simple diagram (Figure 3.1). Annual gross rent is measured on the vertical axis, total annual cost on the horizontal. The curve, which I will refer to as a revenue-cost curve, shows the annual gross rents obtainable by varying the level of operating outlays (OC) given a constant level of fixed costs (FC). For simplicity it is assumed that rent falls to zero when operating outlays fall to zero. As the building owner moves from lower to higher levels of operating outlay, he moves from more to less revenue-productive input dollars. He earns maximum net income where the slope of the revenue-cost curve is equal to 1. At that point the marginal dollar of operating-cost outlay just brings in one dollar of additional rent. On the cost axis the associated level of cost indicates what might be called the optimum quality of operation.

It is assumed that all properties are owned debt-free and, for the present, that no taxes are levied. Annual fixed costs (FC) therefore consist of planned net income plus the annual charge for replacement needed to maintain a given average period of replacement of structure and equip-

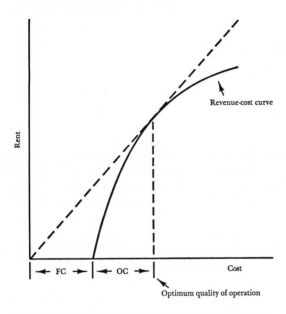

Figure 3.1. Equilibrium of the House-Operating Firm

ment. Since net income is included as a cost, total annual cost will just equal total rent when normal returns are earned. In that case a firm in equilibrium and earning normal returns will operate at the point where the revenue-cost curve is just tangent to a 45° line from the origin.

If the diagram is altered slightly to show rent per room and cost per room instead of total rent and cost, the housing market can be depicted schematically by a set of revenue-cost curves (Figure 3.2) in which the higher fixed costs necessary to build and maintain (in the replacement sense) more spacious or elaborate apartments are generally also associated with the higher operating costs that the tenants of the more luxurious buildings are willing to pay for. Since site rent is a part of planned net income, locational advantages of particular buildings would also be reflected in higher fixed costs and would bring in higher rents.

Effects of Real Estate Taxes on Operating Decisions

We are now ready to analyze the effects of real estate taxes on the quality of urban rental housing. Assuming that we are dealing with a single housing market that falls entirely within one taxing jurisdiction and, moreover, that this housing market and taxing jurisdiction are isolated from all

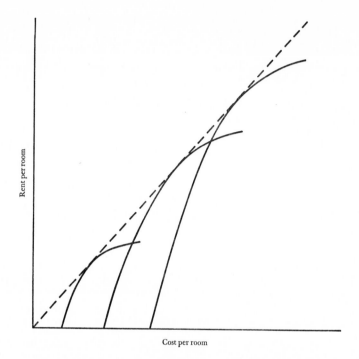

Figure 3.2. Diagram of a Rental-Housing Market (Schematic)

others, then inter-area competition can be ignored. I have chosen to use the method of differential incidence in comparing the effects of various kinds of real estate taxes. Thus, I can treat governmental expenditures as fixed and concentrate on analyzing the changes that take place as one real estate tax system replaces another of equal yield.

The following taxes will be compared: (1) an ad valorem tax on assessed site value; (2) an ad valorem tax on the assessed value of site and improvements combined (the traditional American levy); (3) a proportional tax on the actual (not the assessed) gross rent of site and improvements combined; (4) a tax on the net income of site and improvements combined; and (5) any of the above combined with a tax abatement to encourage maintenance and rehabilitation. With the exception of the net income tax, these alternatives (and a few more) have been or are now employed in many parts of the world and hence must be regarded as feasible systems.[6]

6. See, in this volume, Chapter 11 by Daniel M. Holland and Chapter 8 by A. M. Woodruff and L. L. Ecker-Racz; as well as Heilbrun, *Real Estate Taxes,* chap. 9; and Netzer, *Economics of the Property Tax,* chap. 8.

Let me begin by examining the impact of these taxes on operating decisions. Assuming that a site value tax is already in effect, then the impact of other levies can be compared with the effects of the site value tax. The latter provides a convenient starting point because it is neutral to both operating and investment decisions and cannot be shifted forward to tenants.

It is not necessary to repeat here the familiar explanation of why the site value tax cannot be shifted from owner to tenant.[7] As for its neutrality, the tax is, in effect, a lump-sum payment that the owner must make regardless of the existence, absence, or condition of any buildings on the site. Since the tax is fixed without regard to improvements, it cannot have any effect on the owner's operating decisions. If the situation when the site value tax is in force is compared to a no-tax situation, the only possible difference arises as a consequence of changes on the expenditure side; the tax itself does not cause the optimum operating point for any building to shift.

Suppose now that the voters in the taxing jurisdiction decide to replace the site value levy with a tax on the combined assessed value of site and improvements, at the same level of yield. Will this new tax affect the quality of operation of existing buildings in the short run? Apparently, it will not, if the following argument is valid.

Let us assume that properties are uniformly assessed at full market value or at some given proportion of full market value. Market value, in turn, tends to equal the present value of expected future net returns. It has been shown that the annual net return from a given building is maximized when the building is operated at the optimum level of quality. Above or below that level of quality, present income is reduced. It does not follow, however, that if the owner were to operate away from the optimum quality level, the market value of the property would be lowered. Market value is based upon the market's estimate of the potential earning power of a property and will not be influenced by the failure of a particular owner to realize the property's full potential. Thus, if assessments are based on market value, they will not vary with operating decisions. In the short run, the quality of operation of existing buildings will not be altered if the community changes from a site value tax to the traditional American levy on combined assessed value.

To look at the matter another way, we can say that the amenities provided by operating outlays do not have any capital value. They do not represent stored-up wealth, since their expected life is, by definition, short. Hence, they do not create liability for a tax on assessed capital value. According to the assistant director of assessment in the tax department of

7. The argument is summarized in Netzer, *Economics of the Property Tax,* pp. 33–34.

the city of New York, his department takes no account of the operating condition of a building in assessing its value.[8] I did not undertake any empirical investigation of this point, but I think it well deserves such study.

Suppose that instead of replacing the site value tax with the traditional American property tax, the community had voted to adopt a tax on the actual gross rent of site and improvements combined. Here is a tax that, unlike the first two, would *not* be neutral to operating decisions in the short run. The effect of changing over to a tax on gross rent would be to discourage operating outlays. Owners would now find maximum profits at a lower level of quality of operation than before. I argued, in discussing operating expenditures in the absence of taxation, that owners push them to the point at which the marginal dollar of outlay just brings in a marginal dollar of rent. That same point would provide a profit optimum in the short run under the first two taxes I analyzed. When gross rent is subject to tax at rate t, however, owners will proceed only to the point at which a marginal dollar of outlay brings in $1/(1-t)$ dollars of rent. That point is encountered at a lower level of operating expense since owners proceed in order from more to less revenue productive operating outlays. Thus, compared with the site value tax as a neutral standard, a gross rent tax would cause a general contraction in operating outlays and therefore would reduce the general quality of rental-housing services. Since a tax of 15 to 20 percent on gross rent would probably be needed to match the yield of the present American property tax, the effect at the quality margin would not be trivial.

Next consider a tax on the net income of site and improvements combined. Like a site value tax, this variant will be neutral to operating decisions. The argument is a familiar one in the theory of the firm; taxing net income at so much percent per annum does not induce the owner to operate differently than he would in the absence of taxes. Hence, in the short run, shifting from a site value tax to a net income tax would not alter operating outlays in rental housing.

The last variant I wish to take up is a tax abatement. This device may be very useful in stimulating the improvement of housing quality through its effect on investment decisions, but it is hardly relevant as a means of encouraging operating outlays. An abatement is most likely to take the form of an agreement not to raise the tax base of a property during some limited period if the owner undertakes specified improvements in quality. Such a scheme is meaningless in connection with a site value levy. Under the combined assessed value tax and the net income tax, the owner is already operating at the level of quality that maximizes tax liability. Thus, an agreement not to increase liability further if the owner expands operating

8. Interview with the late Alfred Jacobsen, 8 June 1962.

outlays cannot induce him to do so while those taxes are in force. Only in connection with a gross rent tax would an abatement plan alter operating decisions: its effect would be to remove the tax on rent at the operating margin, thus inducing the owner to expand operating outlays to the same level he would have chosen in the absence of taxes. The unfavorable impact of the gross rent tax on operating quality would be removed.

Effects of Real Estate Taxes on Investment Decisions

Thus far I have analyzed only the operating effects of real estate taxes, and these only as they would appear in the short run. In the longer run taxes will also affect investment decisions; since it is through such effects that tax shifting can occur, I must now discuss tax shifting as well.

Herbert A. Simon has shown that the division of the burden of a tax on urban real property between land and improvements cannot be determined a priori; the proportion of the tax borne by the site owner may be less than, equal to, or more than the proportion of site rent to total rent, depending upon the assumptions of the analysis.[9] For the present purpose it will suffice to say that at any rate a significant part of the burden falls on the rent of improvements. In other words, when the community votes to shift from a site value tax, which is neutral to investment decisions, to a tax on the combined value of site and improvements, the tax on improvements is at best only partly offset by a fall in the rent of land gross of tax, consequent upon taxing improvements. A new burden thus falls upon all projects for investing in structure. For purposes of argument I assume a tax on real property only. Thus, such personal property as producer's durable goods and inventories remains untaxed when the community replaces the site value levy with a tax on the combined value of site and improvements.[10]

9. Herbert A. Simon, "The Incidence of a Tax on Urban Real Property," *Quarterly Journal of Economics*, 57, no. 3 (May 1943) : 398–420; reprinted in *Readings in the Economics of Taxation*, ed. Richard A. Musgrave and Carl S. Shoup (Homewood, Ill.: Richard D. Irwin, 1959), pp. 416–435.

10. In the United States tangible personal property is often, but not always, included in the tax base. The overall effective rate of taxation is well below that on real estate, however, since much tangible personal property is legally exempt, much otherwise escapes taxation, and rates or assessments are often low on the remainder. Netzer estimates that tangible personalty accounted for 17.7% of nationwide property tax revenues in 1957. He estimates the 1956–1957 effective rates of taxation as follows: on manufacturing personalty, 0.7% ; on manufacturing realty, 2.1% ; on the two combined, 1.0% ; on all nonfarm business (excluding all residential real estate), 1.1% ; on nonfarm housing, 1.3%.

Intangible personalty is now so widely exempt from property taxation that it produced, according to Netzer's estimate, only 2.0% of property tax revenues in 1957. See Netzer, *Economics of the Property Tax*, pp. 24–29, 138–153.

I assume that before the imposition of the tax on improvements capital earned the same marginal return in all its uses, due allowance being made for differences in risk. The new tax on improvements therefore pushes the return on investment in housing and other structures below the margin of profitability. Investment in housing ceases until housing rent can rise sufficiently to yield an after-tax marginal return equal to that obtainable on untaxed uses of capital. I have ignored the possibility that a tax on building capital may slightly reduce the equilibrium rate of return to capital in general, the expected normal return on housing investment and, to that extent, the increase in rents necessary to induce new housing construction.[11]

It is worth emphasizing that real estate is far more capital intensive than most economic activities. In 1957 the ratio of capital (as measured by value of all tangible assets) to output (as measured by national income originating in each sector) was 1.9:1 for all nonfarm businesses, excluding residential real estate. For all nonfarm housing the ratio in the same year was 18.9:1, almost exactly ten times higher.[12] Thus, a uniform tax newly imposed on capital value would have much stronger effects on housing than on nonfarm activities as a whole. This will be true, a fortiori, under the assumption that the new tax applies only to real property. Even after allowing for the fact mentioned above, that a fall in land rent gross of tax and a fall in the equilibrium rate of return to capital net of tax might absorb some of the burden of the new levy on improvements, it is evident that the percentage rise in housing rent necessary to shift the remaining burden of the tax forward to consumers would be far larger than the percentage rise in price necessary to achieve the same shift for the aggregate of other activities.

The required increase in housing rent could occur only through shrinking supply (that is, diminution of the standing stock), rising demand, or both. In a declining community the necessary conditions might be permanently absent. In the usual case, however, we would expect demand to increase sufficiently over time so that the remaining tax burden could be passed on from owners of improvements to their tenants.

A rise in demand may, in fact, take place for several different reasons with somewhat different consequences for the quality of housing. For example, the rise may occur as a result of increasing income per capita with no change in population or, by contrast, as a result of increasing population with no change in per capita income. The different consequences to be expected in the two cases can, however, be reached only at the end of a

11. On this point see ibid., pp. 36–37; and Simon, "Incidence of a Tax," pp. 416–422.

12. Netzer, *Economics of the Property Tax,* Tables 2-4, 2-7. If the value and rent of land were excluded from both ratios, the difference between them would probably be somewhat less, but still very substantial.

chain of deductive arguments too long to be attempted here.[13] I will therefore confine myself to more general points.

First, let us look at the effects on the average period of replacement of structure that would follow a changeover from the site value tax to one of the other types.[14] Suppose that before the tax change takes place a given owner was in equilibrium, maintaining the average period of structural replacement that was optimal for his segment of the market. If the community then adopts a tax on the combined assessed value of land and improvements, what will be the effect on the owner's replacement policy? The argument concerning the effect of the traditional American tax is as follows: the structural condition of a building is properly of concern to the tax assessor since replaceable structure and equipment certainly have capital value and this value is greater, the longer their remaining useful life. The older the equipment in a building, the less the annual tax. It follows that each investment in structural replacement adds an increment to the taxable value of the building. Projects for replacement that were on the margin of profitability before the tax change thus fall below the margin after the tax on building value is adopted.

It will be recalled that in the absence of taxes, a given piece of equipment will be kept in use until the annual rental value of the services it renders has fallen far enough so that replacing it will produce a rise in gross rent sufficient to make investment in replacement profitable. Given the general level of housing rent, when a building tax correlated with capital value is imposed, a piece of equipment will have to remain in use longer (that is, depreciate farther) before the necessary margin between its annual rental value and the rental value of its replacement is sufficient to make replacement attractive. Thus, imposing a tax on building value would immediately lengthen the average period of replacement in rental structures.

In the course of time, however, tax shifting will occur. As a result of rising demand, shrinking supply, or a combination of the two, housing rent will rise and this will tend to increase the absolute differentials between the rental values of old and new equipment upon which replacement depends. The higher level of rent, however, in effect puts a higher price on the amenity of "newness" provided by replacement. This amenity is one of the constituents of housing quality. Since the demand for quality is probably quite price elastic (more elastic, indeed, than the demand for housing space), the rise in rent necessary to cover tax payments will, so to speak, reduce the quantity of "newness" demanded.[15] Thus, even after tax shifting has worked itself out, the average period of replacement will be longer and

13. On this point see Heilbrun, *Real Estate Taxes,* pp. 90–104.

14. See note 5, above.

15. For a fuller analysis of the demand for space and the demand for quality, see Heilbrun, *Real Estate Taxes,* pp. 37–45.

housing quality lower than before the changeover to a tax on the combined assessed value of land and improvements.

If the community decided to adopt either a tax on gross rent or a tax on net income instead of the tax on combined assessed value, the results would be much the same as those just recited. Upon impact, both of those taxes would cause an immediate lengthening of the average period of replacement. As in the previous case, tax shifting through a rise in rent would fail to restore the pre-tax situation, since higher rents would, in effect, raise the price of replacement amenities and therefore reduce the amount demanded.

Before concluding the analysis of the effects of tax changes on rate of replacement and on remodeling, I must return to the discussion of the "moving" of buildings. In a world in which buildings last for decades or centuries, while tastes, technology, population characteristics, and the level and distribution of income change continuously, the housing stock is always in the process of adapting to new patterns of demand. Adaptation usually involves moving certain buildings either up or down in the rent-quality distribution, and the move is accomplished by remodeling, by changing the rate of replacement and the level of operating outlays, or by both.

In the preceding section, I assumed that the house-operating firm was in equilibrium at a profit optimum when a change in the tax system occurred and I examined the effects various tax changes would have on that equilibrium position. Now the case is reversed; the tax system is held constant, but a new pattern of demand emerges, that is to say, demand curves shift. The former level of operating expenses and replacement outlays, perhaps even the former design or layout of the building itself, is no longer optimal for the firm. How do various taxes affect the process of adapting to the shift in demand? Since adaptation through change in quality is essential to a well-functioning market, it is important to analyze such tax effects.

When adaptation consists in moving a building *up* in the rent-quality distribution (for example, in response to an improvement in the general character of the neighborhood), it almost always requires a significant commitment of additional capital. The owner is likely to have to overcome past deficiences in maintenance by making a substantial immediate investment in replacement. He will often have to invest in remodeling as well. But even when adaptation consists in moving a building *down,* it frequently requires capital investment. If, for example, the neighborhood population is gradually changing from middle- to lower-income class, owners may wish to break up large apartments into smaller units better suited to local demand. To do so will require investment in remodeling.

The site value tax in no way impedes either remodeling or outlays for catching up on replacement. However, a tax on combined assessed values, on gross rent, or on net income imposes a burden on projects for investing in structure. The owner will elect to move his building by remodeling and by making the investments necessary to shorten the average period of replacement as soon as he finds that the expected return on the necessary investment exceeds the opportunity cost of capital. Under a site value tax the expected marginal return is tax free, but under the other systems the return creates either taxable value, taxable rent, or taxable income. The owner will therefore proceed only when the expected additional return *after* tax exceeds the opportunity cost of capital. The absolute amount of the prospective rise in rent necessary to induce him to invest will be larger by the amount of the expected rise in tax liability. The response of the market to changes in the pattern of demand is thus systematically distorted and the housing stock adapts less efficiently than it might to consumer preferences.

At this point a tax abatement could conceivably come to the rescue. It is assumed that the abatement takes the form of an agreement not to raise the tax base during a limited period if certain improvements are undertaken through remodeling or replacement. Such an arrangement would reduce (although, since the abatement is temporary, not entirely remove) the disincentive to investment that occurs under the three taxes discussed above. The more widely it is used, however, the more likely it is to have adverse effects on revenue, reducing tax receipts below what they would otherwise have been. One of the terms of the present discussion is that tax revenues (rather than rates) are to be held constant. In that case, an abatement on some properties might require the community to raise the tax rate itself, with consequent harmful effects in other directions (for example, on new construction).

Louis Winnick has made the interesting suggestion that an abatement for rehabilitation of existing buildings could be limited geographically to slum areas. Such geographic discrimination, he believes, would concentrate rehabilitation in areas where it is most needed but least likely otherwise to occur. Thus, it would reduce or perhaps eliminate adverse effects on revenue.[16] His argument is that with a tax abatement (and perhaps mortgage assistance) it would be possible to take, for example, a $40-a-month slum apartment and rehabilitate it to rent for $50 or $60 a month instead of the $80 a month that would be required under ordinary cost conditions. The low-income slum resident would willingly pay $50 or $60 for the improved housing. He could never have afforded to pay $80, however, so such abatement-induced rehabilitation does not reduce the demand for ordinary com-

16. Dr. Winnick advanced this suggestion at the TRED conference on 13 June 1966 during the discussion of the preliminary draft of this chapter.

mercially rehabilitated housing and consequently does not reduce property tax revenues below what they would otherwise have been.

This proposal certainly merits consideration. It is one way of grappling with the problem of revenue maintenance under an abatement program. I doubt, however, that it would protect the revenue as effectively as Winnick suggests. Can one, for example, exclude from the rehabilitated building the not-quite-so-low-income families who would otherwise willingly have paid $80 a month for housing of like quality?

I have not dealt explicitly with the effects of taxes on new construction but it is, of course, obvious that those taxes that discourage investment in remodeling will in the same fashion discourage investment in new housing. Likewise, an abatement policy can be extended to new construction to offset in part such tax disincentives; over a certain period, taxes on any new development could be limited to those previously paid on the parcel or even forgiven entirely. Once again, however, a likely result is that tax rates would have to be higher than they would otherwise have been.

Conclusions and Recommendations

The choice among alternative methods of real estate taxation certainly cannot be made solely on the basis of their effects on the quality of existing housing or even on the basis of those effects plus their impact on new construction. Many other criteria must be applied. Those I have examined elsewhere are the following: other resource allocating effects, applicability to owner-occupied as compared with rental housing, administrative feasibility, adequacy and stability of yield, and equity.[17]

Among the taxes considered here only the site value levy and the tax abatement are more favorable to housing maintenance and rehabilitation than is the tax on combined assessed value. While the site value tax emerges as the only variant with no harmful effects of any sort on housing quality, I believe that it must be rejected as an outright substitute for the traditional American tax on two related grounds: adequacy of yield and equity. Land rent is difficult to measure, but if my estimates are correct, revenue from the real estate tax has reached such enormous proportions that it may now almost equal or even exceed the rent of land in some localities. If we were to load the whole burden onto the site value base we might, therefore, expropriate, or very nearly so, the entire rent of land. That is why the proposal to change over to a site value base at the present

17. See Heilbrun, *Real Estate Taxes,* chap. 10.

level of yield raises the equity problem in such an extreme and, to me, disturbing way.[18]

The equity problem would be somewhat ameliorated if removing the tax on buildings were to cause an increase in the rent of land gross of tax. As I have indicated, the theoretical grounds for expecting such an effect are not entirely clear. I am not convinced, moreover, that even with the most favorable assumptions a 15 percent reduction in shelter cost could be expected to stimulate an increase in construction and hence in land rent substantial enough to make a significant difference, given the magnitude of the problem. In short, I am unwilling to recommend taking the plunge, or more accurately, forcing landowners to take it. As I will shortly explain, however, I would not object to lowering them into the water part way.

While a tax-abatement plan would not stimulate improvement in housing quality as much as would shifting to the site value base, it nevertheless remains an attractive possibility. True, it might cause some administrative difficulty and also some loss of revenue. Its principal drawback, I think, is again failure to meet the criterion of equity; an abatement discriminates unfairly between qualifying and non-qualifying property owners. I would agree, however, that none of these objections comes near being decisive.

In conclusion, I would recommend adopting one of the three following reforms:

1. Using the Pittsburgh plan of moving gradually toward a building tax rate set at only half the land rate. Such a plan reduces the disincentive effects of a tax on improvements, while still protecting the revenue, and it reduces the pain to be inflicted on landowners to the point where, if they cannot bear it, at least we economists can.

2. Retaining the present tax on assessed value of land and improvements but combining it with a tax abatement to encourage housing rehabilitation and perhaps new construction.

3. A combination of the first two reforms, involving the following elements: (a) setting a ceiling on building tax rates at their present level; (b) leaving the rate of tax on land value free to rise as necessary in the future; and (c) using tax abatement to encourage rehabilitation and perhaps new construction.

18. For a fuller discussion of these issues, see ibid., pp. 150–154, 162–167; and Netzer, *Economics of the Property Tax*, pp. 208–212.

4 *Urban Renewal and Land Value Taxation*

ARTHUR L. GREY, JR.

The Purposes of Urban Renewal

"Urban renewal," as the term has come to be used since the passage of the Housing Act of 1954, refers to three kinds of activities or programs: redevelopment, rehabilitation, and conservation. It also encompasses a variety of programmatic arrangements that have grown and shifted in emphasis in the course of two decades of operating history.

"Redevelopment" refers to the total physical clearance of land through public acquisition with federal subsidy and the subsequent sale of the open sites thus created in accordance with a plan formally adopted by the local governing body. It was the original element authorized by the 1949 Housing Act, one of the major post–World War II efforts to save American central cities from decline. Actually, of course, the objectives were much more complicated, since the 1949 law was passed through support from a very disparate group of influential interests.[1]

Redevelopment has been, by far, the most active segment of urban renewal. As a consequence, redevelopment is the aspect that has received the most criticism and this, in turn, has led to subsequent modification and broadening of the program. It is not necessary in this chapter (thank goodness!) to review all of the problems which have been encountered in the first twenty years of urban renewal nor to take note of the various intricacies which have been fashioned in response to criticism.

The most serious and frequent criticism of urban renewal has been concerned with its social consequences. When slums were torn down, people had to move, and, while there were federal requirements and standards that this process of relocation was supposed to observe, they were not

1. Cf. Ashley A. Foard and Hilbert Fefferman, "Federal Urban Renewal Legislation," *Law and Contemporary Problems*, 25, no. 4 (Autumn 1960): 635–684. Catherine Bauer Wurster called the 1949 act "mainly a kind of shotgun marriage between the housers and the planners . . . ."—Wurster, "Redevelopment: A Misfit in the Fifties," in *The Future of Cities and Urban Redevelopment*, ed. Coleman Woodbury (Chicago: University of Chicago Press, 1953), p. 9.

often effective.[2] The exigencies of local politics, project economies, and managerial inexperience frequently resulted in substantial neglect of the needs of those who were physically displaced.

Consequently, urban renewal was derisively dismissed as "urban removal" in the black community and among other residents of clearance areas. By the late 1960's federal policies were being broadly modified in response to this criticism.

Urban renewal policy, therefore, falls into three periods:

1. The 1949 act was directed at upgrading the housing stock through the elimination and replacement of substandard dwellings.

2. Beginning with the 1954 law, objectives were successively broadened, with housing, especially housing for the poor, becoming of relatively less importance. By 1961, a full 30 percent of federal urban renewal expenditures were authorized to be entirely unrelated to housing, and an unspecified larger share of urban renewal activity did not result in the development of housing.[3] In this period, the net effect of urban renewal, because new projects tended to lower residential densities and to emphasize nonhousing utilization of renewal sites, was to remove considerably more housing than it added.[4]

Experience and a variety of pressures had dictated the broadening of the objectives of urban renewal. One set of pressures came from the travail of central cities—from their public officials, institutions, property owners, and the least footloose of their business enterprises, as well as from a

2. There is a very extensive literature on this subject, including case histories of specific impacts of the program and more general analyses of urban renewal organization. A critical summary reflecting relocation experience in a range of communities is Charles Abrams, *The City Is the Frontier,* Colophon ed. (New York: Harper & Row, 1967), pp. 132–154.

3. Public Law 87–70, § 308. Another 1961 law, P. L. 87–27, § 14 also exempted any renewal area in a locality which the secretary of commerce had designated as economically depressed. Ten percent of federal funds for renewal might be expended in such projects.

4. Numbers of units demolished by urban renewal areas are estimated to be from two to four times as numerous as the numbers of units built. See Scott Greer, *Urban Renewal and American Cities: The Dilemma of Democratic Intervention* (Indianapolis, Ind.: Bobbs-Merrill, 1965), p. 56.

While modification of renewal policies and programs could reduce personal displacements from homes and neighborhoods, it would by no means affect the causes of all federally assisted dislocations. Fully one-half of the relocation needs caused by federal programs during the mid-1960's were originating in the interstate highway program and other nonrenewal activities. U.S., Congress, House, Select Committee on Real Property Acquisition, *Study of Compensation and Assistance for Persons Affected by Real Property Acquisition in Federal and Federally Assisted Programs,* 88th Cong., 2d. sess., 22 December 1964, p. 272.

variety of civic-minded interests. One picture of the situation will perhaps indicate the nature of this pressure as well as any other:

> The central city includes, typically, a business district; a railway and bus station; a university; Skid Row; a "hill"—which, though it may be flat, has remained socially elevated amidst the surrounding decay; an island of gracious town houses for the sophisticated and well-to-do; a museum housing a superb collection of pictures from every age and country except that in which the museum itself was built; and a park. Around these features and extending far beyond them, miles of seedy tenements and row houses peel and flake, amiable or grim in their degenerate old age.[5]

Another pressure was an awakening to the complexity of the city. The seamless web of urban life might be disregarded in the case of one or, possibly, two modestly sized renewal projects in the average city. Beyond this, reciprocal relations between city and project had to be taken into account systematically. Starting as a better housing program, urban renewal during this middle period became increasingly broad. Perhaps inevitably, it involved all the many problems and infirmities of American communities.[6]

3. By the close of the second decade a new set of forces affecting urban renewal developed from accumulated dissatisfactions and the suddenly greater heed paid to the grievances of blacks and poor in public programs. The 1968 Housing Act abruptly changed the emphasis of urban renewal, which for the preceding decade and a half had been, in application, drifting away from housing and slum problems, although new housing aids were enacted during this time. Implementing regulations provided that "priority consideration" be given to urban renewal projects "which contribute to conserving and increasing the existing housing supply for low and moderate-income families . . . ," or which "develop centers of employment opportunity for jobless, underemployed and low income persons." [7] The emphasis was upon meeting the needs of problem areas and areas of "high social tensions." While these "national goals" for urban renewal were a further addition to the possible ways in which the program might be interpreted, the stated intention was to narrow sharply the kinds of projects that would receive federal approval and funding.[8]

5. Peter Marris, "The Social Implications of Urban Redevelopment," *Journal of the American Institute of Planners,* 28, no. 3 (August 1962) : 151.

6. Greer, *Urban Renewal,* p. 18, states that a "dichotomy" of concentration upon specifics "as symptoms of the larger system . . . runs throughout the history of the urban renewal program."

7. Housing and Urban Development Act of 1968, §§ 2, 1602.

8. Department of Housing and Urban Development, Renewal and Housing Assistance Administration, *Urban Renewal Handbook,* RHA 7202, looseleaf (February 1969).

Economic Processes and Taxation

Urban renewal has been a time-consuming process. Increased appreciation of its social complexities has introduced new delays. In light of this, the comparative subtlety of the economic system, in contrast to the complications of overt administrative processes, commands some interest.[9] Taxation, as one device of economic adjustment, arises as a possible instrument to facilitate improvement without causing personal havoc and social disruption to the slum dwellers whom renewal was originally expected to help. Because of the universality of property taxation, it might be applied to exert an influence over environmental conditions more widespread in occurrence than the concentrations of aggrieved and adverse circumstances to which it is feasible to apply urban renewal.

A different and more sweeping reason for favoring economic processes could be that the imperatives of programs for housing are unpersuasive. Two economic arguments can be advanced against making a special case of housing needs. In the light of doctrines of consumer sovereignty, it might be held that singling out housing reflects a kind of "tunnel vision" on the subject. On the other hand, it might be held that housing quality is an elusive goal, a will-o-the-wisp like any other consumer demand that is a lead function of personal income.

Concerning the first of these arguments, the professional bias that distinguishes the economist is perhaps a preference for increasing personal income as his road to progress in contrast to directing the consumer's expenditure into specified channels: "What would people rather have: a better house, a flashier car, a shinier motorboat, fancier eating, a better education, more travel and expensive vacations, or a host of other things all of which vie for the customer's dollar and affect what he is willing to pay for housing. I am a little reluctant to say that I know or can define what my fellow man's desires are or to prescribe what they should be." [10]

The second point is that the level of aspiration, social and private, out-

9. The best-known version of the argument that renewal is only a feeble substitute for "free enterprise" is that of Martin Anderson, author of *The Federal Bulldozer: A Critical Analysis of Urban Renewal, 1949–1962* (Cambridge, Mass.: The M.I.T. Press, 1964). For a synopsis of his views, see James Q. Wilson, ed., *Urban Renewal: The Record and the Controversy* (Cambridge, Mass.: The M.I.T. Press, 1966), pp. 491–508, esp. p. 506. In a detailed criticism of Anderson's evaluation, Robert P. Groberg, "Urban Renewal Realistically Reappraised," ibid., pp. 509–531, asserts that it is a misconception to view government-sponsored renewal and private enterprise as mutually exclusive alternatives, since the federal program is based upon cooperation.

10. Statement by Karl L. Falk in Housing Act of 1961, U.S., Congress, House, Subcommittee on Housing of the Committee on Banking and Currency, *Hearing on H.R. 6028, H.R. 5300, and H.R. 6423,* 87th Cong., 1st sess., p. 435.

paces the rise in the standard of living. Thus, it is really not possible for new production of housing to draw abreast of what will be regarded as "adequate" in quality as actual achievement. Conversely, criteria of substandardness are always changing as a result of rising incomes and higher consumer expectations. For example, it was estimated that if the Bureau of the Census had applied the same standards to the housing stock of Maryland in 1940 as used in 1950, the quantity of "bad housing" in Baltimore would have been 18 percent higher in 1940 than the figure actually reported.[11]

Finally, it might be contended that taxation measures can rise above some of the political conflict of open advocacy of direct reforms. Resort to taxation, as with any other application of the price system, dampens an incentive here and spurs new commitment there without the "dirty business" of forcing resource choices directly.

Purely economic processes are not a complete substitute for administrative processes in dealing with city problems. The underlying social circumstances are too complex for *single* remedies or approaches to achieve substantially the environmental improvements sought under the name of urban renewal.

Georgian Economics and Theories of Surplus

Every theory must be submitted anew in each generation to the crucible of current conditions. Some will be found wanting and will be consumed in the flames, while others will emerge with their temper restored, their contemporary importance ascertained.

The essence of Georgian thinking that remains relevant for us today is not the theory of economic depression propounded in *Progress and Poverty,* although this statement is not lacking in intellectual virtuosity nor in plausibility for explaining something of the problems of its own time. Nor does this relevance lie in the reiteration of a natural rights doctrine that imputes to land economic attributes categorically different from those of other assets.[12] (Note the emphasis on *economic* attributes.) The doctrine of land value taxation does, however, have an importance and relevance to the discussion of urban renewal:

1. The theory of land value taxation appreciates the efficacy of resolving social objectives within the market system. Taxes are prices; they

11. Robert M. Fisher, *Twenty Years of Public Housing* (New York: Harper and Bros., 1959), p. 62.

12. Cf. George's comments on French physiocratic philosophy in *Progress and Poverty* (New York: The Modern Library, 1938), bk. 8, chap. 4.

are an *economic* resolution. The doctrine of land value taxation is by its nature a very contemporary statement that taxes are not just a means of providing revenue but perhaps more significant as a means for directing the allocation of resources. It is important now when discussions of the urban scene generate numerous (and frequently conflicting) suggestions for direct action, to press the point that the generalized pressure of the taxing system, as a system of rewards and penalties, might command with more authority.

2. The land value taxation doctrine recognizes that value is socially created. It asserts that taxes should fall on surpluses, and, to the extent that relative scarcity causes value to exceed the unavoidable costs entailed in production, it is "fair game" for taxation.

It is a mistake to apply a strict construction to the ideas of Henry George if the above points are to manifest their necessary importance for current conditions.

In using the term "land," we are concerned with a complicated system of rights to use space. There are rights of access, of light and air, and of the alienation or abridgement of the manifold privileges associated with the given terrestial site, above and below it. There are air rights and rights of proportional ownership in an underlying piece of ground beneath apartments under a condominium arrangement. Perhaps the surface rights in the last case are secured only by ground lease, not fee simple ownership. The courts may not have taken any position on the enjoyment of view rights, but it is apparent that buyers and tenants in the real estate market attach a value to unimpeded visual access to an expanse of space. Access to a view is to a considerable extent manufactured by the development of hillside lots as residential sites or the upward penetration of space by tall buildings; similarly, new construction may alter or destroy views and their attendant values. Indeed, what is esteemed about the view may be very largely manufactured. An outlook from a top-floor apartment in a tall building in many cities might be of little interest if the vicinity were in its primordial state. It is partly the habiliments provided the landscape by man that give it value.

For purposes of contemporary discussion, then, "space," not "land" and the rights relating to it, is what is under consideration. Space—like other resources—is combined with others in production and transformed, is susceptible of being used in variable proportions as relative costs dictate, and is not unvaryingly inelastic in its economic supply.[13] Today we

13. Cf. Kenneth E. Boulding, "The Concept of Economic Surplus," in American Economic Association, *Readings in the Theory of Income Distribution* (Blakiston, Pa.: Richard D. Irwin, 1946), pp. 640–641: "Certainly most services of land with the

recognize that the economic supply of land or space is a function of accessibility—the flexibility and the quality of the means of transportation that is generative of competitive sites and that diffuses the values socially placed upon space.

The English tradition in economic thinking was a very long time in breaking out of its narrow viewpoint upon the subject of surplus, a viewpoint that was more appropriate for describing the workings of a subsistence economy. Alfred Marshall's contribution to economic theory in broadening the application of the term "rent" (his terms: "quasi-rent" and "economic rent") to include other forms of surplus is well known. Marshall declared that land rent is only part of "a large genus" of surplus.[14] J. A. Hobson, who criticized Marshall for still maintaining that land was the "chief species" of this genus, insisted on the *generality* of the occurrence of surplus in contradistinction to either classical rent theory or the labor theory of surplus value.[15] Economic theory finally reached a conclusive statement of the ubiquitous nature of surplus in Abba P. Lerner's *Economics of Control.*[16]

If what has been said is in conflict with a cherished tenet of the advocates of land value taxation, the criticism is not that the theory is wrong but that it is incomplete. George himself recognized that surplus was derived from other sources of economic scarcity than land alone.[17]

The purpose of land value taxation is the apprehension of capital gains. No mystique of God-given creation of land can change the fact that these two forms of taxation of surplus—land values and capital gains—should be considered in conjunction with each other. Whereas Marshall Field is quoted as saying that "land is the only way to make money," as long ago as 1900 dividend income in the United States was estimated to have been twice as large as net rents and royalties,[18] and capital gains

---

possible exception of the great river-bottoms are neither original nor inexhaustible. Even the element of *location,* which must seem at first sight to be perfectly inelastic in supply as land cannot be other than where it is, nevertheless is significant only in relation to the location of the human population, which is perfectly capable of shifting."

14. Alfred Marshall, *Principles of Economics,* 8th ed. (London: Macmillan and Co., 1938), p. 629.

15. John A. Hobson, *Economics of Distribution* (New York: The Macmillan Co., 1900), esp. pp. 150, 343, 353, et passim.

16. Abba P. Lerner, *Economics of Control* (New York: The Macmillan Co., 1944), esp. p. 234.

17. See George, *Progress and Poverty,* bk. 8, chap. 3, p. 410, for his views on monopoly and surplus.

18. R. F. Martin, *National Income of the United States, 1789–1938* (New York: National Industrial Conference Board, 1939), p. 21.

have been identified as a significant factor in the development of fortunes in the United States.[19] In the states of New York, Pennsylvania, and Illinois, for which gross receipts from capital gains in the year 1936 were compiled, it was found that *securities* accounted for 74.9 percent, 86.8 percent, and 79.8 percent of the respective totals for each of the states.[20]

These figures represent a period when all capital asset values were low, of course. Real estate speculation has been rife in the 1960's, as in other periods of general prosperity. Yet asset trading in anticipation of appreciation has not been more prominent in real estate than in the securities markets in general and, in 1965, land made up less than 2 percent of the assets of all active business corporations.[21] The definitions and classifications in the available statistics may, of course, minimize or obscure to some extent the importance of real estate assets and asset value change. It would appear, however, from available data as to the types of capital gains, that no little part of the importance that has been assigned to the returns from landholding by many writers must be qualitative in nature.

The taxation of any increase in the value of land should be placed more on a parity with the taxing of capital gains generally. Perhaps these should be taxed at the same rate as ordinary income. Any reform of the American taxing system should seek to establish such congruencies.

Land is a haven of escape from the rates of taxation on ordinary income. Land value taxation would, of course, strike at part of this problem, though not at all. High-bracket taxpayers buy realty and its improvements to enjoy favorable tax treatment, for there is no questioning of the treatment of real estate appreciation as capital gain, and to reap depreciation charges on old assets. The price of real estate and improvements is to some extent raised because of the demand for it as a course of favorably taxed increases in financial well-being (capital gains) or of untaxed income (depreciation). The problems of tax equity and the utilization of urban space are reason enough for concerted tax reform.

Turning to urban renewal, the importance of tax reform as a means of accomplishing its objectives cannot be overstated. Even after two decades urban renewal efforts have aggregated only to a small fraction of the areas of our cities. Usually, their ostensible purpose has been, at

19. Lawrence H. Seltzer, *The Nature and Tax Treatment of Capital Gains and Losses* (New York: National Bureau of Economic Research, 1951), pp. 5–6.

20. Ibid., p. 503.

21. Or $31 billion out of an asset total of $1,723 billion reported by 1,423,980 firms. U.S., Internal Revenue Service, *Statistics of Income 1965*, "Corporation Income Tax Returns" (Washington, D.C.: U.S. Government Printing Office, 1968), p. 17.

least inferentially, to provide better housing. Typically, these programs have had scarcely any impact on the many square miles of existing development that is merely of indifferent quality, although the means have been provided for the programs of reconditioning and conservation that are the distinguishing mark of the 1954 federal legislation. Up to 1966 allocations on all renewal by the federal government had aggregated $5.7 billion (the program was begun in 1949),[22] which implies another $1.9 billion of local-government subsidy under existing formula. Spending for 1967 fell far short of estimated needs ($20 billion).

Application of Land Value Taxation to Urban Renewal

There are four areas of application with respect to which land value taxation will be considered:

1. The redevelopment project, taxation, and its financing: In a publicly assisted redevelopment project with recourse to federal subsidization, the value of existing development is destroyed to make a new site on which construction can take place. It is necessary to estimate the price at which the site can ultimately be sold, in order to estimate the deficit separating this sum from the acquisition of the property with its original improvements, so that the extent of the federal subsidy, which is two-thirds of this negative sum called the "net project cost," and of the local contribution, which is the other third, can be projected.

To do so, the (socially consistent) highest and best use of the property must be established and the value of the property rights derived therefrom appraised. The normal procedure is to ascribe the capitalized sum of all net income, over and above a normal return to be earned on the investment in improvements, to the land. This residual-land technique is congenial with land value taxation, although the premises are different.[23] Since buildings are cleared, landholdings consolidated, and basic physical improvements made through public action, local government is required to obtain the full fair market value for the property upon its disposition for ultimate development.

Taxes, because they are a cost of landownership, will affect the market value of this property to a private owner. Normally, it may be assumed

---

22. Department of Housing and Urban Development, *Statistical Yearbook–1966* (Washington, D.C.: U.S. Government Printing Office, 1968), p. 380.
23. The technique is an example of the application of marginal productivity theory, land being the factor held constant.

that the land will be liable for future taxation at the then prevailing general property rate, although New York (Stuyvesant Town) has exempted property from normal taxation for a stipulated period of time as an encouragement to its private redevelopment.[24]

The calculation of estimated future property tax revenue plays an extremely important part in the redevelopment process. From what is sometimes said concerning the productivity of future tax receipts by redevelopment projects in the course of justifying their being undertaken, one might make the unwarranted assumption that the purpose of redevelopment is to make money for the municipality. In California it is customary under an enabling provision of state law [25] to cover any part of the nonfederal one-third share of the net project cost, not otherwise regained, by the sale of tax allocation bonds. These are to be repaid, according to the statute, with the increased general property tax receipts ascribable to the increased value of property within the project boundaries.

In effect, the local financing is merely a method to amortize initial costs that will be recovered from future tax receipts. There are interesting questions in this connection: Since the local municipality might be given the power to forego the future collection of taxes for an indefinite period, it can increase the amount that will be realized upon resale of project real estate to private developers. Is it advantageous, from the public standpoint, to rocover a larger part of the local share of net project cost now, and, correspondingly, to reduce or eliminate future taxes? In other words, should the municipality accept capitalization or partial capitalization of the taxes?

This is probably not a question anticipated by land value taxation, since here we have government as the *seller* of the land. The answer on practical grounds would be negative, but, analytically speaking, it would have to depend upon a judgment as to what action would be advantageous to the community if it did act (contrary to a point made previously) as an *investor*.

Would the rate of return on the investment in the claim to future taxes (the discount to present value on taxes, if foregone) comfortably exceed the interest rate on the bonds? No answer is offered here, as there are imponderables of risk on both sides, but the question should be raised. Finally, what effect would land value taxation have upon the areas of redevelopment projects, if this system were adopted? For reasons to be

24. Abrams, *The City Is the Frontier*, p. 97, describes the Stuyvesant Town exemption as mainly a giveaway of $4 million per year for the benefit of high-income tenants.

25. Calif. Stats. 1951, ch. 1411.

discussed below, land value taxation should be expected to moderate the need for clearance to be undertaken as a public activity. It would not by any means, however, eliminate the need for clearance projects. Many areas blighted by obsolete patterns of land subdivision and streets could not realize their functional potential to serve the needs of the community without wholesale clearance and reorganization.

In addition, means are needed to assure that properties in former redevelopment project areas are reasonably well maintained henceforth. Land value taxation could contribute to this objective, presumably, although it probably would not, in this instance either, alone suffice to promote a high order of maintenance.[26]

2. Conservation and reconditioning, stimulating improvement, and the process of supercession: As pointed out above, land value taxation should reduce the need for clearance; it should promote improved maintenance in the vast "grey areas" [27] and the selective replacement of structures in established neighborhoods along the lines advocated by Jane Jacobs.[28]

The likelihood of the substantial upgrading of much of the city by these means must not be overrated, however. Many slum holdings are very productive of income and would not be substantially improved or torn down were only the land liable to a tax and at higher rates. The need for the strict enforcement of the building, health, and fire codes of the city as contemplated by the federal requirements for local "workable-program" certification could not be relaxed. The dampening effect of the depreciation credit in the federal income tax (and in state income taxation) upon higher rates of real estate taxation must be considered.

---

26. The efficacy of this program depends upon many other complications, including the comparative profitability of housing markets that evidence economic discrimination (for example, submarkets that do not regard all potential consumers as interchangeable and homogeneous in all respects except the one of relative willingness to pay). "Noneconomic" discrimination (on racial and other grounds) is basic to the practice of economic discrimination in housing markets.

27. It is my belief that this term is used with a good deal of imprecision of meaning. In the foregoing reference it means the portions of the "core" outside the central business district and the older portions of the "inner ring" as these terms are used in the New York Metropolitan Region Study. Cf. Edgar M. Hoover and Raymond Vernon, *Anatomy of a Metropolis* (Cambridge, Mass.: Harvard University Press, 1959) ; and Raymond Vernon, *Metropolis 1985* (Cambridge, Mass.: Harvard University Press, 1960).

28. Jane Jacobs, *The Death and Life of Great American Cities* (New York: Harper & Bros., 1959). For a discussion offering empirical substantiation of the disadvantages of large-scale simultaneous development of areas, see Jack Lessinger, "The Case for Scatteration: Some Reflections on the National Capital Region Plan for the Year 2000," *Journal of the American Institute of Planners,* 28, no. 3 (August 1962) : 166.

The fact that new depreciation accounts can be set up against the useful life of the asset (not its remaining unused tax life) makes older properties (including slums) attractive investments for larger federal taxpayers. One can wish that any depreciation beyond the useful life of the property be "earned" by evidence of extraordinary expenditure for the conservation or improvement of the asset.

Complications are not only on the demand side. *Most* improvements are undermaintained. Can tax changes make a substantial impact, considering the inefficiency of the building industry (including the high cost and limited supply of remodeling service, the low incomes of many occupiers, and the high financing costs)? The point is arguable, but taxation is at least an element in a coterie of remedial possibilities.

One of the subsequent refinements in urban renewal legislation has expressly been to make possible the retention of old and functionally obsolete structures in certain instances instead of assuring their destruction.[29] There have been slowly increasing public pressures to protect historically significant or architecturally noteworthy buildings, even though these at present may be in disrepair, unsightly, unsafe, and not functionally desirable.

Clearly, any modification of the taxing system would need to afford exceptions to spare such properties where this is deemed desirable. There is ample evidence that "the power to tax is the power to destroy" (to give these words a literal meaning). The most enduring buildings in cities are religious and public edifices which enjoy immunity from taxation.

With respect to the problem of historical preservation and in various other instances, judgment of land value taxation is going to depend upon distinctions established between "public" and "private." Many historical sites may advisedly continue in private ownership, if only because their maintenance and operation at public expense would not be accepted by the public. Yet clearly their use has been suffused by the public interest. It may be that under a general system of land value taxation, total or partial exemption from taxes would be a strong inducement to perpetuate the historically significant use of selected sites.

3. The benefited area, the recovery of value in the area outside project boundaries: When special assessment taxation was more commonplace, a technical question was the determination of the assessment district boundaries. The extent of expected benefits in areas adjacent to proposed redevelopment projects should be of greater concern than actually has been the case. One criterion of project selection might well be the expected

29. *U. S. Code,* Title 40, § 461 (h) ; Title 42, §§ 1453n, 1500.

magnitudes of increased value in surrounding areas relative to project expenditure.[30] The value of this "multiplier" might well be a part of the local renewal strategy. While the extent of the area that presumably would benefit from adjacent renewal very probably is rather indefinite *ex ante,* this would not matter in the later collection of taxes on values indicative of the actual effects.

Taxes, even steeply progressive taxes, upon these and other increases in land values would leave locational decisions unaffected. Such taxes would lower values, since the taxes would be capitalized, and could, with certain assumptions, promote development. According to Edwin R. A. Seligman,[31] taxes, by lowering real estate prices, enable more households to contemplate homeownership. This may be a more dubious argument in view of present institutional arrangements in the mortgage market whereby the residential buyer amortizes both his taxes and the land cost. In fact, it seems unlikely that the combination of lower land prices with higher future taxes, in contrast with higher prices and lower taxes, would induce much added interest in the case of income-residential or other investments.

Whereas land value taxation has the same kind of object in view for its burden, we would be mistaken to assume that this tax would have the same effect upon resource use, even if their two rates were substantially the same. (Which, incidentally, they should tend to be in greater degree than at present on the basis of some presumptive graduation of rates.) This is the case, of course, because of the great lag between them in application. Because capital gains taxation is incurred only upon realization, it deters sale and subsequent development.

4. Open space, "maximum development" versus retention of space in nonintensive use: The literature of land value taxation includes this disquieting quotation:

In 1906 Thebarton desired a recreation park. In the center of town was a 134-acre vacant tract owned by an absentee family. The agent was approached

---

30. Along this line see Max R. Bloom, "Fiscal Productivity and the Pure Theory of Urban Renewal," *Land Economics,* 38, no. 2 (May 1962) : 143 ; Arthur L. Grey, Jr., "Valuation Factors in Urban Renewal Projects," *Technical Valuation* (February 1962), pp. 61–67 ; Jerome Rothenburg, *Economic Evaluation of Urban Renewal: Conceptual Foundation of Benefit-Cost Analysis* (Washington, D.C.: The Brookings Institution, 1967), pp. 138–143 ; and Philip H. Friedly et al., *Benefit-Cost Applications in Urban Renewal: Summary of the Feasibility Study,* prepared for the Office of Economic and Market Analysis, Department of Housing and Urban Development (Washington, D.C.: U.S. Government Printing Office, 1968), p. 18.

31. Quoted approvingly by Mabel Walker, *Urban Blight and Slums: Economic and Legal Factors in Their Origin, Reclamation and Prevention* (Cambridge, Mass.: Harvard University Press, 1938), p. 253.

and asked to give a price for a few acres, and the reply was that the land would be available at 150 pounds per acre. This land had cost the absentee owner 12s. an acre, and the only use to which it had been put up to that time was growing two crops of hay and being used as a training track for race horses. The rates paid on these 134-acres under the annual rental-value system were £31–10–0 per year. When Thebarton adopted land value rating in 1907, the rates on this land went to £225–10–0, *with the result that within two years of the increase, more than 200 houses and two factories had been erected on what had hitherto been bare land. Doubtless many other examples could be found to illustrate how land-value rating operates to force underdeveloped land into use.*[32] (Emphasis added.)

This example is supposed to demonstrate the effectiveness of land value taxation in causing intensive development to occur. The actual result, however, defeated the announced urban renewal objective of opening the site to public access, but continuing it in an open-space type of usage.

As a matter of historical perspective, it is useful to remind ourselves that the land value taxation concept sprang out of dismay at the waste occasioned by prevailing motives in landownership and resulting patterns of land utilization. Henry George's theorizing and proselytizing upon this subject is one of two great currents of social reform in regard to land that originated in the late nineteenth century and that have had a persistent effect upon subsequent thought. The other current originated in the ideas propounded by Ebenezer Howard, the founder of the garden city movement.

Howard was an Englishman who addressed his pleas to specifically English circumstances. Yet Howard and George did not form their ideas out of wholly different experiences. A most influential period in Howard's life was his residence in Nebraska as a young man.[33] He returned to England only a short time before *Progress and Poverty* appeared.

Howard disputed the practicality of George's scheme, believing his own reform the more likely because it could start modestly.[34] "Nothing gained by overcrowding" is a much-quoted remark of one of Howard's lieutenants, while George's theories suggest the opposite emphasis. As much as anything perhaps, the differences were inherent in contrasting national circumstances that shaped their views, and Howard acknowledged that he "derived much inspiration from *Progress and Poverty.*"[35]

32. Harry Gunnison Brown et al., *Land Value Taxation around the World* (New York: Robert Schalkenbach Foundation, 1955), p. 12.
33. Ebenezer Howard, *Garden Cities of Tomorrow* (London: Faber and Faber, 1945), Introduction by Lewis Mumford, pp. 29–30.
34. Ibid., p. 139.
35. Ibid.

Contemporary discussion of land reform in English-speaking countries at least owes much to both reformers. The antecedents of land value taxation lay in a former time when private rights in the use of property were practically without restriction. This is no longer true and adequate recognition of the potential of planned controls upon land use is long overdue in discussions of land value taxation.

Henry George was alert to the problem of urban sprawl long before it became the present horrendous problem.[36] He saw land value taxation as counteracting extravagant consumption of space through promoting the actual use of land.

A tax on land alone would penalize the random, unplanned with-holding of land from more intensive development, frequently in the expectation of larger future gains. Such patterns of land use may proceed on a vast scale: "Santa Clara County in California affords a particularly relevant example. Between 1947 and 1962 the amount of land converted into urban use in the county totaled 26 square miles—there is hardly a single square mile in the entire 200 which has not been infected [*sic*] by expensive urban sprawl."[37]

The objections are not only to the attenuation of municipal services at higher cost, but difficulties of conducting agricultural operations on small parcels of land near to city development and the adverse effects upon farming costs of the proliferation of urban taxable values into the country-side. Increasing the holding costs through land value taxation would, because of the discounting effect of future costs upon future returns, dampen the rise in expected land values. Presumably, land withholding would be made less attractive thereby. This benefit is a matter of degree; taxes now tend to have the same effect. Since improvements would be rendered free of taxation, however, this inducement further tips the scales in favor of development. The question that remains is whether land value taxation can make a significant difference amid contemporary conditions of continued metropolitan population growth and geographic diffusion of attendant space demands through the unceasing erosion of barriers to personal and goods mobility that is assured by the combined influence of more motor vehicles and freeways.

The conserving attributes of land value taxation have yet to be given

36. George, *Progress and Poverty*, bk. 8, chap. 3, pp. 413–414: "If land were taxed to anything near its rental value, no one could afford to hold land that he was not using, and . . . settlement would be closer, and, consequently, labor and capital would be enabled to produce much more with the same exertion."

37. J. Herbert Snyder, "A New Program for Agricultural Land Use Stabiliza-tion: The California Land Conservation Act of 1965," *Land Economics*, 42, no. 2 (May 1966) : 31.

a tryout, while financial support for providing planned increments of open space have been an adjunct of the federal urban renewal program since 1959. The partial untaxing of land has, however, been introduced as an incentive to keep farm areas open and in their present use. A 1965 California law grants to petitioning owners of prime farm land, given the assent of the governing body of the city or county of situs, a contract to be taxed on the basis of use rather than market value.[38] Assuredly, the impact of this arrangement would be enhanced if it operated in a context where land value taxation was the general rule. In this way, redevelopment pressure upon farm land would be reduced.

Conclusion

The foregoing are some of the diverse factors to be considered in the application of land value taxation to urban renewal. Generally, it should have an ameliorating effect upon the problems that confront us under the heading of "urban renewal." The merit of land value taxation in this regard should not be construed from any but the broadest interpretation of what is salient about the doctrine, namely: (1) the use of taxation, in the special case of effecting particular public policies, as a set of "push-and-pull" forces of incentives and disincentives; and (2) the appropriateness, in the general case, of taxing surplus, which is that portion of the stream of benefits accruing to the owners of assets that will not cause them to act differently, if abridged.

It appears extremely important, both for the workability and equity of the larger system of incentives and constraints which land value taxation should comprise, that this application be tied in with income tax reforms in regard to capital gains and depreciation. Advances in the automation of information handling should make possible progress in taking account of the taxpayer's *total* burden and behavior in the administration of taxation.

Land value taxation was not conceived, however, as just a narrowly technical doctrine. Its purpose was to subordinate certain private rights to the public interest. George declared that "treating land as private property stands in the way of its proper use. . . . If the best use of land be the test, then private property in land is condemned . . . . It is as wasteful and uncertain a mode of securing the proper use of land as the burning down of houses is of roasting pigs."[39] Urban renewal, it should be noted, developed out of a protracted historical process that has placed societal constraints upon the use of property.

38. Calif. Govt. Code, §§ 51200–51295.
39. George, *Progress and Poverty*, bk. 8, chap. 1, pp. 401–402.

5 *The Political Aspects of Real Estate Taxation in Relation to Metropolitan Growth and Planning*

ERNEST A. ENGELBERT

Introduction

One of the major forces currently shaping the character and growth of urban communities is local property taxation. Together with planning and zoning and the location of public improvements (including highways), property taxation constitutes one of the three most important governmental methods of controlling the pattern of land use. Persons who have had intimate contact with local-government politics know that there are few issues which can stir up the citizenry more than property tax assessments and rates. Whether the assessor is nonpartisanly elected or appointed, his position is among the most politically sensitive of all local-government offices.

It is surprising therefore that in the numerous studies of local government which have been undertaken by political scientists, virtually nothing has been written on the politics of taxation, urban or rural. No analyses exist that tell how political groups employ the instrument of taxation to influence the destiny of urban communities. One searches in vain for behavioral studies that portray the strategies used by various taxpaying groups—the homeowners, renters, retailers, industrialists, and others—or the reaction of these groups to taxes for specific metropolitan functions. Even in the larger sense, the politics of land value taxation and its impact upon the nature of growth and change of the metropolitan community has been overlooked. Insofar as political scientists have studied the property tax system, it has been from the standpoint of administrative organization and procedure. Whatever opinions exist among this profession with respect to the politics of local taxation are based largely upon observations and belief.

NOTE: Acknowledgment is gratefully made to Resources for the Future, Inc., for a grant that enabled me to undertake research on which portions of this essay are based.

Moreover, those who are concerned with the impact of taxation upon the urban land-use pattern will find little in the writings of allied disciplines upon which to draw. Neither in economics nor in planning does one find any systematic body of research upon which to generalize. In a useful survey David T. Rowlands has listed some technical studies completed in recent years which provide pieces of the puzzle, but the overall pattern is still obscured.[1] The dearth of economic analyses has led Mary Rawson to conclude that economists have by and large ignored the importance of the "property tax as a factor in the problems and policies of land use."[2] She states that the issue of land taxation "is under a taboo in the academic world" which grows out of the writings of some of the early economists' aversion to the single tax.[3] Whether or not Rawson's explanation is correct, the fact remains that the economists have not provided urban planners with a taxation framework for land-use decision-making.

The extent to which the financial and physical planning for urban communities is based upon belief and conjecture is reflected in a study by Max S. Wehrly and J. Ross McKeever.[4] After attempting to get data from 178 American cities, these authors concluded that, with the exception of a selected number of communities, cities do not possess adequate records to enable meaningful relationships to be drawn between land-use revenues and municipal services.[5] Although considerable progress has been made in recent years in analyzing the economic base of a number of metropolitan areas, long-range fiscal planning continues to be a weak aspect of municipal administration.[6]

Since essential data are lacking, much confusion and contradiction abounds in the professional literature concerning the impact of property taxation on urban land use. On the one hand, it is contended that lower real estate taxes in the suburbs have hastened the flight of population from the central cities;[7] on the other hand, the residents of the suburbs are

1. David T. Rowlands, *Urban Real Estate Research* (Washington, D.C.: Urban Land Institute, 1959), pp. 80–82. This study is a systematic evaluation of postwar research in urban real estate undertaken for the institute. It includes an annotated bibliography.

2. Mary Rawson, *Property Taxation and Urban Development* (Washington, D.C.: Urban Land Institute, 1961), p. 7.

3. Ibid., pp. 7–8.

4. Max S. Wehrly and J. Ross McKeever, *Urban Land Use and Property Taxation* (Washington, D.C.: Urban Land Institute, 1952).

5. Ibid., pp. 4, 23.

6. See, for example, Seymour Sacks and William F. Hallmuth, Jr., *Financing Government in a Metropolitan Area: The Cleveland Experience* (Glencoe, Ill.: The Free Press, 1961); and Raymond Vernon, *Metropolis 1985* (Cambridge, Mass.: Harvard University Press, 1960).

7. Roswell G. Townsend, "Inequalities of Residential Property Taxation in Metropolitan Boston," *National Tax Journal*, 4, no. 4 (December 1951): 361–369.

reputed to be paying more taxes because of rapid growth and because they encompass a high proportion of residential and low-value properties.[8] The older residential areas within the central city are usually found to bear higher-than-average assessments,[9] while slum properties have the reputation of being profitable because taxes are low in relation to land values.[10] Or to cite still another contrast, governmental units have usually favored tax policies that would attract new industry, yet evidence is also available to show that the concentration of industry may increase disproportionately the costs of municipal services.[11] Other apparent inconsistencies could be presented to show that the impact of property taxation on urban land-use patterns and metropolitan growth is a misunderstood and neglected subject.

The political aspects of property taxation appear to have been disregarded by political scientists for a number of reasons. First, the subject falls in a twilight zone between economics and political science so that neither discipline has given it the attention which it deserves. Second, as has been previously noted, political scientists have concentrated upon the administrative aspects of tax organization and collection usually as part of more general inquiries into the effectiveness of governmental systems. Finally, intensive studies of metropolitan growth and change are largely a postwar phenomenon and political scientists have not yet awakened to the fact that the analysis of fiscal interrelationships of metropolitan governments commands high priority.

The Political Environment of the Property Taxpayer

The Dearth of Political Standards

The evolution of the American system of property taxation has been highly pragmatic. The only political principles that undergird the system are these: (1) the tax must be used for a public purpose, and (2) there should be no discrimination against particular persons or property. Within these limitations, the taxing jurisdiction may take any action it sees fit, restricted only by political expediency. To date, no political standards or concepts have been developed which govern the application of property taxes to land in its various stages of use or development. Insofar as taxing

8. Mabel Walker, "Fiscal Aspects of Metropolitan Regional Development," *Tax Policy*, 24, nos. 6–7 (June–July 1957) : 4.

9. State of New Jersey, Commission on State Tax Policy, *Sixth Report* (Trenton, N.J., 1953), p. 95.

10. Arthur D. Sporn, "Empirical Studies in the Economics of Slum Ownership," *Land Economics*, 36 (November 1960) : 333–340.

11. Julius Margolis, "Municipal Fiscal Structure in a Metropolitan Region," *The Journal of Political Economy*, 65, no. 3 (June 1957) : 225–236.

authorities have attempted to use land taxes to shape the growth of a particular area or community, it has been done on an ad hoc and nonscientific basis. All of this has led one eminent authority to a conclusion that, although made a generation ago, is still valid; namely, that American state property tax systems are "patchworks, adaptations of confused ideas to meet diverse local conditions often sanctioned without a clear understanding of the nature of the property or taxes." [12]

To some extent the reason that no well-defined political framework governs the property tax system is that the average citizen understands so little about its theory or practice. Few persons can be found in the typical community who comprehend the economic distinctions between a land value tax and a tax on improvements, or who could explain the relationships of assessments to values or the phenomena of incidence and shifting. The taxpayer tends to view property taxation not as a financial plan but as a highly personal transaction involving relationships between his property and political officialdom. It is the only major tax that he pays where a considerable element of discretion rests with the tax official. More often than not property owners are wary of highly efficient and scientific tax procedures at the local level since this fosters impersonality and reduces bargaining power with assessors and boards of appeal. It is not uncommon to find them opposing increases in assessment and collection staff, partly out of fear that more staff will result in closer scrutiny of property assessments and values. In short, we find a citizenry that is not too concerned about developing well-defined political standards for property taxation.

Complicating the political picture for the taxpayer in metropolitan areas is the number and diversity of local governments to which he pays property taxes. In rapidly growing urban areas, it is not uncommon for the citizen's property to be subjected to tax by as many as six or more governmental units, including the county, city, and several special districts. Frequently the taxes for a number of these units, particularly special districts, are classified under a numbered tax code area and only by deciphering the code can the citizen tell how much taxes he pays to each unit. Furthermore, he will not be able to make judgments about the fairness of the tax unless he knows exactly which of the municipal services the particular governmental unit provides. In complex metropolitan areas a majority of citizens would be hard-pressed to tell which unit of government provides which services.[13]

12. Jens Peter Jenson, *Property Taxation in the United States* (Chicago: University of Chicago Press, 1931), p. 48.

13. For some findings on community identification, see William B. Storm and Wallace H. Best, "Public Awareness of Metropolitan Problems: Some Survey Research Estimates," in *Metropolitan California: Papers Prepared for the Governor's Commission on Metropolitan Problems,* ed. Ernest A. Engelbert (Sacramento, Calif.: State Printing Office, 1961), pp. 42–46.

Taxpayers also hold widely varying interests and allegiances to specific governmental units depending upon whether they reside near the center or the periphery of the metropolitan area, where the location of their employment is relative to their residences, and what the nature of their property holdings are. Other factors such as the character of the immediate neighborhood, the status of zoning, or the degree of owner occupancy of properties also enter into the taxpayer's personal equation.[14] Because each taxpayer will have different political and economic interests at stake, considerable diversity of outlook over land use within the metropolitan community exists both among classes of taxpayers and within taxpaying areas. Under these circumstances it is difficult for either the citizens or governmental units to formulate any political concepts for property taxation that foster wise community planning.

Common Interests of Taxpaying Groups

Despite the great diversity of interests among individual taxpayers, various groups of property owners do share common concerns regarding real estate taxes within the metropolitan area. To the best of my knowledge no systematic classification of property taxpayers has ever been undertaken for the purpose of identifying dominant attitudes that may prevail in various types of urban communities. If a better understanding of taxpayer motivations toward urban change could be achieved, better tax strategies could be devised to lead to more successful metropolitan planning.

Within the metropolitan area property taxpayers may be classified within two basic frameworks: (1) by residence and place of work, and (2) by occupation and ownership. Certain broad assumptions can be made about the prevailing attitudes of various categories of taxpayers within each group. The assumptions, however, will have different applicability depending upon the complex of urban forces found within each community.

Property taxpayers classified by residence and place of work fall into four major categories: (1) taxpayers who have both residence and place of work in the central city; (2) taxpayers who reside in the suburbs and work in the central city; (3) taxpayers who have both residence and place of work in the suburbs; and (4) taxpayers who reside in the central city and work in the suburbs.

Some of the assumptions that could be made for each category include the following: Categories (1) and (4) generally favor securing more revenue from city sales, income, and business taxes and less from real estate

14. In their study of the property tax in New Jersey, the state tax commission identified ten major factors that were influencing assessments in that state. State of New Jersey, Commission on State Tax Policy, *Sixth Report,* chap. 5.

taxes. Categories (2) and (3), on the other hand, favor higher real estate taxes in the central city and oppose personal income and sales taxes. Residents of the central city look with approval upon tax policies that foster the most intensive use of land in downtown areas. Conversely, residents of the suburbs support taxing arrangements that deter undesirable uses from undermining the basic character of their respective communities. Whereas the residents of both the central city and the suburbs would be more inclined to endorse tax assessments for public improvements in their respective living areas, commuters would be more likely to vote for programs that facilitate intra-urban ties.

More equations enter the picture when taxpayers within the metropolitan area are classified by occupation and ownership. The following categories stand out within this framework: (1) salaried employees, real property as well as nonreal property owners; (2) owners whose major income is derived from real estate holdings; (3) real property and nonreal property owners of small retail, commercial, and professional enterprises; (4) owners and managers of large industrial and commercial establishments; and (5) agricultural and horticultural users of land.

Within these broad classifications of occupation and ownership many different outlooks toward real estate taxes prevail, depending upon where the taxpayer's place of business or residence is located in the metropolitan area, the range and quality of municipal services that are being provided, the income bracket of the taxpayer, and other similar considerations. Generally speaking, the salaried, non-property-owning employees will offer fewer political protests to real property tax changes than to city income and sales tax changes and will place greater emphasis upon the quality of services that the municipal jurisdictions are providing. In contrast, the small property owners usually constitute one of the most vociferous urban pressure groups, more often than not battling to shift the tax load from property taxes to other revenue-producing sources. A recently published study of metropolitan Los Angeles found that not only do property owners hold a "proprietary attitude toward the units of local government," but that they have been a major force both for and against incorporations, annexations, and other local boundary changes.[15]

The small businessman is primarily concerned that the overall tax structure of the metropolitan area does not adversely affect the business climate. If he rents his business property he may be less antagonistic toward property tax increases, despite higher rents, than he is toward sales taxes. He will be particularly concerned that competing businesses within a metro-

15. Winston W. Crouch and Beatrice Dinerman, *Southern California Metropolis: A Study in Development of Government for a Metropolitan Area* (Berkeley, Calif.: University of California Press, 1963), pp. 113–117.

politan area do not get undue economic advantages from different taxing jurisdictions.

Numerous studies have shown that the local tax structure has been a major factor in industrial location not only between but within metropolitan communities. The owners and managers of industrial and commercial firms are interested in how the property tax structure is affecting the pattern of development of downtown areas vis-à-vis the suburbs, whether the tax structure is providing necessary municipal services for both employees and shoppers, and whether there are major inequalities in the assessment processes. Large businesses have many of the same interests as small businesses in achieving uniformity in taxing structure and arrangements of a metropolitan area.

Finally, there are the agricultural users of land, many of whom are farming in metropolitan fringe areas waiting for their land to ripen for urban development. They constitute a group who wish to have land assessed on the basis of existing use rather than real value. In states with rapidly growing urban areas, farmers have received special state tax legislation that protects their occupational status within metropolitan areas. In 1966 the voters of California adopted a constitutional amendment that permits a farmer, at his own option, to have his farm land assessed on the basis of *use* so long as it remains in agriculture.[16]

These, then, are some of the major categories of taxpaying groups, members of which have common interests in property tax policies and administration. Some metropolitan areas will have more visible stratifications of these groups than others, depending upon their respective distribution of economic activities and classes of populations. Moreover, they will be found in varying blocs of political power, depending upon the number and relationships of the taxing jurisdictions within the particular metropolitan community. Altogether they represent, through their economic stakes in property taxation, one of the major forces shaping the land-use pattern.

Public officials have the responsibility of harnessing these sometimes complementary, more often competing, groups into beneficial programs of urban development. Many students of metropolitan government contend that this will never be possible so long as a metropolitan area is fragmented by numerous taxing jurisdictions (counties, cities, and special districts).[17] Others believe that considerable progress could be made if a more dis-

16. Calif. Const. Amend. IV.

17. See, for example, Julius Margolis, *Metropolitan Finance Problems: Territories, Functions and Growth,* Reprint no. 24 (Berkeley, Calif.: University of California, Real Estate Research Program, 1961) ; and Advisory Commission on Intergovernmental Relations, *Governmental Structure, Organization and Planning in Metropolitan Areas* (Washington, D.C.: U.S. Government Printing Office, 1961), p. 15.

criminatory pattern of land value taxation were adopted.[18] Here, much turns upon the economic character of the governmental unit and the types of political strategies for property taxation that are being employed.

Political Strategies for Land Value Taxation in Metropolitan Areas

The Dominant Character of the Governmental Unit

Land value taxation strategies are influenced by the dominant character of the governmental units that comprise the metropolitan area. Although there is a tendency in planning literature to view metropolitan areas of relatively equal size as similar entities, their component units vary greatly in economic profile and political makeup. A metropolitan area may be composed of one or more of the following units: (1) a dominant central city with a relatively diversified economic base and highly dependent cities or suburbs (the Chicago metropolitan area, for example); (2) two or more competing cities with a skewed distribution of economic activities (the Minneapolis–St. Paul metropolitan area); (3) the single-purpose city, exclusively industrial, residential, or agricultural (the cities of Industry, Palos Verdes, and Dairyland in the Los Angeles–Long Beach metropolitan area); (4) the multipurpose satellite city with an intermixture of land uses (the city of Richmond in the San Francisco–Oakland metropolitan area); and (5) the urban unincorporated areas that are serviced by counties and special districts.

Obviously, these urban entities have, by virtue of their dominant character and relative position within the metropolitan area, different land-use objectives. Cities or nonincorporated urban comunities with a healthy economic and environmental base will endeavor to pursue tax policies that will protect their advantages. Conversely, urban units with declining industrial or commercial activities or with low property valuations and high municipal-service costs will endeavor to follow tax policies that will ameliorate their situation. As a result, metropolitan areas represent continuous battles between governmental units and political forces to achieve the most productive and desirable land-use pattern.

Reduced to its simplest terms, the overall tax strategy of a governmental unit within a metropolitan area is twofold: to keep taxes low for all categories of economic activity and quality of municipal services desired and to attain as large a slice of the economic pie as possible. The methods that are employed will depend upon the aforementioned variables: the rela-

18. Leon Silverman, "Municipal Real Estate Taxation as an Instrument for Community Planning," *Yale Law Journal*, 57, no. 219 (December 1947) : 219–242.

tive political power of various taxpaying groups, the industrial structure and landownership patterns, the environmental relationships, and the stage of economic development of the community.

Financial Strategies [19]

Governmental units within a metropolitan area can pursue a number of financial and administrative strategies, all of which have significant bearing upon land use. First we shall look at the major strategies that are employed and then note some of the consequences for wholesome economic growth and development.

Assessing units are able to assess land in different ratios to true value and thereby affect the pattern of land use and real estate development. This can be done in several ways:

1. Assessments can be kept low in relation to true value, which, over a period of time and despite changes in rates, will have the effect of placing greater emphasis upon revenue sources other than property taxes for financing the costs of proliferating municipal services. During the decade 1945–1955 property tax revenues in the New York metropolitan area increased only 73.1 percent, while non-property tax revenues increased 141.6 percent.[20] Over the long run, low assessments have the effect of deterring land from being converted to its greatest potential use.

2. Different assessment ratios can be applied to different classifications of real estate, either as a result of inequities in assessment methods or outright discrimination. For example, studies show that agricultural lands are generally over-assessed in relation to residential properties in metropolitan fringe areas due primarily to inadequate valuation and assessment methods.[21] On the other hand, discrimination may set in when assessing units initiate unjustifiable assessment increases upon specific types of property.[22] The application of different assessment ratios to dif-

19. For the approach taken in this section, I am indebted to Robert C. Wood (with Valadimir V. Almendinger), *1400 Governments: The Political Economy of the New York Metropolitan Region* (Cambridge, Mass.: Harvard University Press, 1961).

20. Ibid., p. 70.

21. See F. E. Hulse and W. P. Walker, *Property Tax Problems in Rural-Urban Fringe Areas,* Miscellaneous Publication no. 135 (College Park, Md.: University of Maryland, Agricultural Experiment Station, 1952), pp. 22–23; and Arthur J. Walrath, "Equalization of Property Taxes in an Urban-Rural Area," *Land Economics,* 33, no. 1 (February 1957): 50–53.

22. The practice of a sudden raising of assessments known as "tax lightning" is so common in New Jersey that Wood found that the New Jersey Commission on State Tax Policy "has officially incorporated the designation into the vocabulary of public finance."—Wood, *1400 Governments,* p. 69.

ferent types of property produces instability in land use and leads, as in the case of farm land in fringe areas, to unwise or premature urban development.

3. Assessing units can place higher evaluations on properties not locally owned, such as utilities or industries, for the purpose of decreasing the financial load on local residents. Once again, this has the practical effect of interfering with economic determinations of the competitive uses of land.

A second major method whereby local taxing units can shape the course of land use is through the granting of concessions or exemptions to specific categories of property or users. All states grant some forms of tax exemptions, notably for public property and property of educational, philanthropic, and religious institutions; twenty-four states grant property exemptions for homesteads, veterans, or personal property; and at least seven states enable taxing units to grant exemptions to industry.[23] In addition, taxing units in many states grant tax concessions for various types of land improvements. Although there is considerable difference of findings and opinions concerning the financial advantages that a community gains from exemptions and concessions, particularly in the case of industry,[24] the land values and property taxes of adjacent areas may be adversely affected by these policies. A municipality, for example, can shape urban growth by granting building permits for a subdivision that qualifies for veterans' tax exemptions or by giving concessions to industries to locate in an economically deteriorating neighborhood. Property tax exemptions and concessions can also be used as political leverage with various categories of taxpaying groups and as weapons of competition with other units of the metropolitan area.

Third, the taxing jurisdiction can affect land use by deliberately limiting the application of the property tax, so that financial burdens will be shifted to other revenue-producing sources. By keeping assessments low, the urban unit more quickly reaches the ceiling of legally permissible tax rates in effect in most states, forcing the community to adopt the sales tax, increase license fees, or find some other source of income. This is invariably

23. Frederick L. Bird, *The General Property Tax: Findings of the 1957 Census of Governments* (Chicago: Public Administration Service, 1960), pp. 19–21; and William J. D. Boyd, ed., "Gaining Industry Major Local Goal," *National Civic Review*, 49 (December 1960): 624–625.

24. For a discussion of this problem, see Walter E. Isard and Robert E. Coughlin, "Municipal Costs and Revenues Resulting from Community Growth," *Journal of the American Institute of Planners*, 32, no. 4 (Fall 1956): 239–255; and Ruth L. Mace, *Municipal Cost-Revenue Research in the United States* (Chapel Hill, N.C.: University of North Carolina, Institute of Government, 1961).

a tactic pursued by small property-owner associations. Alternatively, a comunity can work in concert with other communities to achieve state legislation that will enable the local units to tap new revenue sources (such as a city income tax) and thereby permit restructuring of the local revenue systems. That great variations exist among urban units relative to amount of money raised from property taxes vis-à-vis other sources is reflected in the fact that some cities get less than 20 percent of their revenues from property taxes while others obtain over 70 percent from this source.[25]

Finally, local taxing jurisdictions can modify the application of the property tax to land use by endeavoring to shift more of the burden of revenue-raising to the state. The states command inherent advantages in such fields of revenue-raising as income and corporate taxes. By tapping these revenue sources through increased state subventions and aids, urban communities can reduce the pressures upon the property taxpayer.

Administrative Strategies

In conjunction with financial strategies, governmental units may employ a number of administrative strategies to protect their latitude of property taxation and their tax base. Foremost among these are the zoning and building code restrictions that can be used to control land use: (1) zoning regulations can be drawn to attract desirable and economically productive land-users to specific areas and types of land, and hence repel undesirable land-users who would lower the quality of the neighborhood; (2) zoning can be employed to achieve optimum population densities relative to municipal service levels, and thereby reduce the costs of urban governments; and (3) building code restrictions can be instituted or performance standards (for example, air pollution control standards) established for certain areas which would make it impossible for certain types of land-users to comply. Taken together, these controls provide a formidable weapon that local authorities can and do use for encouraging the best use of land, for enhancing the tax base, and for protecting the interests of specific groups of taxpayers.

A second major administrative strategy that can be employed to modify the political environment of property taxation in the metropolitan area is the creation of special districts. Special districts may be created for any number of reasons other than financial, but it is not unlikely that the financial motive will be strongly present. Particularly for communities that have reached the legal limits for tax rates or debt incurment, the special

25. Allen D. Manvell, "Trends in Municipal Finances," *The Municipal Year-book, 1963* (Chicago: International City Managers Association, 1963), Table 9, pp. 270–287.

district offers a neat way of taxing the same area twice—for the services provided by the general-purpose government and those by the special district. Moreover, it constitutes an excellent way for dividing and conquering taxpaying groups. A special district can provide a municipal service for a specific area which may not be desired by the larger community and which would be defeated if the taxpayers of the total area voted on the issue. Perhaps even more important for the development of land use, a special district can be employed to foster a particular type of economic activity within given areas, particularly when coupled with zoning regulations. For example, the establishment of a sewerage district in an urban-fringe area that is zoned for industrial use might be a means of hastening growth. As of 1960 some 11,415 special districts existed within 212 metropolitan areas of the United States, all to some degree influencing local property tax strategies.[26]

Annexation of land by one taxpaying unit or area by another can be an important tax strategy. As in the case of special districts, annexations may be fostered by groups in a community for many reasons, but the financial aspects are never far below the surface. A city, for example, may seek to annex an adjacent area to secure desirable room for growth to provide a more favorable tax base. Or a city may desire to undertake an annexation for the purpose of controlling what otherwise might be undesirable growth that would adversely affect nearby city taxpayers and properties. An unincorporated area may wish to be annexed to a city to obtain municipal services that could not justifiably be provided by its existing tax base. Or if an area is adjacent to two cities, it may wish to be annexed by one rather than the other because a more favorable ratio of tax rates to municipal services will ensue. Very often, in communities that are beginning to experience rapid population growth, taxpayers will polarize into two groups: newcomers who desire a greater range of municipal services and old-timers who are satisfied with the status quo.

Finally, incorporation has become a major weapon in property tax strategy. Nowhere is this better illustrated than in California where city after city has been spawned in the last decade for the purpose of controlling land use and protecting the tax base. In that state may be found more than a score of cities that have been created solely for the purpose of fostering a single economic activity, such as agriculture or industry, or to protect a desirable residential environment for the commuter. In California, as in other states, the adoption of a state sales tax has been an incentive to incorporate, since cities get a proportionate return of sales tax monies from the state. Many communities also incorporate to prevent becoming

26. U.S. Bureau of the Census, *Census of Governments* (Washington, D.C.: U.S. Government Printing Office, 1963), 1: 11, and Table 13, p. 68.

absorbed by another urban unit with a less advantageous financial setting.

From this brief discussion of strategies, it can be seen that the politics of property taxation can affect not only the pattern of local land use but also the entire course of metropolitan growth. But local officials and tax-paying groups can employ a number of tactics and weapons outside the partisan political arena to foster their respective interests. Assessing officials can play one taxing unit off against another, can time general reassessments to hit different groups of taxpayers, or can discriminate against specific classes of land-users. Local-government officers can hold tax rates down for indefinite periods by delaying the construction of needed public improvements or they can threaten recalcitrant taxpayers with a reduction of specific municipal services. Property owners can exhibit reluctance to make plant investments if assessments or rates are raised excessively, can pressure for alterations in local-government boundaries, or can wage campaigns to recall elected officials.

Property taxation strategies are seldom motivated by the needs of long-range comprehensive urban development. Instead, they are usually shifting in character, depending upon changing coalitions of political groupings, defensive or retaliatory vis-à-vis neighboring communities, and highly influenced by the level of economic prosperity that may prevail at a particular time. A taxing unit within a metropolitan area is fortunate if it can foster a land-use tax pattern which is consistent with its electorate's aspirations. More often than not, however, the sum total of the strategies of numerous taxing jurisdictions within a metropolitan community leads to economic inefficiency and waste and to unbalanced growth and development throughout the entire area.

Metropolitan Consequences Arising from the Present System of Real Estate Taxation

Contemporary textbooks on property taxation dwell extensively on shortcomings in local tax administration. But the consequences arising from the present system of land value taxation go far beyond inequities in assessments or fiscal inadequacies of local units of government. They lead to disarrangements in the total environmental, social, and economic structure of the urban community. Upon the present systems of property taxation and administration must be placed much of the blame for urban disorganization that exists within metropolitan areas.

1. First of all, the present system of local taxation of land produces premature and unwise land-use development within the metropolitan area. Numerous taxing jurisdictions, each encouraging certain types of land im-

provements and discouraging others, produce not only a helter-skelter intermixture of land uses but also an inefficient distribution of economic
activities. To enhance the tax base, communities compete for industry,
commercial enterprises, or residential subdivisions, often causing land to
be developed which is not ripe for urban improvements. Moreover, the
present system of real estate taxation provides a major method whereby
local units of government build artificially segregated land-use communities that are so often detrimental to metropolitan-wide planning and development.

2. The current practice of assessing vacant land and newly developed
properties at lower values than those for well-established areas results in
excessive and unwise urban dispersal. To obtain lower-valued land, builders leapfrog over what might otherwise be suitable acreages for construction into outlying areas, leaving in their wake sprawling communities with
high-cost municipal services. A significant percentage of land within the
perimeters of America's most densely populated cities is still undeveloped.[27]
In 1955, for example, the California State Water Resources Board found
no buildings on 23 percent of the usable land in the long-established city
of San Francisco.[28] Furthermore, a disorderly process of land development
fosters gross speculation, particularly on the part of land developers who
operate on a state- and nation-wide basis and who bear few responsibilities
for fashioning stable urban communities. Inflated land values produced
by speculation forces urban governments to pay excessive prices for land
that must be acquired for such municipal services as streets, school sites,
or parks, and in the case of the latter, the purchase of sizable parcels of
land for recreational purposes often becomes prohibitive.

3. The deterioration of the central portion of cities is hastened by pres-
ent-day assessment inequities that on the one hand cause improvements
in the older, built-up areas to be assessed at disproportionately higher
values than land, and on the other, cause improvements in the heart of
the city to be assessed at higher values than improvements in the outlying
urban communities.[29] Inequitable tax assessments are a factor in the
determination of business firms to move away from downtown areas. Va-
cated properties subvert to less desirable uses and frequently become
blighted. At the same time, the taxation of land at lower values than im-

27. M. Mason Gaffney, "Urban Expansion—Will it Ever Stop?" *Yearbook of
Agriculture* (Washington, D.C.: U.S. Government Printing Office, 1958), pp. 514–
515.

28. Ibid., p. 515.

29. For evidence on this point, see Townsend, "Inequalities of Taxation," pp.
361–369; Wood, *1400 Governments,* pp. 69–71; and Eli Schwartz and James E.
Wert, *An Analysis of the Potential Effects of a Movement Toward a Land Value
Based Property Tax* (Pittsfield, Mass.: Ben Franklin Press, 1958), p. 35.

provements discourages upkeep on properties and leads to urban decay. Although the evidence is not incontrovertible, there appears to be a direct relationship between the profitability of slum property ownership and favorable assessment ratios.[30] As urban dwellers all over America are finding out, far-reaching social consequences, from juvenile delinquency to segregation, are the by-product of property deterioration.

4. The lack of a common system of property taxation throughout the metropolitan area leads to a multiplicity of local governments, each seeking to protect their respective financial advantages and status. New cities and special districts are often created within metropolitan areas for the purpose of getting around rigidities and inequities in the local financial structures. The Advisory Commission on Intergovernmental Relations found that metropolitan areas that were most heavily dependent upon the property tax had the greatest "difficulties in terms of equity and administration in raising revenues sufficient to support governmental services," and they concluded that "relatively small taxing areas, the uneven distribution of valuable industrial properties, and the low correlation in many instances between the location of the domicile and the consumption of governmental services altogether compound into a most difficult and potentially unfair situation."[31] The overall result of an increasing number of independent taxing jurisdictions within what are essentially intradependent metropolitan areas is financial hardship and administrative chaos. To be sure, shortcomings in the administration of the property tax are not solely responsible for the balkanization of local government, but they warrant greater blame for governmental disorganization than students of urban affairs have heretofore recognized.

5. The overall structure of local government is gradually being undermined by the inadequacies of the property tax system. Taxing units in financial distress become increasingly dependent upon the state and federal government for aid in the form of shared revenues or grants, and with financial aid from higher levels inevitably comes increasing administrative controls over subordinate units. Local units could command greater independence than they now do if they properly exploited the property tax. The case for state and federal financial aid is justified on the ground that local communities do not have an adequate tax base from which to raise their own revenues. But this justification simply does not hold in the face of the gross undertaxation of land so prevalent throughout the nation. As a hard-hitting editorial in the national building trades magazine *House*

30. One of the few studies available on this subject is Sporn, "Empirical Studies." See also the discussion in Rawson, *Property Taxation,* pp. 28–29.

31. Advisory Commission on Intergovernmental Relations, *Governmental Structure,* p. 15.

and Home points out, "undertaxation of land is the No. 1 reason most cities are in financial trouble." [32] The editorial notes that, "as late as 1914 land carried nearly half the total tax load—local, state and national. Today the land values in our cities and suburbs add up to something like over a quarter of our total national wealth, but land is so under-assessed and under-taxed that it pays less than one-twentieth of the total tax bill, and more than half that twentieth is deductible from the landowner's state and federal income taxes." [33] Urban local units are in no position to complain about state and federal intervention when they so grossly fail to exercise their powers and responsibilities in the most important field for local independence—the right of local taxation.

6. Finally, the present pattern of real property assessment and taxation by urban units produces pathological and unhealthy political divisions within metropolitan areas. Assessments of different classes of properties at different ratios of true value, segregation of communities on the basis of narrow land-use interests, and the lack of metropolitan area-wide administrative uniformity among taxing units all engender unwarranted rivalries and controversies among taxpaying groups and localities. An unwholesome environment results in which political manipulations and maneuvering by officials and citizens thrive. The overall goals of desirable metropolitan planning and development become obscured by the disintegrative political struggles that take place.

Conclusion

I have highlighted some of the undesirable consequences for metropolitan planning and development resulting from an inadequate system of land value taxation. The American system of property taxation has, historically speaking, evolved pragmatically in a political environment of needs and pressures rather than on the basis of any well-conceived or long-range urban policies. Today we find a situation where local taxation of land has become—by virtue of multiple taxing districts, great variations in tax base, and diverse application of standards—one of the major factors in the economic and social disorganization of the metropolitan community.

Neither the professions of political science nor of city planning have given sufficient attention to the employment of real estate taxation as an instrument for metropolitan reform, despite the fact that it constitutes

32. "Three big changes in housing policy that will affect us all," *House and Home,* 19, no. 2 (February 1961) : 85.
33. Ibid.

one of the most important vehicles that the local community possesses for guiding urban growth. Practitioners of these two professions have devoted too much effort to master planning and administrative reorganizations without coming to grips with the financial adjustments that would have to be undertaken for proposed reforms to succeed.

Many fiscal and administrative changes could be proposed in local tax structures which would facilitate wise urban land-use development, but three are particularly significant for metropolitan areas: [34]

1. A single assessment district should be established for an entire metropolitan area and taxing units within the area should be given uniform taxing powers. Where more than one county is involved, the state should create multicounty or special metropolitan assessment districts. Where metropolitan areas encompass more than one state, the states should cooperatively foster and adopt uniform assessment standards. Metropolitan area-wide assessment districts composed of units with uniform taxing powers provide the best basis for having all classes of land covered by the same valuation standards. Not only would discrimination between classes of property and neighborhood areas be reduced, but land-use studies and financial planning within the total metropolitan perspective would be facilitated.

2. State limitations on local property tax rates should be abandoned. State limitations are for the most part legal fiction and constitute an undesirable interference with local fiscal management. Since taxing units in urban areas provide the bulk of governmental services, they should be given greater freedom in revenue-raising, particularly in the field of property taxation, where under-valued land still constitutes the best revenue potential for local governments.[35] Placing more responsibility upon local governments for raising revenue would not only decrease local dependence upon the states and federal government, but in the case of property taxation would lead to more desirable distinctions and improvements in the assessment and taxing of particular classes of land.

3. Real estate taxation should be based upon a differential tax on land values. The present system makes no distinction among "incremental values resulting from urban development, the values of land already de-

---

34. For a comprehensive review of desirable local tax reforms, see the series of reports issued by the Advisory Commission on Intergovernmental Relations on this subject.

35. An editorial comment in the *National Civic Review* notes that the municipality is currently "low man on the totem pole" with respect to revenue-raising powers despite the fact that it is in "the unenviable position of rendering more than 90 percent of essential services to citizens...."—Paul T. O'Keefe, "Low Man on the Totem Pole," *National Civic Review*, 50, no. 7 (July 1961): 344.

veloped, and the values of improvements." [36] Taxation of land on the basis of site value rather than on existing use has many advantages for metropolitan communities: (a) the underassessment and underevaluation of land, a practice so common in metropolitan areas, would be counteracted, which would provide more money for local units; (b) idle or less productive land would be forced more quickly into more productive uses, reducing thereby the opportunities for unwarranted speculation; (c) based upon the experiences of Australia and New Zealand, the upkeep of improvements would be fostered and property deterioration and blight reduced; and (d) more rational and even urban growth would occur throughout the metropolitan area, and real property taxation could be related more effectively to zoning and other land-use controls as a positive tool for urban planning and development.

Admittedly, the foregoing proposals for changes in the prevailing patterns of real estate taxation do not command strong "grass roots" political appeal, but they will certainly be more acceptable to the public than some of the more drastic reforms that are being recommended in many urban areas for new forms of metropolitan government. As a matter of fact, the public has not been educated by public officials to the benefits that would ensue from a consciously-developed program of property taxation. One thing is certain, however; if locally controlled government is to survive, then some standards of urban land-use development other than those of political expediency will have to govern the field of real property taxation.

36. Lyle C. Fitch, "Metropolitan Financial Problems," *The Annals of the American Academy of Political and Social Science*, 314 (November 1957): 70.

6 *Property Taxation and Multiple-Family Housing*

MAX NEUTZE

Multiple-family housing is usually analyzed as a capital-intensive means of providing accommodation. This is, of course, important, but another feature, the time at which multiple-family housing appears as an area is urbanized, is also important. The first part of this chapter attempts to characterize multiple-family housing as a land use that generally appears rather late in the process of urbanization, and the returns from which are rather uncertain. By contrast, in the process of redevelopment, it is probably the earliest available and "safest" land use. In the second part the effects of property taxation are discussed. Do they encourage apartment development as compared with single-family houses, or suburban apartments as compared with redevelopment in central-city areas for apartments? I will deal with only two alternative forms of property taxation: proportional taxation of site value and of the total value of land and improvements.

The Timing of Apartment Construction

At the outside fringe of urban development very low-density, single-family houses are found, often with lots of one to five acres. A static theory of urban land use would explain this by pointing out that such extensive users of land must seek land that is inexpensive and that this can be found on the fringes of cities in areas where the major urban amenities and centers of employment are rather remote. But a static theory cannot explain the relatively large tracts of land that are vacant or used for farming, closer to the urban core than much of the low-density housing. Agriculture uses

NOTE: This chapter is more than usually a product of the conference. I benefited greatly from the discussion and changed the draft presented there very considerably. I have also been assisted by discussion with colleagues at Resources for the Future, especially Lowdon Wingo.

land much less intensively than any urban use and should not in theory be able to occupy these more accessible sites.

Static theories concerning land-use decisions fail to consider that land uses are indivisible in time; that is, most urban land uses require fixed improvements which have an economic life of many years. If a particular land use is expected to persist for only a short time, it is less able to compete for land because its annual costs will be higher, owing to the high rate at which the structures involved must be depreciated. If it were efficient to build buildings that had a very short life expectancy, the future would be much less relevant to current land-use decisions, and land speculation would lose much of its function and its profitability. The profitability of alternative uses of a particular plot of land is very much a function of the use of neighboring land and the accessibility of employment opportunities and shopping, recreational, and cultural facilities. Consequently, the use of land for roads and the characteristics of those roads appear to be very important.

Apartments, like shopping centers, factories, and office buildings, use land intensively and can afford to pay more for it than single-family housing. Apartment builders can afford to be selective in the sense that they can choose locations that are very accessible to customers, transport, or particular amenities.[1] Not only can they be selective but competition will force them to be. Since the returns from these land-intensive uses are sensitive to accessibility and to the use of adjacent land, those who make an incorrect choice will tend to be put out of business. The buildings will last for a long time but others will not copy their choice of location.

In a situation of urban growth the individual landowner must make the decision whether to use his land for single-family or multiple-family housing. Because of the time-indivisibility of this type of decision, it depends not only on the use of other land at the time the decision is made but also on the land's use for some considerable period into the future. There is always a good deal of uncertainty in predicting future events, and predicting future land use during urbanization is particularly difficult. This type of decision is made not only on the basis of the most likely returns, but also takes into account the whole distribution of possible outcomes of each decision. Assume for the moment that everyone prefers to live where access to urban facilities is easy and that the relative accessibility of any lot over the lifetime of typical housing becomes clearer as urbanization

1. Accessibility means different things to different kinds of land-users. The shopping center must be on a major road. Even different kinds of apartments vary in their requirements. Low-cost apartments will benefit from being close to public transport and employment centers. The most important consideration for at least some high-income apartments is accessibility to recreational and cultural facilities.

progresses. Then the two types of housing have the following characteristics:

1. Single-family housing is a relatively safe land use. Since it is, in a sense, the residual use of urban land, there is less danger that competition from more favorably located sites will make it necessary to sell the houses at a loss or to hold them so long that the profit disappears.

2. Multiple-family housing is a less certain venture, although in some areas the expected returns may be high. It will, however, be very sensitive to future land-use changes. A wrong guess about future trends can easily produce losses through high vacancy rates or by forcing rent reductions.

Rather than build either single- or multiple-family housing, the landowner can adopt a third strategy, namely, to "wait and see." Holding land out of current development involves a sacrifice of income but can produce very significant capital gains if changes in the use of other land increase the expected future earning power of the withheld land. There always remains the minimum loss alternative of building single-family houses. Traditionally, the advantages of physical accessibility have been such that apartments were rarely if ever constructed at an early stage of urbanization. Even if a landowner knew for certain that his land would be most profitably used for apartments in ten or fifteen years, it would still pay him to wait for some time before building. In some circumstances it may pay to build single-family houses first and later replace them with apartments.[2] Today, however, accessibility seems to depend more on closeness to a good highway that can be used for travel to a wide variety of places, rather than on physical closeness to employment, shopping, and other such facilities.

It is possible for one type of landowner to have it both ways. For the very large developer changes in the use of other land need not be entirely an unknown variable. If his development is large enough he can internalize many of the decisions that the small developer must regard as external. Thus, a block of a thousand or so apartments can include many of its own recreational facilities and some of its own shopping. Moreover, the very large developer is in a position to influence the development of adjacent sites. He makes them very attractive for developers of shopping centers and can influence the provision of streets and parks, perhaps by providing part of the land or finance required.

There is evidence that some apartment dwellers are becoming less interested in accessibility to traditional urban facilities, at least those repre-

2. These short-run land-use decisions are explored more fully in my book, *The Suburban Apartment Boom* (Washington, D.C.: Resources for the Future, Inc., 1968), pp. 3–5, 58–59, 109–113.

sented by the central business district and traditional suburban centers. As long as they have indirect access, through nearness to a good highway, they are more concerned about closeness to open space of various kinds. But apartments still use a small proportion of the urban area and are sensitive to changes in the use of other land. Apart from the very large developments, and the "open space" oriented apartment, there is an incentive to delay developments until the future shape of the urban area becomes clearer. The vast majority of apartments, even in the suburban areas, are built on land that has been bypassed by single-family homes or cleared of single-family houses. For the land-user the decision whether to build single-family houses or to wait in the hope that later developments will make the area suitable for apartments depends on the rent foregone—the cost of waiting—and the expected increase in the value of land—the returns from waiting.

The urban land market is notoriously imperfect in the sense that many landowners are unaware of the price that they could get if they sold their land, are unaware of its real earning opportunities in different uses, or are unable to sell or to choose the most profitable use for various reasons. Nor are the imperfections all on the side of sellers or owners. I do not propose to discuss these imperfections here.[3] Nor do I think they should be exaggerated. The land market in most large suburban areas is very active and, although land is a very diverse asset, a large group of potential buyers and developers watch very closely for any "bargain."

If we reflect for a moment on the way different landowners evaluate the future and on their attitude to risk, we can say that speculation in apartment land (the operation of withholding land when single-family housing is its currently most profitable use and taking the associated risk) will occur on the land thought most likely to be suitable in the future for apartment development. Speculation will also occur on land that is progressively less suitable, until the consensus of the market evaluates the gains to be equal to the costs. Such land can be regarded as "marginal" from the present point of view.[4] In the second section of the chapter the effects of the property tax on this margin will be examined.

3. Three of the major imperfections—zoning, building codes, and other regulations—are man-made. I have discussed their implications, ibid., chaps. 4, 8.

4. If S_t is the expected annual net return in each year if the land is used for single-family housing, M_t for multiple-family, and A_t for the best interim use; i is the rate of interest; uncertainty is neglected; and year $t = n$ is the best year to build apartments; then for "marginal" land

$$\sum_{\infty}^{0} \frac{S_t}{(1+i)^t} = \sum_{n}^{0} \frac{A_t}{(1+i)^t} + \sum_{\infty}^{n} \frac{M_t}{(1+i)^t}.$$

The equation assumes an infinite building life simply for convenience.

But first let us turn to apartments as a second- or later-generation urban land use. In and around the city center and suburban centers are areas of relatively old single- and multiple-family housing. Some redevelopment is occurring in these areas, mainly through the slow spread of offices and relatively high-cost apartment buildings. The profitability of this type of redevelopment is also very greatly affected by changes in the use of other land.[5] As a result, the new offices and apartments are mainly found close to existing redevelopment and spread along each side of major routes leading into the central business district. If there is to be any very great expansion in the rate of redevelopment of these so-called "grey areas," most of it will have to take the form of apartments for lower-income families than can afford those now being built. Conversely, if there is to be a marked growth in the number of central-area apartments, it must be through accelerated redevelopment of these areas.

The role of apartments in subsequent generations of urban land use is almost the exact reverse of its role in the first. If redevelopment is to occur, builders of moderate-income apartments are likely to be able to pay the least of any viable second-generation land use and therefore to assume the role of residual land-user that is played by single-family housing in the first generation. (There seems little prospect of low-income families being able to afford unsubsidized new housing of any kind, and certainly not in these areas of high-priced land). The two major reasons for the slow rate of urban redevelopment appear to be the sustained demand for cheap accommodation from low-income families and racial minorities and the interdependence, because of externalities, between redevelopment decisions. Land is being held out of redevelopment while the owner waits for favorable changes in the use of other land to make the redevelopment of his own land profitable. In this sense, speculation results in land being held out of moderate-income apartments in central areas in much the same way as it results in land being held out of single-family housing on the fringe. It is again helpful to examine the effects of property taxation on the incentive to speculate.

The Effects of Property Taxation

Attention is confined in this section to the long run and to a comparative analysis. Problems of transition from one type of tax to another are neglected, and the level of governmental expenditures is assumed constant. Site value and capital value taxation can be considered as alternative ways

5. This provides one of the most important justifications for a policy of urban renewal. See Otto A. Davis and Andrew B. Whinston, "The Economics of Urban Renewal," *Law and Contemporary Problems,* 26 (Winter 1961): 105–117.

of financing the same level of services. In addition, I assume that there is such a large volume of untaxed assets that the type of property tax does not affect the rate of interest. This would certainly be the case if, for example, one city were to change its basis of property taxation. In the three parts of this section I will examine in turn the effects of property taxes on land speculation, on the distribution of landownership, and on the intensity of land use. Each has implications for the volume and location of multiple-family housing.

Property Taxation and Speculation

Speculation is defined as withholding land from the use that would bring the highest current returns in order to reap the advantages of a higher sales price or higher annual returns from some other use later. Many of the advocates of site value taxation have held that it would discourage speculation by raising the cost of holding land and would encourage redevelopment. In part, this would follow from removal of the present American tax on improvements. To see whether a site value tax has any direct effect, we need to know the effect of the tax on land values. Apart from the case of the large-scale development, which is dealt with later, it seems safe to assume that the tax is fully capitalized.[6]

Assuming a single rate of interest for all land-users, a site value tax will have no influence on the cost of holding land. Let K_t be the value of land with no site value tax at successive times (t), K'_t its value when there is a site value tax at the rate of v, and i the interest rate. With no tax, the annual cost of holding is interest, $K_t i$. The value of the land (K'_t) after capitalization of the tax is equal to $K_t i/(i + v)$. The interest cost when the tax is in force is $K'_t i$ and the tax cost is $K'_t v$, so that the total annual cost is

$$\frac{K_t i}{i + v}(i + v) = K_t i.$$

The question that remains is whether the tax has any effects on the returns from speculation. At first the principle of tax capitalization seems to imply that the returns from speculation will be smaller. This would be e   ed to follow from consideration of the changes, over time, in the   two plots of land, otherwise similar, one of which was devoted to   ily housing in year x and the other of which was withheld until

italization and the exception of large-scale development are both twin R. A. Seligman, *The Shifting and Incidence of Taxation* (New University Press, 1926), chap. 3.

year $x + t$ and then used for apartments. It will be assumed that the two plots of land were marginal in the sense defined above so that both decisions were consistent with profit maximization. The two plots will be called m and s according to whether they were used for multiple- or single-family housing. In year $x + t - 1$, m might be expected to have a greater value than s because its value needs to increase in order to compensate for the lower annual income available during the period of withholding. This in turn reflects a higher annual rate of return from m than s once both improvements have been built. Another reason for the difference is that building on s limits the freedom of the owner to change its use in the light of changing expectations about the use of other land and other conditions. In this last sense, all vacant land is more valuable than it would be if it were improved, if only because of the cost of demolishing the improvements.

If vacant land is more valuable for either of these reasons it will bear a heavier tax. Tax capitalization will then cause a fall in the present value of expected future returns from using land for multiple-family housing in the future, compared with single-family housing now. A simple example can clarify this argument. A plot of land is worth $10,000 if sold for single-family housing this year and should be worth $10,500 if sold for multiple-family housing next year. With 5 percent interest and no tax, a landowner would be indifferent. Now impose a 5 percent tax on land value. The values drop to $5,000 and $5,250, respectively, but the holding costs are still $500—$250 for interest and $250 for the tax. It apparently pays to sell now if there is a tax.

But this diagnosis neglects the fact that, once a plot of land has been improved, it is not possible to distinguish the value of the improvements and of the land except by finding the addition that the improvements make to the value a site would have if it was vacant. The value of a plot of land is its market value if it is bare. In the example given in the previous passage, all land will be assessed at $5,250 in year $t + 1$ and the tax payments, at 5 per cent, will be $262.50. The value of land to be used for single-family housing in year t will be $10,000 (value untaxed) minus $5,000 (value in year t of taxes from year $t + 1$ onwards) minus T_t (taxes to be paid in year t), or $V_t = \$5,000 - T_t$. But $T_t = .05\ V_t$; therefore $V_t = \$4,761.90$; and $T_t = \$238.10$.

The value of land to be used for multiple-family housing is $5,000 (present value of $262.50 per year, after tax, from year $t + 1$ onwards) minus T_t, which equals $4,761.90. This is the same as for single-family housing. Note that this result is independent of the time distribution of net returns from either land use. Note also, as Mason Gaffney has shown in a different context, that tax capitalization is made more effective by rising land values.[7] If, for example, the value of expected returns from m relative to the returns from s rose more rapidly than anticipated at the time the initial decision was made, vacant land would have become more valuable relative to lots with single-family houses. The improvements on s would have suffered a particularly heavy rate of economic depreciation. If site value is always defined as the value the site would have if it were bare, it must be independent of the use or non-use of the site.

One problem arises if the cost of demolition of an improvement is greater than its salvage value. Then the market value can fall below the site value. Under these circumstances tax plus interest, with a site value tax, would exceed interest alone in its absence. Thus, the owner of a slum property earning no income may pay interest on its capital value so that his annual cost in the absence of a tax is Ki. But if the site has a value of $K + k$ ($k =$ net demolition cost), and there is a site value tax at the rate v, the cost of withholding it from development is $Ki + [kiv/(i + v)]$. It seems unlikely that k, which can never exceed net demolition cost, has a very high value for most slum property. It may be most significant for large reinforced concrete structures like car-parking buildings and urban freeways.

A more important problem occurs in the case of the large-scale developer of residential, commercial, or industrial property. In a sense, he relies on the increase in the value of land resulting from his own operations for a significant part of his revenue.[8] If site value taxation is to be neutral with respect to his operations, the assessor must treat the area that he occupies as a whole and assess its value as if it were vacant and other land in its current use. In the case of the shopping center, the large group of apartments, or especially the new town, this will give a much lower value than if the same principle was applied plot-by-plot. Since the plot-by-plot approach is applied to smaller-scale developments, it seems grossly inequitable that it should not also be applied here. The neutrality of a site value tax breaks down here because the Georgian contention that site value is socially created is only partly true. Of course, the problem becomes unimportant in the case of very large new towns that are also discrete taxing units. The annual net return from the investment will be the net of the cost of providing local-government type services no matter how these are financed.

The traditional American property tax that is levied on the market value of the improved site can be treated as if it is levied as a tax on the site, plus a tax on the capital value of the improvements. As Herbert A.

7. Mason Gaffney, *Rent Theory, Problems and Practices,* University of Missouri Research Bulletin 810 (Columbia, Mo., 1962), p. 47.

8. Seligman, *Shifting and Incidence,* pp. 285–286.

Simon has shown, this does not necessarily mean that there is a uniform effective rate on both.[9] In particular, it seems likely that part of the tax on improvements will, through reducing the demand for urban land, be capitalized as a lower land value. But, quite independently of the proportion that is borne by landowners, it will remain neutral. The tax on improvements, of course, directly affects the intensity of land use. Although speculation generally has as its objective a higher intensity of land use in the future, this is not necessarily so.

Property Taxation and the Distribution of Landownership

I have argued above that a tax on site value does not affect the cost of holding land. In effect, the taxing authority appropriates a part of the value of the site and rents it to the owner at an annual charge equal to the tax. The rate at which the tax is capitalized is determined by the market in which buyers are presented with a large number of possible flows of future returns. The highest bidders will be those for whom a flow of future returns has the highest present value, namely, those with the lowest discount rate. Of all assets on the market that promise future returns, untaxed land promises flows that are more sustained into the future than virtually any other asset. Hence, buyers of future flows of returns who have a low rate of discount will have a comparative advantage in bidding for land as compared with other assets.[10]

But rented land is a quite different type of asset. Rent is paid periodically as the returns or the satisfaction accrues. Consequently, there is no delay between paying and receiving the returns, and the discount rate does not enter into the decision. Therefore, those with a higher discount rate can occupy rented land, often rented from those with a lower discount rate. Land with a site value tax is in effect partly owned and partly rented, depending on the level of the tax. Capitalization of the tax reduces the present value because periodic returns are reduced by periodic tax payments. A low discount rate is less of an advantage in bidding for

9. Herbert A. Simon, "The Incidence of a Tax on Urban Real Property," *Quarterly Journal of Economics,* 57, no. 3 (May 1943): 398–420; reprinted in *Readings in the Economics of Taxation,* ed. Richard A. Musgrave and Carl S. Shoup (Homewood, Ill.: Richard D. Irwin, 1959), pp. 416–435.

10. Gaffney has explored this matter in some detail in *Rent Theory,* pp. 39–42; and in "The Unwieldy Time-Dimension of Space," *The American Journal of Economics and Sociology,* 20 (1961): 465–481. See also Daniel Holland, "The Taxation of Unimproved Value in Jamaica," in National Tax Association, *1965 Proceedings of the Fifty-Eighth Annual Conference on Taxation,* ed. Walter J. Kress (Harrisburg, Pa., 1966), pp. 442–470.

highly taxed land, and its ownership will not become so concentrated in the hands of those with a low discount rate.

Bidders for land with a low discount rate generally have rather large assets, commonly a high income and a high marginal rate of income tax. Because their assets are large they tend to have a low marginal valuation of capital. If their income is also high, the subjective marginal utility of money to them is also likely to be relatively low so that they do not need to live off their capital. They can keep up the rate of return on their capital by lending and by renting land and other assets, but both operations are costly so that the net return is markedly below the cost to the borrower or the renter. A high marginal income tax rate lowers the net earning power of funds in all uses and, consequently, the opportunity cost of capital.

By contrast the bidder with a high opportunity cost of capital has few assets, generally a lower income and marginal income tax rate. In particular, he is either a borrower or a renter, or both. He is in the land market, as a rule, for somewhere to live or to practice his business. The alternatives are to buy or to rent. His costs of borrowing or of renting are higher than the returns to the lender or owner because of administrative costs, associated in particular with ensuring the security of the loan, collecting the rent, and administering the lease. For him a lot costing $2,000 with a site value tax of $100 per year is a much more attractive proposition than a lot costing $4,000. If he has to pay 6 percent interest on a mortgage, the annual cost will be reduced from $240 to $220. The required deposit will also probably be lower. Conversely, the bidder who intends to become a landlord will very likely find the property less attractive. If his net return from rent on the lot plus $16,000 house is $800 per year and his discount rate 4 percent, the tax will reduce the net annual return to $700 (the administrative costs are unlikely to fall much when the tax is introduced). Since $640 is the return on capital invested in the house, only $60 a year comes from the lot, the present value of which is only $1,500. Hence, his bid will be lower and the bid of the "borrower" higher.

What effect would such easier land purchase terms for "borrowers" have on the volume and location of multiple-family housing? At first sight more widespread homeownership would appear likely to accelerate the migration to the suburbs. This conclusion is strengthened by the fact that very little other than single-family housing is owned, and investment in new rental housing is, for economy in administrative costs, very largely confined to multiple-family housing. Condominiums and cooperative apartments make it possible to own part of a multiple-unit structure, but there are many inconveniences. Similarly, new townhouses are being constructed for renting, and many existing one-family homes are rented either for fortuitous reasons or, in the case of slum property, for very good financial reasons.

Apartment building would be made less attractive, but so would the ownership of low-income housing for rental purposes. With the fall in its value more low- and medium-income families would be able to afford to buy this property, and with the fall in its earning power in its present state, redevelopment would become a more attractive alternative. For central apartments the two influences would, to some extent, offset one another. Of course, it is only investment in land that becomes relatively less attractive as a result of a site value tax. Central-area apartments use little land and, certainly in areas ready for redevelopment, its price would fall markedly. But with homeownership made easier, suburban land prices would not fall as much, so that suburban apartment building would also be discouraged quite markedly. The effect on the total volume is unknown.

This can be interpreted as an effect of land taxation on the rate of redevelopment of slum property, but it only operates because of costs of operations in the capital market, which produce a gap between typical borrowing and lending rates and between rental costs and the return to the landlord. Low-income housing near the central city is occupied mainly by families for whom the opportunity cost of capital is very high and may be infinite if their security is small enough. A government offer to advance a part of the value of the property without security and at much lower than their borrowing rate of interest, puts them in a much stronger position to buy, and hence lowers the price they are prepared to pay to rent. It has many elements in common with a scheme of low-interest finance, although the property is financed rather than the buyer.

The Property Tax and the Intensity of Land Use

So far we have focused most attention on a site value tax and on the effect of the part of a tax on land and improvements that is borne by the landowner. Except through their effects on the incentive for large-scale development and on the distribution of landownership, they do not affect the use to which land is put. When a tax is imposed on improvements, however, only a part of it will, in general, be passed back to the landowners. Another part is borne by the occupants, because the reduced supply of accommodation will increase its price. Even in the long run some part is likely to be borne by the owners of nonland factors of production that produce accommodation, depending on the elasticity of supply of such factors. But in the long run their supply is probably relatively elastic and the main burden is borne by occupants and landowners, its distribution depending mainly on the elasticity of demand for accommodation.

The extent to which land improvement and redevelopment are discouraged by a high tax on improvements has been debated in related literature, but there is little doubt that it has a significant effect in some areas.[11] The political pressure for concessions is evidence of its effect. Certainly, this half of the prescription of reduced taxes on improvements and increased taxes on land has the most straightforward effect on the rate of redevelopment. In general, then, a tax on the improvements to bare land discourages building and redevelopment. It also discourages high-density development and reinforces the tendency of low-discount-rate landowners to concentrate their resources in land, where the tax can be fully capitalized, even if at somewhat higher than the investor's rate of discount.

What effect will the tax on property improvements have on the extent of metropolitan decentralization—will it tend to increase or reduce central-area densities? The answer appears to hinge on the relationship between land area and building space in the utility functions of final consumers and the production functions of producers. If they are substitutes, the tax on buildings will prompt the use of less "building-intensive" and more land-intensive forms of accommodation, thereby reducing urban densities. In this case the share of a tax on combined value of land and improvements borne by occupants and on factors used in building is greater than the share of buildings in total value. If they are complements, land prices will fall with the volume of building and landowners will bear part of the tax on buildings. It also seems quite plausible to believe that property taxes have prompted households and businessmen to seek locations where land is cheaper—in the suburbs. If "accommodation" is regarded as a single commodity, this would occur, even though land costs have fallen rather than risen. In one sense, they will be reducing their expenditure on accommodation by moving to the suburbs, but, at least in the short run, increasing their expenditure on communication.

I have assumed so far that there is a tax on accommodation but not on communication. Intra-city transport and utilities provide communication, and if their land and fixed assets are taxed, the demand for proximity (a close substitute for communication) will increase. Publicly owned

11. See Morris Beck, "Urban Redevelopment: Influence of Property Taxation and Other Factors," in National Tax Association, *1964 Proceedings of the Fifty-Seventh Annual Conference on Taxation,* ed. Walter J. Kress (Harrisburg, Pa., 1965), pp. 239–249; and M. Mason Gaffney, "Property Taxes and the Frequency of Urban Renewal," ibid., pp. 272–285.

utilities and transport are not taxed and roads, by far the most important provider of communication, also are not taxed. A site value tax on roads would have no effect on their price, according to our theory, if they paid the opportunity cost of the land they occupy. Taxes on road users are sufficient to pay the capital cost of expanding the system and the maintenance costs of the whole system. But the opportunity cost of the space occupied by older roads—its rental value—can be very high in central areas and does not enter this calculation. The true opportunity costs, at least in large cities, may be much higher than tax revenue.[12] In other words, communication of some types at least is not bearing its full cost, leading to a lower demand for proximity and a higher degree of dispersion than is desirable. One form of communication, vertical transport, is fully taxed—a further discouragement to high-density development.

Conclusions

The tax on site values would have the following effects (effects which that part of the tax on land and improvements borne by the landowner already has) :

1. It would discourage large-scale developments, especially of apartments or new towns where a good deal of the expected returns take the form of increases in site value. This effect would be felt only when the rules of assessment for site value taxation were applied to units smaller than the complete development.

2. It would reduce the attractiveness of land as an investment asset to those with a low opportunity cost of capital and increase it to those whose opportunity cost is higher. Consequently, land would be redistributed from the wealthy to the less wealthy.

3. It might discourage speculation to a minor extent if the site value exceeded the market value of land and its improvements because of a positive net cost of demolition. Thus, the actual cost of holding slum property might rise.

Both 1 and 2 above are likely to reduce the attractiveness of large-scale apartment developments, particularly in suburban areas. Although it is probably less important, 1 also applies to large-scale tract building of single-family homes. Central-area redevelopment would also receive a boost from factor 2 because slum property would become a less attractive

12. William S. Vickrey, "General and Specific Financing of Urban Services," in *Public Expenditure Decisions in the Urban Community,* ed. Howard G. Schaller (Washington, D.C.: Resources for the Future, Inc., 1963), pp. 62–90.

investment and hence more readily available for redevelopment; factor 3 would have a similar effect. Such a tax would be expected to concentrate apartment development more into the central areas of cities, but it could either increase or reduce the total volume.

The tax on improvements to land has the following effects: it reduces (1) the total volume of such improvements because demand falls when the tax is passed on, in part, to the occupants; (2) probably the extent of concentration in central cities because land-users substitute communication for building space; and (3) the density of improvements by putting a tax on vertical transport, while much horizontal transport not only pays no tax but does not even pay an economic rent.

Each of these effects probably reduces apartment development more than single-family housing and certainly penalizes apartments built near the central city.

PART II

Land and Building Taxes:
Five Case Studies

INTRODUCTION

In studying the effect of land and building taxes on economic development, it is highly desirable to examine whatever empirical information may be available on the subject. Relevant information does not often, if ever, describe and analyze tax instutions that conform to ideal types. Economic development is a product of natural, cultural, and historical circumstances that vary in time and place. Consequently, patterns of economic development differ among states and countries at a given time and vary for each state and country with the passage of time. One would expect, also, to find tax institutions affecting land and buildings that are quite different in various countries.

Scholarly interest in the economic growth of lesser developed countries is running high today. Some of these countries have certain features of their property taxes designed to encourage economic development. Part II, therefore, contains five studies; the first examines the stimulation of agricultural development in the United States, while the remaining four emphasize the taxation of land and buildings in other countries and its relation to economic development.

In the first case study Albert T. Henley reviews the application of land value taxation to the financing of irrigation districts in California. The taxation of land and improvements to finance irrigation facilities by special districts began in 1887. In 1909 taxes were removed from private improvements (and buildings). Henley refers to various reports comparing the economic and social development of several rural communities, some based on dry farming and others based on irrigation farming financed by land value taxation, and finds that the economic development of those communities based on dry farming has lagged seriously and prospered little. In contrast, the consequences of financing irrigation by taxing land values (only) of nonirrigated land in the area as well as irrigated land has stimulated rapid economic development and has fostered a high level of prosperity. The effect on land values, incentive, land use, and opportunities to farm is predictable according to economic theory. Henley harbors no doubt about the effectiveness of the irrigation district tax and benefit plan in achieving rapid and desired economic and social progress in California.

Australia and New Zealand provide an unusual opportunity for observing and studying different kinds of property taxes in operation, often side by side. New Zealand and all but one of the Australian states tax land values only, while their local governments either tax land alone or both land and improvements. The tax base is either a capital value or rental value. In Chapter 8 A. M. Woodruff and L. L. Ecker-Racz explain how the special taxation of land values at the federal (Australia), national (New Zealand), and state levels was largely motivated by the desire to break up large landholdings rather than to provide a significant amount of revenue. Land tax rates were progressive and the tax given added effectiveness with the enactment of a progressive income tax that did not allow the deductibility of land taxes. Exemptions to the land tax were allowed for resident owners of small estates.

In 1952 the federal government of Australia turned over its land taxes to the states. The national government of New Zealand retained the land tax because its state governments had been abolished in 1875. The national tax does not have rates as progressive as the state land taxes in Australia and it also is deductible against income in the national income tax. Today the national (New Zealand) and state (Australian) land taxes affect business decisions only when high land values are involved; this almost always occurs with respect to urban land. Local property and land taxes known as "rates" are proportional with few exemptions—in contrast to the state (Australian) and national (New Zealand) land taxes, which are progressive with many exemptions. The bases of taxation are improved capital value, unimproved capital value, and assessed annual value. Woodruff and Ecker-Racz explain why valuers (assessors) prefer a "site value" basis (which would include invisible improvements) rather than unimproved capital value.

Most of the assessment of property is administered by the state governments in Australia and the national government of New Zealand, and has produced a remarkably high level of professional competence. Professional training and the passing of a rigorous examination are required to qualify as an assessor (valuer). Assessors find little difficulty in assessing property at full value and separating land from building value. In fact, Woodruff and Ecker-Racz find that a tax on the unimproved capital value of land is easier to administer than a tax on improved real estate. Furthermore, it is claimed that site values are still easier to assess than the unimproved capital value of land and the reasoning of valuers supporting this view is presented.

It does not appear to Woodruff and Ecker-Racz that the various property and land tax systems have had a major influence on the pattern of urban land use and development. A partial explanation may be found in the fact that tax rates are low except for more valuable properties. Another lies in the many tax exemptions and abatements which were enacted previously, because without them the property taxes were exerting a great deal of pressure on owners to raise their land use or to sell. The prevailing view of tax professionals in Australia and New Zealand, however, is that taxing land values alone (unimproved capital value) is superior to taxing both land and improvements. It is maintained that the former encourages development and does nothing to discourage it, as is the case with the latter.

In Chapter 9 John Strasma focuses our attention on Chile, which today has the heaviest and most effective taxation of real estate in all of Latin America. Its administration of the tax can also be regarded as the best in the area. Even so, property taxes yield a relatively small part(6.3 percent) of Chilean public revenues.

As is typical of most underdeveloped countries, a large part (37 percent) of total governmental revenues in Chile are raised from transaction taxes and customs duties. The personal income tax provides twice as much revenue as the property tax. The income tax is unique in having two parts, one that taxes income from various sources at different rates and a second that taxes income on an overall basis. A very interesting aspect of Chile's tax system is the recently (1964) enacted tax on personal net wealth that eliminates at least in part the effect of income tax loopholes and evasion. Income taxes may be used as a deduction for up to 50 percent of the annual obligation of the net wealth tax.

Between 1855 and 1957 agricultural land and improvements were subject to the property tax. After 1957 the tax on most improvements was eliminated. A major problem is caused by the serious chronic inflation in Chile, which has left assessments far below market value. Some progress, although inadequate, has been made to correct this situation.

After the 1961 earthquake in Chile, the Organization of American States assisted that country in reassessing most of its agricultural and urban land with the use of photography. This technique has helped greatly in identifying property, in making a more complete listing of property, and in studying soils to estimate the best potential use of land, and has also raised the accuracy of assessments. Each hectare of land is assessed in terms of one of twelve qualities of land as well as in terms of location to market and transportation availability.

The urban property tax includes improvements as well as land. In order to stimulate low-cost housing, however, most urban housing built recently has been exempt from part of the income tax, from rent control, and from part of the real estate tax. These and related measures have resulted in an abundance of privately built housing for all but the low-income groups. An additional building incentive measure is the surcharge on vacant lots, which rises for each year that a lot is held idle after it is first transferred by the subdivider.

While the capital value of land may be taxed annually as part of the real estate tax or on land alone, attempts have also been made to tax land value increments only once, either when produced (as with special assessments) or when "realized" (as with the capital gains tax). In Chapter 10 William G. Rhoads and Richard M. Bird present a meticulous description and analysis of the valorization tax in Colombia, including some comparisons with similar taxes in Ecuador and Mexico. The valorization tax is similar to "special assessments" in the United States or "betterment" taxes in England, which attempt to capture land value increments when they occur because of public improvements in order to pay for those very improvements. There are, however, some important differences as well as similarities between the valorization tax and special assessments.

While the property tax is relatively light in burden, the valorization tax in Medellín (population 700,000), where it has been most seriously and successfully used, produced just as much revenue. The tax has achieved notable public developments in that city, in particular a wide network of broad streets and boulevards including water, sewers, street lighting, and landscaping. The tax has just recently been applied to urban renewal where property owners adjacent to urban renewal project areas are expected to receive land value increments upon completion of contemplated projects.

Although special assessments in the United States have not enjoyed as much professional and popular support recently as in former years, the valorization tax as practiced in Colombia, especially in the city of Medellín, is encouraging. Both professional and popular support has been given to the tax as practiced there and under the prevailing conditions. Rhoads and Bird analyze the factors that seem to account for the considerable success of the tax, the significant and strategic administrative practices of the tax as well as the urban conditions (social, technical, and economic) that are conducive to that success. Other lesser developed countries may well learn much from Colombia's experience.

In Chapter 11 Daniel M. Holland presents a description and analysis of the property tax in Jamaica, which is in the midst of a transition from the taxing of improved values (that is, the value of land and buildings) to unimproved value (the value of land alone). The introduction of this case study gives a number of reasons why developing countries, particularly, might well have an interest in the potentials of taxing unimproved values of property (land values).

The Jamaican experience in taxing the unimproved value of land helps to answer doubts that have arisen in countries taxing buildings as well as lands, as to its administrative feasibility. It shows that achieving quality and efficiency in assessing the unimproved capital value of land is not only feasible but administratively easier with trained assessors and practical definitions for improvements and the unimproved capital value of land. An interesting innovation that has resulted in an administrative advantage in assessing land is the use of fiscal procedures and maps (including photographic) rather than the far more costly and time-consuming legal cadaster. Since a majority of landholdings are fragmented, the work of valuation is further simplified by subjecting all land valued at less than £100 to a standard token tax only.

One objection to taxing the unimproved capital value of land is the fear that it might create hardships for some low-income persons owning land currently in a low level of use but whose market value is high because of the high potential income that might be produced if the land were used in an alternative way. Jamaica's provisions for granting relief in some hardship cases and not in others represent a reasonable compromise between a practical problem and the desire to create an incentive to put valuable land to a higher use.

Holland also analyzes the economic and practical aspects of a number of other features and problems of Jamaica's tax on the unimproved capital value of land. Among them are the progressive rate structure of the tax, the reluctance to increase local-government (parish) tax rates, the relative unresponsiveness of the tax base to economic growth, the problem of "super-development," and the proposal to establish service rates (charges) based on the improved value of property. The latter is part of the broader question of whether any one tax, even that on unimproved capital values, should bear the full costs of developing social overhead capital.

Lastly, Holland points up the dangers of Jamaica's prolonged period of transition and suggests the advisability (after transition) of increasing the rates and reducing exemptions so that the tax will be felt by more landowners than the present small minority. Unless that is done, very few landholders will be given a tax incentive to use land more efficiently and the underutilization of land will not improve. The possibility of achieving economic development by taxing land values depends upon the ability to achieve tax rates high enough to motivate owners to make decisions for greater investments in improvements.

Looking at the five case studies as a group, it is evident that the special taxation of land is motivated by a variety of reasons, including those of achieving greater equity, of influencing land tenure, or of stimulating economic development. Experience in taxing land has revealed certain problems and how best to deal with them. The practical administrability of taxing land values is generally unquestioned. The compatibility of taxing land values with economic development is either taken for granted or enthusiastically supported. Further comments will be made in the conclusion of this volume about the lessons that can be learned from the taxation experiences of various countries mentioned in the case studies.

7 Land Value Taxation by California Irrigation Districts

ALBERT T. HENLEY

Californians have had long experience in the use of a device of local government known as an irrigation district. This is one of a class of greatly diverse forms of public districts that in some states of the United States are in wide and growing use and in others almost unknown.[1] Districts as such are something of a mystery to most people, although they are in fact a simple conception. Simple and ingenious, they provide a means of accomplishing two basic ends: questions relative to projects of preeminently local import may be locally decided and tax-burden boundaries may be adjusted to conform with those of expected project benefit. In the case of California irrigation districts, which tax all the land whether the owner irrigates or not and tax only land while exempting improvements, there has been a kind of side-benefit of extraordinary importance to the state. It is this last that will be the subject of this chapter.

The Evolution of California Public District Legislation

Districts range from entities with a single, defined purpose to those empowered to provide a broad, general, utility service. Such agencies have been organized under established general statutes and also, as a recent tendency, under special district acts.

"General act districts" are in the vast majority in California. Here, the basic enabling legislation is already on the books and merely provides a means of forming a local governmental agency by local initiative and defines the form and powers of a district so created. "Special act districts" are created by legislative act and may or may not require con-

NOTE: I wish to thank the editors of the *American Journal of Economics and Sociology* for permission to use material from my article "Land Value Taxation in California," found in 27, no. 4 (October 1968): 377–386.

1. California is second only to Illinois in numbers of created districts. On the other hand, Art. X, § 2 of the Alaska constitution restricts the delegation of taxing powers to cities and boroughs exclusively.

firmation or consent by local election of those who are to be served by them.

A chronological survey of general districts acts shows a definite movement from narrow to wide declarations of purpose. In 1866 when reclamation districts were authorized as the first such enactment, they were permitted the single function of reducing swamps and tidelands to use.[2] The same is true of three types of protection district acts (1880, 1895, 1907)[3] and three types of drainage district acts (1885, 1903, 1919).[4]

Similarly, the subject Irrigation District Law, first adopted in 1887 and in widespread use today, is largely limited to authorizing the provision of a water supply.[5] In 1911 followed municipal water districts, concerned primarily with domestic water service,[6] and in 1913 county water districts[7] and California water districts.[8] Both of these latter were permitted to reclaim land as well as to distribute water for any beneficial use.

It was not until 1921, with the passage of the Municipal Utility District Act[9] and the Public Utility District Act,[10] that use was made of a public agency, not incorporated as a city, which could nevertheless perform a wide variety of services for its inhabitants. This steady development culminated in the Community Services District Law, passed in 1951.[11]

Special district legislation has had a more recent history. The dominating form here is the county-wide district, often called "county flood control and water conservation districts" or "county water agencies." All reflect, in greater or lesser degree, the first such statute, which was the Los Angeles County Flood Control Act, enacted in 1915.[12]

The Elements of Public District Legislation

Speaking generally, a district may be negatively defined as a "local governmental entity which is neither a city, county, township nor village."[13] In positive terms such units have been defined as

2. Calif. Stats. 1865–1866, ch. 570.
3. 1 Calif. Water Code Ann., acts 6172, 6174, 6175.
4. Ibid., acts 2200, 2202, 2203.
5. Calif. Water Code, §§ 20500–29978.
6. 1 Calif. Water Code Ann., act 5243.
7. Calif. Water Code, §§ 3000–3901.
8. Ibid., §§ 34000–38501.
9. Calif. Pub. Ut. Code, §§ 11501–14509.
10. Ibid., §§ 15501–17776.
11. Calif. Govt. Code, §§ 61000–61891.
12. 1 Calif. Water Code Ann., act 4463.
13. California, Senate, *Preliminary Report of the Senate Interim Committee on Study of Districts* (Sacramento, Calif.: State of California, 1959), p. 7.

organized entities, possessing a structural form, an official name, perpetual succession, and the rights to sue and be sued, to make contracts, and to obtain and dispose of property. They have officers who are popularly elected or are chosen by other public officials. They have a high degree of public accountability. Moreover, they have considerable fiscal and administrative independence from other governments. The financial and administrative criteria distinguish special districts and other governments from all dependent or subordinate districts and from most authorities which, lacking one or both of these standards, are not governmental units.[14]

A distinction must be made between independent districts and dependent districts. The quotation above relates to the former. A dependent district is not autonomous in governmental or fiscal control, but is an adjunct of a county. All districts share the features of a defined area, a governing body, legal identity, and certain powers, including those of serving the public in defined ways, raising revenue for maintenance and operation, and servicing the district's obligations.

Taken as a group, special act districts are organized by the state legislature with local confirmation often added. General act districts are usually organized by a process of petition by proponents to a higher element of local government followed by public hearing, an election, and a formal declaration of a favoring vote and of consequent formation.

In the matter of a governing body, the usual choice for either type of district, special act or general act, is between: (1) a board, elected at large or from divisions of the district; (2) a board appointed by a higher level of government; (3) a board identical with that of a higher level of government acting ex-officio; or (4) where a district is composed of constituent units—that is, of smaller districts, cities, or both—the board may consist of selectees of such units.

The governing body of an independent district, when established, is ordinarily able to act autonomously, as a city council acts, subject to the direct control of its local voters and to indirect supervision by the state.

The boundaries of a district should, of course, include the area to receive its services and benefits, without regard to artificial political boundaries. Sometimes a finding of benefit to included lands is required. Often the several areas of a district need not be contiguous.

Districts, including irrigation districts, often have the valuable power to create, by appropriate proceedings, zones or subdistricts, called improvement districts, in which burden and benefit of a purely local project can be made precisely coterminous.

The most usual definition of the voters of a district is that they shall be residents and electors thereof. Restriction of voting rights to land-

14. John C. Bollens, *Special District Governments in the United States* (Berkeley, Calif.: University of California Press, 1947), p. 1.

owners is, however, a feature of certain district legislation in use in California. In that event, votes normally are assigned on the basis of assessed valuation of land owned.

Assuming a power to make ad valorem levies, district legislation must designate (as between land alone, land and improvements, or all property) the precise values that are to be assessed. A distinction is to be recognized between taxing for maintenance and operation purposes (which may or may not be specifically limited to a declared number of cents per hundred dollars of assessed valuation) and taxing to support regularly issued bonds or certain duly authorized contracts (which taxes are by their nature limitless).

Districts are always declared to have a legal existence, a seal, the power to sue and be sued, and the like. Districts may be empowered to contract with other public agencies including states and the federal government. They act in furtherance of a list of purposes as inclusive as the chosen statute may permit.

California Irrigation Districts

Of public districts in California the most used and useful have been those formed since 1887 under the "Wright Act," known officially since a 1917 amendment as the Irrigation District Act.[15] I have stated elsewhere that "the discovery of the legal formula of these organizations was of infinitely greater value to California than the discovery of gold a generation before. They are an extraordinarily potent engine for the creation of wealth." [16] The legislation did not lack the tribute of emulation. Sixteen other western states have enacted irrigation district laws closely modeled upon the Wright Act.[17]

California irrigation districts follow generally the form of independent local agencies described in the preceding section. These special features should be noted, however:

1. Voters: All of the prospective electors who qualify to vote under the state's election code are eligible to vote in irrigation district elections. Un-

15. Calif. Stats. 1887, ch. 34; amended as the "Wright Bridgeford Act," Calif. Stats. 1897, ch. 189; codified as Calif. Water Code, §§ 20500 et seq. It is to be noted that although there is more irrigated land included in irrigation districts, there exist in California today more *numbers* of districts of other types.

16. Albert T. Henley, "The Evolution of Forms of Water Users Organizations in California," *California Law Review,* 45 (1957): 665, 667.

17. Wells A. Hutchins, *Irrigation Districts: Their Organization, Operation and Financing,* Department of Agriculture, Technical Bulletin no. 254 (Washington, D.C.: U.S. Government Printing Office, 1931).

like the majority of other state enactments in this field, California irrigation district law permits the incurring of debt upon a vote without regard to landownership. An improvement may be approved and the land burdened to finance it against the will of the holders of a majority of the lands of the district. "The essence of the Wright Act ... was the permission given to a part of the residents of a given area to incur indebtedness for which all the lands in such area were held liable." [18]

2. Revenues: The second unusual feature of these agencies is their method of burdening the benefited to pay for the benefit. Revenues are secured chiefly through "assessments" upon the land. The term as used here is not quite synonymous with "taxation." Having been levied to finance a local improvement, an assessment need not be equal and uniform, whereas a tax is required to be both. The original 1887 act called for assessing all real property. In 1909 an amendment provided for exemption of improvements in all districts thereafter created. Existing districts were permitted to come under the new provision upon a favorable vote of the landowners. Most did. All active California irrigation districts today assess land only.

Districts also may and do charge "tolls" for delivered water within and without the district. They may, and a fortunate few do, generate and sell electricity. With the consent of their electors they issue bonds and contract with other levels of government, undertaking in either case a financial obligation for which the liens of land value assessments are the basic security.

Irrigation districts levy and collect assessments independently of the county machinery. Usually the district will assess all irrigable land uniformly and give a much lower value to nonirrigable parcels, that is, to farm land the system cannot reach or which cannot use the water. Town lots that will not conceivably be irrigated were thought by some of their owners to be immune, since a district is only to be created of lands "susceptible of irrigation." [19] The claim did not avail them. Town lots are benefited and may be assessed, said the court, because their value depends upon the productivity of the surrounding farm lands. [20]

In summary, district assessors tend to create classifications and assess uniformly within them; that is to say, they somewhat arbitrarily find that irrigation works are of equal benefit to each acre or provide an equal additional value to each acre in each classification so assessed.

18. Ibid., p. 71.
19. California Irrigation District Law, Calif. Water Code, § 20700.
20. *Modesto* v. *Tregea,* 88 Calif. 355 (1891).

The Effect of Irrigation Development under the Wright Act

It is assumed that a system which permits or rewards the holding of large tracts of land out of production or with extremely limited unit return is less desirable socially than a system that by economic pressure tends to produce resident, productive ownership of subdivisions of such tracts. A careful study made in 1946 of the conditions found in two rural communities of California comes to this conclusion: "the size and character of the farm holdings and operations is responsible in no small degree for the conditions in those cities. On the one hand, in the community surrounded by big farms the social, cultural, and economic attributes of life are developed to a lesser degree than in the other community which is in the midst of an area made up primarily of smaller farms independently operated where the community welfare is of a higher order and more wholesome in every particular." [21]

The study found the city of Dinuba to be sociologically superior in every way to the city of Arvin. The two were highly comparable geographically and in resource potential and yet their differences were striking. The author states:

> In the realm of social conditions, the two towns showed great divergence. In a series of measures of community character one community was found to meet the standards normally accepted for community life in America far better than the other . . . .
>
> It is the position of the present writer after detailed sifting of the evidence presented in this study, that large scale farming does, in fact, bear the major responsibility for the social differences between Arvin and Dinuba.
>
> The study of Arvin and Dinuba shows . . . that quality of social conditions is associated with scale of operations; that farm size is in fact an important causal factor in the creation of such differences, and that it is reasonable to believe that farm size is the most important of these differences. [22]

A word of caution here: the great difference between the Dinuba and Arvin areas in 1946 was that the former had an established irrigated farm economy while the latter did not. To assess with precision the effect of land value taxation would require that an area with available irrigation service *but not organized under the Wright Act formulae* be contrasted with Dinuba. Dinuba lies in the Alta Irrigation District formed in 1888. Arvin's area was not organized under the Wright Act.

21. Walter R. Goldschmidt, *Small Business and the Community: A Study in Central Valley of California on Effects of Scale of Farm Operations,* Report of the Senate Special Committee to Study Problems of American Small Business (Washington, D.C.: U.S. Government Printing Office, 1946), p. viii.
22. Ibid., pp. 112–114.

From the evidence, however, it seems reasonable to believe that the financing of irrigation works by land value taxation was a causal factor in producing the smaller farms Walter R. Goldschmidt has found so beneficial in social effect. For one thing, that result was not an unintended one; it was expected to follow. The Wright Act was "purposely drawn to assist the development of small farming." [23] The pressure to use the land or to sell to those who will derives from the simple fact that if you are in a California irrigation district your land (assuming it is in reach of water service) will be assessed for water development costs whether you take the water or not. To which add the further fact that if you use the land only minimally or let it lie barren for a speculative rise, you pay the same number of dollars per acre as your neighbor who makes a heavy investment in improvements. Both of these difficulties were fully recognized by the old-time cattle barons and "dry farmers" and many fought the application of the Wright Act to themselves by every means at their command. It is instructive to note, for example, that when the Modesto Irrigation District was organized in July 1887, the favorable vote on the question was 700 to 156. The opponents "claimed that of the 156 votes cast against irrigation more than 150 were cast by landowners holding 70,000 acres out of 108,000 comprising the district." [24]

Finally, there is the evidence of observers. In 1914 the Modesto Chamber of Commerce in the Modesto Irrigation District issued a statement regarding the effect of irrigation financed by a tax that exempts improvements. A few lines follow: "as a result of the change [to exemption of improvements] many of the large ranches have been cut up and sold in small tracts. The new owners are cultivating these farms intensively. The population of both country and city has greatly increased .... The new system of taxation has brought great prosperity to our district. Farmers are now encouraged to improve their property. Industry and thrift are not punished by an increase in taxes." [25]

The breakup of the ranches around Modesto did not wait for the new exemption of improvements, however. That change in assessment practice did not effectively occur until 1912. Yet in 1907 the *Stanislaus County Weekly News* told its readers that "the great wheat fields have been gradually diminishing for several years, but the last year was marked by a

23. Ibid., p. 20.

24. Benjamin Franklin Rhodes, Jr., "Thirsty Land: The Modesto Irrigation District, a Case Study of Irrigation Under the Wright Law" (Ph.D. diss., University of California, 1943).

25. Quoted in Commonwealth Club of California, *Transactions*, 9, no. 4 (1914): 300. A statement to the Oakdale City Council in Oakdale Irrigation District is to the same effect. Ibid., p. 302.

wonderful change. Like magic the wheat fields of a year ago have been transformed into great vineyards and orchards of fruit of all kinds . . . . The past year has been one of great activity in land division; many large tracts have been subdivided and populated by new people . . . ." [26]

The following comment is from a 1929 publication of the state of California relative to Wright Act districts:

> When it is realized that land in the districts is assessed at least for district bond interest, and generally also for maintenance and operation, regardless of whether it is irrigated, it is very clear that the presence in any district of large areas that are unirrigated results in great hardships. Obviously the first necessary step in eliminating that hardship is to get the land into production under irrigation, and in most cases this requires more farmers with sufficient means to carry the farm development and operation costs while waiting for the larger income irrigation and more intensive development make possible. Even a considerable lag in settlement is to be expected, but the difficulties resulting from an excessive lag constitute one of the problems that must be counted on, along with the problems of construction and finance, when planning new irrigation district development.[27]

It is obvious that the financing practices of California irrigation districts urge the landowner away from somnolence or the hope of mere speculative gain in two ways. He is nudged from behind by the assessment on his land to do something that will permit him to pay it. At the same time he is beckoned by the promise that his effort and investment to make the land produce will not be penalized, since such improvements are not taxed.

Conclusion

Districts, as a device of government, provide a local decision-making process together with a means of conforming the burden of an expensive local project to its benefit. Some, notably California irrigation districts, offer additionally a method of formation and decision that deprives a minority of large-scale landlords of what seemed a traditional veto to progress. Such districts are the beneficiaries of a formula of finance having two important features. One is that the costs are laid upon all land in the district to which irrigation service could be brought (or which will indirectly benefit) regardless of the use the owner may choose to make

26. 4 January 1907. Quoted by Rhodes, "Thirsty Land," p. 120.

27. Frank Adams, *Irrigation Districts in California,* California State Department of Public Works Bulletin no. 21 (Sacramento, Calif.: State of California, 1929), p. 36.

of the available service. The second is that the orchards, vineyards, and buildings of the industrious owner are not assessed, only his land, valued as if unimproved. Where invoked, these have combined to change a semi-arid land from its normal permanent slumber as an area of absentee baronies to one of prosperous independent farms and rural cities offering social as well as economic rewards to the state.

The foregoing must be taken as valid only for the special situation that existed in California's undeveloped areas in the past. The Wright Act formulae do not appear to have the effect of breaking up large modern corporate farms, but the pressure to bring the assessed acres into production remains.

I do not contend that without irrigation districts the development of the Central Valley of California would never have taken place. If water had been brought to the land by other means of financing (by a central government or a private company, for example) and offered for sale at so much per acre foot canal-side, the development of an irrigated agriculture would probably have occurred—but glacially. It seems likely that great areas would remain today in minimal use. That the change was swift and thorough was due in substantial part, it would seem, to the effective elements of district-wide, land-value-assessment practices inaugurated by the Wright Act.

8 Property Taxes and Land-Use Patterns in Australia and New Zealand

A. M. WOODRUFF and
L. L. ECKER-RACZ

Widespread preoccupation with blight and ugliness in and around American cities is focusing attention on the contribution of the property tax to this disorder. Because the property tax, as used in this country, typically applies both to the value of land and of the improvements upon it, and since its weight in relation to market values is rising, there is a general presumption that it exerts an influence on land-use patterns, particularly on the investor's incentive to improve his land with costly structures. But how much influence and in what direction? And can that influence be channeled into desired directions by differentiating among tax rates applicable to different components of the property tax base? Hawaii is just embarking on a ten-year transition from uniform taxation of land and improvements to a gradual de-emphasis of the burden imposed on buildings and other improvements. Australia and New Zealand are believed to provide an opportunity to observe different kinds of property taxation in

NOTE: This chapter is the result of a field trip to Australia and New Zealand made in the fall of 1964 under the generous sponsorship of the Lincoln Foundation. The authors express their appreciation also to the many commonwealth, state, local planning, financial, and tax officials and to representatives of business firms in Australia and to their counterparts in New Zealand for informative interviews. We are particularly grateful to the chief assessing officials of the Australian states (except Tasmania, where we did not call) and New Zealand, generally titled valuer generals, and to Dr. J. F. N. Murray, Chairman, Commonwealth Valuation Boards of Australia, who not only made themselves available for a detailed interrogation in their own countries, but subsequently reviewed a draft of our findings, meeting as a group at Claremont College, California. The particulars on legislation and litigation were supplied by Harry Manning, Australian Department of Interior, ACT Services Branch. The staff work for this entire project was the responsibility of Erin M. Woodall. This chapter is an edited and adapted version of our "Property Taxes and Land-Use Patterns in Australia and New Zealand," _The Tax Executive,_ 28, no. 1 (October 1965) : 16–63.

operation. In these countries the states tax land only while local governments either tax land alone or land and improvements, and either on the basis of capital value or, as in England, on the basis of rental value. The different systems, moreover, can frequently be observed side-by-side.

While differential tax treatment of land and improvements is practiced in a number of other countries, notably in South and East Africa, the Australian and New Zealand experience is presumed to have more significance for Americans because of the similarity of their cultures to that of America. In addition, Australia has a federal form of government with a constitutional structure patterned on the United States. On closer observation, however, the differences prove to be as striking as the similarities. This phenomenon may explain why from afar so many trained observers, unfamiliar with their institutions, read into the Australian and New Zealand property tax experience lessons not found there. An explanation of the differences is essential to an understanding of the operation of these faraway property taxes.

Homeownership in both countries is more widespread than in the United States, and housing in urban areas is more nearly standardized.[1] Apart from relatively small luxury neighborhoods occupied by top-salaried business and professional people, most of the gainfully employed live in private housing in the £4,500 range (plus or minus a thousand) [2] or in rental housing built and operated by the government (in no sense to be confused with American public housing).

Intergovernmental Relations

The higher levels of government tend to accept residual responsibility for local-government needs. The Australian states have managed to pass a part of that responsibility upward to the federal government (necessarily so, they are wont to say, since they are barred from both income and sales taxation). While Australia has a federal system with a constitutional framework resembling America's, operating similarities are few. Fiscal powers are concentrated far more extensively in Australia than in America

1. In 1961, 70% of the occupied private dwellings in Australia and 69% of the private houses in New Zealand were owner-occupied.

2. When this chapter was written in 1964, both Australia and New Zealand used the pound as the unit of currency. Since then both countries have changed their currencies to the decimal system, the new "dollar" being two to the former pound. The Australian pound equaled about $2.25 and the New Zealand pound about $2.50. The equivalent of a £4,500 (about $10,000) Australian house would cost close to $20,000 in a medium-sized American town.

and this, coupled with the British system of cabinet responsibility, produces strong unitary direction in government finances.

As Table 8.1 makes clear, the level of governmental operations and the load borne by all taxes, including those on property, are conspicuously lower than in the United States. In per capita terms, converted to dollars, Australian taxation at all levels of government is little more than half of that in this country. The load of Australian state and local property taxes is diminished further by the fact that federal grants, financed from other taxes, are twice as large in per capita terms as in the United States.

Table 8.1—Per Capita Governmental Receipts and Expenditures, Fiscal Year 1963

	Australia	United States
Federal taxes	$161.42	$374.39
State and local revenues	215.46	402.22
State land taxes	5.24	3.67
Local property taxes	23.71	103.61
All other taxes	41.04	129.19
Public enterprise income	35.80	119.17
Federal grants	90.74	46.58
Federal expenditures	234.61	589.03
State and local expenditures	266.99	404.59

Source: Prepared by L. L. Ecker-Racz after conferences with representatives of the treasury department of Australia.

Because New Zealand has only national and local government, its situation is simpler but the central government is equally dominant. Loan proposals of local authorities, other than tax anticipation borrowings, have to be approved by the Local Authorities Board composed of the secretary of the treasury, the Commission of Works, and five other members appointed by the governor general. In addition, the borrowing activities of certain other "semigovernment" local authorities are subject to special regulation by appropriate central government agencies.

This leadership role of the federal government in Australia and the central government in New Zealand in governmental finances is relevant to the question of property taxation because it provides a cushion to absorb the burden of public needs left unmet when property taxes at the local level and land taxes at the state level are kept low, relative to American tax rates, with corresponding limitations on the tax resources of these governments. In short, property tax revenue productivity is not as critical to the well-being of the Australian and New Zealander as it is to that of the American.

Local-Government Finances

Taxes on property are used at both the state and local level in Australia and at the national and local level in New Zealand. Local authorities are limited to property taxes and user charges but the revenue from these is supplemented by substantial grants from higher levels of government in both countries. In 1960 property taxes in Australia provided 98 percent of tax collections and 60 percent of all revenue collected for local general-government purposes except for loan receipts. Including local authorities' user charges collected for utility or other special services,[3] property taxes represented only 36 percent of the total, while user charges and sales of products supplied 38 percent. (See Table 8.2.) The

Table 8.2—Local-Government Revenues in Australia, 1959–1960 [a]

Type of revenue	General government	Business enterprises	Total
Property taxes	84,092	6,629	90,721
Other taxes	1,541	. . . . . .	1,541
User charges	28,646	96,987	125,633
Grants-in-aid	22,281	. . . . . .	22,281
Miscellaneous	5,626	5,392	11,018
Total	142,186	109,008	251,194

[a] All figures in this table are in terms of thousands of pounds.

Source: See note to Table 8.1.

distribution of taxes at all levels and their relationship to the gross national product of Australia as compared to that of the United States in 1963 is shown in Table 8.3.

The two largest sources of local-government revenue in New Zealand are property taxes and public-utility charges, rents, and licenses. (See Table 8.4.) The proportions, however, differ among the various types of local authorities. Property taxes supply larger portions of total revenue in cities, counties, and town districts and in river, road, and drainage districts, and smaller portions in boroughs, harbour boards, and a number of other special-purpose, "semigovernment" districts. Grants are half as important as property taxes for New Zealand and a quarter as important for Australian local governments.

3. These included revenues collected by "semigovernment" authorities for water supply and sewerage, electric and gas supply, transport services, hydraulic power undertakings, abattoirs, quarries, iceworks, and a miscellaneous group of governmental enterprises, including off-street parking, municipal markets, amusement parks, hotels, and cinemas.

Land taxes were introduced at the national level in New Zealand and at the state and commonwealth level in Australia in the late nineteenth

Table 8.3—Federal, State, and Local Tax Collections in Australia and the United States, Fiscal Year 1963 [a]

	Australia		United States	
Tax	Percent-age of total tax collected	Percent-age of total GNP	Percent-age of total tax collected	Percent-age of total GNP
Federal, Total	*81.4*	*18.1*	*69.6*	*17.7*
Income taxes	45.7	10.1	47.6	12.1
Sales, excise, and customs	30.7	6.8	9.8	2.5
Trust accounts	3.6	0.8	9.9	2.5
Miscellaneous	1.4	0.3	2.3	0 6
State, Total	*11.6*	*2.6*	*15.2*	*3.9*
Motor vehicle charges	3.3	0.7	3.9	1.0
Death and gift taxes	2.3	0.5	0.4	0.1
Land taxes	1.4	0.3	0.5	0.1
Sales and excise taxes	3.6	0.8	6.2	1.6
Income taxes	. . .	. . .	3.1	0.8
Miscellaneous	1.2	0.3	1.2	0.3
Local, Total	*7.0*	*1.6*	*15.2*	*3.8*
Property taxes	6.3	1.4	13.3	3.4
Sales and excise	0.8	0.2	1.1	0.2
Miscellaneous	. . .	. . .	0.8	0.2
All Governments	*100.0*	*22.3*	*100.0*	*25.4*

[a] Percentages in this table have been arrived at by rounding.

Source: See note to Table 8.1.

Table 8.4—Local-Government Revenues in New Zealand, Fiscal Year 1963

Type of revenue	Amount [a]	Percentage of total
Property taxes	31,222	21.9
Public utility charges and licenses	62,745	44.2
Grants-in-aid	16,684	11.7
Other receipts	31,414	22.2
Total	142,065	100.0

[a] Figures in this column are in terms of thousands of pounds.

Source: See note to Table 8.1.

and early twentieth centuries, but their revenue importance diminished over time. Australia abolished this tax as a federal source of revenue in 1952. By fiscal 1960 the state land taxes were providing slightly less than 12 percent of all state tax revenue, while stamp duties, death and gift taxes, and motor vehicle user charges were each contributing over 20 percent or, collectively, 72 percent of the total. Land taxes also are a minor source of tax revenue for the central government in New Zealand and provided less than 3 percent of total tax revenue in 1963, compared with 40 percent supplied by income taxes.

Types of Property Taxes

For property tax purposes, the Australian states and the central government in New Zealand tax only land values, excluding improvements. Local-government levies on property, with few exceptions, take one of three forms: (1) a tax on the capital value of property (land and improvements); (2) a tax on the annual rental value of property; or (3) a tax on the unimproved value of land.[4] Other bases are used by special-purpose, semigovernment bodies both in Australia and New Zealand; for example, rabbit eradication boards normally tax on an acreage basis or on the number of sheep and cattle carried, while harbour boards levy improvement rates on the basis of cargo tonnage. Some local governments use one form exclusively; some use one form for general purpose rates and another for special purposes or for services like water, sewerage, and public utilities.

Because of the multiplicity of local-government authorities, streets and roads exist in some Australian states where properties on opposite sides are rated on different bases. Moreover, since communities can change from one method to another by plebiscite in New Zealand and in some Australian states, these countries afford opportunities for observing the effects of changes in methods of taxation. Since the property owner generally does not have as deep an interest in his local government as he would have if the education of his children or his welfare payments depended on it, and since only ratepayers vote in these plebiscites, property tax questions generally seem to be voted on the basis of the pocketbooks of the individual ratepayers. Details of these elections are described in a later section.

4. As in Britain, at the local level "rate" and "rating" are synonymous with "tax" and "taxing."

The Introduction of Land Taxation

The introduction of land taxation in both Australia and New Zealand dates from around the turn of the century [5] and, in each country, was part of a movement parallel to "trust-busting" in the United States. It had much the same motives and support as the trust-busting movement in America. Some of the same words were used; references were made to "malefactors of great wealth" and the need to protect the interests of the small and weak against the abuses of the rich and powerful. In Australia and New Zealand, unlike in America, the rich and powerful were land-owners who had preempted very large acreages. During the latter half of the nineteenth century some of the preemption was "free selection," for all practical purposes synonymous with squatting. Some of it was by legitimate grant from the crown through various intermediate crown agencies or crown agents.

In any case, the result was ownership of rural land by a relatively very small number of individuals who controlled vast holdings. The strength of subsequent Labour governments in both countries was traceable in part to the abuses of the landowning minority during this formative period.

Late in the nineteenth century a ready-made solution was found in the writings of Henry George in the form of a tax that would fall on the relatively small number of economic royalists. The idea was immensely popular with a growing and increasingly articulate number of persons who considered themselves economically abused. After considerable internal debate in the various Australian state parliaments and after federation in the commonwealth parliament, the land tax was introduced.

The original Australian federal land tax was levied at steeply progressive rates on "unimproved capital value." (See Table 8.5.) Since the income yield of the land was very low, it was roughly equivalent to a capital levy. Federal land tax rates were computed on the total value of land held by any one individual anywhere in the country. If the same person owned land or held a lease in his own name from the crown in several different states, the total value was aggregated and the rate applied accordingly. In other words, the tax was so devised that the maximum rate would apply despite geographical dispersion of holdings, and the fact that an owner could not break up his holdings by vesting title in a series of different corporations was affirmed by legislation and subsequent deci-

5. Australia Federal Tax, 1910; New South Wales, 1895; South Australia, 1885; Queensland, 1915; Victoria, 1910; Western Australia, 1907; Tasmania, 1905; New Zealand, 1878.

sions of various Australian courts. The owner, however, could subdivide his holdings by deeding parcels to individual members of his family or to others and some "straw" holding undoubtedly occurred.

Table 8.5—Rates of Australian Commonwealth Land Tax

Fiscal year	Rate formula		Maximum rate	
	Residents [a]	Absentees [b]	Absentees	Residents
1911– 1914	$\dfrac{1 + \text{taxable value d.}}{30,000}$	$\dfrac{2 + \text{unimproved value d.}}{30,000}$	6d. for every pound beyond £75,000 (2.50%)	7d. for every pound beyond £80,000 (2.91%)
1915– 1918	$\dfrac{1 + \text{taxable value d.}}{18,750}$	$\dfrac{2 + \text{unimproved value d.}}{18,750}$	9d. for every pound beyond £75,000 (3.75%)	10d. for every pound beyond £80,000 (4.16%)
1919– 1922	same as 1915– 1918	same as 1915– 1918	9d. for every pound beyond £75,000, plus a 20% supertax (4.50%)	10d. for every pound beyond £75,000, plus a 20% supertax (5.00%)
1923– 1927	same as 1915– 1918	same as 1915– 1918	same as 1915– 1918	same as 1915– 1918
1928– 1932	a 10% reduction from 1915–1918 rates			
1933	a 40% reduction from 1915–1918 rates			
1934	a 55% reduction from 1915–1918 rates			
1939– 1940	$\dfrac{\frac{1}{2} + \text{taxable value d.}}{37,500}$	$\dfrac{1 + \text{unimproved value d.}}{37,500}$	4½d. for every pound beyond £75,000 (1.87%)	5d. for every pound beyond £80,000 (2.08%)
1941	same as 1915– 1918	same as 1915– 1918	same as 1915– 1918	same as 1915– 1918
1942– 1951	same as 1915–1918, plus 20% on values of £20,000 or more	same as 1915– 1918	same as 1919– 1922	same as 1919– 1922

[a] Since residents were allowed one exemption of £5,000 of unimproved value, the taxable value in the case of residents was the unimproved value of all land owned in excess of £5,000.

[b] Absentees paid a flat rate of one pence per pound (0.4%) up to £5,000 of unimproved value.

Source: See note to Table 8.1.

The original federal land tax statute also provided for self-assessment of individual landholdings with the proviso that the commonwealth government had the right to acquire the property at the declared value. A

High Court ruling, however, that the commonwealth government could acquire land only on "just terms" prevented this self-enforcing assessment administration from being implemented.

Australia also pioneered the use of progressive income taxes on the federal and state level at about the same time, and land tax payments were not deductible for income tax purposes. The social purpose of both taxes was the same and the combination of the two, both progressive, was neither a political nor a fiscal accident. The progressive income taxes sharpened the impact of the progressive land taxes.

At the time of its introduction, the land tax would have fallen with almost the same severity on the large rural landowners whether it had been levied on improved or unimproved capital value. Improvements other than timber clearance were as minor in relation to total value as they were at the same time on the large ranching properties of the American West, so that within the ranch-owning framework, the same social objective might have been accomplished by a tax on improved capital value provided the rates were on the same steeply progressive basis. On the other hand, had the tax applied to improvements it would have fallen with great severity upon the rather sparse industry just developing and on the properties of department stores, hotels, and other valuable city projects. Since the governments of neither Australia nor New Zealand desired to discourage urban development, the tax on unimproved land value did promise the desired social and economic impact without simultaneously burdening urban landowners who were favored by the then policymakers for their substantial contribution to economic upbuilding.

As a matter of historical record, the land tax did work in the direction intended and as the a priori reasoning of the classical economists, repeated by Henry George, indicated it would. It stimulated the breakup of the large estates, although other economic and social factors also operated simultaneously and in the same direction. The establishment of smaller and more intensely cultivated farm holdings was actively encouraged by the commonwealth and state governmental programs of soldier settlement, irrigation schemes, and closer settlement policies, while the retention of large estates was further discouraged by the imposition of high death duties. Collateral evidence confirming the social and economic impact of the land tax appeared in the decision of the High Court of Australia in 1911 in *Osborne* v. *the Commonwealth of Australia*.[6]

Osborne challenged the land tax on the grounds that it was a social measure designed to break up large estates rather than a revenue measure, that it was having a damaging effect on the commonwealth and more

6. See 12 Commw. L. R. 321; R. & McG. 486; 19 Austr. Digest 332 (May 1911); 17 Argus L. R. 242.

specifically on the appellant, and that it should be held *ultra vires*. While
the High Court agreed with the allegations of the appellant regarding the
significant social impact of the land tax far in excess of its importance as
a revenue measure, it nevertheless held that the principles of parliamen-
tary government had not been violated. Accordingly, the court declined
to make a finding of *ultra vires* and upheld the land tax with its progressive rates. This finding, which carried the force of a United States Su-
preme Court decision, settled this point, but there was a great deal of
subsequent litigation in both countries regarding the administrative handling of the tax. This later litigation chiefly involved valuation questions,
especially the definition of the words "unimproved capital value."

As a revenue producer, the land tax was never impressive. (See Table
8.6.) During the period prior to and including World War I, vast estates

Table 8.6—Commonwealth of Australia Land Tax Revenues, 1939–1963

Fiscal year	Amount [a]	Percentage of total tax revenues
1939	2	2.7
1944	4	1.3
1948	4	1.0
1950	4	0.8
1952	6	0.7
1963	0	0.0

[a] The figures in this column are in million of pounds.

Source: See note to Table 8.1.

were subdivided both by devise to separate heirs and by sale of portions
of property to different individuals; this reduced the number of taxpayers
subject to the maximum rate. At the end of the war the movement had
progressed far enough so that the maximum rate applied only to a relatively small number of taxpayers. Simultaneously, exemptions were introduced at the bottom so that the land tax would not apply to resident
owners with small holdings.

As most of the very large estates disappeared and as the exemptions
crept up from the bottom, the remaining middle band subject to the land
tax encountered moderate rates so that, as then administered, the tax
produced a relatively low yield. During World War I, the commonwealth
government depended increasingly on the income tax and less on its land
tax. This trend continued during the 1920's and 1930's and was greatly
accelerated during World War II, when the states surrendered their authority to levy income taxes to the commonwealth. Finally, in 1952 the
commonwealth relinquished the land tax to the states.

In New Zealand, where such shadows of state government as had existed before were abolished in 1875, the central government retained the land tax and allowed payments under it to be deducted from the central government income tax, but the land tax has declined in importance as a revenue producer and as an economic force. Unlike the Australian state land taxes which in most cases rise to fairly steep rates of seven and eight pence to the pound (3.33 percent) in the higher brackets (Table 8.7), the New Zealand land tax has a maximum rate of only four pence to the

Table 8.7—Rates of Selected Australian State Land Taxes, 1963 [a]

Unimproved land value subject to tax	Queensland		New South Wales		Victoria	
	Base tax on 1st Column	Rate per £ on balance	Base tax on 1st Column	Rate per £ on balance	Base tax on 1st Column	Rate per £ on balance
0–500	....	1d.	....	1d.	....	....
500–999	£2 2s.	1¾d.	....	1d.	....	....
1,000–1,999	£5 15s.	2¾d.	....	1d.	....	....
2,000–2,499	£17 4s.	4¼d.	....	1d.	....	....
2,500–2,999	£26 1s.	4¾d.	£10 8s.	1½d.	....	....
3,000–3,999	£35 19s.	5¼d.	£10 8s.	1½d.	....	....
4,000–4,999	£57 16s.	5¾d.	£10 8s.	1½d.	....	....
5,000–14,999	£81 15s.	6¼d.	£26–67 14s.	2–2½d.	....	1d.
15,000–19,999	£81 15s.	6¼d.	£119 16s.	3d.	£62 10s.	1½d.
20,000–29,999	£472 8s.	6¾d.	£182 15s.	3½–4d.	£93–135 8s.	2–2¼d.
30,000–34,999	£472 8s.	6¾d.	£338 11s.	4½d.	£182 5s. 10d.	2½d.
35,000–39,999	£894 5s.	7¼d.	£432 6s.	5d.	£234 7s. 6d.	2¾d.
40,000–44,999	£894 5s.	7¼d.	£536 9s.	5½d.	£291 13s. 4d.	3d.
45,000–49,999	£894 5s.	7¼d.	£651 1s.	6d.	£354 3s. 4d.	3½d.
50,000–64,999	£1,347 8s.	7¾d.	£776–1,057	6½–7½d.	£427 1s. 8d.	4d.
65,000–69,999	£1,831 15s.	8¼d.	£1,213 11s.	8d.	£427 1s. 8d.	4d.
70,000–79,999	£1,831 15s.	8¼d.	£1,213 11s.	8d.	£760 8s. 4d.	4½d.
80,000–99,999	£2,347 8s.	8¾d.	£1,213 11s.	8d.	£760 8s. 4d.	4½d.
100,000 and over	....	7½d. on total value	£1,213 11s.	8d.	£760 8s. 4d.	4½d.

[a] Rates are on land not used for primary production. In Western Australia and Tasmania maximum rate is 7 pence; in South Australia 7½ pence.

Source: See note to Table 8.1.

pound for taxable values in excess of £20,000. (Table 8.8.) In addition, a rebate of 50 percent of the tax was granted in 1963.

The final outcome, both in New Zealand and Australia, is that the land tax is a significant factor in private business decisions only in cases involving high values of land and almost exclusively urban land. In these cases, however, it can be quite important since commercial and industrial property, particularly in central-city areas, reaches the top tax rate fairly quickly and this rate, both in absolute and percentage terms, is enough to influence owners.

Table 8.8—New Zealand Land Tax Rates, 1963

Taxable values	Rates (per £)
Up to £10,000	1d.
£10,000– £15,000	2d.
£15,000– £20,000	3d.
Over £20,000	4d.

Source: See note to Table 8.1.

Bases of Local Rates

As stated earlier, most local rates in Australia and New Zealand are levied on one of three bases—improved capital value, unimproved capital value, or assessed annual value. In both countries, local property taxes are called "rates." In Australia the former federal and present state levy on land is called the "land tax," as is the New Zealand central government tax on land. The distinction between a tax and a rate is unimportant to Americans because in the United States both would be called taxes. It is retained here, nonetheless, to distinguish between local and other levies. The chief economic difference between rates and taxes—aside from the fact that they are levied by different levels of government—is that local rates are proportional with few exemptions, whereas land taxes are progressive with frequent exemptions.

"Improved capital value," as the name implies, is the total market value of land and buildings and is roughly the basis on which property has traditionally been assessed in the United States. In Australia, improvements also often include appliances or plant machinery permanently affixed to the building that cannot be removed without structural damage. A series of court decisions established "improved" and "unimproved capital value" as what a willing buyer would pay and a willing seller would accept, assuming reasonable knowledge on the part of both. For all practical purposes this is the willing buyer-willing seller rule laid down by American courts.

"Unimproved capital value" is defined somewhat differently in each of the various Australian states and in New Zealand (Table 8.9). In Australia, the unimproved value of a parcel is generally considered to be what the land would be worth in the open market if all other conditions were the same but the improvements did not exist. Improvements generally are defined to include both visible and invisible site improvements except in New South Wales, where some invisible improvements are statutorily merged with land value. The problem of valuing nonstructural improvements is proving difficult in practice. Valuers consider the concept of "un-

Table 8.9—Definitions of Unimproved Capital Value and Assessed Annual Value for Rating Purposes in the Australian States and New Zealand [a]

Unimproved capital value	Assessed annual value

New South Wales

The capital sum which the fee simple of the land might be expected to realize if offered for sale on such reasonable terms and conditions as a bona fide seller would require, assuming that the improvements, if any, had not been made.

Assuming the land may be used or may continue to be used for any purpose for which it was or could be used at the time of valuation and such improvements may be continued or made on the land as may be required to enable the land to continue to be so used; provided this does not prevent consideration of possible uses if the above improvements had not been made.

Nine-tenths of the fair average annual value of the land with improvements, if any, provided such assessed annual value shall not be less than 5 percent of the improved value.

"Fair average annual value" is what the property will fairly bring in as an average gross annual rental on the basis of the owner paying all outgoings.

Queensland

Same as above

Provided that unimproved value shall in no case be less than the sum that would be obtained by deducting the value of improvements from the improved value.

Value of improvements is added value the improvements give the land, irrespective of their cost, including the value of any hotel license; provided the added value does not exceed the replacement cost of the improvements at the time of valuation.

Not used.

Victoria

Sum which the fee simple of the land, unencumbered by any mortgage, might in ordinary circumstances be expected to realize if offered for sale on such reasonable terms and conditions as a bona fide seller would require, assuming that the improvements, if any, had not been made.

Value of improvements, subject to certain exceptions, includes all work done or materials used by the expenditure of capital or labor for the benefit of the land insofar as the effect is to increase the selling value of the land and

Amount which the property may be reasonably expected to let at from year to year, deducting owner's rates and taxes, average annual cost of insurance, and other expenses required to maintain the ability of the property to command actual gross rental value.

Provided the net annual value is at least 5 percent of the improved capital value.

Table 8.9 (continued)

Unimproved capital value	Assessed annual value
the benefit is not exhausted at the time of valuation; provided the value does not exceed the cost of the improvements. Improvements by public bodies not included unless paid for by the owner other than by rates or taxes.	

South Australia

The capital amount for which the fee simple of the land might be expected to sell if free from encumbrances, assuming the actual improvements, if any, had not been made.

Improvements defined as visible and some invisible improvements (such as draining and clearing) the benefit of which is unexhausted at the time of valuation.

Annual value is defined as 75 percent of the gross rental value of the land, including improvements or 5 percent of its capital value, whichever is the greater.

Western Australia

The capital sum which the fee simple of the land might be expected to realize if offered for sale on such reasonable terms and conditions as a bona fide seller would require, assuming the improvements had not been made.

Provided there be a reasonable deduction for profitable expenditure by the owner or occupier on visible and effective improvements which, though not upon the land, might have been constructed for its drainage, etc. or more beneficial use.

Full, fair, average amount of rent the property will let for from year to year, assuming letting is allowed by law, less 40 percent for rates, repairs, insurance, and other expenses.

Providing the annual value shall not be less than 4 percent of the capital value of the fee simple in the case of improved property and not less than 10 percent of the capital value in the case of unimproved property. Unimproved property is land with improvements valued at less than 50 percent of the unimproved value or £50 or less per lineal foot of land.[b]

Tasmania

Capital sum which the land, if it were held for an estate fee simple free from encumbrances by an owner who is at liberty to dispose of it as and when he so desires, might be expected to realize if offered for sale on such reasonable terms and conditions as a bona fide seller would require, assuming that the improvements had not been made. Definition of improvements same as in Victoria.

Gross annual income which the owner of the land might reasonably expect to obtain by letting the land with improvements, if any, to a tenant without fine upon reasonable terms and conditions.

Table 8.9 (continued)

Unimproved capital value	Assessed annual value

New Zealand

The sum which the owner's estate or interest therein, if unencumbered by any mortgage or other charge, might be expected to realize if offered for sale on such reasonable terms as a bona fide seller might be expected to impose if no improvements had been made.

Definition of improvements same as in Victoria; omitting phrase "providing the value does not exceed the cost of the improvements"; value of improvements means the added value the improvements give to the land at the time of valuation.

Rent at which property would let from year to year deducting therefrom 20 percent in the case of houses and buildings and 10 percent in the case of land; provided that annual value is equal to at least 5 percent of the capital value of the fee simple.

---

a Paraphrased from the relevant statutes to give a reasonable flavor of the intent of the law. In each state the statute is long and complex. The statutes are as follows: New South Wales, Valuation of Land Act, 1916–1961; Queensland, Valuation of Land Acts, 1944–1958; Victoria, Land Tax Act, 1958; Western Australia, Local Government Act, 1960–1962; South Australia, Land Tax Act, 1936–1961; New Zealand, The Valuation of Land Act, 1951; Tasmania, Land Valuation Act, 1960.

b Assessed annual value may not exceed 6 percent of capital value under the Metropolitan Water Supply and Sewerage and Drainage Act; or 6½ percent under the County Areas Water Supply Act; or 7½ percent under the Water Boards Act.

Source: See note to Table 8.1.

improved land," as defined in most Australian states and in New Zealand, an anomaly and advocate the use of "site value," which would include invisible improvements. Invisible improvements of agricultural land include clearing of forests and, in cases where this occurred as long as a century ago, the extent and present value of the clearing are fairly hard to determine. With respect to rural land the appraisal of the invisible improvements is an abiding and persistent problem.

A case that occurred in New Zealand illustrates a further problem produced by the prevailing definition of unimproved capital value. The harbour board in Auckland reclaimed some forty acres of marsh land along the foreshore which then became valuable commercial property. Since this land had previously been either valueless marsh or actually under water, its value in its original state was zero and it escaped taxation until an act of the New Zealand parliament specified that land reclaimed from the sea should be taxed on the basis of comparable unimproved values rather than its own "original" state. This act, however, left an odd loophole since it referred only to land reclaimed from "the sea." Shortly thereafter some land was reclaimed from Lake Taupo and the court held that the statute did not apply to land reclaimed from fresh water. Hence, any land reclaimed from any lake is exempt from land taxes and local rates based on unimproved capital value. Redefinition of unimproved value as site value would avoid this type of problem as well as the problem of invisible improvements. Recently drafted taxation statutes in Jamaica, Trinidad, and Barbados refer specifically to "site value" rather than to unimproved capital value.[7] These statutes, in large part, were drafted by United Nations experts, chiefly Australians. The use of site value is in response to the difficulty of definition indicated in Table 8.9.

The other commonly used base for local rates is "assessed annual value," which is not used in the United States although it has long been used in the United Kingdom. "Assessed annual value" or "net annual value," as it is called in the Australian state of Victoria, is the amount of rent that the property could be expected to return during a "normal" year, assuming that both the landlord and the tenant enjoy the freedom of the market and are not bound by rent-control regulations. The statutory definition of assessed annual value varies among the Australian states and New Zealand, with varying percentages deducted to approximate net rental value, but most states specify that it may not be less than 5 percent of improved capital value.[8] This makes it necessary for valuers to ascertain the improved capital value of property. In point of fact, single-family residences generally are assessed for rate purposes at 5 percent of the improved capital value in most Australian states and commercial and industrial property usually higher.[9]

The concept of assessed annual value made a great deal of sense in England during the eighteenth and much of the nineteenth century because a large proportion of taxable realty was owned by landlords who themselves occupied only a small portion of it and leased the balance. Lease figures thus were readily available and taxes based on assessed annual value had many aspects of a proportional income tax. Assessed annual value was transplanted to both Australia and New Zealand by people with English backgrounds and persists in both countries where the English influence is the strongest.

Assessment Administration

In Australia and New Zealand the assessing function is largely centralized under state or central government valuation departments, which provide

7. Information in this paragraph is from Vincent Brent, who in 1964 was a member of the United Nations Advisory Team that assisted in developing the site value concept.

8. The minimum is 4% in Western Australia.

9. Exceptions include New South Wales, which has rent control under a landlord and tenant act.

comprehensive valuation services for a variety of public purposes in addition to taxation. These central departments are responsible for the valuation of all property in New Zealand and in the Australian states of New South Wales, Queensland, and Tasmania, but have somewhat less authority in the other Australian states of Victoria, South Australia, and Western Australia. When assessed annual values are used for local rates in New Zealand, they are often established by local valuers; local valuers are used also in parts of Australia. In addition, many semigovernment bodies establish interim valuations for rating purposes when new properties are constructed or added to existing systems, but generally these are not parallel assessment systems, since the interim values are reviewed by the central valuation department at the time of the next general reassessment and its values are used thereafter.[10]

A valuer general heads the central valuation department in New Zealand and in the Australian states of New South Wales, Queensland, and Victoria, but his counterpart is a commissioner of land tax in South Australia, a senior valuer in Tasmania, and a chief valuer of the commonwealth taxation department in Western Australia.[11] These officials supervise large staffs except in Tasmania, which is considerably smaller, and in Victoria, where the valuer general has only supervisory authority and the actual assessing is done by state certified local valuers. The state of New South Wales, with a staff of 450 (including 200 valuers), has the largest organization, followed by Queensland with 200, Western Australia with 144, South Australia with 87, and Tasmania with 24; approximately half of the staff in each case are valuers. Victoria has 160 municipal valuers and a valuer general's staff of 12, including 6 valuers.

The heads of these valuation departments and their staffs are permanent public servants in both Australia and New Zealand, with all the rights this provides, including a prestigious position. In these countries, permanent public servants are accorded the kind of traditional respect their counterparts had earned in the United Kingdom, and it is evident in each country that this respect is well deserved. Of particular interest is the fact that these valuation officials enjoy complete independence of action in the performance of their assessment duties under the basic statutes establishing these central valuation departments. When questioned specifically on the point, the valuer generals and their deputies simply could not conceive of a system under which valuation departments could operate without civil service protection. They were completely aghast at the notion

10. An exception to this general rule is the State Water Supply Department in South Australia, which maintains its own assessment system for water rates.

11. In Western Australia the functions of the federal and state valuation authorities were combined in the Commonwealth Taxation Department in 1921, making the chief valuer a federal rather than a state public servant.

that a valuer might submit himself to election at the hands of persons whose property he was valuing for tax purposes. One valuer likened such a system to one in which an engineer is elected to design a bridge.

The duties of these valuation departments in most cases extend beyond the establishment of values for local rating or state land tax purposes. Their values are also used as important evidence in "resumption proceedings," the process that in the United States is called condemnation through the exercise of eminent domain. They are used also as evidence for death duties, for stamp duties on deeds of conveyance, and for gift taxes. Moreover, the figures established by the valuer general are respected by banks and other lenders to an extent unknown in America. The processes of appraisal and assessment in Australia and New Zealand are both simply called "valuing" and far less distinction is made between them than in the United States. The valuer general's figures enjoy a degree of respectability in the business world not generally accorded assessments in the United States.

Valuers, both in private practice (appraisers in American terminology) and within the civil service (assessors), belong to the Commonwealth Institute of Valuers in Australia and the New Zealand Institute of Valuers in that country. The Australian institute is organized along geographic lines with separate state divisions. These professional organizations publish quarterly journals devoted to discussions of valuation problems and have been doing so since the 1930's. The presidency and other important positions in these organizations are frequently held by a valuer general or one of his deputies. It is as common to find the presidency in the hands of a valuer in public service as a valuer in private practice. To conceive of a parallel situation in the United States would be difficult for most assessors and appraisers. They would find it difficult to imagine a situation in which the senior management of the American Institute of Real Estate Appraisers would be in the hands of assessing officers or that the International Association of Assessing Officers would become dominated by appraisers; even more difficult to conceive is that the two organizations would happily merge.

These institutes establish professional qualifications for valuers, including a rigorous examination that must be passed in order to qualify for membership. The examination requires formal academic work, which is provided by technical colleges and the Commonwealth Institute of Valuers in Australia and by the University of Auckland and Canterbury University in New Zealand. The University of Auckland has a three-year course for urban valuers and Canterbury University has a similar course for rural valuers. There is no requirement, such as exists in much of the United States, that a valuer in private practice must also hold a broker's license and must have participated in real estate brokerage. Indeed, the view was expressed that brokerage experience is not necessarily helpful in the training of a professional valuer. Having once acquired the professional designation given by these institutes of valuers, the valuer considers himself a professional man at least the equivalent of a C.P.A. and is accorded a corresponding measure of respect.

Prior to the establishment of the valuer general's department in New Zealand and the state valuation departments in Australia, local municipalities and shires established their own values and some local valuing still persists. Local authorities in New Zealand can employ local valuers who can either establish assessed annual values with a minimum of central control or can set assessed annual value at 6 percent of the improved capital values established by the valuer general. Alternatively, the local-government authority may request the valuer general to prepare its local assessment roll.

In Australia, the degree to which assessing is done centrally and the amount of supervision given local valuers varies among the states. The valuer general in New South Wales, Western Australia, Tasmania, and Queensland has state-wide authority, and, except in New South Wales, the valuer generals or their counterparts establish values throughout their respective states. The valuer general of New South Wales establishes values in only about half of his state, but this half contains 92 percent of the state's population. Such local valuers as survive in New South Wales are generally unsupervised. In Victoria, since the passage of the Valuation of Land Act of 1960, the valuer general has had considerable influence over local valuing though not actual control, and state-wide minimum professional qualifications and certification of local valuers has prevailed. Federal valuers are in charge in the Northern Territory and in the Australian Capital Territory, which embraces Canberra and a large area around it.

There is a noticeable trend toward state valuation systems in Australia, but how rapidly it will be adopted by the remaining states of South Australia and Victoria and extended to embrace all property is not easily predicted. Considerable professional rivalry exists between the permanent civil servants in the valuer generals' offices and the part-time local valuers with little or no special qualifications or training, and the average professional competence of the latter is earnestly questioned by the former.

On the strength of long-established tradition, property values for assessment purposes are set at full market value with a small margin for reasonable differences of opinion and market irregularities. The need for a margin of error was recognized by the South Australian Court when it stated that property values should be at the lower end of the margin for

tax purposes and at the upper end of the margin for resumption.[12] Since
this point has been discussed in American tax literature in recent years
with a general consensus that full value assessing is not practical, it is interesting to note that valuers in Australia and New Zealand find no difficulty in establishing full market values. With the exception of New South
Wales, values within a common jurisdiction are set as of a common date
specified by statute and revised triennially or quinquennially.

Both countries levy a transfer tax at the time any property is sold.[13]
The valuer general is asked by the registrar of deeds to comment on any
sale that appears out of line and is responsible for seeing that the transfer
tax is levied on a reasonable consideration. Both for this reason and as
a basis for establishing values for tax and rating purposes, every sale is
reported in detail to the state valuation department. Assessments closely
follow sales, and sales ratio studies are used as in America. The report on
each sale gives more detail on the transactions than is common in the
United States, including the amount of cash, the amount of credit, and
any other factors that might have influenced the price. In some jurisdictions the sales report includes a breakdown between land and building
value to which the buyer and seller have agreed. Sales are generally
plotted on cadastral maps.

Valuer generals in Australia and New Zealand find the same difficulties
with sales ratio studies that their counterparts experience in the United
States. They report that sales in fairly recent subdivisions conform closely
to pattern and that a frequency distribution of such sales generally establishes a peaked curve with relatively short tails. On the other hand, in
neighborhoods where the prevailing character of use is changing either
from residential to commercial or industrial or from agricultural to residential, the pattern of sales produces a flat curve with long tails.

In the case of property in a neighborhood changing from residential
to higher value uses, several of the valuer generals report an interesting
phenomenon, long suspected by American assessors and appraisers, but
never established with certainty. It is evident from sales reports that different buyer-seller pairs make entirely different divisions between land and
building values even with respect to adjoining or closely adjacent properties. If the property purchased includes buildings to be demolished to make
way for other improvements, the buyers and sellers generally agree that
all of the value is in the land or, if demolition is planned in the near future,
a substantial portion of the value is attributed to the land. If, on the other
hand, the buyer intends to occupy or rent the building, the buyer is apt
to attribute more of the value to the building and the seller will not neces-

12. 1947 Commonw. L. R. 358.
13. Both countries use the Torrens system of title registration.

sarily agree. Judgments as to allocation of value between land and buildings are not influenced by income tax considerations because there is no tax on capital gains and no allowance for depreciation, which works to the advantage of the owner of an old house. Hence, there is no tax inducement to overstate building value as there is in the United States.

The professional competence of the valuers and their civil service status have special interest to Americans in the light of the recommendations for property tax improvement recently made by the United States Advisory Commission on Intergovernmental Relations.[14] About half of these recommendations are directed to improving the quality of assessing work. The commission stressed the importance of having assessment districts large enough to warrant full-time employment of qualified personnel so that unqualified semiamateurs would not be called upon to assess the occasional valuable property found in predominantly rural or residential districts. The experience of Australia and New Zealand underscores the merits of these recommendations. Bankers, valuers in private practice, and real estate brokers unanimously confirmed the uniformly high quality of valuation work done by permanent public servants in Australia and New Zealand. Much of this superior quality undoubtedly is associated with large centralized valuation departments with broad valuation responsibilities for a variety of public purposes, civil service status, extensive training, and the stiff-necked professional pride of valuers.

Local Rating Systems and Land Use

As already stated, most local governments in Australia and New Zealand levy rates on either improved capital value, unimproved capital value, or assessed annual value. In addition, water rates and charges allied with them (such as sewerage and drainage rates) are levied by semigovernment bodies in Australia and ad hoc authorities in New Zealand; these are not always levied on the same basis as local-government rates. The interesting fact to these observers is that the three systems coexist in a haphazard fashion. (See Tables 8.10 and 8.11.)

In Queensland (for all practical purposes) local rates are based on unimproved capital value as are all rates levied by local governments in New South Wales. In Western Australia most shires have adopted the unimproved capital value system, but only a few cities and towns have. The assessed annual value system is used in many local shires in Victoria and

14. Advisory Commission on Intergovernmental Relations, *The Role of the States in Strengthening the Property Tax*, 2 vols. (Washington, D.C.: U.S. Government Printing Office, 1963).

Table 8.10—Bases for Local Rating in Australia, 1962

| State | General rates | | | | Special rates |
	Cities	Boroughs [a]	Towns	Shires [b]	
New South Wales	Unimproved land value	Unimproved land value	Unimproved land value	Unimproved land value	Assessed annual value—3 metropolitan water and sewer authorities; improved capital value by a few local authorities
Queensland	Unimproved land value		Unimproved land value	Unimproved land value	Unimproved land value
Victoria	30—unimproved land value; 21—assessed annual value	6—unimproved land value; 8—assessed annual value	3—unimproved land value; 2—assessed annual value	10—unimproved land value; 128—assessed annual value	Assessed annual value—3 metropolitan authorities; unimproved land value—rural water supply [c]
South Australia	9—assessed annual value; 6—unimproved land value		12—assessed annual value; 15—unimproved land value	77—assessed annual value; 23—unimproved land value	Assessed annual value in urban areas; unimproved land value in farming areas [d]

Western Australia	Assessed annual value except 5 with unimproved land value [e]	Assessed annual value except for a few with unimproved land value	Unimproved land value except in township areas with assessed annual value	Assessed annual value [f]
Tasmania [g]	Assessed annual value	Assessed annual value		Assessed annual value
Australian Capital Territory	Unimproved land value			Unimproved land value [h]

[a] Boroughs are not used in Queensland, South Australia, and Western Australia.

[b] Comparable local authorities in South Australia are called district councils.

[c] These include Melbourne and Melbourne Board of Works and two sewerage authorities; rural areas are served by the State Rivers and Water Supply Commission.

[d] State-administered by the Engineering and Water Supply Department.

[e] The endowment lands district of Perth uses unimproved land values.

[f] Administered by two state departments.

[g] Tasmania has only cities and municipalities, the latter including both rural and urban areas.

[h] Municipally operated.

Source: See note to Table 8.1.

Table 8.11—New Zealand Local-Government Tax Systems, Fiscal Year 1964

Territorial local authorities	Unimproved value		Capital value		Annual value		Total
	Number	Percent	Number	Percent	Number	Percent	
Boroughs and cities	123	85	10	7	11	8	144
Town districts							
Independent	11	79	2	14	1	7	14
Dependent	3	88	4	50	1	12	8
Counties	76	66	40	34	0	0	116
Road districts	1	33	2	67	0	0	3
New Zealand as a whole	214	75	58	20	13	5	285

Source: See note to Table 8.1.

South Australia and throughout the state of Tasmania. About half of the cities and towns in South Australia and Victoria use the unimproved capital value system, the other half the assessed annual value system. In New Zealand most rural rates are levied on unimproved capital value, while the urban areas vary. Wellington bases rates on unimproved capital value, but its largest adjoining suburb, the city of Hutt, uses assessed annual value. The city of Auckland uses the assessed annual value system, while its suburbs use varying rates.

This picture, however, is further complicated by the fact that most autonomous urban special authorities rate on assessed annual value or improved capital value in New Zealand and in Australia outside of Queensland. (See Table 8.12.) In New South Wales, where territorial local-government rates are based on unimproved capital value, the three metropolitan water and sewerage boards rate on assessed annual value. On the other hand, water and sewerage rates levied by semigovernment bodies in rural parts of Australia are often, though not always, based on unimproved capital value.

Many have tried to find empirical support for one or the other system of rating from the experience of Australian and New Zealand communities. A considerable number of claims have been made, but careful investigations generally have concluded that differences traceable to the method of taxation on the local level could not be conclusively determined.[15] The frequently reiterated claim that rating on unimproved capital value is responsible for a rapid pace of community development could

15. A similar conclusion was reached in a recent study by an American Fulbright scholar at the University of Sydney. See James P. Holl, "A Survey of the Effects of Valuation and Rating Systems on Australian Suburbs" (Ph.D. diss., University of Sydney, 1961).

Table 8.12—Bases of Rating for Water Supply and Sewerage Purposes in Australia, Fiscal Year 1964 [a]

Cities	Water				Sewerage			
	Occupied land		Vacant land		Occupied land		Vacant land	
	Basis	Minimum	Basis	Minimum	Basis	Minimum	Basis	Minimum
Brisbane	3d. in £ on U.C.V. taxable value	£8	As for occupied	£8	2½d. in £ on U.C.V. taxable value	£8 10s.	As for occupied	£8 10s.
Sydney	10d. in £ on A.A.V.	£5	As for occupied	£ on A.A.V.	£5 9½d. in £	£5	As for occupied	£5
Melbourne	8d. in £ on N.A.V.	10s.	As for occupied	10s.	½d. in £ on N.A.V.	No minimum	As for occupied	No minimum
Adelaide	7½% on £400; 5% on balance	£6	As for occupied	£6 if supplied; £2 10s.	6¼% on A.A.V.	£5	As for occupied	£2 10s.
Perth	1s. in £ on N.A.V.; nonresidential, 1s. 6d. in £	£1	As for occupied	£1	1s. 9d. in £ on N.A.V.	£1	As for occupied	£1
Hobart	4d. in £ on A.A.V.	No minimum	As for occupied	No minimum	3d. in £ on A.A.V. including draining	No minimum	As for occupied	No minimum

[a] A.A.V. = assessed annual value; N.A.V. = net annual value; and U.C.V. = unimproved capital value.

Source: See note to Table 8.1.

not be substantiated by direct observation. The following section explains why this is so.

Virtually every respondent in this inquiry was questioned directly or indirectly as to his opinion on whether local rating had any significant effect on the pattern of land development in any particular community. The replies from the valuer generals or their counterparts and members of their staffs in five of the six Australian states and from the valuer general in Wellington and his deputy in Auckland were almost unanimously negative. The answers from the commonwealth valuers operating out of Canberra, from the tax economists associated with the Australian commonwealth government, and from mortgage lenders, real estate operators, members of the National Capital Development Commission in Canberra, and planners in five of the six Australian states were uniformly negative.

The overwhelmingly negative opinion recorded in the previous paragraph is confirmed by our own observations as we rode diligently through the suburbs of Melbourne, Auckland, and Adelaide, where some of the property is rated on unimproved capital value and some on assessed annual value. Of particular interest is the so-called Toorak area in Melbourne, which is a prestige residential neighborhood divided between the cities of Prahran and Malvern. Prahran rates on assessed annual value and Malvern on unimproved capital value. The people of Toorak are more impressed with the fact that they live in Toorak than with the fact that part of Toorak is under one system of rating and part under another. We rode back and forth across the boundary line between the two parts of Toorak and were unable to distinguish any difference in appearance between the two. Similarly, in Auckland, we noted municipal boundaries that run down the middle of streets and were unable to observe significant differences between the appearance of property on one side where rating is based on unimproved capital value and on the other where it is based on assessed annual value.

Based on the opinions expressed by the valuers, planners, real estate operators, and others, and our own observations, the conclusion seems well supported that there is no clearly visible difference between localities that use unimproved capital value rating and those that use assessed annual value or improved capital value.

Why the Rating System Does Not
Affect the Urban Pattern

Since no significant visual differences appear between communities that use one system of rating as compared with those that use another, the investigators turned to the far more intriguing question of why differences did not emerge. The fact that urban semigovernment rates (outside of Queensland) are generally levied on assessed annual values or improved capital values partially blunts the effect of unimproved capital value rates. However, on this basis Queensland in general and Brisbane in particular should have developed differently from Victoria in general and Melbourne in particular; the facts are otherwise.

Part of the answer lies in the low percentage relationship between local rates and the total amount of improved capital value. Since most state land taxes have a significant effect only on the relatively few more valuable properties, the meaningful relationship in most cases is between local rates and capital value. Throughout Australia and New Zealand, local rates (including those of semigovernment) average between one-half of 1 percent and 1 percent of improved capital value on residences. Compared with percentages in most urban centers in the United States, Australian and New Zealand tax rates are very low. Bankers, real estate men, and planners are unanimous in declaring that local rates are not a prime consideration for builders, buyers, or developers, although in a few cases rates and the land tax together probably affected decisions concerning commercial and industrial location. In general, however, the local rate is minor compared with the other considerations—too low to have any effect on the pattern of community development.

On the other hand, the introduction of tax exemptions and abatements from the land tax in most Australian states and in New Zealand provides persuasive evidence that rates and taxes levied on unimproved capital value were beginning to have exactly the effect foreseen by Henry George and others. Cases arose in the older parts of virtually every large Australian city in which elderly and relatively impoverished pensioners found it difficult to retain their homes in neighborhoods where land values were rising as commercial and apartment uses replaced single-family residential uses. As George and his followers predicted, the unimproved capital value tax penalized owners who attempted to retain the land in less than its highest and best use, yet many caught in this situation were not in a position to acquire another home. This generated a political situation that government found intolerable and the parliaments of each Australian state enacted "hardship" exemptions to permit such people to retain their homes despite the fact that surrounding property was being converted to commercial, apartment, and other more profitable uses. A similar tax concession was authorized in some Australian states for residential property whose conversion to a more profitable use was prevented by zoning.

These "hardship" provisions vary from state to state in Australia, and exist only to a slight degree in New Zealand, although there is a body of opinion in the second country that a more generous provision would be desirable. Statutory authority for a rate reduction in hardship cases exists in New Zealand but is seldom used. In Queensland, tax relief for hardship cases is authorized in the form of a reduction in the valuation of owner-occupied residences to the level justified by their existing use, but in practice only half of the increase in valuation is remitted. New South Wales likewise grants concessions on the attributable portion of the full value assessment of residence owned and occupied by pensioners and on occupied residences in changing-use areas penalized by zoning regulations. In Victoria and South Australia, arbitrary abatement of rates is granted by local councils upon the owner's application in hardship cases.

Most Australian states and New Zealand also grant a tax exemption to urban farm land to reduce the pressure of local rates on truck gardeners and other agricultural users in urban areas where residential development is increasing land values. In Queensland, individuals owning a farm of not less than five acres, if the land is used for farming, are permitted to pay local rates at the rural rate, which is half the residential rate. A similar exemption is given farms of not less than two and one-half acres in New South Wales. Such tax relief is granted at the discretion of the local councils in Victoria and South Australia, but, in the latter case, only after application has been made by the owner. A New Zealand urban farm rating act of 1932 as amended allows land that is used for agricultural purposes and is considered either unfit for development or for which demand for development is considered unlikely for at least five years to be granted special rates by the local councils, provided the major portion of the property owner's income comes from the land.

Individuals benefiting from the hardship exemption in New South Wales or the agricultural provision in South Australia are subject to retroactive taxation for a five-year period preceding sale. However, there is no provision for the recapture of local rates abated for hardship reasons in South Australia or Victoria.

While special tax concessions of this kind might have developed under any property tax system, the pressure for relieving pensioners and farmers is probably especially compelling when property is taxed on the basis of unimproved capital value. Many Australian tax officials felt that the hardship exemption would not have been passed except for the unimproved capital value basis. A hardship exemption has been written into the Jamaican model tax law as an essential concomitant of its site value system. In other words, land taxation and rating on unimproved capital value is doing just what it was supposed to do, but, as a by-product, creates social pressure to a point where the government considers it prudent to introduce amendments to moderate the impact of the tax. We noted an absence of official sympathy for the owners of large or valuable tracts against whom the state land taxes are aimed in most Australian states. On the other hand, economic distress suffered by a fairly large number of relatively poor people causes considerable concern, especially under Labour governments, and leads to prompt relief measures.

Four reasons explain the lack of visible differences between areas where rates are levied on unimproved capital value as compared with other methods: (1) the generally low level of rates; (2) the mix of local rates on land value and semigovernment rates on other bases; (3) the hardship exemption for certain types of homeowners allowing the payment of rates at former or lower levels; and (4) the agricultural exemption extending similar benefits.

The Slum Question

The argument is frequently advanced that the use of unimproved capital value as a rating base is closely associated with the relative lack of slum property in Australia and New Zealand. In fact, the cities of Australia and New Zealand do not have slum property in the sense that American cities do.

One reason is the type of housing found in Australia. The cities grew fairly slowly from the founding of the colonies until the several gold rushes of the middle and late nineteenth century. The resultant activity set off a boom in real estate construction, the evidences of which are still abundantly visible throughout every city in the commonwealth. The typical urban residence of that period was the so-called terrace house. This is a one- or two-story structure and would be called a row house in American terminology. The individual structures are from sixteen to about twenty feet wide with masonry party walls and the buildings are about forty to fifty feet deep on lots that generally are eighty to one hundred feet deep. These houses were built without basements and originally depended upon fireplaces for heat. Some one-story houses have a small loft, but most consist simply of three or four rooms in a row, built railroad flat style. Two-story structures are versions of the same thing. Many of the two-story structures have elaborate cast iron or wrought iron balcony grillwork of the type highly esteemed in the older parts of New Orleans. Most of the older terraces were built out to the sidewalk or very close thereto with any private land at the rear. Most of the yards are enclosed by fences or masonry walls.

Another factor was the early imposition of building codes. The first building code in South Australia, including provisions favoring low-density housing, for example, was passed in 1881. Construction in New Zealand followed somewhat the same pattern except that there were relatively fewer terrace houses and relatively more detached houses, even in the nineteenth century. In neither country are there any of the three-, four-, and five-story tenement structures of the kind built in large numbers in the eastern cities of the United States during the latter part of the nineteenth and the early part of the twentieth century to house the hordes of incoming European migrants.

In addition to the fact that the physical characteristics of Australian and New Zealand cities prohibit housing as many families per acre as is common in the congested parts of any American multistory slum, social programs in these countries, while not totally eliminating poverty, go a long way toward eliminating its visible evidence. Unemployment in both countries is virtually unknown and has been for thirty years. For all practical purposes, the government of each country is dedicated to the proposition of full employment and, in the opinion of those questioned, would quickly contrive a public program to alleviate the situation, should unemployment develop. Combined with full employment are social programs that virtually guarantee universal free medical care to the needy (the elderly, widows, and orphans), and racial discrimination is almost unknown. These factors collectively have eliminated the major cause of urban congestion as Americans know it: the people's financial inability to secure reasonably adequate housing.

In addition, governmental bodies throughout Australia and New Zealand are actively building housing. The Housing Trust of South Australia builds roughly one-third of all the houses constructed each year in that state. This is in no sense public housing comparable to that of America. In South Australia some of these houses are offered for rent and, although a minor means test is utilized in connection with the initial rent, it is an insignificant hurdle compared with the means test used by the American public housing authorities. Furthermore, once in residence, a tenant can make as much money as his abilities permit without fear of eviction, or he can purchase the house. The South Australia Housing Trust sells most of its houses outright through mortgage arrangements that make purchase possible for individuals with modest incomes. A private mortgage lender in either Australia or New Zealand typically provides a first mortgage of £3,500 on a £4,500 dwelling. This would be backed in South Australia by a £500 second mortgage negotiated through the trust and a £500 down payment. Public construction of private homes is one of the explanations for 70 percent homeownership in Australia and New Zealand, and an additional reason for a relatively slumless society.

The South Australian Housing Trust has clustered its rental houses in groups of about two hundred, which stand out from the larger areas of owner-occupied houses because they are noticeably less well maintained. In addition to one-family houses for sale or rent, the trust builds a relatively small number of flats and disperses these throughout the community rather than massing them. The trust had a particularly happy experience with the new town of Elizabeth, which it built and which now accommodates some fifty thousand residents. While opportunities for improvement could be noted on touring Elizabeth in 1964, this was by far the most attractive of the contrived communities which we visited in Australia and New Zealand and stood as a considerable achievement among planned "new towns."

One is impressed also with the relative cleanliness of the Australian and New Zealand communities. The junk and litter characteristic of American slums is conspicuously absent. Even in what obviously are the poorest and most insalubrious areas, standards of municipal tidiness are considerably higher than in the United States, and local government is far less inclined to tolerate mess and litter. This suggests that if American municipalities were disposed to spend a little more money collecting garbage, cleaning streets, and removing litter from vacant lots, the visible appearance of congested American neighborhoods might be immeasurably improved and they would look less "slummy." In addition, some local councils require that housing be kept in good repair, which leads to enforced renovation by occupiers.

In summary, the lack of obvious slums may be attributed to several factors:

1. Cities in Australia and New Zealand lack the multistory tenement houses that characterize the older parts of American cities; hence the practical possibility of crowding to the extent of American slums is lacking and the replacement of worn-out housing with industrial or commercial uses is facilitated.

2. The general welfare of the lowest income segment of the population seems to be relatively higher and economic conditions that force overcrowding in American slums are not widely present.

3. Housing trusts maintain a supply of housing and at a cost within the means of a somewhat larger segment of the public than is provided by the housing industry or by public housing authorities in the United States and the percentage of homeownership is substantially higher.

4. The high standards of municipal tidiness keep poor neighborhoods looking fairly clean.

5. Racial discrimination forcing impoverished groups to cluster in ghetto conditions is lacking in all-white Australia and small in New Zealand.

Against the background of these influences in the slum question, the part played by the tax factor appears to be relatively minor.

It should be recorded that the local viewpoint on slums does not accord with our evaluation. Although we failed to find any real slums, many Australians and New Zealanders thought they already had a slum problem. Wide interest was expressed in urban renewal, and we were vigorously and frequently queried about financing methods used in the United States and the problems of those displaced. The counter inquiry of why the areas under discussion were thought to need renewal generally brought the reply that the houses were well over a hundred years old, of frame construction, and deteriorating. Physical deterioration is indeed visible in a number of instances and in a few cases is extreme with weather boarding falling off the sides of houses, gaping holes in roofs, and broken windows. There is much more of this in New South Wales than elsewhere, due to a peculiar set of circumstances to be discussed later. On the other hand, few houses now lack interior plumbing, and central heat is unimportant, since electric or gas space heat is adequate anywhere in the larger cities. Few areas would be called blighted by American standards, but a substantial amount of urban renewal was underway in Australia, particularly where it generally appears to be associated with an effort to put close-in land to more productive uses than old terrace houses.

Quite possibly Australia or New Zealand may actually have something like American-type slums in the course of the next twenty years, although one- and two-story houses can never produce Harlem-like neighborhood congestion. Australia is currently experiencing a substantial influx of "New Australians," some of whom have been accustomed to the congested living that characterizes the poorer sections of many European cities. Difficulty of language and cultural assimilation is encouraging them to crowd together in far greater congestion than even the poorest of native Australians. This is true of a number of ethnic groups that have collected in the older residential neighborhoods. Small and inexpensive restaurants provide old-country menus and help preserve European manners, languages, and habits. Australian planners express concern over the congestion that is beginning to occur in some of the older residential districts when "New Australians" take over. They want to know more about the effect on cities of the waves of migration into the United States.

New Zealand has had some movement of the Maori and Cook Islander population from the country to publicly constructed housing in Auckland, Wellington, and Christchurch. The Maoris and Islanders are not subject to anything like the discrimination suffered by dark-skinned people in the United States, but they are beginning to develop a degree of unpopularity by bringing into clear visibility in the city housing projects living habits which went unnoticed when they lived in rural areas. Having been accustomed to congested living, they tend to occupy urban flats to a degree of density not contemplated by the planners. Occasional protests by the management of the projects that each flat is to be occupied by not more than one family are reputedly met with the reply that all of the people in the flat, at times twenty and more, are related to each other.

While quantitative data are not available, over-congestion of buildings is beginning to appear both in Australia and New Zealand. These early signs, although not conclusive, suggest also that the lack of slums is due to a combination of forces of which the tax system is only one.

In New South Wales the physical condition of housing in the poorer neighborhoods appears to be more dilapidated than elsewhere, although the scope of the investigation precluded the possibility of a quantitative or definitive finding. Australian respondents confirmed the observation and attributed the condition to a rent control law passed in 1939. This law, virtually iron-clad in its operation, set the net return to the landlord-owner at August 1939 levels, and incumbent tenants enjoying the benefits of controlled rent sublet one room for more than the controlled rent on the whole house. This serves as an incentive to the build-up of a profitable rooming-house industry and is, at least in the opinion of several respondents, a factor in generating quasi-slum conditions in parts of Sydney. Incumbent tenants can be dislodged only with their own consent and owners frequently "buy them out" at quite high figures in order to demolish and make room for something else, move in themselves, or sell the house at the "vacant-possession" market price.

Rent control has been a factor in the lack of private construction of rental housing except at very high rent levels and under stipulation between owner and tenant that the provisions of rent control not apply. Meanwhile, the public authority has built quantities of rental housing, also exempt from controlled rent, and the private market has concentrated on single-family sale housing or "strata-title" flats, a variant of the American condominium.[16]

As experienced elsewhere, conditions of controlled rents set up a complex of economic forces that tends to freeze the status quo, since owners cannot gain possession of their property to demolish and rebuild. Controlled rents also encourage minimum standards of maintenance. Efforts

16. Incidentally, "strata-title" flats pose a technical problem in the assessment of rates based on land value since the value of the underlying land cannot be apportioned equally among the strata. The various strata may not be of equal value; that is, the ground floor may have more than average value due to non-residential use, or less, because a lot of it is taken up by an elaborate entrance, while a top floor with a view may be worth more than a lower floor without one.

to repeal or substantially amend the New South Wales rent control law, however, have been unsuccessful. Similar laws existed in other Australian states, but have been either repealed or greatly modified.

The "Native" View on Rating Methods

While almost everyone queried found few visible differences between communities levying rates on unimproved capital value as compared with those levying on assessed annual value or improved capital value, a very substantial majority expressed themselves in favor of the unimproved capital value system, and a significant number as *strongly* in favor of it. When pressed on this point, they generally repeated one of the arguments which had been advanced by George nearly a century ago: rating on unimproved capital value encourages development and does nothing whatever to discourage it. This basic line of reasoning was spun out in numerous versions, but the encouragement of development was always central to the argument.

A second line of argument is advanced by a smaller number, chiefly tax professionals, who favor rating on unimproved capital value because it is administratively superior. J. F. N. Murray, the highly regarded author of the leading Australian textbook on valuation techniques, holds that: (1) equity in valuation can be more easily achieved when the rating is based on land rather than a combination of land and building; (2) considerable economies can be achieved if the valuer general does not need to maintain records on the character of buildings; (3) most of the errors in valuation involve buildings and not land; and (4) use of cadastral maps not only readily permits equilization of land values but reference to such maps makes it very simple for an aggrieved owner to determine whether he is treated equitably. In consulting with the United Nations concerning tax systems for new nations, where ownership records are good enough to permit clear identification of taxable holdings, Murray strongly advocates site value taxation because of its simplicity and the relative ease with which inexperienced civil servants can be trained to do the job.[17]

The argument commonly heard in America that site value rating is administratively impossible because of the difficulty of assessing land apart from the buildings on it, is not heard at all in Australia and New Zealand. Many decades of experience have convinced even the most hardened skeptics that while it may be considerably more difficult to appraise the

17. This paragraph is based on several personal conversations with J. F. N. Murray during October 1964.

land component of a single improved parcel apart from the building on it, the reverse is true when great numbers of properties have to be evaluated for tax purposes. Involved calculations need be made only for selected bench-mark properties and the values established for the bench marks may be extrapolated to all properties, very much as American assessors customarily build up land value maps. The "land value atlas" or "cadastral map" is the device for accomplishing the extrapolation. Both Australian and New Zealand tax professionals, including a few who either oppose site value taxation or are lukewarm to it, are agreed on its administrative simplicity.

The case against unimproved value rating was heard, but less frequently. Its opponents argue that buildings contain a great deal of value especially in the central cities that should not be allowed to go untaxed; that the unimproved capital value system violates the basic tax principle of benefit received because the people living and working in downtown buildings require services they do not pay for proportionately; and that it also violates the principle of ability to pay since it lightens the tax burdens of those most able to pay at the expense of those least able. The exclusion of improvements under the unimproved value system also means that the tax base has considerably less flexibility than under either improved capital value or assessed annual value systems.

Another argument against site value taxation develops into an argument in favor of assessed annual value. In communities with assessed annual value systems, a peculiar element of progressivity emerges which legitimately places more of the cost of local government on nonresidential property than would be its proportionate share under either unimproved capital value or improved capital value. Assessed annual value is set at not less than 5 percent of improved capital value in New Zealand and in most Australian states or an approximation of actual net annual rental value, whichever is the greater. In practice this means that assessed annual value of residences is usually 5 percent of improved capital value, but that of commercial property ranges from 6 to 8 percent and industrial property tends to fall at or above the 8 percent level. Under these circumstances and by design of the system, commercial and industrial property pays a great deal more, sometimes nearly twice as much, in proportion to its improved capital value, than residences.

The combination of the progressive state land tax and assessed annual value rating produces very marked progressivity. In some boroughs, large factories pay rates of well over 2 percent of capital value on this basis, whereas the homeowner pays less—nearer 1 percent. If the factory or commercial land value is high enough to make it subject to a state land tax as well, the large property owner might pay 5 percent or more of capital value in rates and taxes compared with 1 percent or less for the average homeowner.

In areas such as New Zealand and the Australian states of Victoria and South Australia where local option is permitted, many localities have changed their system of local rating to unimproved capital value, but very few have changed in the other direction. A referendum on what taxing method to employ can be initiated either by the local council or by petition of a given percentage of ratepayers in the district. In some Australian states, such as Victoria, the plebiscite has to be preceded by an official analysis of the comparative amount of tax payable under the different taxing methods. In the state of Victoria, a complete study has to be made by the local valuer under the supervision of the valuer general. Following the study, a statement is sent to each ratepayer showing his tax liability under the present as well as the proposed valuation basis. The change of tax incidence depends on the mix of property in the district. If, for example, the district consists entirely of single-family residences and if the ratio of land to building value is consistently 1:7, then a shift from one basis to any other would have no effect at all on incidence. If, however, the district contains a substantial volume of vacant land (ratio 1:0) or other property with high ratio of land to building, say 2:1, the change to unimproved value shifts the load to properties with a high ratio of land to building value. Conversely, a large improvement like a factory on not very valuable land might have a ratio under the average and gain substantially from a switch to unimproved capital value.

In communities on the edge of a developing metropolis where a thousand or so houses have been built and where most of the vacant land is still owned by individuals who hold fairly large tracts, the usual result of a change to unimproved capital value rating is to reduce the rates of most homeowners and increase those paid by owners of undeveloped land. In the type of case described above, where many homeowners benefit and a relatively few large landowners are penalized, voters have almost invariably favored a change to unimproved capital value, and understandably so.

The converse case arose some time ago in an industrial suburb of Melbourne. This community has virtually no undeveloped land but a considerable number of modest homes together with a number of large factories representing a substantial capital investment in buildings. The official survey in this case revealed that the factory owners and the owners of commercial property would benefit at the expense of homeowners. The referendum failed and the community retained net (assessed) annual value rating.

In another recent case, the municipality of South Melbourne, with a variety of mixed uses, voted about ten thousand to sixteen thousand in favor of a change to unimproved capital value rating. Industrial property in this suburb was generally old and fairly well depreciated so there was not much industrial value to spill over and lighten the load on home-owners. Furthermore, a considerable number of owners of commercial and semicommercial property had building improvement programs in mind and foresaw a rise in their rates if South Melbourne remained on net annual value, whereas their rates would remain unchanged or rise only slightly if the town shifted to unimproved value. Interrogations in this community revealed that the number of "prospective improvers" of property was large enough to produce a class of voter in this election. This case suggests that "transitional" close-in suburbs may be ripe candidates for changing to unimproved capital value rating in the future. It also points up what interesting possibilities can arise out of combinations of uses and resultant values in the various jurisdictional pockets that collectively make up metropolitan areas in Australia, New Zealand, and America.

In communities on the edge of a developing metropolis, there is a general trend toward unimproved value rating, but no such trend is observable in the prosperous developed communities on the edge of the metropolitan core where a signficant investment in large buildings lightens the burden of individual homeowners.

Since many of the referenda favoring unimproved capital value occurred in localities on the edge of expanding cities where rapid residential growth is taking place, it is not surprising that communities with unimproved capital value rating generally show a faster rate of development than those with other systems. Conversely, many of the older suburbs in the Melbourne and Adelaide metropolitan areas where the growth rate is slower because most of the property is already developed, voted to retain the assessed annual value system. The advocates of unimproved capital value rating make considerable use of the argument that their form of rating stimulates growth and offer the higher growth rate of the outer ring communities with unimproved capital value rating for evidence. The contention that unimproved capital value rating stimulates growth of an undeveloped area is easily supported a priori, but the correlation between growth and the system of rating in the suburbs of Melbourne and Adelaide is in large part accidental and does not of itself constitute empirical verification of the a priori case. Although Sydney, which rates on unimproved capital value for territorial local-government purposes, has had a higher growth rate than Melbourne, which uses assessed annual values, Adelaide, which rates on assessed annual value, has had a higher growth rate than either. If the system of rating were the determining factor, Brisbane, which rates only on unimproved capital value, should have had the highest growth rate of all the major Australian urban centers, but it did not.

The fact that political leadership found it expedient to introduce the hardship exemption in such areas as New South Wales and Queensland constitutes further strong support of the a priori arguments in favor of unimproved capital value rating. It must have been effective to have made relief from its impact a political necessity.

The Advocates of Change

The use of unimproved capital value in Victoria is advocated chiefly by the General Council for Rating Reform. It maintains a modest continuing organization and systematically advances the traditional Henry George arguments. Its literature, however, appears to ignore the administrative advantages of unimproved capital value rating. Outside the state of Victoria, groups advocating unimproved capital value rating are less well organized but are usually associated in one way or another with the Henry George movement. Advocates of unimproved capital value rating for territorial local-government purposes not infrequently favor the use of assessed annual value for water, sewerage, and allied rates imposed by semigovernment authorities.

The opponents of unimproved capital value rating are less well organized and far less articulate than its advocates. The advocates of the assessed annual value system are associated with conservative business and financial interests, but their stand generally lacks the fervor of those who urge the unimproved capital value system. In local situations where a change to unimproved capital value would benefit a few and hurt many, the opposition to a change generally represents a spontaneous upwelling of local feeling rather than a systematically directed movement.

Our Evaluation

At tax rate levels now prevailing in Australia and New Zealand, the economic and social impact of property taxation based on unimproved capital value is minor. No differences are perceptible between communities that use unimproved capital value rating and those with other taxation systems. The earlier graduated land taxes, however, as originally ad-

ministered by the Commonwealth of Australia, the Australian states, and
the central government of New Zealand, were a decided factor in the
breakup of large landed estates and contributed to the realization of these
governments' political objectives. Since their decline in importance during recent decades, the land taxes have been exerting a significant influence in only a relatively few cases involving large and valuable tracts of
land.

The Australian and New Zealand cities today show few visible differences attributable to the type of local rating system, as distinguished from
the (states') land taxes. We attribute this absence of visible differences to
(1) a low level of tax rates made possible by the relatively low total cost
of the functional responsibilities borne by local governments and the opportunity these governments have to shift fiscal burdens to higher levels
of government; (2) hardship provisions in most Australian states that,
under certain conditions, allow single-family houses in transitional areas
to be retained in their existing use without incurring tax penalties; (3)
agricultural exemptions that permit farms in urban areas to be similarly
retained in the face of impending developments; and (4) the dilution of
the effect of unimproved capital value rating in many urban areas by bas-
ing charges for sewerage and similar services on assessed annual value or
improved capital value.

The very fact that governments in Australia found it politically expedient to introduce exemptions to blunt the impact of unimproved capital
value rates and taxes on low-income homeowners and farmers is persuasive
evidence that this method of property taxation did have the potential of
the kind of economic impact foreseen by its advocates.

The case for the use of unimproved capital value for the base of property taxation on grounds of administrative simplicity, efficiency, and resultant equity between individual owners and classes of owners is also
impressive, if only because professional administrators representing as a
group nearly three hundred years of collective experience are satisfied
that substantial savings could be realized in valuation (assessment) costs
and assessment quality could be raised if unimproved capital value were
the only base used for local and state property taxation.

The fact that a number of Australian and New Zealand communities
have been voting to change to unimproved capital value basis for property taxation has less implication for the inherent superiority of that system over others, as it generally reflects taxpayer desire to minimize tax
bills. Communities vote to shift to unimproved capital value when they
are on the outskirts of a developing metropolis and a majority of homeowners stand to benefit at the expense of a few. The reverse is true in

older prosperous sections of metropolitan areas where the shift would be in the opposite direction and store and factory owners would benefit at the expense of the more numerous homeowners.

Possibly our most meaningful finding from the viewpoint of the lesson it holds for the United States pertains to the quality of valuation (assessment) work by the valuer generals' departments in Australia and New Zealand, which compares with the best rather than the average in the United States. It is signficant that the superior quality of Australian and New Zealand assessments appears to be due largely to (1) the consolidation of this function in single departments covering areas large enough to support qualified experts; (2) the professional quality of the personnel; (3) the civil service status of these officials and their independence from political influence; and (4) the centralized valuation departments' multifunctional approach to valuation for all or most public purposes.

On the whole, taxation of real property on the basis of unimproved land values appears to have had much of the economic impact foreseen by George and the classical economists. This economic impact would have produced more visible evidence had it not been blunted by exemptions and diluted by the use of assessed annual value or improved capital value by semigovernment bodies (outside of Queensland). The social by-products, however, were not always entirely desirable and at times caused politically intolerable levels of individual hardship. We are obliged to reserve judgment on the view expressed by Australian and New Zealand tax experts that such pressures as this tax exerted were directed more consistently in constructive directions than if both land and buildings had been taxed.

9 *Property Taxation in Chile*

JOHN STRASMA

Chile, beyond all doubt, now has the best-assessed, heaviest, and most effective taxation on real estate in Latin America. For both urban and rural property, the tax laws and their administration combine heavy annual fixed-cost tax burdens with exemptions to encourage investment in low- and middle-income housing and in productive farm improvements.

This is not to say that the present structure and administration are perfect; there are many problems left, as with the property tax everywhere else. Furthermore, I do not yet know whether this theoretically attractive tax structure is producing the economic effects predicted by a substantial body of economic theory.[1]

The Structure of Chilean Taxation

As in most underdeveloped countries, a very substantial part (37 percent) of Chile's total governmental revenues comes from transactions taxes and customs duties. The transactions tax is of the turnover type, at 6 percent for most goods and services, with rates rising to 20 percent for certain items considered luxuries.[2] Evasion of this tax is widespread, and there is considerable evidence both of pyramiding of the tax and of vertical integration to reduce the number of taxed transactions.

The large, American-owned copper mines contribute substantial revenues (13 percent), on a sliding incentive scale whereby the effective rate

NOTE: I am greatly indebted, for data and critical comments, to Norman Nowak and Peter Griffith, of the Tax Modernization Project of the Agency for International Development in Santiago. The opinions and responsibility for accuracy of the facts in the present chapter, however, are solely my own.

1. This is the subject of current research by the author sponsored by the Land Tenure Center of the University of Wisconsin and the Institute of Economic Research of the University of Chile, with the cooperation of the Chilean Bureau of the Budget and Internal Revenue Service.

2. The transactions tax on goods and services was recently codified in *Diario Oficial*, Law 16,466, 29 April 1966.

drops as output rises above that of a base period. This arrangement is now being revised, as a Chilean government corporation acquires a 25 to 51 percent partnership in specific mines and undertakes the new power, road, and other investment necessary to expand capacity to about double present levels. Another project, still in the drafting stage, will provide incentives and taxes to encourage the development and exploitation of privately held mineral reserves not now in production.[3]

The personal and corporate income tax produce a substantial share of total revenues; the structure was simplified considerably in 1963, together with a lowering of schedular rates on profits and a sharp increase in the progressive rates on the upper brackets of personal incomes.[4] Equally important, the new government is enforcing the tax vigorously, with eighteen persons being tried in 1966 and several already serving jail terms for tax fraud.[5]

The structural and financial importance of Chilean taxes is shown in Table 9.1. It is also worth noting here that, at about 30 percent of the national income of some $450 per capita, Chileans bear about the same relative tax load as do United States citizens.[6]

The Taxation of Wealth in Chile

Following a series of tax reforms over the last decade, property of most kinds is subject to substantial and sophisticated taxation in Chile. The income tax discriminates according to source, and a separate tax on personal net wealth nullifies or reduces the extent of many loopholes and forms of evasion under the income tax. Some types of capital gains are taxed, and inheritances, gifts *inter vivos,* and transfers of real estate are subject to taxes similar to those in more industrialized countries. Finally, both urban and rural real estate are subject to a substantial tax (by Latin American standards), based on a recent national reassessment that is described at some length below.

3. The Chilean project, as well as similar recent legislation in Bolivia and Peru, is currently being studied in the field by graduate students from the University of Wisconsin. Scholars interested in further details on this subject may address Professor Donald Clark, School of Engineering, University of Wisconsin, Madison, Wisconsin 53706.

4. Both the reforms and the entire income tax code, as revised, appear in *Diario Oficial,* Law 15,564, 14 February 1964.

5. *El Mercurio* (Santiago), 2 January 1966.

6. Ibid., 22 April 1966. Social security taxes are included.

Table 9.1—Composition of Chilean Fiscal Revenues, 1966

Tax	Percentage
Transactions tax	23.8
Personal income taxes [a]	13.7
Copper mines tax	12.9
Import duties	12.8
Business profits taxes	8.7
Production excises	7.1
Property taxes	6.3
Services tax	5.3
Stamp taxes	5.2
Nontax revenues	4.2
Total	100.0

[a] These taxes include the "minimum presumed income tax," which is similar to a net wealth tax with a credit for income tax paid.

Source: Dirección del Presupuesto, as reported in *El Mercurio* (Santiago), 6 April 1966.

The Income Tax

The Chilean income tax includes both a set of schedular taxes according to the source of income and a global progressive tax on total personal income from all sources. Corporate profits are subject to a schedular tax at 30 percent, while unincorporated business profits are taxed at 20 percent and the net income of independent professionals (such as lawyers or doctors) at 7 percent. For employees, the schedular tax is withheld at the rate of 3.5 percent by their employers. The rate differences reflect both a politically expedient aim to favor "earned income" and recognition of the fact that businessmen and professionals are allowed to deduct the costs of earning their income, whereas the worker is not.

The higher rate on corporate profits reflects the fact that the progressive complementary tax on personal incomes does not affect retained corporate profits, whereas owners of partnerships and sole proprietorships must pay both the 20 percent schedular tax and the global progressive tax on all profits, even if reinvested in the firm. Professionals were formerly subject to a 22 percent schedular rate; this was cut to 7 percent in the 1964 reform, and administrative measures were designed to eliminate some of the evasion taken for granted when the rate was originally set at 22 percent.[7]

7. The fact that professionals still pay 7% while wage-earners pay 3.5% may reflect a congressional suspicion that a certain evasion persists and that it is administratively impossible to prevent it.

The income tax favors neither tenants nor owner-occupiers. The latter must declare an implicit income equal to 5 percent of the assessed value of their homes in the schedular tax on income from capital (taxed at 20 percent). The balance, 80 percent of this presumed income, is added to other incomes subject to the progressive complementary tax. Real estate tax paid, however, is credited against the schedular tax, thus annulling it completely for owner-occupiers, as well as for landlords whose reported net rental income, subject to the 20 percent schedular tax, does not exceed 10 percent of the assessed value of their real estate.[8] The net effect, then, is to include the implicit income of owner-occupiers in the progressive complementary tax. It also provides neutrality vis-à-vis other sources of income from capital by preventing the taxing of income from real estate under both the property tax and the schedular income tax.

The "global complementary" progressive tax on personal income from all sources rises from 10 percent on the first five "sueldos vitales anuales" (SVA) to 60 percent on all income beyond eighty SVA.[9] There are *no* deductions.[10] Although various kinds of income are exempt from the complementary tax, the list is much shorter than the list of incomes exempt from schedular taxation.[11]

8. Landlords must declare actual net income from real estate as shown by their accounts. Since the real estate tax rate is 2%, it offsets the 20% schedular tax on income up to 10% of assessed values. No refunds are made when the real estate tax exceeds the schedular tax due. Owner-occupiers have a low presumed implicit income (5%), but are not allowed to deduct repairs, mortgage interests paid, and so on. When accounts are not kept or do not satisfy the revenue service, it may also presume a net income of 10% of the assessed value of agricultural property and 7% for other property—such as vacation cottages—not qualifying as a regular residence of the owner.

9. The "sueldo vital" is the legal minimum wage for white collar workers. In 1966, it was 3,141 escudos per year. At the then current "brokers" exchange rate, this was about $675 per SVA. Annual escalator adjustments keep the "sueldo vital" reasonably constant in purchasing power over time, despite inflation.

10. For an analysis of the rate reduction that would be possible if the United States eliminated all deductions, see Joseph A. Pechman, "Erosion of the Individual Income Tax," *National Tax Journal*, 10, no. 1 (March 1957): 1–25. Chilean taxpayers do receive a tax credit of .3 SVA for married persons declaring jointly, .15 SVA for single family heads, and .05 SVA for each recognized dependent. Bachelors without dependents have a credit of .1 SVA. Thus, in Chile the tax saving per child is $33.75. It does not increase progressively with the total taxable income of the parents. Note also that the designation of tax brackets in an escalator-clause unit reduces distortion of the tax structure by Chile's secular inflation.

11. The 1964 reform uses an ingenious mechanism to prevent exemptions from reducing the marginal rate applicable to taxable income: the taxpayer must declare all income, determine what percentage of it is taxable, and find the tax payable by applying that percentage to the tax that would be due and payable if *all* of the income were subject to the tax.

Capital gains have been subject to taxation since 1964; the rate is 8 percent on gains on assets acquired before publication of the law and 20 percent on gains on assets acquired after publication. To ensure that only real gains are taxed, the base is increased to include the cost of improvements made, decreased for depreciation, and adjusted according to the change in the consumer price index during the period held. As profits from stocks and bonds are exempt, taxable gains are largely limited to real estate and interests in partnerships.

The Wealth Tax

In addition to taxing income derived from capital at higher schedular rates than income derived principally from labor, the government has enacted and implemented a new tax, payable during 1965, 1966, and 1967, on personal net wealth as of 31 October 1964.[12] Half of the global progressive income tax paid, however, is credited against the wealth tax due. The net result is that those persons who have declared and paid progressive income tax on an amount approximately equal to 16 percent of their net wealth on the base date pay no wealth tax at all. But those who have either evaded the personal income tax or taken full advantage of its many exemptions find themselves subject to a substitute tax, rising progressively from 20 to 35 percent, on legally presumed taxable incomes of 8 percent of the net wealth declared for the base date.[13] Against this tax due, they may credit one-half of whatever progressive income tax they did pay.

The only important exemptions are agricultural improvements—livestock and implements—since farms (except corporate farms) enter at their assessed value, which is based solely on land (see below).

None of the proponents of this tax have claimed that it catches wealth abroad, although legally such assets must be declared. However, the tax did restore some progressiveness to a structure that was so eroded by incentive schemes that only 11,000 persons declared taxable incomes above 18,000 escudos ($6,000) in 1964, whereas the national accounts show that 117,000 persons earned that much.[14] Of the 88,000 persons

12. *Diario Oficial,* Laws 16,250 and 16,282, published in 1965. The first payment was due 9 September 1965; subsequent annual installments were raised by the amount of increase in the consumer price index, to keep them in constant purchasing power. The base date was just before the present government took office; use of a fixed date seeks to avoid discouraging further saving and investment. Real estate is included at its 1965 assessed valuation.

13. The first 24,000 escudos ($6,000) were exempt—as was one taxi or truck, if operated by its owner. The tax was renewed in 1968, with higher exemption levels.

14. Carlos Garcés, *La Nación* (Santiago), 13 September 1965.

declaring their net wealth, some 600 reported net wealth over 1,000,000 escudos ($250,000), and paid an average of 40,000 escudos ($10,000) in tax for the first year.[15]

Taxes on Inheritances, Gifts, and Other Transfers

There is no estate tax in Chile; the amounts received by heirs (or as gifts *inter vivos*) are subject to a tax rising from 5 percent on the first 2 SVA to 55 percent on amounts over 320 SVA. These rates apply to spouses and linear relatives; collateral relatives pay the tax with a 20 percent surcharge, and nonrelatives pay with a 40 percent surcharge. For linear descendants and spouses, the first five SVA are exempt, while others may deduct only one SVA.

While most goods and services are subject to a transactions tax of 6 percent (as already mentioned), real estate transfers are taxed at 4 percent. As in other countries, the value reported is often below the true sales price (but must be at least equal to the current assessed valuation). This custom may have been jolted in April 1966, when the first person was jailed for false declaration of a transfer price.[16] This transfer tax is independent of the capital gains tax, already mentioned, and it is customary to split the transfer tax equally between buyer and seller.

Incentives

In spite of this impressive set of taxes affecting property, apart from the real estate tax as such, one must also note a large number of exceptions and exemptions. Most low- and middle-income urban housing built in recent years is exempt from schedular and progressive income tax, from rent control, and from the national government's share (75 percent) of the real estate tax of 2 percent of assessed value. (Other housing is subject to an annual rent ceiling of 11 percent of assessed value, and landlords can evict tenants only after lengthy court proceedings.)

While these exemptions were intended to stimulate low-cost housing construction, no limit was imposed except that the area per unit should not exceed 140 square meters (about 1400 square feet). Subsequent amendments insisted that finishing and fixtures be simple—which has led in some cases to temporary installation of cheap fixtures until after the inspectors leave.

The income tax privileges had to be substantial in order to woo capital

15. The exchange rate at the 1965 wealth tax payment date ("brokers" rate) was about 4.00 escudos per dollar. In 1964 (see above) it was nearer 3.00 per dollar, while by 1966 (see note 9) it was almost 5.00 per dollar.

16. *El Mercurio* (Santiago), 1 May 1966.

from other privileged activities, such as fishing and fish-meal processing (almost complete exemption from profits taxes). The housing law competed by exempting not only the rental income derived from the ownership of "economical housing," but also the profits of firms constructing such housing. Individuals were even permitted to deduct amounts invested in the purchase of such housing from current taxable personal income.[17] As if that were not enough, tax inspectors and exchange-control authorities were forbidden to ask owners and builders how they had obtained capital invested in such housing.

As a direct result of these incentives, there is now an abundant supply of modern two- and three-bedroom apartments and bungalows for the middle- and upper-class Santiago resident. Housing that low-income groups can afford remains scarce, however, with only public agencies making a real effort to increase the supply.

The new housing units are generally exempt from the national government's 75 percent share of the real estate tax for the first ten to twenty years; to maintain the desired incentive vis-à-vis other investments, owners may deduct the property tax that would have been payable in absence of exemptions from the schedular tax on income from capital. With exemption from both property taxes and income taxes (schedular and complementary), an enormous block of capital disappeared from the tax base entirely in the course of the Alessandri administration (1959–1964). It only reappeared in part when the new government enacted a wealth tax (see above) that gives a tax credit exclusively for the progressive complementary income tax actually paid.[18]

The Taxation of Real Estate

Land has been taxed in Chile since well before it gained independence in 1818; tax rolls and fairly continuous assessment and taxation of both urban and rural real estate were established by 1855. Since 1927, property has been revalued (after a fashion) about every six years—one of the highest frequencies in Latin America.

Agricultural Property

Starting with taxes paid in 1957, Chile switched from a tax on both land and improvements to a tax based exclusively upon the value of the

17. This provision exempted much income previously taxable, as well as exempting newly created income; it proved so costly that it was repealed at the end of 1964.

18. Persons owning one modest apartment probably fall within the exempt amount under the wealth tax. See above, note 13.

land ("casco del suelo"), plus vineyards on irrigated land and mansions (defined as owners' houses assessed in excess of 12.5 SVA or about $8,440).[19] As an incentive for further investment in land itself, clearing, drainage, and similar works are not to be reflected in higher assessed values for the land before 1974 unless the land changes owners.

The chronic problem of inflation, which left assessments far below market values in the very year they were promulgated, was also faced in the revision that took effect in 1957. The law provided for the creation of a mixed commission, giving equal votes to landowners (two representatives of the Chilean equivalents of the Farm Bureau and the Grange) and to the government (one each from the Internal Revenue Service and the Ministry of Agriculture). The impartial chairman and tie-breaker was to be the dean of the Faculty of Economics of the University of Chile.

This commission was to determine the amount of net profits earned by agricultural landowners in 1956, capitalize this sum at 10 percent, and determine the total tax base for land taxes to be paid in 1957. The reassessment made by the Internal Revenue Service between 1954 and 1956, based solely on the land and making use of a rough land classification and owner declarations as to the extent and shape of their holdings, served only to establish relative values of individual properties. The total was adjusted in 1957 and in each succeeding year so as to equal the capitalized value of the net sector income as determined by the commission.[20]

In a series of maneuvers still far from clear, the commission rejected a memorandum supplied to it in 1956 by the national accounts section of the Chilean Development Corporation (CORFO), indicated by law as the source of data for their determination. The commission then produced its own estimate by averaging the national accounts figures for 1954 and 1955, without correcting for price inflation. From that figure, the commission subtracted various "costs" that it felt the national accounts section had not allowed for properly. For example, it subtracted the land tax itself—assuming implicitly that the land tax should be deemed a cost of production rather than a direct tax to be borne by landowners.

The figure resulting from the 1956 meetings, which served as the basis

19. *Diario Oficial*, Law 11,575, published in 1954. Since further plantations of vineyards on irrigated land are prohibited, they have acquired a considerable monopoly value, which is deemed taxable. In addition, because of the ban on new plantings, there is obviously no disincentive effect if they are taxed.

20. That is, if a *fundo*'s original assessment in 1956 was 0.0001 of the total assessed value of all Chilean farmlands in that year, the tax in 1957 and each subsequent year would be 0.0001 of the presumed capital value of all Chilean farmlands, obtained by capitalizing the commission's profits estimate for the previous year at 10%.

for taxes paid in 1957 on the new assessments, was about one-third of the net income for the sector as determined in the national accounts. Similar maneuvers held assessed values at about a third of the level obviously intended by law for succeeding years; the most flagrant abuse was perpetrated between 1960 and 1962. In that period, while the consumer price ,index rose 37 percent and the national accounts showed money income of the sector well over 1959 levels, the commission announced that landowners' money income had actually fallen each year.[21]

The reason for the commission's behavior is not clear. As one critic said, the landowners would never have let the government fix wheat support prices with calculations like those used to fix the tax base.[22] One hypothesis, however, is that the representative of the Ministry of Agriculture assumed that he was supposed to vote in favor of the interests of the people served by that ministry—the landowners—rather than in favor of the revenue interest of the government or in respect for the clear intention of the law.

Partly driven by revenue needs and partly by awareness of the gross undervaluation, the Chilean congress approved regular rate increases, going from an average of 2.02 percent in 1958 to 3.16 percent in 1962.[23]

Reassessment by Photo-Interpretation and Soil Classification, 1962–1965

In the aftermath of the 1961 earthquake that devastated the southern end of Chile's Central Valley, the Organization of American States raised $550,000 in donations by other American governments. By the time the money was available for spending, however, immediate relief needs had been met by other aid and domestic resources, so the OAS decided that the best use for the money would be the aerial photography of the devastated zone, for use in planning reconstruction and development. As the project advanced, the photos and resulting maps were found to be so useful for various purposes, including tax assessment, that the project was expanded to include Chile's major cities and almost all of the agricultural land.

21. See Kurt Ullrich and Ricardo Lagos, *Agricultura y Tributación* (Santiago: Instituto de Economía, Universidad de Chile, 1965), p. 84, Appendix A.

22. Ministerio de Hacienda, "Retasación de los predios agricolas y reajustes automáticos dispuestos en la ley 11,575," mimeographed (Santiago, 1958), p. 2.

23. Ullrich and Lagos, *Agricultura*, p. 83. For further information on taxation and agriculture in Chile, see José L. Pistono, *Tributación Agrícola en Chile, 1940–1958* (Santiago: Instituto de Economía, Universidad de Chile, 1960). This publication has recently been reprinted; both editions contain the same data and analysis of the quasi-tax and quasi-subsidy elements of price supports and controls, as well as material on taxation and government investment in agriculture.

The total cost of the project came to the equivalent of $5.4 million. The Inter-American Development Bank provided a loan of $2.1 million, which, together with Chilean budgetary contributions, made it possible to identify property boundaries, verify ownership in the field, and measure all areas greater than one hectare (with a planimeter, on the photos). The project also determined land use at the time of photography (some thirty-four different classifications) and, by combining photo-interpretation with compiled soil studies, field samples, and geological materials, attempted to estimate the best potential land use under prevailing levels of knowledge and capitalization. The United States Agency for International Development helped with data processing and sent advisors to the urban and rural tax reassessment staffs.

As a final product of the OAS project, Chile now has 532 plastic mosaics, each showing some 66,000 acres, covering almost all (85 percent) of the agricultural land in the country. Property boundaries and the owner's name were verified in the field and entered on an overlay, with the tax roll number. Other overlays show the present and estimated potential land use and irrigation works, roads, and so on. While there are slight technical problems leading to some error in measurement of areas by planimeter, the accuracy is far better than in previous assessments. The accurate determination of boundaries and size and the inclusion on tax rolls of land never before declared, could, according to one enthusiast, repay the entire cost of the project (close to $5.4 million) in about five years.[24] And the photographs, mosaics, and the maps made from them have been valuable for planning public works, field surveys, the location of new schools, oil and mineral exploration, and preparatory work for land reform.[25]

Fixing Unit Values in Massive Land Revaluations

Although the objective of the 1962–1965 reassessment was clearly stated as including an approach to true market value of land (maintaining the exemption of improvements), it was clearly out of the question to consider the market value of each property with the detail and discussion (and appeals) inherent in traditional assessment or appraisal. The 1962 Chilean law therefore provides for the determination of tables of

24. Jorge García-Huidobro, in a paper presented at the Seminario Internacional sobre Tributación Agrícola, Santiago, 1963. According to Ullrich and Lagos, *Agricultura*, p. 118, the area included on tax rolls increased by about 10%.

25. For details of the project, see Luís Vera, *Agricultural Land Inventory Techniques: The OAS/Chile Aerophotogrammetric Project* (Washington, D.C.: Organization of American States, 1964).

values for a hectare of each of twelve qualities of land in each *comuna* (township), as well as adjustment factors to allow for the impact on market values and income of the distance and kind of road or river transportation to a principal market.

This procedure ruled out owner appeals based solely on the grounds that the assessment is higher than market value—or, more candidly, than the value on which the landowner is *willing* to pay taxes. It also reduced the former discrimination, in which appeals were handled by people who tended to give more consideration to the wealthy than to small landholders, turning a proportional tax into a regressive one.[26]

These tables of values were debated in 1964 by a new set of commissions, one for each province. This time all members were university-trained technicians in agriculture, although some were nominated by landowner groups and some by governmental agencies. In preparation for the meetings, the Internal Revenue Service assigned fourteen men to spend eight months of field work developing draft tables. These were based on income and capital values of some two thousand farms, plus interviews of a 10 percent sample of the landowners themselves, for a discussion of the value figure declared by the owner in 1962 at the start of the reassessment.[27] Since sales prices declared for transfer tax purposes were deemed worthless, the Internal Revenue Service also assigned other appraisers for 140 man-months of work gathering some seven thousand sale prices from other sources; these were also used to prepare the draft tables of land values for each *comuna*.[28]

The commissions met in late 1964, considered the tables proposed by the Internal Revenue Service, and proposed changes, usually reducing the values by 25 to 50 percent. (The service proposals were usually four to five times the levels prevailing in 1963, as well as those declared by owners in 1962.) The finance minister then studied the commission recommendations and the rebuttal arguments of the service and forwarded the tables with his own recommendations to the president of the country, who was the final arbiter.

---

26. Oscar Dominguez analyzes the reasons for this favoritism in *La Nación* (Santiago), 14 August 1965.

27. The owner was required to estimate the market value of his land and to give his idea of the area of his land falling in each of the twelve soil classes, which were described in a four-page technical folder that went with the declaration. Most owners declared market value to be slightly more than the current assessed value; they had no incentive to declare a more realistic value.

28. Extensive details of the reassessment of agricultural land, including the formation and functioning of the commission, are given in William J. Cecil, "End of Tour Report," mimeographed (Santiago: Tax Modernization Mission of the Agency for International Development, 1964), esp. pp. 42–43.

Although all parties had their say, through representatives in the commissions, there was (and is) no appeal to the courts against the unit values so determined. Landowners could appeal during the first sixty days after the new assessments were announced, but only on grounds that (1) their land area is less than that shown on the rolls; (2) the distance or quality of road is not as shown; or (3) the distribution of their land by soil classes is inaccurate. Since each of these points is a matter resolved quickly by generally accepted techniques, the appeals process was rapid and the Internal Revenue Service was quite willing to agree when the owner was right. While appeals rejected by the service may be carried to the courts, the legal basis for appeal remains limited to these three points, and the outcome is not likely to change.

The area not covered by the aerial photography was assessed by more traditional methods; the assessment was completed late in 1965.

Reassessment of Urban Property

The reassessment of urban property followed the general lines of the rural assessment project, except that improvements were fully valued. About one million units were involved, compared to some 250,000 farm properties. Valuers were given manuals that included pictures of typical types of buildings, with values per square meter of various standard types of construction, in "very good," "good," "poor," and "bad" condition. These unit values, as well as depreciation factors, site values along each street, and formulas for depth values were proposed by the Internal Revenue Service, debated by provincial commissions, and promulgated by the president, as was done for rural land.[29] The work of the valuers was thus confined to a visual classification of type and condition and to inquiry when the area or date of construction recorded in previous assessments did not match what they saw.

Appeals can be filed only on grounds that the area of house or lot is overstated, the age is understated, or the building type is misclassified. The values are intended to approach full market prices, but there is no provision for appeal just because the owner alleges that his assessment exceeds that level.

The development of urban property is still favored by various measures, even though improvements are fully assessed. In addition to the income tax and land tax exemptions mentioned before, new "economical" hous-

29. The urban phase of reassessment is described in E. G. Haislop, "End of Contract Report," mimeographed (Santiago: Tax Modernization Mission of the Agency for International Development, 1965). The report includes a copy of the *Manual for Valuers* and other materials developed in the reassessment project.

ing is generally exempt from 75 percent of the tax insofar as the value of the improvement is concerned. This is the national government's share of the rate of 2 percent of assessed value; the local-government share is maintained to cover local services, such as sewerage disposal and street lighting.

Building is further encouraged by a surcharge on vacant lots, which rises from 1 to 6 percent in annual increments and supposedly begins in the year following the first transfer by a subdivider. (It is not clear whether it is sufficient to file for a building permit, or whether one must actually complete a building in order to stop the operation of this surcharge. A spot check found enforcement to be uneven among different municipalities making up greater Santiago.)

Conclusions and Research Plans

From the preceding, it is obvious that the assessment and taxation of real estate in Chile is fairly well conceived and is an integral part of a complete system of income and wealth taxation. The exemption of most on-farm improvements is recommended in much of the literature on agricultural taxation in underdeveloped countries. The assessments are recent, and the valuation methods and appeals system are streamlined. Nonetheless, there are a variety of intriguing problems inviting serious research:

1. To what extent can aerial photo-interpretation be used to determine whether present land use is so deficient that a farm deserves priority attention in Chile's land reform? And to what extent can the photo-interpretation estimates of land-use potential be used for planning cultivation programs, at least initially, on idle or underutilized land that is expropriated by the land reform agency? In other words, can the data already compiled for land-assessment purposes help relieve the shortage of skilled technical staff and thereby help raise food output, or at least keep it from dropping, in the initial stages of land reform?

2. What are the effects of the fixed-cost taxes on land use and tenure? The combined impact of the net wealth and land taxes rises progressively from about 1.6 to about 3.9 percent of market value of the land (but a lower percentage of total farm value, including improvements, of course). Is this enough to cause intensified land use? The presumptions in the income tax penalize tenancy. Whereas owners not obliged to keep full accounts are taxed on the basis of a 10 percent presumed income, tenant-farmed land is presumed to yield a total of 16 percent (4 percent for the tenant and 12 percent for the landlord) of assessed value, for purposes of

both the schedular and the progressive complementary tax—has this had
any impact on tenure patterns? And on the eve of a fairly sweeping redistribution of idle or underutilized land and water rights from some three
thousand large *fundos,* with a vigorous debate as to the procedure and
terms of payment, how far can one hope to detect effects of tax pressure
on land use and tenure?

3. Has the policy, now over ten years old, of taxing agricultural land
but exempting most improvements, actually stimulated enough additional
farm investment to justify the loss in fiscal revenue? What is the resulting
effective ratio of tax to market value of farms including improvements?
How effective is this incentive, as compared with cheap long-term credit
that could be given with the revenue from an all-inclusive tax? Likewise,
should urban improvements be taxed more lightly, at the expense of
increased taxes on site values? Has the annual surcharge on lots long
vacant been effective? Has it been applied efficiently in all cities, or indeed in any? Has it, perhaps, led even to too much building, in areas
where zoning and planning has yet to provide for orderly growth and
preservation of amenities?

4. To what extent can and should the techniques and tax policies used
in Chile be considered by other countries? Is the revenue and the effective
progression provided by the personal wealth tax sufficient gain to offset
the psychological shock of the tax, which some blame for a slowdown in
investment? (The stock and real estate markets fell, in part just capitalizing the tax.) Are the photo-interpretation techniques as good as those
in charge of the project claim? Even with several thousand field tests and
soil samples, can one really have confidence in land-use-potential studies
made wholesale? And what problems arise in the use of a land classification developed for conservation purposes in the United States, but used
in Chile for lack of one referring specifically to the economic potential
of different types of Chilean farm land? And why were the aerial photos
of the cities *not* used in the reassessment of urban property?

5. How can these wholesale techniques and land records best be made
useful in land reform and agricultural development programs? They
offer enormous advantage in time saved. But, as compared to traditional
methods, are there serious errors or problems when compensation payments to expropriated landowners, as well as initial farm plans for the
beneficiaries, are based on studies carried out basically for tax purposes?

10 *The Valorization Tax in Colombia: An Example for Other Developing Countries?*

WILLIAM G. RHOADS and
RICHARD M. BIRD

Introduction

One of the most striking phenomena in developing countries today is their rapid growth in population and urbanization. Many cities grow continuously at rates seen only in boom periods in developed countries. This rapid urbanization has put a tremendous strain on municipal finances: extremely heavy investments in roads, sewers, aqueducts, street lighting, parks, and schools are needed if the city is to remain suitable for human existence, but there is no capital market from which funds can be borrowed, and the national governments cannot provide adequate assistance to finance capital investments.

In the countryside in many countries an analogous situation exists. With a rapidly growing population, agricultural development must take place at a rapid rate, often requiring heavy investment in transportation facilities to open up agricultural areas and in projects for drainage, flood protection, and irrigation to make more land productive.

A major contribution that property taxes can make to economic development is to help finance the heavy burden of these capital improvements. Like most countries, Colombia has a conventional property tax

NOTE: The authors were members of the Agency for International Development Mission in Colombia and the Colombian Advisory Group of the Harvard Development Advisory Service, respectively, when this chapter was written in mid-1966. The views expressed are those of the authors only, and in no way represent those of the United States government, the Harvard Development Advisory Service, or the Colombian government. A condensed version of some of the argument in this chapter has previously been published in William G. Rhoads and Richard M. Bird, "Financing Urbanization in Developing Countries by Benefit Taxation: Case Study of Colombia," *Land Economics*, 43, no. 4 (November 1967): 403–412.

that is used primarily to provide municipal revenues. This tax has not yet been a major factor in financing economic development.[1] Rates have been low, assessment has been haphazard, and collection has been poor, with the result that total yield has been low and that, partly for this reason, municipalities in Colombia have not played a strong role in economic development. Public education, for example, is financed almost entirely by the departmental (state) and national governments.

In addition to the usual role of property taxes in providing municipal revenues, Colombia has perhaps had more proposals for special taxation of idle agricultural land to force land reform than any other underdeveloped country.[2] Although one complicated scheme was actually made law a few years ago, the property tax's incentive role in economic development has not really amounted to much. On both counts, then, with regard to its revenue productivity and to its incentive use, the property tax in Colombia has not as yet made much of a contribution to economic development, although there is some hope for improvement as a result of efforts now underway.

It is an alternative tax on property in Colombia, the "impuesto de valorización" or valorization tax (similar to the "special assessment" or "betterment tax" in English-speaking countries), which, even though its yield is less than that of the regular property tax, has already played an important part in financing urban economic development in Colombia and may well play an even more important part in the future. This valorization tax is interesting from both a theoretical and a practical point of view, but it has been almost totally ignored in taxation literature in recent years, in large part because of its relative unimportance in advanced countries.[3]

1. For a general account of property taxes in Colombia see Richard M. Bird, "Local Property Taxes in Colombia," in National Tax Association, *1965 Proceedings of the Fifty-Eighth Annual Conference on Taxation,* ed. Walter J. Kress (Harrisburg, Pa., 1966), pp. 481–501. Additional information may be found in Harvard Law School International Program in Taxation, *Taxation in Colombia,* World Tax Series (Chicago: Commerce Clearing House, 1964), chap. 4; and in the Organization of American States and the Inter-American Development Bank, Joint Tax Program, *Fiscal Survey of Colombia* (Baltimore: The Johns Hopkins Press, 1965), chaps. 6, 7.

2. Albert O. Hirschman, *Journeys towards Progress: Studies of Economic Policy-Making in Latin America* (New York: Twentieth Century Fund, 1963), chap. 3, gives an excellent account of these proposals.

3. For example, five standard American public finance texts consulted devote an average of only four pages to special assessments or land-value-increment taxes. These writers tend to stress the arbitrariness and administrative difficulties of special assessments (which all too often in the United States were bond issues to finance improvements for speculative real estate subdivisions) and to favor land-value-

The second section of this paper explores briefly the theory of the valorization tax, showing why it seems particularly suitable for use in such developing countries as Colombia. The third section then examines in some
detail the operation of the valorization tax in Colombia, describing its
history, revenue importance, administration, and future. Finally, the conclusion contrasts Colombian experience with that in two other Latin
American countries and brings together the lessons to be derived from
Colombian experience as to the extent to which the theoretical usefulness
of the valorization tax can be realized in practice in developing countries.

Theory of the Valorization Tax

Urban Areas

Since the primary purpose of a tax in a developing country is to raise
revenues for public use, the revenue needs of urban areas must first be
examined. In developing countries, cities typically grow very rapidly. In
Colombia the average rate of urban growth is 5 percent a year, and the
major cities discussed in this paper—Bogotá, Medellín, and Cali—grew
in the last decade at average annual rates of 7.7, 6.2,[4] and 7.5 percent,
respectively. The rapid growth of these cities arises from their development of dynamic manufacturing and commercial sectors and also from
the increasing importance of education, health, and other activities that
are most efficiently carried on in urban areas.

This urban growth takes place at a time when the public capital requirements for creating efficient cities with "satisfactory" social services
are very high, but domestic saving is low and there is a shortage of capital.
City growth in developing countries today is usually based on transport
by urban buses. For efficient transportation, the narrow streets of the
central city—in Latin America a heritage from colonial days—must therefore be widened and new streets opened. On the edge of the growing city,
streets must be extended rapidly to new factories and new housing, often
single-family homes being developed slowly from original squatter settle-
ments by owners lacking the organization, financing, and technical capacities to build more compact multifamily structures even if they wanted

---

increment taxes levied after the completion of the work rather than special assessments levied before the work is finished. As discussed later, the Colombian
valorization tax is really a hybrid of these two concepts as usually expounded and,
in actual operation, appears to suffer from few of the problems stressed by the
textbook writers.

4. Medellín only. The growth rate of the Medellín metropolitan area was somewhat higher. Only Medellín of the major Colombian cities has a significant fraction
(one-fourth) of its metropolitan area population living outside the central city.

to do so. If the city is to be a location of low-cost production, it needs these streets to provide rapid bus transportation. It also needs adequate water and sewerage systems to protect public health, and street lighting, parks, and schools for training and social betterment. All these investments require large amounts of capital, yet they must be provided if the city is to fulfill its potential for economic development. This investment is desirable not only for the benefits that it gives in better living conditions and more efficient production in the city but also because it requires a great deal of unskilled labor, thus helping to ease the always heavy urban unemployment in developing countries. In addition, such public-works investment generally uses few imported materials and therefore puts less pressure on the balance of payments than most other types of investment.[5]

There is no organized capital market where domestic funds can be borrowed for long periods at low interest rates to meet these heavy capital requirements. At best, some improvements can be financed by borrowing from international lending agencies (such as the International Bank for Reconstruction and Development, the Agency for International Development, and the Inter-American Development Bank), but these agencies are usually reluctant to finance local currency costs of investment and, as already noted, import requirements for these urban investments are low. Some investment funds may be provided from central government subsidies, but these are likely to be inadequate, given the usual fiscal difficulties of the central government in a developing country. Nor can the city rely heavily on the ordinary local property tax, for property assessments are usually out of date and inequitable and the administration and collection mechanisms are weak, while legal mechanisms to enforce payment are lacking. Finally, the city cannot call on private enterprise to finance these investments through subdivision laws which require the urban developer to provide streets, water, sewerage systems, and so on at his own expense. Even if such subdivision laws exist (as they in fact do in Colombia), many people purchasing lots do not have the money to pay for complete public improvements; consequently, the subdivision law must permit new subdivisions lacking street pavement, complete water services, and sewerage connections if the people flocking to the cities are not to be forced into already overcrowded existing housing or else forced to set up shantytowns without any urban controls (or services) at all.

The same factors that lead to the financial difficulties of the rapidly

5. For a forceful exposition of the position that rapid urbanization should be promoted as a means of accelerating economic and social development, see Lauchlin Currie, *Accelerating Development: The Necessity and the Means* (New York: McGraw-Hill Book Company, 1966). Part II of this book applies these ideas to Colombia.

growing city in a developing country—the large influx of population and the rapid growth of modern industrial, commercial, and service sectors— also lead to a rapid rise in property values. This fact can be used to advantage to finance a major part of the needed municipal investment through a valorization tax on this increase in value.

The rapidly growing city in a developing country always has many potential projects with such a high social productivity that the benefits to site values from which the financing is supplied may in many cases greatly exceed the costs of the project itself. While in theory the tax can recover an amount equal to the entire increase in site values, in practice something less than this is attempted, given the desirability of securing payment of the tax before the investment is made and the uncertainties of estimating what the ultimate increases in site value will be. Even allowing an ample margin for error in estimating benefits, the tax can usually recover the investment and operating costs of the public agency without exceeding the realizable benefit to any individual landowner from the increased site value of his property. This presumption in the law—a major reason for the distrust of the textbook writers—has in fact worked out quite well in Colombia, for reasons discussed in more detail below.

A valorization tax may be contrasted with a traditional property tax assessed on site value and with a special capital gains tax on increases in site value. In theory a property tax assessed on site values can collect the entire net rent of the land and may be viewed as taking away from the landowner the net revenue from all unearned increments in the site value of his property. A capital gains tax on increments in site values can also recover the total increment in site value, although payment usually takes place only when the increment in value is realized by sale. The practical difficulties of taxing unrealized gains on an accrual basis are well known. Neither the site value tax nor the gains tax on increment in site value is designed to raise the revenues to provide the public investments that will lead to an increment in site value—although if a capital market existed, these taxes could be used to repay loans made to finance these public investments.

Another difference between site value taxation and valorization taxation is that, in theory, the valorization tax recovers only those benefits from direct public investment that enhance the value of land, while site value taxation also reaches increases in private site values that may arise in a large, heavily populated urban area from the external economies of face-to-face contact and of the mobilization of an efficient work force. Hence, in theory the present value of maximum valorization taxes in a growing city can never be as high as the present value of the maximum site value tax.

The valorization tax has the political advantage that it is clearly on a benefit basis. The taxpayer is making no sacrifice, for the value of his property will rise by at least the amount of the tax he must pay. This is an important consideration where political resistance to paying taxes is high, as it is in most developing countries. In practice, since the tax is paid before the investment takes place and before site values increase, the estimates of the increase in value must be sufficiently accurate or the upward trend of land values because of urban growth must be so rapid that the forecast of benefit exceeding tax will be true in almost all cases. In effect, the increment in site value from rapid urban growth and (assuming some money illusion) inflation provides a cushion in case the increment arising from the public investment alone turns out to be inferior to the valorization tax paid.

From urban land use and transportation theory, it may be predicted that a valorization tax, justified as it is on a benefit basis, will be successful only if the urban area is growing rapidly and if no drastic changes in transportation technology take place. The main use of valorization taxes has been to provide new or improved streets in urban areas, an investment needed to keep production costs low in urban areas with existing transportation technology, as noted earlier. Theoretical analyses of improved urban transportation providing more rapid access to the central business area show that ordinarily site values in the fringe areas of the city with improved transport will increase, and, *ceteris paribus,* site values in the central areas and other fringe areas will fall as a result.[6] If benefit taxation is to be successful, there *must* be an obvious connection between the cost and the benefits to the taxpayer. For this reason it should be difficult to use a valorization tax in a static or slow-growing city, since suburban and urban-fringe dwellers will not be convinced that the increases in their site values are coming from improved roads located far away in the older central portions of the city. If, however, increased transportation efficiency lowers production costs sufficiently in the city to attract new industry and economic activity to central areas at a rapid pace and if urban population increases rapidly, then urban land values in central areas will rise also and will not fall in fringe areas without improved transport. Thus, central city landowners will be willing to pay valorization taxes. The relationship between public investment and site values may be indirect, but the property owner will know from experience that better streets in front of his property or near it will increase the value of

6. See the different theoretical models in Lowdon Wingo, Jr., *Transportation and Urban Land* (Baltimore, Md.: The Johns Hopkins Press for Resources for the Future, Inc., 1961) ; and William Alonso, *Location and Land Use* (Cambridge, Mass.: Harvard University Press, 1964).

his land, and he will be willing to pay a valorization tax even though he cannot distinguish between the increases in site values resulting from particular public investments and those resulting from rapid urban growth in general.

The minor role played by valorization or special assessment taxes in the urban areas of developed countries and the consequent neglect of the tax in public-finance literature may thus be accounted for in part by the slower growth of cities in developed countries, with, consequently, less connection visible between public improvements and increases in site values. Other factors explaining the difference between the potential usefulness of the valorization tax in advanced and less developed countries are the existence of capital markets, so that public improvements may be easily financed and paid for out of regular revenues over time, and the existence of subdivision laws that force many public improvements to be made at private expense.

Rural Areas

Much the same favorable situation for valorization taxes may exist in the rural areas of developing countries. Large areas of rich land may be without any transportation but horses and mules, and construction of a road or railroad may have such dramatic effects on land values (by lowering transportation costs) that a large proportion of the cost of the new road or railroad can often be paid for through valorization taxes. In addition, projects to increase the value of agricultural land through dikes to prevent flooding or canals to provide drainage may have very high benefit-cost ratios in developing countries, so that financing them with valorization taxes may be feasible. In the United States, on the other hand, few if any areas still lack modern transportation and the benefit-cost ratios of land reclamation projects are notoriously low; consequently, the scope for valorization taxes in rural areas is much less.[7]

Investment and Saving

From the point of view of stimulating saving and investment, the valorization tax also seems desirable in developing countries. The proceeds

7. See Otto Eckstein, *Water Resource Development* (Cambridge, Mass.: Harvard University Press, 1958), for examples and an explanation of how benefit-cost ratios are inflated in the United States. The potential use of special assessments in the rural areas of developing countries is discussed briefly in Haskell P. Wald, *The Taxation of Agricultural Land in Underdeveloped Countries* (Cambridge, Mass.: Harvard University Press, 1959), pp. 221–223. His appraisal is overly negative because of the particular form of tax he assumes (cf. also the discussion of the CVC project in the text below).

of the tax are used almost exclusively for investment and the nature of the tax is such that if it is to be successfully used the investment must be highly productive and increase land values. In fact, the valorization tax may be considered a forced investment where the taxpayer benefits from the increased site value of his land resulting from the public improvement financed by the tax. Income distribution in developing countries is highly unequal, and much urban land is owned by the wealthy upper classes. While these groups could be major sources of saving, they often consume a surprisingly large fraction of their income.[8] Thus, the valorization tax often falls heavily on a group which has the potential to increase its savings considerably and might well do so to pay the tax, although this is also the group with best access to the credit markets so that they might instead borrow the existing savings of others.

Incentive Effects

The incentive effects of the valorization tax are also favorable to investment and development. As a tax on pure site values, the valorization tax does not penalize development of unimproved land, and in practice its use will also probably lessen reliance (currently or in the future) on the regular property tax, which does penalize such development.

The payment of the valorization tax itself is probably an even more important stimulant to investment, however, in practice and perhaps also in theory. It is often stated that in theory a tax on site values should have no incentive effects on land use since it does not affect the most profitable use of the land.[9] This statement, however, implicitly assumes that land is always an investment good. In fact, in developing countries much land is held idle not for speculative purposes, but to provide pleasure and prestige to its owners, so that it is in a real sense very often a consumer

8. See Nicholas Kaldor's comments on the savings habits of Chilean property owners in "Problemas Económicos de Chile," *El Trimestre Económico,* no. 102 (April–June 1959), p. 495. The extent of present income inequality in Colombia is indicated in Chapter 11 of the OAS and IDB, Joint Tax Program, *Fiscal Survey,* where it is claimed that 1% of the labor force received 12% of the income, while at the lower end of the income scale 65% received only 26% of the income (p. 224). The upper income class may be separated economically and psychologically into a new class of industrialists who often save a great deal of their income and a traditional class of landowners who save very little.

9. Among recent authors, Dick Netzer, *Economics of the Property Tax* (Washington, D.C.: The Brookings Institution, 1966), p. 205; and Daniel Holland, "The Taxation of Unimproved Value in Jamaica," in National Tax Association, *1965 Proceedings of the Fifty-Eighth Annual Conference on Taxation,* ed. Walter J. Kress (Harrisburg, Pa., 1966), p. 457, have accepted this argument.

good. Under regular site value taxation, the income effect (there is no sub-stitution effect) of site value taxation can be expected to lower consumption (since land is probably not an inferior good); land formerly used for consumption purposes may be put to productive use as a result of the tax. For the valorization tax the analysis is different, since payment of the tax is matched by an increase in the site value of the land. The improvements financed by valorization taxes increase the value of the land for productive purposes, not for prestige consumption, however, and as a result the valorization tax and public investment combined increase the opportunity cost of using land for consumption purposes, and the substitution effect in this case tends to more productive use of the land.[10]

In practice, the effect of site value taxes in forcing more intensive land use may depend most on the lack of liquidity and capital markets facing many landowners and on the common failure of landowners to calculate carefully the most profitable use of their land.[11] Owners may underutilize land when not faced with cash payments, but when the valorization tax must be paid, they may either realize the opportunity cost of holding the land idle and hence put it to more profitable use, or they may have to sell it to someone else who will do so. Since the valorization tax is a relatively large tax assessed over a short period of time, its effect in forcing better land use through the liquidity and attention-to-use effects should be stronger than a regular site value tax, where the rate may be too low to threaten the liquidity or arouse the interest in land use of any but the largest landowners.

A factor as important in the underuse of land in developing countries as the existence of large estates held for prestige purposes may be the large amount of land held by absentee owners, usually professional and commercial people from the cities, who cannot find good farm managers and who do not themselves have time to provide good management.[12] The analysis is the same as in the prestige case: under pure site value taxation the income effect might be expected to lead to greater owner work effort, probably in managing his land, while under the valorization tax the owner must supply greater effort and develop his land if he is to realize in cash the greater gross income it can now provide,

10. The argument assumes that there is no "Veblen effect"; that is, it is not considered *more* prestigious to hold out of use land whose productive value has risen. Also, if the benefit exceeds the tax, the income effect will tend to increase all consumption, including that of land used for prestige purposes.

11. These factors are well discussed in Holland, "Taxation in Jamaica," pp. 457–460.

12. This point is made in a number of mimeographed reports on Colombia available from the Land Tenure Center of the University of Wisconsin.

or else sell the land to someone who will develop it.[13] He also has the option, of course, of reducing expenditures from other income in order to pay the tax (see above). If the property is in fact sold as a result of the tax, the net effect on saving depends in part on the disposition of the sales proceeds by the former owner.

Administration

From an administrative point of view the valorization tax may seem attractive to developing countries, for land cannot easily be hidden from taxation (though landowners can—an important factor in countries with the Latin tradition of *in personam* taxes). The tax is collected in large sums from a relatively small number of taxpayers, which makes enforcement easier even though it may make compliance more difficult. The crucial factor in administration is that the tax and the public improvements go hand in hand. If poor administration leads to badly planned or executed projects, projects which are not executed promptly, or poor allocation of taxes among landowners, and if, as a consequence, a significant number of taxpayers find that the tax they have paid is more than the increase in the value of their property, the tax may easily be discredited and appear to be only an arbitrary and capricious capital levy.

Summary

In summary, the valorization tax in theory seems an attractive one for developing countries. It is suitable only for financing public investments that will be demonstrably productive. It has a clear benefit justification to help muster political support for the tax. Its effects on saving should be at least neutral and may be positive. Its incentive effects should be favorable. It should be relatively easy to collect. But it will require skilled administration if it is to work in practice as the theory indicates, and skilled people are often the scarcest resources in developing countries. That this administration is not beyond the reach of an underdeveloped country is demonstrated by Colombian experience; whether it is the best use of these resources is another question.

13. The effect of valorization taxes on the *amount* of land held for speculative purposes is uncertain: if the increase in land values due to the public improvements leads speculators to believe that the land has matured and is ready for development, the amount of land held for speculation might fall; if, on the other hand, they believe that the improvements make the land more attractive for future development, the amount held for speculative purposes might increase. This question is not further discussed in the present chapter.

The Valorization Tax in Colombia [14]

History and Development

While the antecedents of the valorization tax go back to 1887, when the first law authorizing taxation of those benefited to pay for public works was passed,[15] it is only in the last twenty-five years that the valorization tax has become of practical importance in Colombia.

The first laws in 1887 and 1921 authorized valorization only for flood control and land reclamation projects. The tax could cover only the cost of the public investment, and it was to be assessed on the basis of appraised land values. These laws were poorly drafted and little used. In 1936 the law was extended to cover municipal improvements in Bogotá. Two years later all major cities were authorized to carry out public works and to impose the valorization tax. The laws required land valuations before and after the investment to determine the benefits and again limited the tax to the cost of the public investment. It was at this time that the first valorization activities were undertaken in Bogotá. The law was still both too vague and too restrictive for wide application, however, and it was not until 1943 that the valorization tax was established in the form in which it is found today in Colombian municipalities.

Law 1 of 1943 allowed all municipalities to charge a valorization tax on all public improvements, whether financed by the municipality, department, national government, or other public agency, up to the total amount of the benefit received, without reference to the cost of the public improvements. This law also left it open to the municipality to determine the methods by which the benefit in increased land values to the property

14. This part of the chapter is based on personal interviews with, among others, Dr. Carlos Cardona H., director of valorization in Bogotá; Dr. Guillermo Martinez and Dr. Juan Velez U., director and financial chief, respectively, of the valorization department in Medellín; Dr. Jorge Restrepo U., director of valorization in Medellín, 1945–1949, and former mayor of Medellín; and Dr. Alvaro Restrepo T. of the private consulting firm Valorización y Asesorias, Ltda. in Medellín. We are most grateful to all these gentlemen for their assistance. In addition, for legal and other background information we have relied on Alberto Fernandez C., *El Impuesto de Valorización en Colombia* (Medellín: Tip. Bedout, 1948); and Rafael Mora R., *Régimen de Valorización Municipal y Renovación Urbana* (Bogotá: Editorial ABC, 1966); as well as on various documents supplied by the valorization offices in Medellín and Bogotá and by Valorización y Asesorias, Ltda. These offices have also provided many of the figures used in this section. A pamphlet by Dr. Jorge Restrepo U., *El Impuesto de Valorización en Medellín* (Medellín, 1957), has also been useful.

15. This law and the others found in the following section are cited in Harvard Law School International Program in Taxation, *Taxation in Colombia*, p. 135, note 36.

owner would be determined; gave municipalities almost complete freedom to establish the organization and methods for administering the
valorization tax; made it clear that any public improvement which increased land values could be covered by the valorization tax; and gave
the municipalities clear rights to collect the tax, providing the sanctions
of embargo and seizure of property if the tax were not paid. A year later
the Council of State ruled that municipalities had the right to assess and
collect the valorization tax as soon as the plans and budget for a project
had been prepared and approved and before actual work had begun on
the improvements. An additional section in the 1943 law stated that the
municipalities must give the property owners taxed the right to be consulted in the formation and execution of the project and in the determination of the way in which the valorization tax was to be distributed.

It is on the basis of this broadly drawn law, which provides almost
complete autonomy to the municipalities, that the modern valorization tax
has been developed in Colombian cities. The primary check on abuse of
the municipal valorization tax is provided by the ability of local citizens
to put effective pressure on the city government and the valorization
agency rather than by legal safeguards against abuse written into the law.

While the laws for municipal valorization give great freedom of action
to municipalities, the laws for flood control, drainage, and irrigation and
other projects executed by the departments, the nation, or regional development authorities remained quite restrictive until June 1966. By law
the valorization tax in these cases could not be assessed and collected until
after the public work was completed. The total tax was limited to the
cost of the investment plus at most 33 percent of the difference between
the total benefit to land values and the investment cost. The tax had to
be in proportion to the benefits, as calculated by special valuations of
the properties before and after the work was done. In June 1966 a new
law gave national and departmental valorization authorities the same
freedom of action enjoyed by municipalities.[16]

In Colombia the valorization tax has been of most importance in the
cities. Medellín pioneered the modern use of the tax, and most of the
other major cities in Colombia have valorization programs. The major use
of valorization in cities has been in the construction of new streets or

16. The law and its regulatory decree were drafted for the government by
private consultants from Medellín and closely followed current practice in that
city. The law explicitly allows for valorization financing of only part of a project
if total benefits to property owners are less than costs. Although several departments
have announced highway valorization projects under the new law, there is no
practical experience as yet with the law, and we do not discuss it further in this
chapter.

widening of existing ones to form a network of main arterial roads. In connection with these programs, paving, sewers, street lighting, tree planting, roadside parks, and stream control projects have also been included. Attempts to construct schools and parks by valorization have not been successful because land values could not be reliably predicted to rise enough after the projects were completed to cover the costs of the programs. Some valorization agencies have had to drop these programs.[17] Recently, some agencies have been authorized to undertake urban renewal projects, but the first projects are only now being started, so there is as yet no basis for judging the feasibility of conducting urban renewal by this procedure.

In the rural areas valorization was first used for swamp drainage projects and continues to be used for water projects and highways by departments and regional agencies. A recent project financed by valorization was the construction of dikes to protect lowlands near Cali from floods by the CVC (Cauca Valley Corporation), a regional power and water agency modeled on the TVA. Although in the end fruitlessly, serious consideration was also given to financing part of the Magdalena Valley railroad by valorization, and the use of valorization to finance new intercity highways was the main reason for the enactment of the new national valorization law.

Revenue Importance

Considered in relation to other sources of taxation in Colombia, the valorization tax is a very minor tax. In 1963, the latest year for which data are available, the yield of municipal valorization taxes in Colombia was only 81.4 million pesos, or slightly less than 2 percent of all tax revenues, which in turn were about 10 percent of the gross national

17. This experience provides an interesting contrast to that in Minneapolis, where it has been said that "neighborhood assessments" work well for parks and playgrounds but very poorly for roads. The reason given is that "people seem willing enough to pay their share of improvements that will make their neighborhood a pleasanter place to live in, but balk at paying for improvements that will mostly make it easier for people from elsewhere to drive by."—"Are property taxes obsolete?" *Nation's Cities,* 3, no. 3 (March 1965) : 29. This statement ties in very well with what was said earlier about the need for rapid city growth if road works are to be successfully financed on a valorization basis. It also demonstrates that parks and playgrounds are basically a consumption expenditure in Minneapolis and could probably be better financed on a straight user-charge basis, except insofar as the provision of such amenities is a part of redistributive policy. Incidentally, the municipal planning office in Medellín recently proposed that a city park system be developed with valorization financing.

Table 10.1—Use of Municipal Valorization Taxes, by Department, 1963 [a]

Department	Valorization tax [b]	Implicit mill rate [c]	Percentage of municipal taxes	Percentage of municipal current revenues
Antioquia [d]	32.9	3.7	29.7	9.9
Atlántico [e]	7.5	3.9	27.0	13.2
Bolivar	0.2	...	1.8	0.4
Boyacá	0.1	...	1.1	0.5
Caldas	2.0	0.4	5.9	2.6
Cauca	...	...	...	...
Córdoba	0.1	...	1.5	0.8
Cundinamarca	0.3	...	1.8	0.7
Chocó	...	...	...	...
Distrito Especial [f]	28.5	2.5	21.1	6.1
Huila	0.4	0.4	6.4	3.0
Magdalena	0.8	0.4	9.5	5.4
Meta	...	...	...	...
Nariño	0.3	0.2	6.7	3.6
Norte de Santander	1.4	1.2	12.5	5.4
Santander	3.7	1.6	18.2	10.4
Tolima	0.7	0.3	4.7	2.7
Valle [g]	2.5	0.3	4.6	1.4
Colombia as a whole	81.4	1.5	17.0	5.9

[a] The dotted lines in this table indicate negligible data.

[b] The figures in this column are in terms of millions of pesos.

[c] These rates are based on the total assessed property value, including property exempt under the property tax, some of which is taxable under the valorization tax. These mill rates in relation to assessed values are therefore on the low side.

[d] Contains Medellín.

[e] Contains Barranquilla.

[f] Contains Bogotá.

[g] Contains Cali.

Source: Unpublished data from Banco de la República, Instituto Geográfico "Agustín Codazzi," Departamento de Planeación Departamental (Antioquia), and Departamento de Planificación Distrital (Distrito Especial).

product.[18] Related to total assessed property values, the rate of the tax was only 1.5 mills per peso of assessed valuation. (See Table 10.1.) Since assessments on an average are something like 50 percent of market value, the true rate is about half this. Table 10.2 shows valorization taxes for all Colombian municipalities in 1959–1963 in relation to property

18. The Colombian peso was worth 5.7 and 7.4 U.S. cents at the most important exchange rates in 1966. Its value had dropped from about 15 cents in 1960 and 25 cents in 1955.

taxes, total taxes, and total current revenues. During this period valorization tax collections were from 22 to 67 percent as large as property tax collections, and the tax provided from 12 to 23 percent of total municipal tax revenues. For the three years 1956–1958 statistics are available only for the twenty-four largest municipalities in Colombia. During this period valorization tax collections were about 50 percent of their property tax collections and provided about 20 percent of their total tax collections.

Table 10.2—Importance of Municipal Valorization Tax, 1959–1963 [a]

Year	Valoriza-tion tax [b]	Percentage of property tax	Percentage of municipal taxes	Percentage of municipal current revenues	Implicit mill rate [c]
1959	75.7	66.8	23.2	10.4	2.5
1960	44.5	35.0	15.0	5.7	1.3
1961	38.9	22.0	12.3	4.4	1.0
1962	49.7	29.0	12.9	4.8	1.0
1963	81.4	40.3	17.0	5.9	1.5
Average, 1959–1963	. . .	38.6	16.1	6.2	1.5

[a] The department of Chocó is excluded.

[b] The figures in this column are in terms of millions of pesos.

[c] See Table 10.1, note c.

Source: Unpublished data from Banco de la República, Instituto Geográfico "Agustín Codazzi," Departamento de Planeación Departamental (Antioquia), and Departamento de Planificación Distrital (Distrito Especial).

These aggregate figures are somewhat misleading, however, in view of the wide variation in the degree to which the tax is used. A better idea of the importance of the valorization tax to large cities may be obtained from the data for Medellín, Bogotá, and Cali. In Medellín, the city which pioneered widespread use of the valorization tax in Colombia, the valorization organization has regularly budgeted income about equal to the total regular income of the city government (the public utility enterprises are not included in this comparison) as shown in Table 10.3. In recent years, however, the valorization organization has only raised and spent about half of the amount budgeted, while general fund income has been close to the budgeted levels. Although the 1966 budget is 67.7 million pesos, in May 1966 we were informed that the estimate of income for the year had been reduced to 52 million pesos. The valorization department plans to make future budgets more realistic. It is not known if the budget shortfalls were this large before 1956. In any event, the valorization tax has supplied from around one-third to perhaps one-half

Table 10.3—Medellín: The Importance of Valorization Taxes, 1956–1966 [a]

Year	Valorization investment expenditure	Valorization operating expenses	Valorization taxes and other current income	Implicit mill rate (taxable property)	Total income	Total budgeted income	Total budgeted income Medellín general fund
1956	...	...	8.9	(6.5)	18.4	20.0	20.1
1957	...	...	16.0	(10.0)	18.0	24.9	24.8
1958	...	...	17.2	(9.8)	19.6	24.7	27.8
1959	...	...	...	....	...	28.9	36.2
1960	19.4	1.6	19.7	(6.7)	19.7	38.4	36.2
1961	14.5	1.8	19.5	(6.7)	19.7	37.3	42.1
1962	16.8	2.7	16.5	(4.9)	19.9	50.1	50.0
1963	55.6	4.2	36.7	(9.5)	52.6	87.1	66.9
1964	51.7	5.1	54.7	(11.8)	59.6	88.4	82.1
1965	24.9	7.1	36.9	(6.8)	44.5	88.1	96.6
1966	...	...	50.0 [b]	(8.0) [b]	52.0 [b]	67.7	...

[a] The figures in this table are in terms of millions of pesos. The dotted lines indicate data not available.

[b] Projected.

Source: Unpublished data in Departamento de Valorización and Departamento de Catastro, Medellín; Jorge Restrepo U., *El Impuesto de Valorización en Medellín* (Medellín, 1957).

of the total income of the city of Medellín and a rather higher percentage of the total tax revenues of the city. In Medellín the average mill rate for the regular property tax in the last ten years is slightly less than six mills; the valorization tax, with its average implicit mill rate of 8.0 for the last ten years, is therefore actually a larger source of revenue than the property tax.[19]

Bogotá has been the next heaviest user of the valorization tax, as shown in Table 10.4. The implicit mill rate of the valorization tax in Bogotá has been, however, only about one-third to one-half of that in Medellín. In Cali, the third largest city, with a population about equal to Medellín's, the valorization tax has been weak. In 1963 the yield of the valorization tax in Cali was only 2.0 million pesos. This was less than 7 percent of total municipal tax revenue and represented an implicit rate of less than one mill on taxable assessed valuation.

19. Properties under 10,000 pesos are exempted from the property tax, but not from the valorization tax. The implicit mill rate for the valorization tax on the broader base is about 7.5 mills. (See also Table 10.1, note c.)

Table 10.4—Bogotá: The Importance of Valorization Taxes, 1959–1965 [a]

Year	Valorization tax [b]	Percentage of property tax	Percentage of all taxes	Implicit mill rate
1959	21,585 [c]	69.5	...	3.2
1960	15,304	37.4	21.0	2.5
1961	17,906	44.0	25.3	2.4
1962	16,379	28.6	14.3	2.0
1963	33,562	54.2	24.8	3.7
1964	22,122	...	...	2.1
1965	21,793	...	...	...

[a] The dotted lines in this table represent data not available.

[b] Figures in this column are in terms of thousands of pesos.

[c] National statistics show valorization taxes of 39.2 million in 1959 for Bogotá. No explanation of the discrepancy is available.

Source: Unpublished data from Departamento de Valorización, Bogotá; Instituto Geográfico "Agustín Codazzi"; and Departamento de Planificación Distrital (Distrito Especial).

It is possible to test crudely whether the valorization tax tends to substitute for other taxes in Colombia or to be a net addition to municipal revenues. Table 10.5 contains per capita revenue data for the three cities, which tend to indicate that the valorization tax may add to total tax revenues, rather than substituting for other taxes.

Table 10.5—Municipal Tax Revenues Per Capita, 1963 [a]

	Medellín	Bogotá	Cali
Valorization tax	54	22	3
Property tax	42	40	28
Total taxes	115	88	50
Taxable real property (assessed values)	5,750	5,950	4,230

[a] The figures in this table are in terms of pesos.

Source: See Tables 10.1, 10.3, and 10.4; Departamento Administrativo Nacional de Estadística, *Anuario Estadístico de Medellín, 1963* and *Cali en Cifras* (Bogotá, 1965).

Valorization in Medellín [20]

The administration of the valorization tax is most highly developed in Medellín, which will therefore be taken as a basis for describing

20. Medellín is the capital of the department of Antioquia, whose citizens are widely known as energetic businessmen. See Everett Hagen, *On the Theory of Social Change* (Homewood, Ill.: The Dorsey Press, 1962), chap. 15, for an account of Antioquia and the Antioqueños.

Colombian practice. Brief comparisons will then be made with the operation in Bogotá and other cities.

Medellín is a city of seven hundred thousand persons, located on both
sides of a river in a narrow valley. It is a manufacturing city, diversifying
from a base of textile industries. Because of growth, the urban area now
spreads into four or five other municipalities in the valley and all the
familiar problems from fragmented jurisdiction are beginning to arise.
Medellín has not yet solved them, but through the semiautonomous
Institute for the Development of Antioquia, attempts to form municipal
compacts and joint organizations are underway.

The valorization department of Medellín is independent of the municipal government in most respects. It is controlled by a nine-man board
composed of city officials, city council members, and two private citizens.
The department itself has about one hundred fifty employees. All projects
are originated by the department staff, which prepares preliminary reports on all aspects of a project and recommends it to the board for
approval. Under Colombian law, all large cities must have city plans, and
while some do not comply, Medellín has had a long-range plan since
1948. All valorization projects are selected and planned in accordance
with the city plan and with the advice of the city's planning department.
The major and most visible achievement of the valorization department
has been to construct a network of broad streets and boulevards throughout the city. In conjunction with the boulevards, sewers, street lighting,
and landscaping have also been provided.

Since the projects must increase land values by at least the amount of
the tax if the valorization plan is to be successful and enjoy continued
support, careful attention is given from the beginning to this aspect. Thus,
benefit-cost analysis is an integral part of planning all projects. There is
a tendency to make projects large, so that sections can be included in the
project which would not be justified by themselves, but which can be
covered by other parts of the project that are more attractive. For example, parks, as noted above, can only be included as a part of major
street development projects.

After the board has given preliminary approval to a project, the department prepares a detailed plan. Since the residents of the area involved
must be included in the planning and execution of the project by law,
the board calls an election for them to choose a representative. No quorum
is required for the election. If no one is elected, the board appoints a
representative. If the elected representative fails to act on any matter,
the board can go ahead and make decisions without him. This representative has the right to appoint an expert to intervene in all technical questions of the project, particularly the assigning of the tax among property

owners. If a disagreement arises between the property owners' expert and the department, it must be settled within less than thirty days or the board has the right to make a final decision, which cannot be appealed. In effect, the property owners' representative has only the weapon of the voice of reason or politics in influencing the development of the valorization project.

The procedures for determining the area of benefit and assigning the valorization tax are aimed at finding formulas that will seem fair to the taxpayers, rather than "scientific formulas." The most important considerations in determining the area of benefit are that it seem reasonable to most people and that it be large enough so that the tax on properties at the edge of the area will be low and so the marginal taxpaper will not get angry because his neighbor next door or across the street is not in the benefit area and does not have to pay any tax; yet the area must not be so large that the taxpayer feels he gets no benefit from the distant public improvement. Once the area of benefit is determined, several methods may be used to assign relative taxes. One formerly used, and perhaps used still, is to prepare a number of maps of the area and assign an arbitrary number to the value increment per unit area in the point of highest benefit and a similar index at the lowest point. A number of other points are marked on the map, and perhaps half a dozen persons who are familiar with property values in the city are asked independently to assign relative numbers to the other points on the map on a scale between the two arbitrary values. When all have done so, they get together, examine their results, and work out a final set of arbitrary value increment numbers. By interpolation and extrapolation from these numbers, each property is assigned a value increment number which is then multiplied by the area of the property to obtain its "equivalent area." No attention is paid to buildings or improvements in carrying out these calculations.

At other times, a distinction is apparently made between the "zone of direct benefit" and the "zone of reflected benefit," and an attempt is made to allocate the cost between the two zones first, before assigning the tax to each property. When the public improvement is a road, the benefit may be assumed to be constant along a line parallel to the road, with some modifications. For such simple improvements as paving existing streets, the cost is often assigned on a frontage basis alone. Valorization officials admit that public improvements may lower site values for some properties near the improvement (for example, commercial properties on side streets when a main street is improved), and occasionally they must adjust the tax downward to reflect this when complaints come in from property owners. In general, however, the Medellín valorization officials state that there is such a large backlog of needed public improvements and property

owners are sufficiently anxious to have them built because they believe
they will increase property values, that taxpayer protests are minor and
have no limiting effect on the volume of valorization projects undertaken. The officials feel they must be careful in their approach and flexible
in their methods when assigning valorization taxes, but that all property
owners will be willing to pay at least a small tax to obtain the improvement.

Although the city regulation permits a tax of up to 75 percent of the
total increase in land values, in practice the total tax is set equal to
project cost (including 10 percent for contingencies) plus 20 percent for
administrative costs.[21] Property used for religious purposes is exempt from
the tax. The departmental government pays valorization tax on its
property. By law, the municipality is also supposed to pay on its property,
but in fact the transfer is really the other way as the valorization department pays 1.5 percent of its budget to the municipal government for
compensation of taxes on properties it has acquired and for municipal
services. Other public properties are generally exempted and, if the project
warrants it, the entire cost may be placed on the nonexempt properties.
When the total amount of tax to be collected is determined, it is divided
by the total "equivalent area" of all properties to obtain the tax rate per
unit of "equivalent area," and the tax bills are prepared.

When the project receives final approval from the board, the terms for
payment of the tax are also set. The board may allow up to one hundred
months to pay and may set down-payment requirements as it wishes, in
accordance with its opinion on the ability to pay of the people in the
area. Areas with poorer property owners get a longer period to pay. Interest of 8 percent per year is charged on unpaid balances, and the taxpayer, if he wishes, may pay the entire amount at once, with a discount
of 3 percent for each year paid in advance. Since interest rates in private
markets start at about 12 percent and go on up in Colombia, there is
little incentive for advance payment. A typical payment requirement is
20 percent down and two years to pay the remainder. If the taxpayer is
short of cash, he may arrange to pay his tax in whole or in part in land,
although this is seldom done. Taxpayers who can prove financial strin-
gency may make special payment arrangements with the board at its
discretion. Flexibility is the essence of the whole payment system in

21. As seen in Table 10.3, operating expenses (not including interest payments
on loans) in Medellín have been over 12% of current income in recent years. Much
of operating expense is design and engineering expenses for projects, so administrative expenses for the valorization tax itself are much less than 12%. However, administration costs for local taxes in Colombia are high ; for example, the operating
expense of the cadastral office in Medellín is 6% of property tax collections.

Medellín. All payments go into the rotating fund of the valorization department, and construction of the project must start within two years of the final approval of the project or payments are refundable. This valorization fund is completely separate from the general fund of the municipality.

To provide working capital the valorization department can issue bonds or borrow money from private banks; at the end of 1965 its debt was 27 million pesos. At that time its cash on hand was less than 0.2 million pesos. The department planned to issue 34 million pesos in bonds in 1966. Since these bonds sell at a discount of 10 percent, pay interest of 9 percent on the face value, and are exempt from all taxes, they are occasionally purchased by well-off people who cannot otherwise hide their income from the tax authorities. They are also purchased by insurance companies in order to satisfy legal obligations on their portfolio composition. But, in general, the valorization bonds will be bought only by those who expect to have to pay the valorization tax in the near future, since one year after purchase up to 50 percent of the valorization tax obligation may be met by bonds at their face value.

While in the short run the scale of operations of valorization is limited by the lack of working capital, the more important limits seem to be set by the amount of tax which the board estimates can be collected in a year without overstraining the finances of the taxpayers (or arousing strong opposition from them) and by the quantity of projects which the department staff can successfully prepare and administer in a timely fashion. The department staff state they would like to expand their operations somewhat, but that major increase would be undesirable. It is not clear what (in their opinion) the major limiting factor is.

In addition to its regular program, the valorization department administers two other funds. One is a newly established program to provide light, water, sewers, paving, and so on to poor neighborhoods. (Under Medellín's subdivision law, the poorest new developments need not have paved streets and only a communal water supply need be provided.) The beneficiaries of these works will repay the department over a ten-year period. The working capital will consist of twelve million pesos from municipal sources. The 1966 income was budgeted at two million pesos for this fund. The third fund, for urban renewal, was not operational then, although the department had hopes of selling twenty-five million pesos of bonds to finance its working capital in 1966.

While the principle of valorization taxes is well established in Medellín, the administrators seem very sensitive to public attitudes toward the tax and are careful to maintain public support. In 1966 a major project in downtown Medellín was to tear down a number of buildings and build a wide boulevard. Because the project aroused some criticism from influential citizens, the board was proceeding extra carefully in selecting its new projects in order to avoid losing any further support for its program.

Partly because of the high value put on voluntary taxpayer cooperation and the flexible way in which payment periods may be fixed, relatively few taxes are collected by coercive action. Less than 1 percent of the accounts are passed to the enforcement section of the municipal treasury for action, and almost all of these settle before formal action is taken, usually by making informal arrangements to pay over the rent of the property until the tax debt is satisfied. In 1965 perhaps 15 properties (out of 18,000 affected) were sold at auction as the ultimate sanction.

The success of valorization taxation in Medellín seems to depend on a law free from procedural roadblocks, a competent permanent staff, and an administration which is sensitive to popular attitudes toward the projects it undertakes. A major fight was necessary to establish the valorization tax in Medellín against the opposition of large landowners who wanted to avoid paying for the public improvements benefiting their land,[22] but when valorization proved able to provide a much larger number of well-planned and executed projects than had been possible previously, this opposition largely ended. The administrators in Medellín emphasize the importance of carefully building up the valorization program over time, starting with small works that can be completed on time and as promised and avoiding any dishonesty or financial mismanagement in the program.[23]

Valorization in Bogotá

The other city in Colombia where the valorization tax is used extensively is Bogotá, the national capital of some 1.8 million population. In addition to being the financial and governmental center of Colombia, Bogotá is also the largest manufacturing center. The city is governed as

22. We were told that one leading citizen (and landowner) even wrote a book against valorization called *The Robber Municipality* (*El Municipio Ladrón*). Valorization officials claim he died a very rich man from the increases in his property values brought about by valorization projects.

23. The failure of valorization programs in London in the late 19th century, for example, appears to have been due mainly to poor management rather than to any basic defect of the program or to the less favorable conditions for valorization in developed countries cited earlier. Ralph Turvey, *The Economics of Real Property* (London: George Allen and Unwin, 1957), chap. 9, notes that the Municipal Board of Works, which handled valorization in London, was popularly known as the "Municipal Board of Perks."

part of a special district, which covers a large enough area so that problems of overlapping jurisdiction in the metropolitan area are only now arising and are still very minor. The valorization department was established in 1959 (replacing a valorization office established in 1944) and with one hundred fifty employees is the same size as that in Medellín. Valorization in Bogotá is devoted mainly to construction of the "Plan Vial," a long-range plan to provide the entire metropolitan area with boulevards and highways. The valorization department also opens up many short new streets to rationalize the street pattern left by private developers, and a separate fund is used to pave existing streets in the poorer neighborhoods. A fund for urban renewal is only now being implemented.[24]

Valorization in Bogotá is similar in many respects to Medellín in its organization, but the requirement that the city council approve all projects is an added hindrance. In fixing zones of influence and coefficients to be applied to properties in the zone, Bogotá takes on the whole the same pragmatic approach as Medellín, although the use of zones of equal value parallel to new highways seems to be more popular than in Medellín. The total tax is determined as the cost of public works plus 20 percent for administration.

Like all valorization offices, Bogotá has faced difficulties in raising working capital, and its rotating fund has issued valorization bonds, of which twenty-four million pesos were outstanding in December 1965; in addition, bank loans of nine million pesos had been obtained. All payments of valorization taxes *must* be made in valorization bonds, which are sold at a stabilized price of 91 percent of face value. The bonds are received in payment of the tax at 110 percent of face value during the first three months after the tax is payable, at par for the next three months, and thereafter at the market value. The taxpayer has the option of paying the tax in installments if he so requests. Taxpayers with income of less than fifty thousand pesos are allowed by law from six months to five years to pay the tax, depending on the size of the tax assessed compared with their income, while higher income taxpayers receive from six months to twenty months to pay.

In Bogotá the valorization department has attempted to secure payment from the city for municipal property, but has been unsuccessful; in 1966 the city owed the valorization fund forty million pesos for valorization work and failure to pay has severely hampered the operations of the

24. The law establishing this fund has an interesting provision for "voluntary renewal," according to which the owners of 70% of an area may get the city to expropriate the rest of the area in order to combine large properties for approved urban development projects. This power is now undergoing its first test in Bogotá.

valorization department. Construction of the city's only limited access expressway by valorization was held up for several years because the neighboring Hotel Tequendama, owned by the Military Retirement Fund, was exempt from the tax and the valorization department lacked alternate sources of revenue to finance the expressway. The department does receive one-half of one mill of the property tax collections, however, in contrast to Medellín. In addition, the department has decided that some costly works, such as expressway interchanges, cannot be charged to the neighboring properties and must be financed from general funds. It is argued that taxpayers cannot bear the burden of constructing major portions of the road system all at once, so that the interchange costs might successfully be spread over a large number of taxpayers, and that when the system is constructed a small section at a time, a limited number of taxpayers cannot absorb the tax. Apparently, the department is afraid that it cannot declare a very wide zone of benefit for expressway interchanges to cover their costs by valorization because taxpayers would protest at an apparent lack of benefit to them from some works.

The valorization office reports no difficulties in enforcing payment. If the tax is not paid, the office has the right to seize the property and collect rents until the tax is paid or to sell it. Many properties are apparently embargoed but fewer (one or two a year) are sold than in Medellín. The department has its own judge to handle seizures to enforce payment, and, since the volume of taxpayers is small enough, enforcement is prompt and effective, although more formal than in Medellín, in part perhaps because of the greater impersonality of large metropolitan areas. The city has four tax judges for general enforcement purposes, but they cannot keep up with a workload covering all city taxes, with the result that property tax collections in particular lag badly.

The major limitation on the volume of valorization work in Bogotá is lack of working capital, caused in part by the failure of the city to contribute its full share to the valorization fund, but also by past difficulties in managing the valorization bonds, which weakened the financial strength of the fund.

The separate fund for paving streets in Bogotá requires that local "community action" councils in the neighborhood pay 30 percent of the cost of the paving job before the pavement work is started. The other 70 percent of the cost will be paid by the city (except in the case of bus routes in poor areas, where the city bears the whole cost). This work is supported by an annual grant from the city government. The local councils use their own private methods to get all householders on the street to be paved to pay their share of the 30 percent down payment. This program is paving streets in short stretches, with little plan or reason. When paved, the job is guaranteed against failure for four years by the contractor, and the local public works department is responsible for maintenance for the next six years. Only after ten years can valorization be used to repave streets.[25]

Other Colombian Experience with Valorization

We were not able to investigate the operation of the valorization tax in Cali, the third largest city in Colombia, where it has been much less successful. The following reasons have been offered by various sources for the lower level of valorization activity in Cali: First, the valorization rotating fund has been unable to obtain working capital to finance its operations, which is attributed in part to the fact that a fully independent valorization department with a competent staff has never been established in Cali. This in turn is ascribed to the fact that the owners of large amounts of vacant land on the edges of Cali are unwilling to pay valorization taxes for the new roads needed to open up their land and have had the political power to prevent establishment of a strong valorization program in Cali. They apparently expect these improvements to be financed from general funds, even if it means a much lower rate of construction.

Although the municipality of Cali has had little success in financing capital improvements by special charges, the independent municipal-utility enterprise has done much better, partly because of its operating success and consequent ability to obtain initial financing from the international lending agencies.[26] Given some initial funding, the municipal utilities have found it quite feasible to recoup capital costs along with consumption charges on a user-charge basis. In fact, the initiative for requesting the extension of water or power lines has been, in large part, left to the inhabitants of the areas affected, who must get together (under the auspices of the community action groups mentioned earlier) and agree on a financing plan acceptable to the enterprise. Piecemeal provision of services has been avoided, it is claimed, by acceding to the requests of different neighborhoods—all of which are said to want services—only in accordance with the general development plan for the service. The only sanction possible under this system is to cut off the service once the work

25. The Harvard Law School International Program in Taxation, *Taxation in Colombia,* p. 135, states that valorization taxes are paid more or less continuously in Colombia for what would usually be considered to be municipal maintenance expenditures. We have found no real evidence for this statement. (See, however, the discussion on Mexico City below for some evidence of such practices.)

26. This information is largely based on an interview with Hernán Borrero, manager of municipal enterprises of Cali. The scope of the Cali enterprise is similar to that in Medellín, covering water and sewerage, electricity, and telephone. It is not known whether the enterprises in Medellín and Bogotá (where there are four separate enterprises) follow the same financing system as that outlined in the text.

has been done, but there are said to be very few problems since the idea of purchasing water or electricity service on the installment plan is now well understood and accepted. Only community services are charged for on this scheme; thus, water pipes more than twelve inches in diameter, electricity substations, and the like are charged to the general funding of the enterprise. The Cali municipal enterprise also makes some use of the municipal valorization office by, for example, financing a major extension of the water network in 1966; but the manager feels unable to do so on a wider scale both because of the present weakness of the office and because of the confused land title situation in many of the poorer areas of the city. The financing system actually employed is in many ways an acceptable substitute for valorization and could perhaps be more widely used in connection with the "workers' subdivisions" mentioned earlier in which the urban developer is not at present required to provide most urban services.[27]

The valorization program has also been rather small scale in Barranquilla, Colombia's fourth largest city, according to a recent report by Lauchlin Currie and Associates.[28] Revenues from valorization in 1964 amounted to about 3.3 million pesos, an implicit rate on the property tax base of less than 1.6 mills. The Currie report attributes the low level of valorization activity in Barranquilla to lack of working capital and to continuous political interference. The valorization board lacks independence, and taxpayers can petition the city council for exemption from the tax, petitions which are apparently frequently granted. (If true, this is a violation of a national law stating that exemptions for private citizens can only be granted to properties which are the owner's sole asset and valued, *after* the assumed increase in benefits, at less than thirty thousand pesos.) Dilatory court procedures are also used to delay or evade payment of the tax.[29] Currie recommends that the valorization program be made a part of the autonomous public utility enterprise of Barranquilla in order to reduce the present political interference in the program.[30]

27. A recent analysis of pricing for electric utilities in Colombia by Ralph Hofmeister of the University of Minnesota points out that the costs of local distribution systems for utilities are joint costs that cannot be assigned to individual users, and that the local distribution system is best considered a "Samuelsonian" public good whose costs should be covered by taxation. He recommends use of special assessments. See Hofmeister, "Observations on the Tariff Policies of the Electricity Supply Companies Affiliated with 'Electroguas,' " mimeographed (Bogotá: Los Andes–Minnesota Project, 1966).

28. Lauchlin Currie and Associates, *Plan Socio-Económico para el Atlántico* (Bogotá: Imprenta Nacional, 1965), pp. 200–209.

29. The relatively slower growth rate of Barranquilla, only 4.5% per year in the last decade, may also have made valorization more difficult in that city.

30. Currie and Associates, *Plan Socio-Económico,* pp. 200–209.

The experience of the Colombian cities indicates that the freedom of action provided by the national laws allows Colombian cities to have successful valorization tax programs, *if* the valorization agency can be created with sufficient autonomy to withstand political interference and to build up a technically competent staff. Pragmatic methods of successfully selecting projects and assessing the valorization tax have been worked out, but the financial management of even the most successful programs seems weak, for the discrepancies between actual and budgeted operations are large, and working capital for operations is lacking. It has not been possible to examine the financial self-sufficiency of the valorization funds to see if they will be adequately financed from valorization tax payments and budgeted public contributions or if they are using up their working capital, but there is reason to doubt the financial soundness of many of the funds. The main limitation to successful valorization programs in Colombia, however, is the lack of trained personnel to run them.[31]

The difficulties of applying valorization taxes under the more stringent laws for nonmunicipal agencies are well illustrated by the attempts of the Cauca Valley Corporation to collect valorization taxes from a dike project which, by preventing seasonal flooding, opened up much new land for urbanization on the outskirts of Cali.[32] Although the project was authorized in 1958, and by 1962 the work had been substantially completed and over ten thousand people were living in the formerly flooded areas, no valorization tax had yet been collected by the middle of 1964. The difficulty lies in the fact that the law required special property valuation surveys before and after the dike was built, and these surveys were not completed until mid-1964. Only then could the tax per property be determined and collections begun. The interest rate charged to the taxpayer on the investment between the time it was made and the time the tax was assessed is only 6 percent, whereas the purchasing power of the currency has dropped by about 10 percent per year during the period since con-

31. A private consulting firm (the Valorización y Asesorias, Ltda. mentioned earlier) has recently been established in Medellín to help set up valorization offices in other cities. So far its activities have been confined to Colombia, although there was apparently one inquiry from Caracas in Venezuela. On the absence of valorization in Caracas, see Carl S. Shoup, C. Lowell Harriss, and William S. Vickrey, *The Fiscal System of the Federal District of Venezuela* (New York: n.p., 1960), p. 65.

32. The project and the attempts to finance it by valorization are described in detail in Antonio J. Posada F. and Jeanne de Posada, *CVC: Un Reto al Subdesarrollo y al Tradicionalismo* (Bogotá: Ediciones Tercer Mundo, 1966), pp. 189–190. When this was written in 1966, a movement was on foot to make more use of valorization at the departmental level. New roads on the edges of large cities and crossing several municipalities were proposed and new valorization offices were set up in Antioquia, Valle, and Santander.

struction; consequently, the tax cannot cover the total costs of the work in real terms, and the delay in collection has forced the CVC to finance works to be recouped eventually through valorization taxes for three or more years from other sources in a situation of a chronic shortage of credit.

An Example for Other Developing Countries?

Valorization in Ecuador [33]

Finally, by way of contrast, we shall briefly describe the valorization tax systems in two other Latin American countries—Ecuador and Mexico.

In the past, special improvement taxes have not been very important in Ecuador. A new municipal law passed early in 1966 is intended to expand the number of public works that may be financed by valorization. This new law has several features of interest in relation to the Colombian system outlined earlier. Like the Colombian tax, the Ecuadorean tax is levied on the benefit (increase in value) *presumed* to be derived by property owners whose holdings border on the work or lie in the zone of influence laid down by the municipal council. Also more or less like the Colombian system are the funding and payment systems prescribed for this "special improvement levy," as it is known. There appears, however, to be no provision for the establishment of independent valorization offices responsible for both the execution and the financing of projects, on the Colombian model. The proposed Ecuadorean system also differs significantly in other respects, such as in the treatment of exempt property and the treatment of different types of public works.[34]

33. The information in this section is based on Ecuadorean law and on discussions held in Quito in February 1966 by Bird, particularly with Lic. Carlos Davalos R., former Director Técnico de Administración in Ecuador.

34. Three minor differences might also be mentioned: (1) In no case may the total tax exceed 50% of the increase in value of the property between the period immediately before the work and that in which the tax due is determined (which looks considerably more restrictive than the municipal system in Colombia). (2) Municipalities are also empowered by the new law to levy a tax at rates ranging from 10% to 42% on capital gains arising from the sale of real property, *provided* that no special improvement levy has been imposed. If it has, only the excess of the capital gains tax over the valorization tax is payable, a procedure which may be contrasted with the deduction of valorization taxes from the capital gain for purposes of the national capital gains tax in Colombia. (3) Municipalities may also make agreements among themselves to allow each other to collect valorization taxes or to do so jointly, or the national government may require some joint arrangement to be made ; this would seem a desirable provision in the Medellín area, for example.

All properties, taxable or exempt, must be included in the initial distribution of the special improvement levy. The share allocated to national government properties exempted from the property tax must be met by direct payments from the national budget. Other exempt properties must be paid for from the common municipal funds. This treatment seems logical although, given the usual pressure on both national and municipal budgets, it will probably not work well in practice (witness the failure of Bogotá to live up to its own laws in this respect). The Medellín practice of sometimes allocating the costs properly attributable to exempt properties to nonexempt ones has little to be said for it in theory, although it may be practically acceptable if the benefit-cost ratio of the project is high or the cushion provided by rapid urban growth is large enough. The Ecuadorean tax is a charge on the property rather than on the owner (like the new national tax in Colombia), thus avoiding some of the difficulties of *in personam* taxes in areas of confused land titles like so much of Latin America, both urban and rural.

The other interesting feature of the new Ecuadorean system—for which there is apparently no parallel in Colombia (except perhaps the Cali municipal enterprise's system of technical division of projects into general and local components)—is the different treatment of different kinds of public works. These are classed in eight groups, in each of which the cost is to be allocated in a different manner. In the case of urban paving, for example, 30 percent of the cost of the work is to be met from the general municipal budget, 20 percent pro-rated among bordering properties on a frontage basis, and 50 percent pro-rated on fronting properties in proportion to the cadastral value (of land and improvements). Similar specific formulas are used for the other seven types of improvements.

A number of comments may be made about this system. One is that there is no logic in the use of the cadastral-value base for a valorization tax since there is no reason at all to suppose that the increase in value due to the improvement will be related in any systematic way to the initial value of the properties benefited, even supposing what is hardly ever true in Latin America—that these initial values are themselves rationally distributed. Another point is that there *is* some reason for different treatment of different kinds of works and particularly, in some cases, for the allocation of some of the cost to the general fund.[35] The case for general fund financing probably becomes stronger as urban areas become more de-

35. The report by the Advisory Commission on Intergovernmental Relations, *Performance of Urban Functions: Local and Areawide* (Washington, D.C.: U.S. Government Printing Office, 1963), contains an interesting (nonoperational) discussion of the degrees of "localness" of the benefits from different kinds of public improvements.

veloped. However, it is most unlikely that rigid specification of different percentages, as in Ecuador, is desirable since relevant circumstances will vary so much from project to project. Partly for this reason, greater flexibility in allocating benefits, as in Colombia, seems desirable. One might argue that the Colombian system could be improved by a more explicit recognition on the municipal level of the fact that the local benefits of projects do not always exceed their total cost—a fact that is clearly already recognized in practice. On the whole, however, it seems clear that Ecuador has more to learn from Colombia than the reverse.

Valorization in Mexico City [36]

Taxes similar to the valorization tax have long been used in Mexico City. In 1961 the so-called "planning tax" yielded 10 percent as much as the real property tax, or less than 2 percent of total municipal revenues.[37] This tax apparently applies to all properties benefited by major public works, including governmental and religious properties, although as usual there is often a losing fight on the question with such public bodies as the railroads. The only explicit exemption in the law is for foreign diplomatic missions when reciprocity is granted (as in Colombia, where, however, the nation is supposed to pay for such properties). In addition, properties classified as of special historical interest get a reduced rate (as they do

36. This section is based largely on work done by Bird in 1962–1963 as part of a project on urban financing in developing countries undertaken by the Harvard Law School International Tax Program under the direction of Professor Oliver Oldman. Some of the results of this project have since been published in Oliver Oldman, Henry J. Aaron, Richard M. Bird, and Stephen L. Kass, *Financing Urban Development in Mexico City* (Cambridge, Mass.: Harvard University Press, 1967). Chapter 3 of this book, which discusses the Mexico City special assessment system in detail, is even more critical of Mexican practice than we are. Perhaps largely because of their awareness of these deserved (for the most part) criticisms, the Oldman book reaches, we think, overly pessimistic conclusions on the general usefulness of special assessments in the urban areas of developing countries. (See pp. 109–110, 124–125.) We would also like to point out that, for reasons developed earlier in the text, we disagree with the position apparently taken on p. 116, that cadastral values should as a rule be used as the basis for special assessments.

37. Mexico, Finance Law of the Department of the Federal District, *Diario Oficial*, 31 December 1941. This tax replaced an earlier form of increment value tax in 1950. The earlier tax was supposedly unsatisfactory because (1) it was difficult to calculate and in any event arbitrary; (2) it was felt that the property tax reached the increments in land values anyway; and (3) it was a cause for taxpayer resentment when more money than the cost was collected in connection with some project and the surplus used elsewhere. This explanation of the change seems improbable, however, since the same remarks could be made about the present Mexican tax. See Oldman et al., *Financing Urban Development*, p. 111.

under the property tax), presumably because in this case it is not desired to induce more profitable use of the land.

The planning tax due on any particular property is devised by means of rather complicated formulas to determine the affected zones and the allocation within them. These formulas appear to be rigidly applied in all cases, even though their arbitrariness virtually assures that no public improvement will actually affect property values in the precise, specified pattern.[38] The virtues of more flexibility in these matters, so apparent in the operation of valorization in Medellín, are thus completely lost in Mexico City. The notification and payment systems are rather similar in both countries, with some discount being allowed for advance payments. This discount procedure seems more acceptable for valorization works, where otherwise money would have to be borrowed and interest paid, than in the case of regular property taxes.

Many works which are financed by the planning tax also give rise to the so-called "cooperation fees," which yielded a little over 1 percent of total current revenues in Mexico City in 1961. These fees are levied on a flat frontage basis for sewers, sidewalks, water lines, street lighting, and street paving when the street is part of the internal road network of the district. Occasionally, such works have been financed by assigning the proceeds of these charges to the lending institutions and empowering them to collect their money directly.

On the whole, the system of financing public works by benefit taxes does not appear to have worked well in Mexico's capital up to now, as is indicated both by the small revenue yield and by the number of complaints made about those taxes that are levied.[39] It has been argued, for

38. This is probably in part the explanation for the finding in various American studies in the early part of this century that special assessments were badly correlated with value increments. See Harold M. Groves, *Financing Government,* 5th ed. (New York: Holt, 1958), p. 376 ; and International City Managers' Association, *Municipal Finance Administration,* 5th ed. (Chicago, 1958), chap. 10. Incidentally, to the other reasons for the relative lack of use of valorization financing in the United States today, we might add the traumatic experience of the 1930's when land values generally fell, public improvements or no public improvements. Since Keynesian thinking is now accepted, it is unlikely that this experience will be reproduced in the United States, but it remains true that valorization will work much better in prosperous times. In developing countries, inflation may play the role of prosperity for our purpose.

39. In Mexico, unlike Colombia, the national government has traditionally subsidized the capital city, and much of the public investment in Mexico City, including highways, has been financed from national government revenues. Opposition to valorization in Mexico may simply reflect realistic expectations that the city can escape the tax burden for improvements if a little pressure is put on the national government.

example, that taxes must be paid several times on the same increase in value—through the planning tax, the cooperation fees, and increased property taxes. The basic property tax is apparently usually increased because of the interchange of information between the valorization office (in the public works department) and the property tax office (in the treasury). There is no such formal notification procedure in Colombia as far as we know. Assuming a real property base has any rationale at all for tax purposes, one would suppose that property taxes should in fact be increased as a result of public works which increase land values, whether or not the work itself is financed by taxes on the value increments. But as a matter of public relations, the issue is not so clear, and it may be worth foregoing the smaller benefit for the greater one.

It has also been said in Mexico City that the operation of the valorization tax system has had undesirable effects both allocationally and distributionally. The existence of these taxes may make property owners in certain areas less desirous of having public works than would otherwise be the case. We saw that an analogous situation has also held back the operation of the system in Cali. This effect is not necessarily bad if the existence of taxpayer resistance means that works to be financed by this system must have high benefit-cost ratios and be clearly beneficial to all, as is more or less true in Medellín and Bogotá. It is less desirable if it leads to underspending on such works owing to "spite" resentment of taxes, to ignorance of the full benefits, or to the belief that a good enough cover-up of true preferences for public goods will eventually lead to the provision of the improvements from the general funds. In addition, where, as in Mexico City, rent controls prevent landowners from reaping higher returns from their property, they are unlikely to favor improvements to benefit their tenants at their expense.

The distributional effect of financing a work by benefit taxes rather than general taxes is clearly to favor the general taxpayer at the expense of those benefited. In some instances, this shift may be considered socially undesirable. This argument has been used against benefit financing in Mexico City. It has, for example, been claimed that heavy transit traffic has led to continuous works being charged to areas inhabited by poor people rather than to the well-off fringe districts.[40] It has also been suggested that the poor inhabitants of the small villages swallowed up in the course of the growth of the metropolitan area were forced to sell out (though presumably at higher prices) in order to meet the heavy charges

40. See the discussion of this point in Oldman et al., *Financing Urban Development*, p. 117. In fact, there is generally no benefit financing of repaving in Mexico, although it is presumably as logical to finance the maintenance of existing values as the creation of new values in this way.

connected with the extension of the urban service network. As always, the distributional argument for the provision of some particular consumption good, whether it be food, housing, or urban services, at subsidized prices is weak unless the general benefit is assumed to outweigh the local benefit (in which case all the improvement cost should not be financed by valorization), or the specific subsidy is the only politically or economically feasible way of providing an income subsidy (as may indeed be true in developing countries characterized by very unequal income distributions and by the political power of the better-off).

Without discussing the not-so-happy Mexican experience further, we may sum it up by saying it shows again the overriding importance of careful planning and good taxpayer relationships if the valorization tax—no matter what its theoretical merits or its real relation to increments in land values—is not to be perceived as a harsh and arbitrary charge by those it reaches.

An Appraisal of the Valorization Tax

Taxing on the Basis of Benefit

The valorization tax appears to have been most successful where the greatest efforts have been made to put it on a true benefit basis, as was done in Medellín. To do this seems to require the following elements: (1) freedom from any fixed formulas for distributing the tax among property owners; (2) careful study of projects at the initial stage to determine those that will truly bring increased site values equal at least to the cost of the project; (3) participation of property owners in the planning and execution of projects without giving them obstructionist or veto powers; (4) careful costing of projects; (5) prompt construction of projects; (6) prompt and complete collection of all taxes assessed on the property owners while the project is being built; (7) extensive publicity of valorization construction projects; and (8) a general statement of the rules for hardship cases permitting, but not requiring, reduction in tax or delayed payment in certain circumstances. The development of a valorization system is also a matter for careful planning; Medellín's experience indicates the importance of starting with small projects that can be completed quickly and with certainty and thus earn taxpayer trust; at a later stage it might be better to concentrate on large multi-faceted projects. While there are no empirical studies available to show how closely valorization tax assessments have corresponded to subsequent increases in site value in Medellín, there is a general feeling on the part of officials and other observers that the tax has been on a basis proportional to benefits. Preserving a popular identification between the tax and the benefits by all possible means is repeatedly emphasized in Medellín. If one believes Abraham Lincoln's dictum that "you can't fool all of the people all of the time," the valorization tax over the long run must have approached a benefit basis in fact as well as in belief. This means also that, as was noted above in discussing the proposed Ecuadorean system, some explicit recognition should be given to the likelihood, especially at later stages of urban growth, that the benefits from works projects capitalized in private property values may not always suffice to pay for the project, although its general social productivity may still be very high. It is important for effective functioning of the tax, however, that any such provision be couched in general rather than rigidly specific terms.

Exemptions

There is little reason for exempting any property from the valorization tax. The exemptions of government property have given windfalls to private-interest public groups such as military pension funds.[41] Failure of other governments to pay assessments has seriously hurt the financial soundness of valorization in Bogotá. Exemption may be justified for small landowners who are illiquid and cannot raise the cash to pay their assessments, but this problem can usually be solved in practice by giving small landowners longer periods to pay (in effect requiring them to pay less, especially in inflationary periods) and by making special arrangements in hardship cases. Valorization may force improvements on some owners that they do not want, forcing them to sell out and move elsewhere, but in theory at least they should sell out at a profit and suffer no financial harm, although there may be some loss of consumer surplus from valorization, as from any change in supply and demand conditions.

Earmarking of Revenues

Public finance textbooks tend to condemn earmarked revenues because they limit the flexibility of budgeting in a government, glutting some activities with too much revenue while other activities starve. This can only be avoided if the rate of the earmarked tax is changed regularly to bring it into line with actual revenue needs. This is the case with the valorization tax. Further, the financing of investments from the earmarked valorization tax gives an added incentive to examine the prospective benefits of

41. The exemption of publicly owned property is sometimes justified on the grounds that this property has no commercial value. While this position may recognize the realities of political life, it has no base in economic analysis. The use of land for public rather than other purposes has an opportunity cost equal to its highest value in alternative uses, and increases in this cost due to public works should be, in theory, explicitly recognized in making decisions on the location of public facilities.

projects more closely than would otherwise be done and hence promotes good budgeting and project appraisal procedures.

Benefit taxation may be made politically popular in the way outlined in the text above. A charge may then be made, however, that those activities which can clearly be financed on a benefit base will receive too much support, at the expense of other activities which for technical reasons cannot be benefit financed. Too much emphasis on benefit taxation may also limit the scope for income redistribution through taxation. The force of these charges is lessened to the extent that benefit taxes can be shown to be (in addition to other taxes) expanding the size of the public sector, rather than substituting for other more general taxes. On the basis of admittedly crude and impressionistic evidence (see Table 10.5), the valorization tax does seem to be a net addition to public financing in Colombia. The need in Colombia is for additional technically sound benefit taxes to expand the public sector, not for less use of those now existing.

Relation to Other Taxes on Property

As discussed above, the valorization tax is supposed to be applied on the basis of the assumed increases in pure site value; the continued popularity of the tax when well administered seems to indicate that this aim is achieved.[42] The valorization tax is compatible with a capital gains tax on increments in site values, provided the valorization tax is included in the original cost of the property when calculating capital gains, as is in fact done in practice in Colombia. Assuming that the valorization tax and the capital gains tax together recoup for the public sector the increment in land values, it may seem unfair to have a regular property tax which taxes site values and improvements, since valorization projects raise site values and hence the property tax on the site. On the other hand, public improvements have maintenance expenditures, and the cost of maintenance should be paid by those who benefit. Also, it will rarely be the case that all increments in land value can be taxed away by the valorization and capital gains taxes, so some scope will be left for site value property taxation. Finally, it must be recognized that most property taxes are used to finance municipal services for people, who in turn live in and use buildings and other improvements, and if taxes are to be benefit based

---

42. As noted earlier, such authorities as Groves and Netzer appear to favor a land-value-increment tax over the valorization tax recommended here; that is, they favor a tax assessed on benefits actually received as a result of the work to one on benefits that it is presumed will arise in the future. The valorization tax is preferable in developing countries because of the lack of a capital market for financing public works, the more favorable attitudes of taxpayers to benefit taxes, and the growth-inflation cushion of rising property values.

(at least in part), much of the property tax should be on improvements, so that development will pay its proper share of taxes. In the face of ignorance as to the relative weight of these points, it would seem a priori best to tax land and improvements at the same rate, especially since site value is already reached by the valorization and capital gains taxes.

In practice in Colombia the values of valorization-financed improvements are not automatically included in the assessed values of properties. Owing largely to the continued inflation, the municipalities now are pressing for more regular reassessments anyway. If the target of a four-year cycle or less is achieved, the lag between completion of a project and an increase in its assessed value will not be a long one. In any event, as noted earlier, if real property is a rational base for taxation in developing countries—as it would seem to be on both benefit and distributional grounds—there is every reason for taxing increases in site value, however caused, under the regular property tax as soon as possible.

Effects on Income Distribution

In terms of the usual definition, the valorization tax is probably a progressive tax, since it is in proportion to property, and property ownership is more unequally distributed than income in almost all countries. Using the more inclusive concept of the "fiscal residuum," the tax is neutral, for all taxpayers would receive benefits equal to or greater than the payment. Compared with alternative ways of financing public improvements if valorization is not used, the valorization tax probably favors the poor over the wealthy and yields a more equal income distribution. This presumption is somewhat confirmed by the fact that the strongest opposition to valorization taxes in Colombia has come from some of the wealthier groups in the country.

Conclusion

The valorization tax as it exists in Colombia seems to have a useful but limited role to play in economic development. It is effective in financing certain specialized types of public investment at one stage in the economic development of a country. For the tax to be useful, the country must have reached a stage where urbanization is proceeding at a rapid rate and large modern cities are being formed and where modern agriculture and transportation are rapidly being introduced. The country must also have developed capable administrators, real estate men, and engineers who can handle the complicated machinery of the valorization tax. City planning must also have become feasible.[43] Yet the country must not have yet reached the stage of maturity where capital markets have developed which can take over the job from valorization, and where the city has become so large and intricate that the relation between public investment and increases in site value is too complex for valorization financing to work. This stage probably will not be reached throughout Colombia for many years, but there are signs that it may already be approaching in Bogotá.[44]

There are many other countries already in, or soon to be in, Colombia's stage of development, and this country's experience may be of interest and use to them. At present in Colombia the interest in extending the valorization system to new uses and increasing its importance in current uses is high. Colombians feel that the experience in Medellín and elsewhere in the last twenty years has established both the general principles and the specialized methods needed for successful valorization programs. The success of the present attempts to extend the valorization tax will probably depend more on the quality of administration of the new programs than any other factor. While there is little information available on the effects of valorization taxes, on the basis of what little we know, it may be safely concluded that the expansion of valorization taxation in Colombia and in other similar countries should be favorable for general economic development.

43. It is, of course, essential to relate the works financed by valorization to a coherent city plan if the full benefits of this form of financing are to be realized without the disadvantage of "piecemeal" improvement. The financing and execution of the work should be under the responsibility of a single entity, for reasons discussed earlier. This entity should be as autonomous as possible (except for its relation to the planning department), in order to enable it to hire and retain the capable, skilled people success requires, free of the usual fiscal and political constraints of public administration in developing countries.

44. Even at this more advanced stage there is still a role, though a lesser one, for valorization taxes in the financing of works with an irregular local-general benefit split. Possibly land-value-increment taxes might by this time be more suitable. See Netzer, *Economics of the Property Tax*, p. 213.

11 A Study of Land Taxation in Jamaica

DANIEL M. HOLLAND

Introduction

Jamaica, an island country in the Caribbean, has since 1957 been engaged in an important effort in land taxation. The country is changing the basis of its property tax from improved value (that is, the value of land and buildings) to unimproved value (the value of land alone). About 40 percent of the island's land is not yet taxed on its unimproved value, and, while the shift has lagged behind the schedule initially set, the process is continuing. The government has every intention of eventually putting the whole country on the new base.[1]

Jamaica, which achieved independence in 1962, is a member of the British Commonwealth. Its 1.7 million people, who inhabit an area of

NOTE: A portion of the research on which this chapter is based has been supported by Regional and Urban Planning Implementation, Inc., under a contract from the Agency for International Development. The opinions expressed and conclusions reached are, of course, solely my own.

I am indebted to many people for help at various stages of this study. In particular, I wish to thank the Honorable Financial Secretary, P. W. Beckwith, and Mr. W. S. Chang, Commissioner of Valuations, for arranging a series of visits and giving so generously of their time and counsel during my visit to Jamaica and for numerous useful insights and criticisms. To William L. White and David Pyle I am grateful for a critical review and helpful suggestions, and to John Copes (who served as the first commissioner of valuations in Jamaica) for a similar service, as well as for two letters that, as the reader will note, served as a very valuable source of information.

I wish to thank the National Tax Association for permission to use verbatim or in only slightly modified form a number of sections from "The Taxation of Unimproved Value in Jamaica," *1965 Proceedings of the Fifty-Eighth Annual Conference on Taxation,* ed. Walter J. Kress (Harrisburg, Pa., 1966), pp. 446–470. This chapter is the result of an extensive revision, updating, expansion, and improvement of the earlier paper.

1. As Jamaica defines the term, "unimproved value" is equivalent to "site value"; the phrases will also be used synonymously in this chapter.

about 4,400 square miles, are engaged primarily in agriculture. A mountain ridge runs down the middle of the island, so that the country is considerably more densely populated than the gross figures on land relative to population would indicate.[2] Moreover, most of the agricultural holdings are small, but the relatively few large properties account for a large fraction of total land. And the population is increasing at just under 2 percent per annum. It is understandable, therefore, that the country is concerned with efficient land use. Nor is it only agricultural land that this concern covers. The island has several towns and one urban area—Kingston, which, together with the suburb of St. Andrew (known collectively as the Corporate Area), has a population of 450,000—which exhibits the usual stigmata of undisciplined urban growth—sprawl, leap-frogging, pockets of decay, and so on.

Jamaica is a developing country whose growth in the last decade has been very rapid. But she is not a rich country and is faced with a number of severe problems, particularly protracted and heavy unemployment. This, of course, lends no uniqueness to Jamaica. Rather, the interest that attaches to her experiment in land taxation transcends this particular country's importance. She falls in the group of countries who must take special pains to improve their economic circumstances and has chosen site value taxation as one of the mechanisms suitable for this purpose. Since Jamaica's problems are similar to those found in many developing countries, her experience in taxing unimproved value could carry a lesson for them. Moreover, all countries, no matter what their stage of development, are interested in possible alternatives to the usual property tax—which is, in essence, an excise tax on construction. As a result, Jamaica's experiment should be a matter of general interest.

Not that Jamaica's experience will be simple to interpret. For in actuality the tax change is not merely a switch from one base to another. Associated with the substitution of unimproved value for improved value as the base of tax, there has been a complete revaluation of properties (which was sorely needed since there had been no general revaluation since 1937 and even then it had not applied to all properties). Consequently, relative tax burdens have changed both because of the change in tax base and because of the revaluation of all properties as of a common date. Jamaica's experiment is difficult to evaluate for this reason and a number of others,

2. See John MacPherson, *Caribbean Lands* (London: Longmans, Green and Co., 1964). The proportion of unproductive land is high—about 42%. Part of the reason lies in "the mountainous nature of the country—half of which lies above 1,000 feet—the steep, rocky slopes and the large tracts of poor thin soil . . . ."—Ibid., p. 31. In addition, "over large areas, forests have been cut for lumber, burned for charcoal and cleared for cultivation, thus exposing the land to rapid tropical weathering."—Ibid., pp. 38–39.

including (1) a depressed land market over the last several years (especially from 1962–1964, with some improvement since), really the "morning after" a fairly strong boom; (2) the fact that very little has been published so far on the results of the tax change; and (3) the fact that the new basis has not yet been introduced in the metropolis. Any judgments will necessarily be hedged and equivocal. There is one saving grace, however. Rates were set so that property tax collections in the first year of the new basis were equal to those of the preceding year. In this sense, then, we have a controlled experiment—the substitution of one basis of assessment for another, with revenues held constant.

Despite the difficulties, Jamaica's experience seems well worth analyzing. Very few countries have attempted to tax site value, although there is a long history of vigorous advocacy by some dedicated persons and groups as well as somewhat more dispassionate but nonetheless affirmative support from economists and students of public finance.[3] And it could be argued, I think, that developing countries should have a particular interest in the potentials of taxing unimproved values (which means also, of course, exempting improvements). For this a number of reasons may be given:

(1) Compared with the usual kind of property tax, site value taxation encourages development of land and construction thereon.

(2) In the process of development particular actions of the government and the natural progress of society will cause the values of sites to rise. The holders of land get the benefit, but they have not undertaken expenditures or expended effort sufficient to account for the enhancement in values. Windfall gains or, in more loaded language, "unearned increments" are very appropriate targets of taxation. Revenue is raised, income is redistributed, and economic decisions are not affected.

(3) As a general rule, underdeveloped countries will have a large number of unimproved sites and could therefore more conveniently establish unimproved values for developed sites by analogizing from the market

---

3. A representative sample of citations of recent origin which support site value taxation or some variant of it to some degree, at least, would include the following: Carl S. Shoup et al., *The Fiscal System of Venezuela* (Baltimore, Md.: The Johns Hopkins Press, 1959), pp. 339–340; James Heilbrun, *Real Estate Taxes and Urban Housing* (New York: Columbia University Press, 1966), pp. 171–173; Dick Netzer, *Economics of the Property Tax* (Washington, D.C.: The Brookings Institution, 1966), p. 217; Dick Netzer, "The Property Tax and Alternatives in Urban Development," *The Regional Science Association Papers and Proceedings*, 9 (1962): 192; Mason Gaffney, "Property Taxes and the Frequency of Urban Renewal," in National Tax Association, *1964 Proceedings of the Fifty-Seventh Annual Conference on Taxation*, ed. Walter J. Kress (Harrisburg, Pa., 1965), pp. 272–285.

value of comparable vacant sites than could countries that are more heavily built up.[4]

(4) In a number of developing countries decisions on land use mirror numerous values other than those of the market and tend in a real sense to be uneconomic (for example, sentimental attachment to large land-holdings as the basis of a way of life). Taxing unimproved value could induce more rational decisions on the part of landholders.

(5) Developing countries, perhaps more than others, experience considerable speculative holding of land. Since excessive speculation mirrors the imperfections of the market, this would be expected. In addition, once again particularly in developing countries, there is a heavy demand for land as an inflation hedge. Thus, a rapid rise in land prices as a country develops is a real possibility. This expectation, together with capital market imperfections and other factors that cause investors to have different discount rates, introduces "distortions" in land use and development that a tax on unimproved value would tend to moderate.[5]

There is another reason for particular interest in property taxes for developing countries—an interest not specifically in site value, but simply in property taxation as against other forms of taxation. As a broad generalization, in developing countries local governments have been laggard in providing for a portion of the social overhead (roads, for example) and have not generated the fiscal resources to permit an enhanced role. In particular they have failed to draw on property taxation to anything but

4. This point has been made by U. K. and J. R. Hicks, who suggest that the stage of economic development might very well be an important determinant of the appropriate base for property taxation. See, for example, U. K. Hicks, *Development From Below* (London: Oxford University Press, 1961), p. 360; and J. R. Hicks, "Unimproved Value Rating—The Case of East Africa," in *Essays in World Economics* (London: Oxford University Press, 1959), p. 242.

On the other hand, John M. Copes, an Australian valuation expert who served as Jamaica's first commissioner of valuations, disagrees with this judgment and believes that he would be joined on this point by his Australian colleagues who are experienced in unimproved land value assessment. They are able to value rates in areas that are completely developed, such as the central commercial districts of Kingston, for example, where there are no vacant sites per se. For one thing, there are always a number of sites that are substantially vacant in the sense that their improvements are obsolescent and of little or no value. For another, it is generally possible to make satisfactory valuations of the total property and of the improvements thereon and thus arrive at the unimproved value. Copes asserts that "in Australia we have found that the unimproved values system engenders the sales evidence, particularly in cities such as Sydney. Considerable activity occurs in the market where progressive land tax applies to higher value sites upon which the improvements are obsolescent."—Quoted from a letter from John M. Copes to the author of 16 January 1967.

5. This point is developed at greater length below.

a minimal degree. Yet real property, being both visible and immovable, is the "natural" object of taxation for local governments.[6]

In brief summary, for the reasons stated and with an eye particularly on the lessons that could be learned for other developing countries, I have studied Jamaica's experience with unimproved value taxation. It goes without saying that the evidence gathered and presented here can hardly constitute the basis for a definitive report, particularly since the shift to the new basis is in midstream and has not yet been tested in Kingston. One should not, however, disclaim too much. In my judgment, it is possible to reach some conclusions from what has happened so far and to suggest in addition where the main problems lie and what they are like. In the rest of this chapter, therefore, I will first deal with Jamaica's particular experience in site value taxation and then consider more generally the problems and questions posed by this kind of tax. Economic effects are analyzed in the appendix to this chapter.

Instituting the New Basis

Background History

In adopting unimproved value as the base for its property tax, Jamaica is finally implementing a royal commission recommendation made many years ago; even prior to this report considerable sentiment in support of site value taxation existed in the country. As evidence of this sentiment, I have been informed that a set of valuations on the unimproved basis was prepared as far back as 1901. In 1943 the Bloomberg Commission, a royal commission enjoined to inquire into problems of property valuation and taxation, recommended that Jamaica adopt a system of unimproved value taxation and sketched out an administrative framework for implementing its recommendations. Jamaica's current practice reflects the Bloomberg Commission's main recommendation and some of its specific suggestions as well. A report by a mission of the International Bank for Reconstruction and Development supported the principle of unimproved value taxation, but did not discuss it at any length.[7]

6. See Joseph Froomkin, "Fiscal Management of Municipalities and Economic Development," *Economic Development and Cultural Change,* 3, no. 4 (July 1955): 309–320, for a discussion of the point that the process of economic development has suffered because of insufficient provision of social overhead by local governments. For evidence suggestive of too small a reliance on property taxation in developing countries, see the data in Alison M. Martin and W. A. Lewis, "Patterns of Public Revenue and Expenditure," *Manchester School,* 24, no. 3 (September 1956): 235.

7. International Bank for Reconstruction and Development, *The Economic Development of Jamaica* (Baltimore, Md.: The Johns Hopkins Press, 1952).

A note of disagreement was struck by two British economists, J. R. and U. K. Hicks, who in 1954 had been asked to study the problems of governmental finance in Jamaica. Their report included an extended discussion of property taxation in which the conclusion was reached that both on administrative grounds and for reasons of economic efficiency, temporary exemption of new construction from the tax on the capital value of the property (that is, the combined value of land and improvements) such as Jamaica then had (and, of course, still has in the parishes that remain on the old basis) would be preferable to a tax based on unimproved value.[8] (The Hickses' recommendation is discussed at greater length in a later section of this chapter.) Finally, in 1956 a report by J. F. N. Murray, an Australian land valuation expert and land economist, who had been appointed a United Nations advisor to the government of Jamaica on problems of valuation and taxation of land and to recommend a procedure for a speedy and economical revaluation of all land in Jamaica, strongly supported unimproved value taxation on grounds both of administrative ease and desirable economic effects and laid out a set of procedures and administrative arrangements that should be followed to this end.[9] Murray's main recommendations and many, but not all, of his specific suggestions were accepted. They are incorporated in the Land Valuation Law, the basic legislation underlying unimproved value taxation, which was adopted by Jamaica's parliament in December 1956,[10] and also constitute the underlying basis for the procedures adopted by the valuation division of the Ministry of Agriculture and Lands, the unit set up to get on with the work of developing the unimproved value assessments.

8. J. R. and U. K. Hicks, *Report on Finance and Taxation in Jamaica* (Kingston: Government of Jamaica, 1954). They did, of course, urge an immediate revaluation of all properties to obtain a set of consistent and up-to-date assessments.

9. J. F. N. Murray, *Report to the Government of Jamaica on Valuation, Land Taxation and Rating* (Kingston: Government of Jamaica, 1956). In fact, while suggesting primary reliance on taxing unimproved value, Murray also suggested that the local rates (local-government service charges) be based on improved values. (More of this below.) "Dr. Murray was the senior member of a team of two Australian experts in land valuation who were appointed United Nations Advisors to the Government of Jamaica on valuation and land taxation—the other member being Mr. J. M. Copes, who was appointed to implement Dr. Murray's recommendations. As the first Commissioner of Valuations, Mr. Copes organized and directed the program of revaluation from 1956 until early 1961."—Wilfred S. Chang, "Recent Experience of Establishing Land Value Taxation in Jamaica," in *International Seminar on Land Taxation, Land Tenure, and Land Reform in Developing Countries*, ed. Archibald M. Woodruff, James R. Brown, and Sein Lin (W. Hartford, Conn.: John C. Lincoln Institute, University of Hartford, 1967), p. 212.

10. Jamaica, Land Valuation Law, 1956, no. 73.

Defining the Tax Base

The objectives of the Land Valuation Law of 1956, as evidenced by the proceedings of Jamaica's House of Representatives, encompassed the classical case for site value taxation. The use of this base was supported because it: [11]

(a) did not tax a person on the efforts he put into the land;
(b) provided a means of taxing values created by the community at large;
(c) discouraged the withholding of land from use.

The law defined unimproved value and established the machinery for getting valuations made on this basis. Responsibility for carrying out the provisions of the law is vested in a commissioner of valuations who "shall, in each district, make a valuation of the unimproved and improved value of every parcel of land." [12]

Unimproved value was defined as: [13]

(a) in relation to unimproved land the capital sum which the fee simple of the land might be expected to realize if offered for sale on such reasonable terms and conditions as a *bona fide* seller would require;
(b) in relation to improved land the capital sum which the fee simple of the land might be expected to realize if offered for sale on such reasonable terms and conditions as a *bona fide* seller would require, assuming that at the time at which the value is required to be ascertained for the purposes of this Law the improvements as defined in this Law do not exist....

Further, the law states that "'improvements' in relation to land means those physical additions and alterations thereto and all works for the benefit of the land made or done by the owner or any of his predecessors in title which, as at the date on which the improved or unimproved value is required to be ascertained, has the effect of increasing its value.

11. Chang, "Taxation in Jamaica," p. 213.
12. In 1959 the decision was made to value on the unimproved basis only. This matter will be discussed in a later section of this chapter.
13. Chang, "Taxation in Jamaica," pp. 220–221. The law further provides that "the unimproved value shall in no case be less than the sum that will be obtained by deducting the value of the improvements from the improved value at the time as at which the value is required to be ascertained for the purpose of this Law."—Ibid., p. 221. In other words, as Chang explains, two methods of valuation are prescribed for determining the unimproved value of an improved property, and the higher figure must be chosen. "The first may be termed one of abstraction where the improvements are assumed to be non-existent. The second as contained in the proviso is a method of subtraction whereby the unimproved value can be obtained as a residual by deducting the value of improvements from the improved value."—Ibid., p. 222.

"Provided that the destruction or removal of timber or vegetable growth shall not be regarded as an improvement." [14]

In summary, then, under Jamaica's law unimproved value is defined as the value of the raw land per se without any improvements, such as houses, factories, crops, etc., that may have been put on it. The exclusion of the removal of the original land cover from the category of improvements is a major simplification in the law and, in effect, means that Jamaica is taxing site value rather than unimproved value. [15]

While value is not the same as market price, the price a property would fetch if vacant and unimproved is good evidence of value and can be considered most generally to be the kind of valuation that is attempted. Unimproved does not mean value in current use, but what a site might currently go for in a legitimate market transaction that, presumably, takes cognizance of the uses to which a site might be put. The courts in Jamaica have explained it thus: "These cases establish that 'value' of the land is its market value, that is, what a man desiring to buy the land would have had to pay for it on the prescribed day to a vendor willing to sell it for a fair price but not desirous of selling it. In arriving at this value, all the advantages which the land possessed, present or future, in the hands of the owner, may be taken into consideration; but its potentialities must be considered as possibilities and not as realized in the hands of the purchaser." [16] That is to say, in determining unimproved value, the

---

14. Ibid., p. 221.

15. Thus, while in this chapter "site value" and "unimproved value" are used as synonymous terms, and while Jamaica's statute refers to the tax as based on unimproved value, technically the tax base in Jamaica is neither site value nor unimproved value. Rather, it is something between them. The point is this: site value includes, but unimproved value does not include, invisible improvements such as drainage, the cost of clearing land, and so on. Jamaica's Land Valuation Law, 1956, defines unimproved value to include the cost of clearing but exclusive of invisible improvements such as drainage and reclamation. As A. M. Woodruff and L. L. Ecker-Racz note, "The problem of valuing nonstructural improvements is proving difficult in practice . . . . Invisible improvements of agricultural land include clearing of forests and, in cases where this occurred as long as a century ago, the extent and present value of the clearing are fairly hard to determine. With respect to rural land, the appraisal of the invisible improvements is an abiding and persistent problem."—Woodruff and Ecker-Racz, "Property Taxes and Land Use Patterns in Australia and New Zealand," *The Tax Executive*, 28, no. 1 (October 1965): 34.

The complexities in terminology on this matter will, in general, be ignored in this chapter. Thus, as noted, the terms "unimproved value" and "site value" will be used synonymously to avoid confusion even though Jamaica designates hers a tax on "unimproved value," when, in fact, it is more appropriately to be considered a tax on "site value."

16. From the opinion of Mr. Justice Lewis, in the case of *Commissioner of Valuations* v. *Conrad Hall,* as reported in the *Daily Gleaner* (Kingston), Monday, 27 July 1963.

commissioner of valuations can peer into the future but with no greater or less precision and insight than that incorporated in the collective wisdom that determines the market price. The citations in this case draw on decisions in a number of Commonwealth countries; the availability of this body of law based on long experience in valuation for compensation as well as taxation purposes is a real help to Jamaica in administering the tax on unimproved value.

Concerning the feasibility of taxing unimproved value a curious situation has existed for a long time. Stout assertions of the theoretical impossibility (or administrative impracticality) of meaningful valuations of land per se, separate and distinct from the improvements thereon, have flourished in the face of the continuing fact of separate valuations of land and improvements in a number of taxing jurisdictions. Thus, C. C. H. Hipgrave, a professional valuer from the United Kingdom, observes: "Some members of Commissions of Enquiry and some leading economists have stated that it is either impossible or very difficult to assess with any degree of accuracy the value of a hereditament divorced from the improvements thereon. If these statements were true then it would appear that many valuers are obtaining remuneration under false pretenses and, particularly, in those countries where the unimproved value system has long been established, the taxpayers and the courts are being hoaxed." [17]

He goes on, however, to give his own judgment that "provided trained staff are available, and the definition of 'improvements' is so worded as to include only those improvements which are reasonably capable of accurate assessment, any doubts on this point can be disregarded." [18]

In fact, as James Heilbrun notes, the whole issue is more sensibly viewed as an empirical question. That is to say, the relevant question is not "Can it be done?" but "How well can it be done?" [19] In Jamaica, apparently, it has been possible for the office of the commissioner of valuations to come up with assessments of unimproved value that, in the main, are acceptable to most taxpayers and that generally seem to be regarded as "fair." While it is difficult to gauge such matters with any precision, I would judge that there is no real discontent with the valuations on the new basis (on the constrained spectrum of attitudes to taxation which runs from indifference at the upper end to revolution at the lower, this is a rather positive response). For the main run of cases, the valuations on

17. C. C. H. Hipgrave, "Feasibility of Land Value Taxation: Experience in Commonwealth Countries," in *International Seminar on Land Taxation, Land Tenure, and Land Reform in Developing Countries,* ed. Archibald M. Woodruff, James R. Brown, and Sein Lin (W. Hartford, Conn.: University of Hartford, 1966), p. 251.

18. Ibid.

19. Heilbrun, *Real Estate Taxes,* pp. 134–135.

the new basis seem to strike people as appropriate. There have been some disputed cases, of course, and some problems in equity. The Land Valuation Law provided an objection and appeals procedure for valuations, while matters of tax relief for "hardship" cases are dealt with by the Land Taxation (Relief) Law.[20] These mechanisms seem to have been generally satisfactory. (More about appeal and relief below.) Finally, it should be noted and kept in mind that a number of factors helped create a favorable reception for the new valuations and taxes based thereon. These factors are also discussed more particularly below.

Jamaica's experience, of course, is some evidence in support of the feasibility of site value taxation, but in fact, a more positive administrative case can be made for it. Generally, skepticism of the practicability of site value taxation has been more characteristic of students in countries not using this base. The pervading opinion in countries with extensive experience in taxing site value is not merely that this is a feasible method, but that in fact it is superior administratively to improved value taxation. Thus, A. M. Woodruff and L. L. Ecker-Racz, after studying property taxation in Australia and New Zealand, concluded as follows:

> The argument commonly heard in America that site value rating is administratively impossible because of the difficulty of assessing land apart from the buildings on it, is not heard at all in Australia and New Zealand. Many decades of experience have convinced even the most hardened skeptics that while it may be considerably more difficult to appraise the land component of a single improved parcel apart from the building on it, the reverse is true when great numbers of properties have to be evaluated for tax purposes. Involved calculations need be made only for selected bench-mark properties and the values established for the bench marks may be extrapolated to all properties, very much as American assessors customarily build up land value maps. The "land value atlas" or "cadastral map" is the device for accomplishing the extrapolation. Both Australian and New Zealand tax professionals, including a few who either oppose site value taxation or are lukewarm to it, are agreed on its administrative simplicity.[21]

Again on the subject of administrative feasibility or convenience, Woodruff and Ecker-Racz report that, while the main arguments advanced in support of site value taxation related to its encouragement of development:

> A second line of argument is advanced by a smaller number, chiefly tax professionals, who favor rating on unimproved capital value because it is administratively superior. Dr. J. F. N. Murray, the highly regarded author of the leading Australian textbook on valuation techniques holds that: (1) equity

20. Jamaica, Land Taxation (Relief) Law, 1960, no. 4.
21. Woodruff and Ecker-Racz, "Property Taxes," pp. 57–58.

in valuation can be more easily achieved when the rating is based on land rather than a combination of land and building; (2) considerable economies can be achieved if the Valuer General does not need to maintain records on the character of buildings; (3) most of the errors in valuation involve buildings and not land; and (4) use of cadastral maps not only rapidly permits equalization of land values but reference to such maps makes it very simple for an aggrieved owner to determine whether he is treated equitably. In consulting with the United Nations concerning tax systems for new nations, where ownership records are good enough to permit clear identification of taxable holdings, Murray strongly advocates site value taxation because of its simplicity and the relative ease with which inexperienced civil servants can be trained to do the job.[22]

In a letter to the author (7 April 1966) from which I quote, John M. Copes, the Australian land valuation expert who served as Jamaica's first commissioner of valuations from 1956 through the early part of 1961, puts the case for unimproved valuation more positively, asserting not simply that it can be done, but that it can be done more easily than improved valuation, and by reference to Puerto Rico, which uses the improved value base, he stresses particularly the smaller demands on manpower made by unimproved valuation:

> The finding of Improved Capital Values does not readily lend itself to mass valuation techniques, in that each improvement must be recorded and considered separately and there is no repetitive process, except perhaps in moderately priced housing estates. For taxation purposes the approach should be to firstly find the value of the site, and the improvements should be assessed at the added value which they give to the land.
>
> For a developing country there is the problem of assembling a large staff to be trained for the purpose of referencing and valuing these improvements. In Puerto Rico over 700 persons were employed in 1949–60.

This is a heavy requirement of very scarce personnel. In Jamaica the number of trained professionals utilized was considerably less than this.

Valuation Procedures

Valuing on the new basis started in the parish of St. Catherine in June 1957 and, as of April 1959, this parish and St. Ann as well went on the unimproved basis. St. Mary and Portland followed in April 1960, St. Thomas and Trelawny in April 1961, and St. Elizabeth in April 1965. Currently unimproved valuations are in process in Manchester and Clarendon, and it is expected that they will be started soon in Westmoreland

22. Ibid., p. 57.

and Hanover.[23] This leaves only two parishes—St. James, in which the highly developed resort area of Montego Bay is located, and the Corporate Area (that is, Kingston and St. Andrew), which is a major conurbation, containing over one-fourth of the country's population.

Thus, the change to the new basis has not kept up with the schedule seemingly implicit in the Land Valuation Law of 1956, which, by providing for a fresh valuation every five years, suggested that the whole country would be on the new basis within that timespan. Part of this lag is due to a "pause" in the valuation process (reflected in the hiatus between 1961 and 1965 in the chronology above) attendant upon the unseating of the party that sponsored the taxation of unimproved value. The present government, however, intends to continue to introduce the new base in the rest of the country, although it has not announced any expected date of completion and, in particular, it has not been stated when valuations will start in St. James and the metropolitan area (Kingston and St. Andrew). It is these latter developed areas, of course, that pose a two-faceted problem: (1) unimproved values should be more difficult to estimate for highly developed properties; and (2) where unimproved value is the sole basis of taxation, properties whose capital value is very high relative to their unimproved value, as is the case with central-area urban properties, would enjoy a considerably lower tax than formerly. Wilfred S. Chang refers to this as the "problem of super-development," [24] and it is discussed briefly below.

The details of referencing and valuing sites are interesting and important, but it was not possible to go into them very deeply during my brief stay. Some discussion of these matters is necessary, however, in view of the major interest in drawing from Jamaica's experience lessons that might be useful to other countries. Fortunately, both the first commissioner of valuations (Copes) and the current one (Chang) have provided information.[25]

A major conclusion from what was done in Jamaica is the wisdom of choosing procedures that may be "second best" in theory but "first best" in practice. Basically, Jamaica was able to get off the ground because at a number of steps in the process where there was a choice between an unalterably correct or completely thorough procedure and one that fell short of perfection but could be basically satisfactory, Jamaica opted for

23. Chang, "Taxation in Jamaica," pp. 227–228. He notes that the number of valuations already completed comprise about half the total for the whole country and account for 60% of Jamaica's land area.

24. Ibid., p. 238.

25. Copes in a very helpful and informative letter to the author dated 7 April 1966 (from which I will quote) and Chang in "Taxation in Jamaica."

the latter. And because of this it was possible to get started, whereas in two previous instances when site value taxation had been recommended—1949 and 1951—nothing eventuated because the cadastral survey or maps of a high order of accuracy that were considered necessary at that time for valuations on the unimproved basis were beyond Jamaica's fiscal and manpower resources.

Thus, Copes draws the following conclusion from Jamaica's experience in his letter of 7 April 1966: "Whereas countries have balked at introducing a valuation programme because their survey advisers have contemplated maps at high degrees of accuracy, with attendant high cost and time lag, this need not be so . . . the costs of flying and producing suitably large scale mosaics and orthomaps (planemetric photomosaics) is low in relation to producing maps of high degree survey accuracy, and most countries would find little difficulty in financing this aspect of a programme."

This time, then, Jamaica aimed at carrying out a valuation that would be practical, not one that would have all the features of a legal cadaster. One might call their procedure a fiscal, as differentiated from a legal, cadaster. They developed information sufficient for tax purposes, but less precise and, of course, less demanding of scarce capabilities than a cadaster necessary for establishing title. Thus, to quote from Copes's 7 April 1966 letter again, "It is an important aspect of the Land Valuation Law that the Valuation Roll does not set out to be a record of titles. It is a roll of 'owners' as defined, and the Commissioner can place on the roll a person who he believes to be the owner on the basis of the best evidence available."

Finding and referencing all properties started with maps to the scale of 1:12,500 developed from aerial photographs. For some properties, generally those larger than twenty acres, precise information can be obtained from title searches at the Registrar of Titles; their boundaries are entered on the maps. The remaining properties are then "found" and plotted with the help of information obtained by field teams who draw heavily on key local people who know their particular area and the history of holdings in it. This information will not, of course, be very precise, but with the total area specified and all properties having proper and findable titles entered, the rest can be satisfactorily sketched in by a process akin to rounding out the remaining words in a crossword puzzle.[26] Chang

26. Chang, "Taxation in Jamaica," p. 227. Of the maps developed from aerial photography Copes remarks in his letter of 7 April 1966: "These maps are, of course, not to the high degree of accuracy of a Cadastral Survey conducted with the objectives of recording title descriptions, but with the paucity of maps in Jamaica they have served many other purposes for Government other than valuation . . . ."

judges that "by and large the survey methods employed are not very precise and much of the mapping exercise could be regarded as controlled sketching." [27] Yet they have proved sufficient for their purpose and, in fact, when completed will serve as the first complete catalog of the country's properties.

A major achievement in all this has been Jamaica's ability to find and value properties with a surprisingly small professional staff; moreover, most of that staff did not exist at the start of the process, but had to be trained. In particular, draughtsmen and valuators were extremely scarce.[28] In fact, as Copes notes, when valuations on the unimproved basis started, in addition to himself there were only two qualified valuers in Jamaica. Both have degrees from London University's College of Estate Management and are associates of the Royal Institution of Chartered Surveyors. Around these two men the staff was built. According to his letter of 7 April 1966, Copes regards "the standard of their professional attainments as possibly the greatest single factor in the establishment of the programme. Other persons recruited were not trained to full valuer status but assigned duties on a tier system of responsibility." In valuating the first six parishes, from the two qualified valuers came "all basic decisions as to the level of value to be applied and the application of these levels . . . . The output of the department was therefore limited to their capacity to supervise." Since then more graduates in estate management have been added to the commissioner of valuations' staff. Because of the unavailability of a sufficient number of professionally qualified valuers, an important role is played by a group of technical personnel. "Technical officers were recruited both within and outside the Civil Service on the basis of qualifications and experience in other fields related to land, e.g., agriculture and building technology," and draughtsmen and technical assistants were trained under a "program initially supervised by a team of United States Technical Assistance Experts." [29] Currently in the Land Valuation Division there are eight professional valuers (including the commissioner), twenty-nine technical valuers, eighteen draughtsmen, and thirty technical assistants, a staff of seventy-seven professional and technical officers.[30]

In 1959, as sanctioned by the law, it was decided to exempt all landholdings worth under £100 from the formal unimproved valuation pro-

27. Chang, "Taxation in Jamaica," p. 227.
28. The shortage of skilled professional valuers in all countries is remarked on by Hicks in *Development From Below,* p. 365.
29. Chang, "Taxation in Jamaica," p. 224.
30. Ibid.

cess.[31] Such properties were simply noted to fall in the under £100 class and were subject to a token tax of four shillings. Because of the great fragmentation of rural landholdings in Jamaica, this decision represented a major simplification.

An idea of the accomplishment to date is furnished by Table 11.1, which also highlights the administrative importance of not requiring a valuation of properties under £100. About 70 percent of the holdings revalued so far—144,458 of a total of 206,611 parcels—fall in this group. This saves an enormous amount of valuation work, but the value of parcels involved is small, less than 14 percent of the value of all landholdings in the seven parishes. Consequently, much is gained and little lost on this score.

The fragmentation of holdings at the lower end of the distribution has its counterpart, of course, in its upper portion. Witness the fact that for the seven parishes just over 2 percent of the holdings by number account for over 50 percent of the value of land. And this pattern is found consistently in each individual parish.

Hardship and Relief

As would be expected, the Land Valuation Law of 1956 specified procedures for appeal by taxpayers who disagreed with the commissioner's valuation. The taxpayer may take objection to the commissioner's valuation and appeal to the valuation board (one for each valuation district), a quasi-judicial body made up of a chairman who has legal qualifications and four other members. Additionally, of course, the taxpayer may appeal the commissioner's valuation to the courts.

Whenever land is taxed on potential rather than actual use, there is the possibility that some taxpayers will find it hard to meet their land tax liability. This is not a question of disagreeing with the commissioner's valuation. Rather, it is a matter of the "hardship" that payment of a tax liability would cause. Grounds for obtaining relief (that is, tax reduction) were set forth in the Land Taxation (Relief) Law, 1960, and amendments to that law passed in 1964.[32] Requests for relief are taken up by the Land Taxation (Relief) Board made up of the collector general, the commissioner of valuations, and one other person. (To date, the last has

31. At the time of this study the Jamaican pound, like its British counterpart, was worth $2.80. In November 1967 Jamaica followed Britain's devaluation of the pound to $2.40.

32. Jamaica, Land Valuation (Amendment) Act, 1964, no. 44.

been a real estate man, but this professional qualification is not required by law.)

The objective of these provisions "is to grant relief where hardship is experienced in paying the tax and where the valuation of the land took into account the potentialities of the land for use other than the purpose

Table 11.1—Unimproved Land Valuations in Seven Parishes

Value of parcel (in pounds)	Number of valuations			Amount of valuation		
	Number	Percentage of total	Cumulative percent	Amount [a]	Percentage of total	Cumulative percent
St. Catherine (1959)						
Up to 100	30,779	74.6	74.6	1,275	14.3	14.3
101–200	5,029	12.2	86.8	734	8.2	22.5
201–1,000	4,631	11.2	98.0	2,020	22.7	45.2
1,001–5,000	797	1.9	99.9	1,562	17.5	62.7
5,001–10,000	90	....	....	627	7.1	69.8
10,001–20,000	47	0.4	100.3	668	7.5	77.3
Over 20,000	31	....	....	2,017	22.6	99.9
Total	41,404	100.3 [b]		8,903	99.9	
St. Ann (1959)						
Up to 100	23,457	69.0	69.0	1,047	11.3	11.3
101–200	5,126	15.1	84.1	783	8.5	19.8
201–1,000	4,290	12.6	96.7	1,868	20.2	40.0
1,001–5,000	898	2.6	99.3	1,962	21.2	61.2
5,001–10,000	90	....	....	638	6.9	68.1
10,001–20,000	45	0.7	100.0	639	6.9	75.0
Over 20,000	56	....	....	2,290	24.7	99.7
Total	33,962	100.0		9,227	99.7	
St. Mary (1960)						
Up to 100	23,584	76.4	76.4	1,018	15.1	15.1
101–200	3,649	11.8	88.2	561	8.4	23.5
201–1,000	2,893	9.4	97.6	1,294	19.3	42.8
1,001–5,000	621	2.0	99.6	1,346	20.1	62.9
5,001–10,000	68	....	....	495	7.4	70.3
10,001–20,000	35	0.4	100.0	519	7.8	78.1
Over 20,000	36	....	....	1,468	21.9	100.0
Total	30,886	100.0		6,701	100.0	
Portland (1960)						
Up to 100	17,319	71.7	71.7	756	16.2	16.2
101–200	3,407	14.2	75.9	131	2.8	19.0
201–1,000	2,902	12.1	98.0	1,167	25.0	44.0
1,001–5,000	357	1.5	99.5	761	16.3	60.3
5,001–10,000	42	....	....	305	6.6	66.9
10,001–20,000	37	0.4	....	560	12.0	78.9
Over 20,000	15	....	99.9	980 [c]	21.0	99.9
Total	24,079	99.9		4,661	99.9	

Table 11.1 (continued)

		St. Thomas (1961)				
Up to 100	15,453	66.7	66.7	712	13.2	13.2
101–200	4,375	18.9	85.6	674	12.5	25.7
201–1,000	2,922	12.6	98.2	1,176	21.8	47.5
1,001–5,000	308	1.3	99.5	637	11.8	59.3
5,001–10,000	33	....	....	238	4.4	63.7
10,001–20,000	36	0.4	99.9	548	10.2	73.9
Over 20,000	22	....	....	1,400	26.0	99.9
Total	23,149	99.9		5,385	99.9	

		Trelawny (1961)				
Up to 100	10,772	59.5	59.5	462	9.7	9.7
101–200	3,654	20.3	79.8	567	11.9	21.6
201–1,000	3,265	18.1	97.9	1,212	25.3	46.9
1,001–5,000	297	1.7	99.6	700	14.6	61.5
5,001–10,000	31	....	....	225	4.7	66.2
10,001–20,000	16	0.4	100.0	236	4.9	71.1
Over 20,000	29	....	....	1,377	28.8	99.9
Total	18,064	100.0		4,779	99.9	

		St. Elizabeth (1965)				
Up to 100	23,094	66.0	66.0	962	14.8	14.8
101–200	7,161	20.4	86.4	1,132	17.3	32.1
201–1,000	4,438	12.7	99.1	1,655	25.4	57.5
1,001–5,000	289	0.8	99.9	688	10.6	68.1
5,001–10,000	39	....	....	275	4.2	72.3
10,001–20,000	22	0.2	100.1	316	4.8	77.1
Over 20,000	24	....	....	1,492	22.8	99.9
Total	35,067	100.1		6,520	99.9	

		Total of the Seven Parishes				
Up to 100	144,458	69.9	69.9	6,231	13.4	13.4
101–200	32,401	15.7	85.6	4,980	10.7	24.1
201–1,000	25,341	12.3	97.9	10,393	22.3	46.4
1,001–5,000	3,567	1.7	99.6	7,656	16.4	62.8
5,001–10,000	393	....	....	2,803	6.0	68.8
10,001–20,000	238	0.4	100.0	3,486	7.5	76.3
Over 20,000	213	....	....	11,024	23.7	100.0
Total	206,611	100.0		46,573	100.0	

a These figures are in terms of thousands of pounds.

b Total and cumulative percentages below or above 100 are due to rounding.

c On the basis of a check of cross-totals, I have changed the amount of valuation in the "Over £20,000" class for Portland to read £980,000 rather than £580,000, as in Chang's paper, and I have adjusted aggregate totals accordingly.

Source: Wilfred S. Chang, "Recent Experience of Establishing Land Value Taxation in Jamaica," in International Seminar on Land Taxation, Land Tenure, and Land Reform in Developing Countries, ed. Archibald M. Woodruff, James R. Brown, and Sein Lin (W. Hartford, Conn.: John C. Lincoln Institute, University of Hartford, 1967), pp. 227–228, 230–231.

for which the land is being used." [33] While one of the purposes of taxing unimproved value is to discourage inefficient use, the application of this principle can run into some hard cases. Particularly sharp have been the reactions of some property owners on the North Shore whose beach land (in the judgment of the commissioner) had potential for luxury hotels. For example, a fisherman who owned one and one-quarter acres of beach on which his shack lay and where he stored his equipment was assessed a tax of £36 on the new basis, a sum that he could not possibly pay out of the income generated by the current use of the land. In general, taxpayers may apply for relief if they are using their land for agriculture and if its valuation took into account other potential uses, or if the land on which a private residence is located has been valued in recognition of its potential for hotel, industrial, commercial, or multiple-residence uses. (The law does not provide relief for land that is vacant or land that is being used for industrial or commercial purposes.) When relief is applied for, the Taxation Relief Board must decide whether it is reasonable that the land continue in its present use and whether paying the tax based on the commissioner's valuation would mean hardship for the taxpayer. Relief certificates are not transferable.

Relief is provided as to tax liability but not tax base. According to Copes's letter of 16 January 1967 to the author, the board

> has no jurisdiction to alter a valuation but only to assess the amount of tax relief for which the applicant may be eligible. The relief ceases should the person sell or he or his widow die. The value on the roll applies to subsequent purchasers or owners.
>
> It has been suggested at times that the amount of the relief should remain a charge on the land, to be collected on a subsequent sale, and in the state of New South Wales, where a similar provision operates, the amount of the relief up to a period of five years is collected on subsequent sale.

Hardship cases involve a difficult question: under what conditions should the personal circumstances of the taxpayer be an important determinant of land tax liability? They pose a problem because the use to which the owner is putting his land, while not optimal, best represents his skill and in many cases, his way of life. He is not capable of developing the property appropriately, and, should he sell it, there may be nothing else he can do. Moreover, particularly with land with hotel potential, selling his land might mean giving up a property that had been in his family for many years, quite possibly to a wealthy person who might very well hold it for further appreciation. Under the circumstances, compromise is appropriate; the relatively few hardship cases might otherwise threaten the success of the tax shift to the new basis.

33. Chang, "Taxation in Jamaica," p. 235.

While a tax on property is just that—a tax on things rather than on persons—"hardship" recognizes, sometimes in curious and unspecified ways, the personal circumstances of the owners of properties and the uses to which they can put them. The necessity to sell at fair market value could constitute hardship for a man skilled in one craft and in one region. This, of course, is the prototype of the hard-core hardship case, say, the fisherman who can do little else and whose beach is located on land that is very suitable for a luxury hotel.

Formal principles of "relief" are hard to spell out, but the tendency has been, in severe cases, not to push taxing based on full value where undue strain would ensue and to favor permitting those committed to a way of life to continue it (to postpone taxation of full value until the property's use has been changed or it has changed hands).[34]

Rates and Rate Schedules

Legislated Rates

Three taxes are levied on the unimproved value of land—the property tax, parish rate, and service rate. The property tax is set by the national government and is the same in all parishes. The parish rate is determined by each parish council subject to the national government's approval and varies somewhat among parishes.[35] The property tax and parish rate together comprise the tax on unimproved value as that term is used in this chapter and account for almost all the revenues from levies laid on land. Service rates are charges for specific and particular services provided by the parish—fire protection, water, lighting, etc.

The property tax is a progressive levy with very high exemptions. All parcels whose unimproved value is £1,000 or less are exempt from it. On all sites with unimproved values exceeding £1,000, a progressive schedule applies with the tax commencing at 1 pence in the pound and reaching 2 pence in the pound by a value of £10,000; 3 pence in the pound at a

34. Illustrative of the tax changes that have led to appeal are the following cases cited to the author which were granted substantial relief:

Old tax	New tax
£52 10s.	£374
4s.	£ 2 4s.
£ 3 15s.	£152
£ 1 16s.	£ 23 19s.

35. The parish rate varies between parishes because it is set at that level which will make parish rate collections plus property tax collections in the aggregate the same as they were in the last year of the old basis.

value of £20,000; 4 pence in the pound at a value of £30,000; and for values above £30,000 (that is, £30,000 in excess of £1,000 or £31,000 in all) a flat rate of 7 pence in the pound is imposed.[36] All this boils down to an effective rate schedule that behaves like the line labeled "Property tax" on Figure 11.1. The tax is at a zero rate on properties up to £1,000, and for holdings with unimproved value greater than this the tax rises with the value of the property approaching in the limit an effective rate of 2.92 percent (that is, 7 divided by 240). The tax is progressive with respect to properties, not with respect to persons; holdings under one ownership are not aggregated for purposes of computing the tax.

Once again we are reminded of the fragmentation of ownership in numerous small plots and the vast size of a small number of larger holdings by noting from Table 11.1 that in the seven parishes currently on the new basis, just over 2 percent of all holdings and well over half of aggregate site value are subject to the property tax.

Although parish rates vary from one parish to another, certain features of the tax are common to all parishes: there are no exemptions; the first £100 is subject to a flat tax of four shillings; the second £100 pays a tax of one-half pence in the pound; and on values in excess of £200 the rate is set to meet the total revenue requirements stated above. In St. Catherine it was put at one and three-fourths pence in the pound; in St. Ann at one pence in the pound. The parish rate then covers all properties and its rate, while progressive, "slides" only modestly, running in St. Catherine, for example, from 0.2 percent on a holding whose unimproved value is £100 to an effective rate of 0.73 percent on a £100,000 site.[37] (See the line labeled "Parish rate" on Figure 11.1.) On the other hand, gentle and modestly progressive as it may be, because there are no exemptions from the parish rate, it is not an unimportant revenue raiser compared to the property tax. For example, in St. Catherine parish, one of the first two to go on the new base, and for which more detailed information than for the other parishes is available, it has been estimated that of the total revenue of £103,000 to be raised in the first year of unimproved value taxation, £60,000 would come from the property tax and £43,000 from the parish rate.[38]

36. The formula involves progression on the basis of one pence in the pound increasing by .0001 pence for every pound increase. Government of Jamaica, Ministry Paper No. 4: *Revaluation of Land and Proposed System of Taxation*, 5 March 1959, gives the following example: on a holding with an unimproved value of £7,864, there would be £6,864 subject to tax at a rate of 1 pence + (6,864/10,000) = 1.6864 pence per pound or a total tax of £48 4s. 7d.

37. At its limit the parish rate approaches 0.73% in St. Catherine and 0.42% in St. Ann.

38. Government of Jamaica, Ministry Paper No. 4.

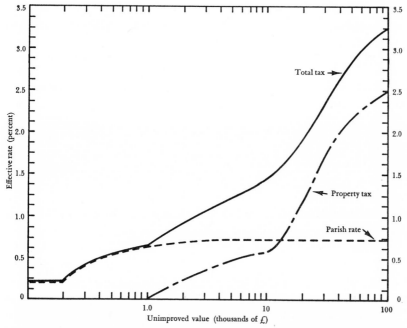

Figure 11.1. Rates of Unimproved Land Value Taxation, St. Catherine Parish

The effective rate at which site value is taxed is the sum of the property tax and the parish rate. As plotted in Figure 11.1, it is a progressive rate schedule (with a couple of kinks that reflect exemptions and unevenness in the legislated rate formulae) that ranges from 0.2 percent on sites whose unimproved value is £100 to 3.24 percent on sites valued at £100,000 (the highest value plotted). This is what the rate schedule looks like, but can we say anything further? Are they too "high" or too "low"? Are they likely to affect the decision to develop a holding? Of course, computed effective rates provide no direct answers to questions of this kind.

Dogmatically, we could choose a value and state that rates below this level are *de minimis* and not likely to have an economic effect.[39] If 1 percent were designated for this purpose, then in the parish of St. Catherine properties of under, say, £5,000 would be subject to rates too "low" to affect the decisions of those who hold or develop properties. Under

39. Actually, this is too naive a way of putting it. The germane datum would be the differential between the rate of taxation on improved value and the rate of taxation on the same property on unimproved value.

Table 11.2—Number, Value, and Rates of Taxation on Unimproved Land Value for Properties in St. Catherine Parish as of 1959

Valuation class (in £)	Properties			Valuation			Effective rate of [a]			Percentage of [b]		
	Number	%	Cumulative %	Amount (Thousands of £)	%	Cumulative %	Property tax	Parish rate	Total tax	Property tax	Parish rate	Total tax
Up to 100	30,779	74.9	74.9	1,275	14.3	14.3	0.00	0.20	0.20	0.0	11.9	5.6
101–200	4,729	11.5	86.4	734	8.2	22.5	0.00	0.20+	0.20+	0.0	2.9	1.4
201–300	1,565	3.8	90.2	401	4.5	27.0	0.00	0.38	0.38	0.0	2.5	1.2
301–500	1,795	4.4	94.6	730	8.2	35.2	0.00	0.52	0.52	0.0	6.6	3.1
501–1,000	1,271	3.1	97.7	889	10.0	45.2	0.00	0.52	0.63	0.0	9.0	4.2
1,001–2,500	624	1.5	99.2	954	10.7	55.9	0.00	0.63	0.63	2.6	12.4	7.2
2,501–5,000	173	0.4	99.6	607	6.8	62.7	0.29	0.63	0.98	3.9	8.2	5.9
5,001–10,000	90	0.2	99.8	627	7.0	69.7	0.47	0.69	1.18	6.2	8.7	7.4
10,001–20,000	47	0.1	99.9	668	7.5	77.2	0.71	0.71	1.43	10.4	9.4	9.9
20,001–30,000	16			410	4.6	81.8	1.15	0.72+	1.87	9.8	5.8	7.9
30,001–50,000	6	0.1		233	2.6	84.4	1.57	0.73-	2.30	7.6	3.3	5.5
50,001–100,000	5			340	3.8	88.2	2.11	0.73-	2.84	13.7	4.8	9.5
Over 100,000	4		100.0	1,033	11.6	99.8	2.51	0.73-	3.24	45.9	14.6	31.1
Total	41,104	100.0		8,902	99.8					100.1	99.9	100.1

[a] Effective rate on lower limit of valuation class.
[b] Columns do not total 100.0 due to rounding.

Source: Government of Jamaica, Ministry Paper No. 4: *Revaluation of Land and Proposed System of Taxation,* 5 March 1959.

this assumption, falling in the category not affected by the tax would be all but four-tenths of 1 percent of the parcels in St. Catherine. However, the small number assumed to be affected would account for 32 percent of the site value. (See Table 11.2.) But even this would be an over-statement of the number and value of sites assumed to be affected by the tax. For with land taxes deductible from taxable income as defined for the personal income tax, the real effective rates of the property tax and the parish rate are lower, particularly for the owners of the parcels of high value, than those plotted in Figure 11.1. This whole discussion is highly conjectural, however, because in fact we do not know at what rate the tax bite really starts to affect landholding and developing decisions. Moreover, there is not much profit in pursuing this kind of hypothesis, for the relevant information here is not the rate of taxation on a given property, but how much this rate differs from what it would be had improved value been the basis of assessment. To this end I obtained some evidence for a few properties in the course of my visit.

Some Illustrative Cases

The data of Table 11.3 all pertain to one parish and cover a few particular instances of valuation and tax rate changes associated with the

Table 11.3—Examples of Valuations and Tax Liabilities on Old and New Bases for a Few Particular Properties [a]

	Valuation		Combined property tax and parish rate	
Nature of property	Old basis	New basis	Old basis	New basis
(1) Large tract of idle land	£6,000	£60,000	£335	£1,836
(2) Large tract of idle land	900	30,000	25	723
(3) Idle seacoast land	9,000	25,000	502	547
(4) Banana and coconut plantations	3,000	90,000	105	2,966
(5) Undeveloped acre plot in subdivision	200	2,250	3 15s	23 7s
(6) Undeveloped half-acre plot in subdivision	300	850	2 12s	5 16s

[a] In the parish in which these properties are located, the parish rate is 2 pence in the pound on all values in excess of £200, a little higher than in St. Catherine, where, as noted above, it is 1¾ pence.

Source: Data made available to the author in Jamaica by several collectors of taxes.

shift in tax bases. The need for a revaluation is dramatically pointed up by the difference between the old and new values.[40] Those on the new basis, although limited to site value, are considerably higher because they were made as of a recent date. At least as worthy of note, however, is the wide dispersion of the ratio of old to new basis. For the large properties it runs 1:10, 1:32, 1:3, and 1:30; for the two small holdings it is 1:11 and 1:3. Sizable tax changes do show up for the valuable properties.[41] The holder of property (1) will now need to expect the value of his property to increase by more than 3 percent per year to offset the tax cost (I am taking the new basis valuation as a "correct" estimate of the value of the property), while on the old basis an increase of only one-half of 1 percent per year would have met the tax cost of holding this land. Now a price rise of about 2.5 percent is needed to offset the new tax, whereas a rise of one-tenth of 1 percent would have met the old tax cost. The decision to hold plot (3) is substantially unaffected by the change to unimproved value taxation. The tax cost of holding plot (4) has changed markedly. To pay for the tax now an increase in its value of 3.3 percent is necessary; on the old basis tax costs really did not enter into the decision to hold it, for a price rise of a little over one-tenth of 1 percent would have been sufficient to pay for the tax. On the very large undeveloped properties, then, the change in taxes would seem to be of an order of magnitude that could seriously affect the landholding and development decisions.

On the other hand, the holders of smaller and less valuable vacant sites seem unlikely to be induced to sell or develop them because of the increased tax liability associated with the change to unimproved value taxation. Thus, despite the tenfold increase in its valuation and the fivefold increase in his tax, the owner of property (5) could earn the tax cost of holding it if its value increased by as little as 1 percent, and an increase of little more than one-half of 1 percent in the value of plot (6) would cover the tax cost of holding it. Another way to look at it is this: Typically, a house of about £6,000 is built on plots the size and value of plot

40. The reader should be reminded that the difference in valuations and tax liabilities is made up of two effects: (a) the revaluation of all properties as of a common date; and (b) the change in the distribution of a given aggregate amount of tax liability among particular properties attendant upon the substitution of unimproved for improved value taxation.

41. To the extent that the holders of these properties appealed and were accorded relief, the data of the table overstate the tax change. At least one of the four large properties did get relief and will have a tax liability lower than that shown in Table 11.3.

(5). Interest rates in Jamaica run at about 8 percent, so the annual interest cost (imputed or actual) of plot and building would be about £650, against which the tax on the land fades to insignificance. But to revert to the difference between the likely effect on these smaller or less valuable sites and the very large or more valuable sites, the same developer who discussed the effect on holders of acre and half-acre plots in one of his subdivisions in the spirit of the last several sentences, also mentioned that he knew of some holders of idle land who formerly paid £50 to £100 in taxes and are now paying £500 to £600, in his judgment a rise large enough to energize them.

So much for likely effects; is there any firmer evidence, can we point to decisions that have, in fact, been affected by the revaluation on the unimproved basis? Needless to say, such information has not been collected by Jamaica's tax authorities, but in the course of my visit I heard of a few cases. A wealthy landholder refused £100,000 for something like thirty to forty acres of good beach land on the North Shore. Then after the property was assessed at £150,000 subject to something like £5,000 in tax, and after upon appeal no relief was granted, the landholder sold the property for £250,000 to someone who was going to develop. In another instance, a property initially valued at £158,000 but upon appeal reduced to £81,000 was sold because the income from the property in the use to which the holder was putting it was insufficient to pay the tax liability. Again, therefore, it was the large and valuable sites that were affected. It was the judgment of the people I spoke with that on most plots the taxes were too low to have any effect. One man felt that rates about twice the current ones would be required to affect the development decisions of the holders of most properties. This is closer to gossip than evidence; yet there can be little doubt that on most properties a real dissuasion to underutilization has yet to be achieved.

The Question of Progressivity

It was noted earlier that the land tax in Jamaica is impersonally progressive, being progressive relative to each parcel, but not as regards any person's total holdings. About this procedure much can be said by way of criticism, but something can also be said in its favor.

The major points against it have been pithily put in the Hickses' report as follows: "It is bad (i) because it is inequitable, since progressive taxes should be levied upon income, or property, *as a whole,* not upon particular sorts of property such as alone can be reached by a land tax; (ii) because it is adverse to development, since it involves the imposition of special taxation on business that tends to prevent the expansion of firms to their most efficient size . . . ." [42]

A less than fully convincing argument on the other side would start with the observation that the progressive feature of Jamaica's land tax provides an incentive for the development of the more valuable plots. And this constitutes a selectively efficient device for development. To argue the point strictly one would standardize for site value per unit of space and observe that the excess of the value of site A over site B is a measure of the outlays on productive resources that do not have to be made in generating a given output, if site A is used as against site B. Therefore, to develop site A instead of site B is to conserve on other factors of production, and this, of course, will mean resources freed for other uses. On these grounds a progressive tax on value per space-unit (acre or something else) of site would be efficient and salutary for growth. But this is not a strong argument because the progression in Jamaica's tax on unimproved value is not as precisely cast as this, running as it does on the value of each site, which itself depends on both value per unit of space and the physical size of the site. An element of the more correct base might be caught by Jamaica's land tax, however, to the extent that the sites of higher absolute value are also the sites of higher value per unit of space—a condition more apt to be met in urban than rural areas.

There is another argument, in my judgment stronger than the one just discussed, for a progressive (with total holdings rather than for each parcel) land tax. It is weak because it rests on the association, admittedly rough and partial, between the value of landholdings and economic power more generally. Its strength lies in its recognition that the property tax is only one component of a country's tax structure.

Specifically, this argument draws attention to the differential effect of a tax on property in the context of a progressive income tax. Given that property taxes are deductible in deriving the income tax base, the net burden of the property tax is cushioned for all income tax payers in direct proportion to the personal tax rates they are subject to. Thus, a 2 percent property tax is effectively a tax of 1.5 percent for a landholder subject to a 25 percent personal income tax rate; it is a tax of 1 percent for a person in the 50 percent bracket; while for the taxpayer subject to personal marginal rates of 75 percent, the property tax would constitute

---

42. Hicks and Hicks, *Report on Jamaica,* p. 146. Their argument applies to progressive property taxation and asks whether the progressivity be on a property-by-property basis or be related to each taxpayer's total holdings.

an annual holding charge of one-half of 1 percent.[43] As Sherman J. Maisel notes, this is equivalent to asserting that a landholder-investor, say, in the 50 percent bracket, will, in effect, be meeting a 2 percent property tax payment should his land increase in value only at the rate of 1 percent, while an investor not subject to income tax will, in fact, need to make a gain of 2 percent in value to cover the property tax.

All this means that even a site value tax in conjunction with an income tax is not "neutral" in its effect on the landholding (or land developing) decisions of different taxpayers. The higher a taxpayer's income, the less his land need appreciate in value to be an attractive investment for him to hold. This "distortion" tends to push land into the hands of the wealthy. And this is a matter that "more equitable assessments would not alter . . . by much." [44] One policy that would change this differential thrust is a purposeful bias in the land tax. If income and landholdings were perfectly correlated, then a degree of progression could be incorporated in the land tax that would just neutralize the differential push of the income tax, and all investors, *ceteris paribus,* would find land equally desirable for holding. In fact, there is not a tight coupling between income and value of landholdings, yet there is some association. Therefore, the progressivity of Jamaica's tax on unimproved value probably does tend to mitigate somewhat the distortions among taxpayers of different incomes in the landholding decision introduced by the progressivity of the income tax. But this effect is probably weak.

Following Maisel's procedures, the nature of the distortion under discussion can be spelled out more generally. By specifying an investor's discount rate (i), we specify also what he can earn on alternative investments. At the end of n years such an investment will be greater than its initial amount by a factor $(1 + i)^n$. Or he can invest in land which, say, at the end of n years will double in value. Assuming further that there are net out-of-pocket carrying costs for investment in land of 0.5 percent [45] and that the initial investment is 1, then for the land case where a doubling is assumed in n years, the value of the investment would be $2 - (1 + .005)^n$, while the alternative would have appreciated to $(1 + i)^n$.

43. Sherman J. Maisel, "Background Information on Costs of Land for Single Family Housing," in *Appendix to the Report on Housing in California* (Governor's Advisory Commission on Housing Problems, 1963), p. 269. The next several pages draw heavily on Maisel's discussion.

44. Ibid., pp. 269, 271.

45. In his illustration, Maisel allowed for a capital gains tax on the appreciation in land value, but my example makes no such calculation because capital gains are not taxed in Jamaica.

If we set these two equal and solve for n, we will have the maximum number of years over which a doubling of price must take place to make land preferable to alternative investments. Since

$$n = \frac{\log 2}{\log (1 + i) + \log (1 + .005)},$$

the maximum number of years is a function of i. More specifically, we have the following results:

| i | n |
(in percent)	
3	20
5	13
10	7
20	3

Clearly, high income taxpayers (those subject to high rates of personal income tax and who therefore have low discount rates characterizing their investment opportunities) will have the greatest inducement to invest in land; on the other hand, holding land for appreciation will be relatively unattractive for those to whom high discount rates apply. Thus, the investor who can earn 3 percent on alternative opportunities would prefer land to these alternatives so long as its price would double in twenty years or less, while the investor whose alternatives were characterized by a 20 percent return could not afford to hold land for appreciation unless he could expect it to double in value in no more than three years. Illustrative data like this, Maisel concludes, "shows why we would expect most landowning for speculative purposes to be done by estates and wealthy landowners." [46]

These data also suggest that investors subject to high income taxes could afford to hold land for appreciation (keep it out of development) even though its prospects of appreciation were relatively slight. To drive this latter point home, we might note that given the same assumptions as stated above, over a ten-year period land must appreciate by 30 percent to cover the costs of investing in it for investors whose discount rate is 3 percent, while those to whom a discount rate of 20 percent applies would require an appreciation of 624 percent in ten years to cover the costs of investing in land.[47]

46. Ibid., p. 271.
47. The costs of investing in land are the opportunity costs measured by i and the out-of-pocket expenses, which are assumed to be 0.5%. Over a ten-year period these costs cumulate to $(i)^{10} + (.005)^{10}$. The figures in the text are the cumulations for i of 3% and 20%, respectively.

In summary, both bodies of illustrative data point in the same direction, viz., that the lower the rate of discount applying to one's investment opportunities the more attractive, *ceteris paribus,* is investment in land. There are a number of reasons why we would expect the investors in a community to have different discount rates relevant to their decisions. One of them, of course, is the progressive income tax.

For countries with progressive income taxes under which site value taxes would be a deductible expense, an argument can be made for having that latter tax progressive, to the extent that there is an association between value of landholding and level of income. For, *ceteris paribus,* the introduction of progressive income taxation "distorts" the landholding decision by making it a function of the marginal rate of personal income tax with the investor's land tax cost, α, transformed to $\alpha (1 - P_j)$, where P_j is the marginal rate of personal income tax. If, therefore, α were made variable, with α_k an increasing function of income, and P_j a decreasing function, $\alpha_k (1 - P_j)$ would be more likely to approach constancy than would $\alpha (1 - P_j)$, where α is an invariant rate. Thus, with α_k progressive, the combined income and property tax would not work toward making it less expensive for the rich to hold land and so on.

The argument strictly applies to the unreal situation of a site value tax progressive with income, but it is not unreasonable to assume that there is at least some correlation between income and the value of property holdings and that, therefore, the point is relevant also to Jamaica's progressive tax on unimproved value.

Both an economic and "practical" justification for progressive taxation of unimproved value have been set forth by Copes in a letter to the author of 16 January 1967. He argues that the effects of progressive taxation (including the "cushioning" effect attendant upon the deductibility of land tax from the personal income tax base) "are recognized by persons at different levels in the tax scale in Jamaica. For instance such persons holding, say, 50 acres of land of a similar quality to an adjoining large sugar estate have shown interest in comparing the rates of tax per acre. Although the lands have a similar value per acre, say £100, it is recognized that capacity, through finance and 'know how' are considerably different for the sugar estate and that the smaller holding should attract a lower tax per acre."

He then notes, "Apart from the economic justification, progressive land taxes are the means through which a new land system can be made nationally acceptable." Taxpayers at the lower end of the scale would, of course, favor a progressive structure, while those at the upper end would find the severity of the tax softened by its deductibility from the income tax base. Moreover, Copes contends, a progressive tax structure has a greater potential for revenue collection than a proportionate tax. And this is particularly the case when legislated rates tend to be sticky, a condition germane to Jamaica (as discussed in the section that follows).

Problems in Local Government

A Revenue "Bind"

Parish councils, the local governments in Jamaica, levy a tax on unimproved value—the parish rate—and since 1956 have received the government's property tax collections as a refund. The revaluation and shift to the new basis have had unfortunate consequences for the parishes, which, while neither an inevitable result of unimproved value taxation nor an essentially new problem, nonetheless serves to point up some possible consequences of an unimproved value base.

It is a fact that the national government, which determines the rate of the property tax and also must approve the parish rates, has long been and still is very reluctant to see a legislated increase in rates. This reluctance stems from the fear that any such increase will lose the party in power some votes, and with the two parties very closely matched, an increase in rates is seen to be politically unwise. Additionally, resistance to rate increases has become traditional as a response to the unsatisfactory state of affairs that the failure to revalue properties since 1937 has caused. For any increase in rates would hit those properties valued recently (either newly constructed or as a result of sale) quite heavily but leave those with values of a much earlier period almost unscathed. Which is to say no more than that when a tax base is considered inequitable, it is hard to get public support for increases in tax rates.

There has been a long history of rate constancy in Jamaica. This condition, found in other countries as well, of course, can be characterized as a rate constraint similar to the "rate-illusion" noted by J. Wiseman.[48]

48. "There is some evidence of the existence of a 'rate-illusion.' Notionally, there is no reason why rates of more than twenty shillings per £ of rateable value should not be common, since rateable value is merely a convenient measure of the relative burden to be placed on different local citizens. But there is a widespread feeling that levies of such a size are improper, and councils are consequently reluctant to impose them. Supporting evidence for the existence of, and belief of councils in such a rate-illusion is provided by the great increase in the total amount raised in rates in the year after the introduction of the new and higher rating valuations, despite a government appeal to exercise moderation. Councils who would not have dared to raise such extra revenues by pushing up rate-poundages felt able to do so when the actual burden on local citizens could be raised without rate-poundages rising simultaneously."—J. Wiseman, "The Future of Local Government Finance," *Lloyds Bank Review,* n.s., no. 45 (July 1957), p. 34.

Further, to ease the acceptance of the new basis and the transition to it, the national government set the property tax and parish rates such that combined collections in each parish would be the same in the first year on the new basis as the year before (although, of course, this total burden would be distributed differently). Thus, a level of rates was decided on, and, given Jamaican attitudes, these rates tend to remain invariant. But the parish councils' expenditure responsibilities and revenue needs continued to grow as they had before.

With rates fixed, the only way for revenues to move congruently with expenditure needs would be for the tax base to grow at a commensurate rate. And on the improved basis this is what tended to happen. But the unimproved base is sluggish and does not respond as markedly to growth.[49] It probably would not even if all sites were revalued annually. But this, of course, is not possible nor was it necessary on the improved basis. Each year's new construction was automatically added to the base and hence helped to keep revenues moving upward. Support for this judgment would seem to come from Woodruff and Ecker-Racz, who, in their study of property taxation in Australia and New Zealand conclude that "the exclusion of improvements under the unimproved value system also means that the tax base has considerably less flexibility than under either improved capital value or assessed annual value system." [50]

On the other hand, there is a body of expert opinion that takes exception to the contention that the site value base is sluggish and does not respond as markedly to growth as the improved value system. For example, in a letter to the author of 7 April 1966, Copes, a valuation expert with considerable experience in developing countries including Jamaica, remarked that "one cannot generalize on this. In Trinidad the average consideration on the sale of Real Property increased by 69 percent between 1957 and 1962. This was considerably in advance of the increase in the cost of construction in the same period, and I cannot agree with Mrs. Hicks that the value of buildings is likely to increase considerably faster than sites. Revaluations in Sydney on the Site Value System showed marked advances in the total roll values, often resulting in little, if any, movement in the rate poundage."

In a similar vein, Chang, the present commissioner of valuations, has expressed the view that the ability of the old basis valuation rolls to produce a fairly steady increase in tax yield without any increase in rates

---

49. Thus, Hicks is of the opinion that "generally speaking the value of buildings is likely to increase considerably faster than sites."—Hicks, *Development From Below,* p. 362. While this judgment appears in a chapter on the taxation of urban land and buildings, it would seem to be of more general applicability to all but strictly agricultural communities.

50. Woodruff and Ecker-Racz, "Property Taxes," p. 58.

stems from some particular imperfections of these valuations and the way they are levied rather than on any greater growth rate of improved value compared with unimproved value. Specifically, in a letter to the author (31 March 1967) he noted: (1) that the graduated rate structure in parishes on the old basis is designed to raise the requisite revenue from an old and inconsistent set of valuations; and (2) that the increase in their tax base (rateable values) comes from revisions attendant upon the transfer of properties and the addition of new buildings, both of which are valued at a higher percentage of true value than the properties previously on the rolls. In the absence of these special conditions, which are neither equitable nor tenable over the long run, he doubts whether percentage annual increases in improved value are larger than those in unimproved value. While no research has been done on this point, in Jamaica, at least, he feels that unimproved values could very well be increasing at a faster rate.

The point, then, that I have made in this section is open to real question. Be that as it may, since the introduction of unimproved value taxation, the parish councils have been in a revenue bind, relieved only by grants-in-aid from the national government, which are felt to be insufficient and, moreover, the growing dependence of the parish councils on this aid threatens their independence.[51] To some this is not so much an argument for the improved basis as it is for using both unimproved and improved valuations—the former to serve as the base for a national government tax and the latter to be the basis for assessing charges to meet some of the outlays of local governments. Something of the sort was originally proposed by Murray—the valuation expert who served as advisor to the government of Jamaica. For this procedure an additional argument can be made.

Charging for the Costs of Development

Murray, whose report served as a basis for much of what has since been done, proposed therein that in the revaluation two values be determined for every property, with the unimproved value to be the base for the land tax at a progressive rate and improved value to serve as the base for service rates.[52] (Service rates and the parish rate should not be confused; the former are particular charges for fire protection, water, lighting, and so on, while the latter is the parish tax on the site value of properties.

51. From a longer-run point of view this development may be considered an intensification of a trend that had set in much earlier. See Hicks, *Development From Below*, p. 142.
52. Murray, *Report to Jamaica*.

Service rate charges are considerably less than parish rate liabilities.) As it turned out, getting the one set of valuations on the unimproved basis took more time than had been planned for both sets; Murray's suggestion was therefore not followed. A government paper explains the reason for this decision and suggests that, in fact, the use of the unimproved basis for all taxes on property will be less likely to discourage development than the use of two bases.[53] This argument, however, is not wholly convincing; encouraging development is an important consideration, but not the only one. If the unimproved basis alone is used, the required outlays imposed on local governments by development are not properly accounted for. To the extent that development is encouraged (that is, sites are developed more intensively) by use of the unimproved basis it is likely that local governments will have to provide a larger flow of services closely tied to the pace of development.[54]

What Murray's suggestion in principle boils down to is a *national* tax to encourage development and a *local* tax for supporting the particular services of local government that increase *pari passu* with development (which in a Jamaican context would serve as a proxy for an expanded set of service rates). For the former, unimproved value makes good sense; for the latter, however, the capital value of a property would seem to be a better measure of the demand it makes on local-government resources. And as things have proceeded in Jamaica, to the degree that the switch to the unimproved basis achieves its objective of spurring development, heavier demands for local-government services will be a necessary result, but local-government taxing on this sluggish base and with its constraints as to rates will not be able to generate the fiscal resources to meet the increased demands. Fiscal strain for local government is not a problem peculiar to Jamaica. Currently in the United States, for example, local-government expenditure responsibilities tend to outrun their fiscal capacities (or their predisposition to use them). But it shows up in particularly sharp focus in Jamaica because of the relative stability of the unimproved value base.

53. "It was found, however, that to attempt to compile two sets of valuation rolls would take so long that it might well have taken more than 10 years to complete the valuation of the whole island. Moreover, it was thought that there was no important reason for insisting that special services in a given area in itself enhances the unimproved value of the land and the removal of all elements that discourage improvement of the land was thought to be better secured by having a single uniform system applicable to every type of tax."—Government of Jamaica, Ministry Paper No. 4.

54. Hicks in *Development From Below*, p. 359, notes as a criticism of unimproved value taxation that "from the point of view of social cost it is rather doubtful policy to provide building owners with urban social services gratis ...."

As noted above, as an empirical proposition, it would appear that Jamaica and other developing countries could, in fact, tax property more heavily. And on equity grounds likewise, an argument for more property taxation can be made. An income tax is likely to be a more imperfect tool for distinguishing among persons as regards capacity to pay in such societies than in economies with a longer record of development. There are grounds for this belief in the efficiency of administration, the pervasiveness and quality of record-keeping, and the degree of involvement of the economy in market exchange. Moreover, property taxation in general, and site value taxation in particular, will get at persons who hold land and are not developing it or making it available for development in a way that income taxation will not. Thus, a tax structure embodying site value taxation and an additional, smaller, and gradually introduced levy based on improved value makes a good deal of sense.

It is not suggested in this section, however, that improvements can be taxed without cost. In all honesty, it must be admitted that the costs could be substantial. Thus, apropos of this proposal, Copes notes that "the cost of making improved values will be more than twice the cost of finding site values, with the result that if the differential is weighed too lightly towards improvements, the result will not be worth the trouble of making the valuations." [55]

Moreover, Copes holds (in his letter of 16 January 1967), "by way of additional qualifications of the argument of this section," that one should not overstate either the extent of local-government overheads in some developing countries, such as those in the West Indies, or the degree to which it is appropriate to charge for them via taxes on improvements. He distinguishes three classes of overhead—economic, trading, and social. The existence of economic overheads (public works, health, fire protection, and street lighting for example) is of benefit to the whole parish and support for them, at least in part, should be more widely based than from individual property owners. Outlays on such trading services as water and sewerage are most appropriately recouped from the users by a metering charge, but if such a charge is not made and a tax is to be used instead, in his judgment there is no strong reason for choosing improved value rather than unimproved value. Social overheads—such as swimming pools, other recreational facilities, and libraries—are prop-

---

55. Letter of 7 April 1966. In a later letter (16 January 1967) Copes points out that "it is difficult even for developed economies to maintain valuation rolls of improved values." In New South Wales, for example, the pressure of increasing development has caused the valuation cycle to lapse from three years in the pre-World War II period to five or six since the end of the war, while thirty years were required in the United Kingdom to carry out the revision completed in 1962.

erly chargeable to improvements rather than land. But such outlays "do not loom large in the budgets in the West Indies."

Summary and Conclusions

In brief summary, site value taxation seems to be working in Jamaica. A number of administrative simplifications help to explain this achievement. Among the most important are:

1. The exemption of small holdings—those valued at less than £100—from the valuation process. This saved an enormous amount of work with only modest effects on revenues and equity.

2. The decision not to undertake a legal cadaster, which would have been time-consuming and expensive, but to be satisfied with simply establishing a roll of ostensible owners.

3. A heavy reliance on a technical corps for a good deal of the referencing and valuation field work, with a consequent ability to get along with very few professionally trained valuers.

It is my impression that, generally, most people have been reasonably satisfied with unimproved value taxation. In part, taxpayer acceptance of the new basis can be attributed to the unsatisfactory state of affairs under the old system.[56] Thus, a consistent set of values on either a site or capital value basis would be preferred to the status quo. Moreover, with total unimproved value tax liabilities fixed to be the same as under the old basis, a majority of taxpayers are subject to a simpler and smaller tax and would be likely to be "satisfied" with unimproved value taxation.[57] Further, as will be elaborated below, rates of taxation are generally

56. The old system relied on voluntary ingivings by the property owner, imperfectly and sporadically checked by the revenue authorities, and which mirrored competitive underassessment, thus making it impossible to include newly constructed or exchanged properties at their market value. All this was further aggravated because there had been no general revaluation of properties over £200 in value since 1937, and none of lower-valued properties (under £200) since 1928. For a discussion of how things stood under the old system, see Chang, "Taxation in Jamaica."

57. As noted above, properties of under £100 are not valued but merely stated to be in this category. From them is due a token tax of four shillings. The tax receipt is frequently "worth" considerably more than this since it serves some of the purposes of evidence of title where no such evidence previously existed. Further, most of the other taxpayers in St. Catherine and St. Ann (the first two parishes to go on the unimproved basis) paid a lower tax on the new basis than the old—at least 90% (70,000 of the 76,000) holdings were in this position. Of course, this is not a necessary result of taxing unimproved value, but follows from the particular schedules of exemption and tax rates chosen.

low and tax liabilities not particularly irksome. In part, the general acceptance of the new basis reflects the fact that most properties valued to date are agricultural and that judgments of land values in this use are probably not subject to as wide a margin of error as land values in commercial and industrial uses. Also, variations in the ratio of value of improvements to site value may not be as large in agricultural properties as in urban properties. Furthermore, some responsibility for the acceptability of unimproved value taxation must be laid to the community consensus on economic development as a high-priority goal. But over and above all these special and particular reasons, the seeming acceptance of site value taxation reflects in my judgment a feeling that the values so far determined are generally about right.

All things considered, Jamaica has started an interesting and, in all likelihood, fruitful transition to taxing site value. What is appropriate for one country at a particular time, however, is not necessarily a wise policy for other countries—even those that are in about the same stage of development. Jamaica needed, in any event, a thorough-going revaluation of all properties and would therefore have about as great an administrative task had she remained on the old basis. Consequently, the incremental cost of shifting to site value taxation was not large. Countries now taxing both land and improvements and with reasonably up-to-date and consistent assessments, but seeking to encourage development might very well find temporary exemptions from their tax (for example, as suggested by the Hickses) a simpler and more "efficient" way to proceed, since only new construction in desired categories need be given the stimulus. Or they might consider a differentially heavier tax on land as in Pittsburgh and as suggested for serious consideration in Venezuela by Carl Shoup and his associates.[58]

In evaluating Jamaica's experience (or any other country's for that matter) a distinction should be drawn between the administration of the program and its accomplishments. In Jamaica, for example, the objective was to institute a tax on site value to encourage development. It is one thing to fashion a system that will tax unimproved value successfully; it is quite another to accomplish the goal of development. For one thing,

[58] "Should Venezuela undertake to tax land more heavily than buildings? The fact that real estate rates are still so low makes the idea more feasible than it would be if rates were already relatively high. And if the tax burden on real estate is gradually increased, the bulk of the increase can be put on land. If the increases are gradual and the assessments competently done, there need be no major disturbance of land values.

"We believe that the theoretical case for a differentiated tax, in a country with rapidly increasing urbanization, is so strong that it merits careful consideration." —Shoup et al., *Fiscal System of Venezuela*, pp. 339–340.

the former is concerned with establishing and administering the base of the tax, while the latter very likely involves the rate of taxation as well. But more than this, as the people I spoke with in Jamaica so frequently emphasized, to place on one tax measure the whole burden of development is both unfair and unwise. For development is the product of numerous factors. If we are thinking of construction, for example, there has to be a demand for the construction, finance has to be forthcoming, and the requisite resources (including foreign exchange for equipment and furnishings) and skills have to be available. With these preconditions of development present, the tax on unimproved value (both via the price effect that follows the removal of the tax on improvements and the income effect that is a function of the site value tax per se) will push forward the point in time at which development takes place, will speed up the pace of development, or will do both. Similarly, the unimproved value tax complements (and is complemented by) zoning and planning more generally. The master plan sets the general pattern of land use, zoning controls particular uses within the framework of the plan, and the unimproved value tax can help determine how rapidly the master plan unfolds. Complementarity also characterizes the relation between site value taxation and monetary and fiscal policy. Thus, for any given level of tax on unimproved value, development will be the more rapid the lower interest rates and the more available funds are. In general, unimproved value taxation affects primarily the pace, not the form of development. More positive controls are necessary for shaping the form.

It is well to point this out because the tax on unimproved value (site value) has suffered from over-zealous supporters to an extent that suggests the old joke whose punch line has the victim ruefully ask, "with friends like this who needs enemies?" But as Mason Gaffney reminded the 1964 National Tax Association Conference, it has also suffered from over-zealous critics.[59] Why criticize a good tax because it is not better? Indeed it is about as good as a tax can be. A tax on unimproved value, as a substitute for taxing improvements, is neutral (or even salutary, given irrationality and imperfections) as among the uses to which resources are put, and it raises revenue. In having these two qualities it is matched only by a head tax. But on another dimension of tax policy-equity or distributional justice, site value taxation and a head tax are far apart, with the former getting the palm. For to tax surplus or unearned increment is equitable in a way that taxing existence is not.

Too often in the past site value taxation has been criticized because it cannot perform miracles. A balanced view would recognize site value

59. Gaffney, "Property Taxes and Urban Renewal," p. 285.

taxation as a member of a family of inducements and controls. And such recognition would remove the sting from the charge that while site value taxation encourages building, "the encouragement is indiscriminate; it may be questioned whether it is right or desirable to encourage all building of whatever sort." [60] This observation is true, but not the complete story. Many possibilities of controlling building exist, and they, together with land value taxation, should be dovetailed to produce the desired result. Thus, with unimproved value taxation providing an underlying pressure for development, zoning can help to determine the specific forms it takes, influencing the direction of mortgage funds can encourage one sector and deter another, and so on. In fact, of course, the role of site value taxation should be congruent with the rest of the economy so that what it attempts to do can be absorbed (made effective) by the rest of the economy. There is not much sense in encouraging development if there is no way to finance it or if a shortage of foreign exchange will prevent the purchase of necessary supplies and equipment.

Given these considerations, Jamaica is wise to temper the transition to unimproved value taxation by relatively modest rates. It is not wise, however, to prolong the transition. The revaluation and change in basis has already been overlong; at the present rate, valuations in the parishes that went on the new basis early could be seriously out of date before the other parishes get on the unimproved base. And since the property tax is a country-wide tax, this would mean serious differentials in tax liability on essentially similar properties. This, of course, is not a viable situation and would threaten the success of unimproved value taxation. No matter how economically sound a tax measure may be, poor administration will defeat it.

Nor should Jamaica consider its present unimproved value tax schedule and structure as "ideal" and not requiring major improvements. Once the changeover has been completed and all parishes are on the unimproved basis, careful thought should be given to increasing rates and lowering the exemptions. As it stands now, exemptions from the property tax are very high. As noted earlier, the data for St. Catherine show that almost all properties by number and about half by value are exempt from the property tax and paying only the very moderate parish rate. Half of site value, therefore, is not subject to a consequential penalty for under-utilization. But a good portion of Jamaica's agricultural, commercial, and industrial enterprises are modest in scale, and no one would argue that this sector could not use a stimulus toward greater efficiency. And

60. Hicks, *Development From Below*, p. 358. Mrs. Hicks goes on to point out that there may already be too much building as an inflation hedge, and more building could aggravate balance of payments difficulties.

higher rates and lower exemptions would increase revenue and permit, among other things, programs to help holders of smaller properties to develop them. In sum, over the long run, land value taxation has to cut deeper into Jamaica's economy than it presently does. As an economy develops and sites become more valuable, this will happen automatically to some extent. But over and above this, more of Jamaica's land must come under a meaningful tax incentive to efficiency, and programs for providing the financial and other resources to implement this incentive need to be developed. Higher rates and lower exemptions from the property tax will be an important step in this process.

There still remains a major difficulty. Yet to be solved is the puzzling problem of super-development, which is most severe in urban areas. In essence, if unimproved value taxation were relied on rigorously and solely, highly developed properties—those with improvements of high value relative to site value—would enjoy a sharp fall in tax burden. This is the condition that figured importantly in the Hickses' preference for temporary exemptions from a tax on improved value as a device to encourage development. And, indeed, many of those who support unimproved value taxation are unwilling to rely on it without modification in the case of highly developed properties.

Thus, Murray suggested that a "method of averting the anomalies which would result from the adoption of unimproved value as the sole basis of assessment would be to levy a special rate upon those properties which possess a high ratio of capital to unimproved value." [61] Specifically, he suggested that the special rate could be levied on "that part of the capital value lying beyond, say, ten times the unimproved value . . . ." [62] And Chang cites two other methods that might well be considered:

(a) a tax on capital values in addition to the taxes on unimproved values;
(b) a statutory definition of the unimproved value of improved land whereby the unimproved value is deemed to be not less than a certain percentage of either the capital value or the value of improvements. [63]

On net balance, however, Jamaica is laying a good basis for land taxation. But it is a good basis on which to build, not on which to rest. She must avoid complacency and the danger of becoming beguiled by the form of the tax change at the expense of making its substance a more effective force for development.

61. Murray, *Report to Jamaica,* p. 11.
62. Ibid., p. 12.
63. Chang, "Taxation in Jamaica," p. 238.

APPENDIX

Unimproved Value Taxation and Development

In a "Perfect" World

Perhaps we can go some part of the way in assessing economic effects on purely theoretical grounds. What does theory tell us the effect should be? Here, it is surprising to find, the picture is not at all clear. According to one point of view, in fact, the argument seems to be that the tax rate on unimproved value is irrelevant. To explain this argument and to help develop some related points, it is necessary to go back to the beginning of the story.

What is happening in Jamaica can be viewed as a two-step process. First, the tax on the improved value of properties is abolished. Such a tax tends to deter development in the sense that some plots have not been built on and others have been developed less intensively than they would have been in its absence. Therefore, removing the tax on improvements is an action that encourages development. Nor is this encouraging action undone by the second step of the process, which involves imposing a tax on site value. For this latter tax, the theory has it, is neutral as among the uses to which resources can be put. The amount of the tax does not depend on the use that is made of the site; if unimproved value is the tax base, the same tax liability will be forthcoming no matter how the site is developed (ruling out, of course, situations in which unimproved value is enhanced by a particular right, such as a license for a gas station).

The first step—removing the tax on improvements—gets rid of a deterrent to development, thereby encouraging construction, while the second step raises revenue but does not undo this stimulating effect. On net balance, then, the process of substituting a tax on unimproved value for one on improvements will in theory tend to encourage development. But notice, the strength of this effect is a function of the tax that is rescinded (that is, the tax on improvements), but does not depend on the site value tax that replaces it. On this line of reasoning, then, in analyzing the economic effects of the switch, the rate of taxation on unimproved value is irrelevant.

True, if the latter tax is capitalized (and this is the assumption usually made in analyzing its economic effects), then the market price of land will have been lowered. And this, it has been frequently asserted, will act as a spur to development. But this simple argument is clearly wrong. For while the selling price of land would decline, the effective cost of development would not. To explain: assume for simplicity that there is only one discount rate applying to all transactions.[1] Then the running cost of land for development purposes is converted by the site value tax from an interest charge to a smaller interest outlay plus a tax payment which together are just equal to the interest charge in the absence of the tax. For

---

1. This assumption, the one usually made in analyzing the effects of site value taxation, is equivalent to assuming that all transactors can borrow or lend all they wish at the same rate of interest. It is relaxed later in the discussion.

example, let the discount rate be 5 percent and let there be a piece of land that promises $1,000 a year (appreciation or net rent). The land will sell for $20,000 and the annual interest cost will be $1,000. Next, impose a site value tax that comes to 20 percent of the annual yield. The land will now sell for $16,000. The annual interest charge will be $800 and the annual tax payment $200; together they will be precisely equal to the annual interest cost before the tax. The running costs of development will not have changed.[2] And, if this is the case, capitalization of the tax and the consequent decline in the selling price of land do not encourage development. This is where matters would stand in a "perfect" world.

In an "Imperfect" World

In my judgment it is hard to believe the strict argument that all that matters as regards the effect on development of changing from improved to unimproved value taxation is the tax on improvements that has been removed. This amounts to asserting that it would make no difference whether the site value tax raises a given amount of revenue, half that amount, or twice or five times that amount. And the strict argument really gets its logical support by assuming away (or neglecting) liquidity considerations and other market imperfections.

Let the world be like it really is (less than perfect), and specifically, let at least some people be unable to borrow (or lend) without limit at a given price; then it makes a difference what level of site value taxation is set. For the higher the rate of taxation, the more pressed owners of sites will be to pay it. Thus, in addition to a price effect favorable to development associated with the removal of the tax on improvements, there will be a liquidity or income effect associated with the site value tax substituted for it. And the strength of this latter effect will depend on the level of unimproved value tax. At any given rate of site value taxation, the owners of vacant or sparsely developed sites will be particularly pressed by the income effect, because on them taxation on the new basis will fall more heavily

2. To explain more generally, let: r = annual rent or appreciation; i = interest or discount rate; t = rate of site value tax (as a percentage of annual rent); V_1 = market price of land before site value tax; and V_2 = market price of land after site value tax.

$$V_1 = \frac{r}{i} \text{ ; therefore, } i\,V_1 = r.$$

$$V_2 = \frac{r}{i} - \frac{tr}{i} = r\,\frac{(1-t)}{i} \text{ ; therefore, } i\,V_2 = r(1-t).$$

In the first instance, the running costs are the interest charges (imputed or actual) associated with the land, and this comes to r. In the second case, the running costs are the interest charge which equals $r(1-t)$ and the tax cost which comes to tr. The sum of $r(1-t)$ and tr is equal to r, which was precisely the running cost in the first instance. In our numerical example, the running costs in the first instance are $1,000 of interest; in the second case they are also $1,000 ($800 of interest and $200 of taxes).

than on the old. To raise the funds to meet their higher tax liabilities these owners will be induced to develop their properties or sell them to others who will. And the price at which they can sell will be lower by the capitalized value of their increased tax liabilities. New holders therefore will buy free of the tax increase. However, as already noted, the cost of the plot to them will not, of course, measure the cost of developing it—in a very real sense that will have remained unchanged.

But this is not the whole of the story if the economy is "imperfect" and capital rationing exists, as it surely does, in all countries and, characteristically, in more pronounced form in developing countries. For if liquidity (the availability of finance) has been a constraint, when the market price of sites falls due to capitalization of the differentially higher tax on unimproved value, a new opportunity is made available. Some developers previously unable to acquire land will now be in a position to do so because a smaller down payment is required of them. In effect it is as if new and additional finance was made available to them; the effect is equivalent to the new purchaser's obtaining a mortgage (additional to what he could otherwise get) on the parcel equal to the present value of the increase in expected tax payments. For this additional "mortgage" there is an annual running charge—the differentially higher site value tax. But the important thing is that an annual payment has been substituted for a capital sum, and people formerly unable to acquire land for development are now able to do so.

The strict unavailability of finance, of course, is just a particular instance of the more general condition that investors (developers) have different rates of discount applying to their marginal investment decisions. There are a number of reasons for this, among them being: (1) a varying propensity for risk assumption; (2) progressive income taxation; (3) discontinuities in market opportunities or knowledge; and (4) differences in financial strength and access to credit (under which heading falls credit rationing).

Thus, we might argue more generally that investors with high marginal discount rates—those developers who are more venturesome than average and consequently have opportunities with an expected yield higher than average—will benefit vis-à-vis the less venturesome or credit-rich investors. These high-discount-rate investors will "see" a real fall in the price of land for development, for the sum of the new market price of a site plus the present value *to them* (that is, capitalized at their discount rate) of the additional unimproved value tax will be lower than the old market price. But this is not a very esoteric point, after all. It is to be expected that if additional "mortgage" finance is made available to them at the same price as it is to everybody, it will be worth most to those who can put it to the most profitable use.

Moreover, there are "noneconomic" actions that a tax on unimproved value could affect in a salutary way. For example, it is frequently alleged that some people hold sites with no real development plans in mind but simply out of a firm conviction that their price will go up or, even more basically, because land is a prerequisite to a certain way of life or station in society. Increasing the carrying costs of land will make them less willing simply to hold and will force a closer examination of alternative courses of action, thus making the current holders more likely to develop their parcels themselves or to sell to someone who would. This constitutes, then, another reason for expecting unimproved value taxation per se to bring new plots into development. This point and those raised in the last several paragraphs are not new, of course, but they have generally received much less attention than they deserve. Mason Gaffney, in an article on urban renewal, points out the importance of liquidity (income) effects of the differentially heavier tax on site value this way. "They (land taxes) are largely neutral in the renewal decision, at least at our present level of analysis. In practice they even tend to accelerate renewal by arousing sleeping landowners, bypassing credit rationing, substituting a visible explicit cost for an invisible implicit one, reducing the liquidity of slow landowners, compelling a more rational attitude toward heirloom land and in general needling landowners to do what their self-interest would seem to have dictated anyway." [3] It is important, I think, that most of these "imperfections" could be expected to be more severe in developing countries than in industrialized nations. This is another reason, then, for arguing the appropriateness of site value taxation—particularly for developing countries.

Let us pause for a moment and summarize what has been discussed so far. It was suggested that an informative way to view the economic effects of the replacement of a tax on improved value with one on site value would be to break it down to a two-step process. First, the tax on improvements is removed; this will have an incentive effect on new construction. Because it will change the rate of return derivable therefrom, we may call it a "price" effect. *The strength of this effect is a function of the tax on improvements that has been rescinded.* The second stage of the process involves imposition of a tax on site value. Such a tax is not really neutral as regards development, although it has no "price" effect. *It does have an "income" or "liquidity" effect, which is a function of the rate of site value tax that is imposed.*

In a perfect world, where everyone can borrow or lend as much as he wants at the going interest rate, only the price effect is important. But in an imperfect world the income effect, as we have argued, would likewise be important. It is helpful to think in terms of price and income effects, especially since each depends on a different tax. Moreover, via the income effect we are able to point to a positive role for site value taxation, a role that is additional to its not undoing the "price" effect due to removal of the tax on improvements.

I know of no better summary of that role than Gaffney's, who, in commenting on the discussion of a paper he had presented in 1961, observed, "My proposal is rather to by-pass the credit system, deflating land prices by means of heavy ad valorem land taxes so that land transfers do not entail heavy financing burdens." [4] The reader interested in this problem is urged to study Gaffney's paper and the discussion of it. In his paper, rich in suggestive insights, he develops more carefully and formally the line of argument that has been pursued in this section.

3. Gaffney, "Property Taxes and Urban Renewal," p. 280.
4. Mason Gaffney, "Ground Rent and the Allocation of Land Among Firms," in *Rent Theory, Problems and Practices,* ed. F. Miller, North Central Regional Research Publication no. 139 (Columbia, Missouri: University of Missouri, 1962).

The material discussed in this section is treated at length by Ralph Turvey in his "two-step" analogy.[5] His analysis, more sophisticated than mine, leads to the conclusion that upon the substitution of site value for improved value taxation, the market price of sites (after capitalization of the new tax) could rise or fall. I assumed that because of the tax base shift the market price of undeveloped and underdeveloped land would be lower. This is not an unlikely result, particularly for the price sans the present value of the new higher future tax liabilities, but it is not inevitable. (If, contrary to the bounds Turvey put on his analysis of the problem, site value tax collections are not constrained to equal the rescinded improved value collections, the higher the site value tax, the more likely the result of a fall in net market price of future tax liabilities.) To the extent, however, that the net price of sites goes up, owners of land will not have to sell as much of it to meet unimproved value tax liabilities. While there would still be some pressure to sell, not as many sites would be sold as would have been the case had their price declined. And there would not be the added incentive to development noted in our earlier discussion in connection with the availability of the equivalent of a "mortgage" at average interest rates to those who can obtain above-average yields on their funds.

Unimproved Value Taxation or Tax Exemptions?

Another Way of Speeding Development

Substituting site value for improved value as the base of the property tax to encourage development can be viewed as a particular application of the general principle that a way to induce people to undertake an action is to exempt it from taxation. But when site value taxation is substituted for taxing improved value, all development is exempt, both those improvements that have been made and those that will be undertaken.

This was noted by U. K. and J. R. Hicks, who, when they studied problems of governmental finance in Jamaica in 1954, expressed their preference for temporary exemptions from taxation (old basis, or capital value of land and improvements) over changing to the unimproved value base as a method of encouraging development. For, as they pointed out, shifting to site value taxation would lower effective rates of taxation on all existing improvements as well as prospective ones. But only improvements yet to be made can respond to this incentive.[6] Moreover, they argued, the temporary exemption of new construction is certainly "cheaper" than site value taxation as an incentive device in the sense that a given degree of building can be encouraged at lower "cost" (revenue loss). They also

5. Ralph Turvey, *The Economics of Real Property* (London: Allen and Unwin, 1957), pp. 76–92.

6. "Why then de-rate the old buildings? You cannot get more old buildings—or, in general, more past improvements—by de-rating them. It is the new buildings, the new and future improvements, to which the case of de-rating applies."—Hicks and Hicks, *Report on Jamaica*, p. 138.

stressed that temporary exemptions would be a more powerful and flexible policy because the de-rating could be considered a privilege "which could be given to such sorts of buildings as it was particularly desired to encourage, but could be withheld (either wholly or in part) from improvements, that are in fact more of a luxury character." [7] And, finally, they felt that an additional superiority of temporary exemption lay in its avoidance of difficult valuation problems that might well characterize site value taxation, although they did not press this point too strongly. [8]

An exemption, though temporary and hence only for a portion of the project's life, could constitute an important incentive. Given the relatively high degree of risk associated with construction projects, a high discount rate applies to expected future revenues, and, therefore, a high value is placed on an earlier recoupment of the investor's outlays. To illustrate, [9] take a housing project that costs $495,000 and is expected to yield $125,000 per year (net of running costs but gross of depreciation) for twenty-five years. The rate of return on this investment is just about 25 percent. Next assume that the tax (old basis, or both land and improvements) on this project would be 20 percent of the annual income. The post-tax expected annual income would then be $100,000 per year, and the property tax would have cut the rate of return on this projected investment from 25 percent to 20 percent. Now suppose that this project is given a temporary five-year exemption from the property tax. Then the rate of return on this investment would increase to 23 percent. [10] In other words, exempting it from taxation for only one-fifth of its economic life would, nonetheless, restore 60 percent of the decline in rate of return caused by the property tax. Another way of looking at the same effect is to consider the payoff period of the investment, a factor businessmen allegedly take to be very important in evaluating investment decisions. Without the tax exemption, the investor will recover his capital in just under five years ($100,000 per year). With the tax exemption, the payoff period is shortened to four ($125,000 per year). It would appear, then, that temporary exemptions could undo, to an important degree, the discouragement to development that would otherwise occur in the face of a tax on the improved value of properties.

How substantial tax exemptions will act as a counter-incentive depends critically on the expected life of the investment, the particular rates of return on investment in housing that have been assumed, and the strength of the property tax as measured by the percentage of net income from the investment that it represents. If the property tax were a much smaller percentage of net income than in the illustrative example (as may well be the case in Jamaica), the effect of the tax concession on the rate of return on the investment would be considerably less. But this does not mean that temporary exemptions are ineffective per se. In principle they seem to be a potentially powerful tool, given a property tax rate tough enough to give them some leverage. Jamaica, however,

7. Ibid., p. 140.
8. Ibid., p. 138.
9. The example that follows is illustrative and nothing more.
10. The Hickses proposed specifically that new improvements be exempted in full for three years and to half their amount for an additional three.

did not follow the Hickses' recommendation that a realistic revaluation on the improved basis be instituted immediately and temporary exemptions therefrom be used to encourage construction. She revalued but on the unimproved basis. Can this choice be justified?

Criticisms of Temporary Exemptions

The case for temporary exemptions is not as strong as we have left it; there is something to be said on the other side. On economic grounds, Murray, in his report, treats the Hickses' proposal brusquely and unsympathetically. Specifically, he makes two criticisms of temporary exemptions as an incentive: (1) Because of the exemption "the vendor would be able to increase his price to the industrialist. Therefore, the rates which should have passed to the community would be capitalized and fall in part, at least, into the hands of the vendor." [11] (2) To the extent this does not happen, there would be "unfair competition between similar types of business" because of the different times at which their facilities were constructed.[12] It was his judgment that a capital gain to the vendor was the more likely outcome. Basically this is an empirical question to which there is no simple answer, although it does suggest, at least, the possibility that windfall gains rather than allocational effects will eventuate from property tax exemptions. And this means that temporary exemptions are not really as attractive as they may seem at first glance.

The question of economic effects aside, there are real grounds for preferring unimproved value taxation to temporary exemptions. The reasons for this preference are the broader sort that hold that the tax structure should be viewed as a device for raising revenue with a minimum of harm to the economy, not as a mechanism to generate differences in tax liability that will cause resources to flow to desired activities. It is all too tempting to suggest that a specified activity, being "good for the economy," should be encouraged by tax abatements. But a look at the history of such incentives is not at all reassuring. With an empirical regularity that suggests an historical law, two kinds of claims inevitably are generated regarding exemptions and all governments capitulate to them. The cries that are raised are "me too" and "give me more." The first represents a horizontal extension, a widening of the incentive as those interested in other activities convince the legislature that they partake so closely of the nature of the encouraged activity as to receive an incentive also; the second represents a deepening of the incentive, its extension for a longer period of time, a larger cut in tax rates, etc. Together they constitute a "Gresham's Law" of incentives as inexorable as the widening of the initial "hole in the dike."

Further elaboration is not necessary. Everyone will recognize the familiar process of tax base attrition and consequent danger of a decline in public support for and cooperation with the tax. Against this background much can be said for the "even-handedness" of unimproved value taxation. It does not deter construc-

11. Murray, *Report to Jamaica,* p. 6.
12. Ibid.

tion and it is tamper-proof or at least hard to tamper with. If, as I believe, Jamaica could very well obtain more revenue from land taxation, it is best to lay down a tax that is "good" and can be increased in rate without exercising a deterrent effect on development, rather than one that is "bad" and needs rate reductions for "good" effects. There is a lot to be said,then,in favor of the choice Jamaica made.

But there is much of merit, also, in the Hickses' position. Had their proposal been adopted, for example, there would be no problem of super-development— essentially undue tax relief to properties very highly developed relative to the value of their sites—which remains to be solved before site value taxation can be extended to Kingston.[13]

The Need for Further Research

Finally, I would like to make a plea for further research, the necessity for which I was made strongly aware of in the course of this study. For too long have discussions of tax effects been "reasonable" conjectures based on introspection. To advance beyond this stage it is necessary to know more about the decision process, the expectations, the costs, the budgetary procedures, and so on that go into land investment and development activities. Only then can we expect to know more about the effects of taxation than we now do.

For example, it is quite likely that there is much more to be said about the relative economic effects of site value taxation and exemptions of improvements than that they both can be used to encourage construction. With consideration of liquidity constraints as our earlier discussion indicates, a real difference shows up. And it could be that with uncertainty another difference appears. The unimproved value tax is like a fixed charge; it is due whether an investment turns out close to its expected value and optimal or not, or even if no investment at all is made in improvements. The tax on improved value is more contingent. If things go well and the investment really pays off, a heavy tax will be due, but if a less desirable outcome eventuates, the tax liability will be smaller. There must, then, be some difference in the effect of the two taxes on the evaluation of risky opportunities. One possibility here is that the unimproved value tax (being lump sum) is subtracted from every component of the possible revenue stream, while the improved value tax enters as a proportionate subtraction. For example, if the contemplated investment's possible net returns except for tax is a random variable $(\widetilde{E})$, then with the unimproved value tax the tax-transformed random variable will be $\widetilde{E} - \alpha$, where α is the lump-sum tax, while the

13. In their report the Hickses noted particularly that although "there is undoubtedly some tendency (at least in an urban area) for the more expensive buildings to be put up on the more expensive sites, ... there is likely to be some tendency for the value of buildings, relative to their sites, to be highest in the case of the wealthiest property-owners, so that a de-rating of buildings would reduce taxation on those who are more able, and raise it on those who are less able, to pay."—Hicks and Hicks, *Report on Jamaica*, p. 137.

improved basis tax-transformation will be $k\,\widetilde{E}$, where k is equal to $1 - \beta$ and β is the rate of tax on the improved basis. Clearly, one can choose a β that will make the expected value of the two random variables equal, but the two transformations will have different variances which suggest different effects on investment in improvements.

Or to cite another instance, we really do not know how heavy tax rates have to be before they become important considerations in land development decisions. But it is not necessary to extend the list. Enough has been said to substantiate the point that it is basic for assessing the effects of different kinds of taxes and the choice between them to find out what the landholding and developing decisions are really like.

CONCLUSION

A systematic study of the property tax with respect to economic development requires the study of the components that make up the tax base. The need for this is generally accepted regarding the taxing of intangibles and personal property. However, the need for separating the effects of the ad valorem tax on land and improvements (which comprise the real estate tax) is not as obvious and has received far less attention. The fact that improvements are fixed to land makes it natural to regard the joint factors as though they were a single or homogeneous factor for production, use, or taxation. The components of the real estate tax, however, have individual and dissimilar economic characteristics and therefore must be differentiated in economic analysis, including the study of the tax effect.

Land and improvements differ fundamentally in terms of origin, need for economic incentives, and quantitative and qualitative characteristics (such as permanence, limited supply, and flexibility in level of use). As a consequence, the long-run effect of an ad valorem tax on land differs from a tax on improvements. This is particularly so in terms of land use, investment in improvements, and efficiency in the allocation of resources, all of which are vital facets of economic development.

Taxing land values produces three primary effects, all of which are of great importance for economic development: the capitalization, holding-cost, and fixed-cost effects. The first of these refers to the depressing effect of the tax on land market prices in an amount equal to the capitalized value of the tax, the second to the cost of owning land due to land taxes, and the last to the fact that the tax burden to the owner of a given site is unrelated to the value of the specific improvements on that site.

An ad valorem tax on buildings increases their costs, and these will be passed on in the long run in the form of higher prices to the users of building facilities. Consequently, a tax policy designed for economic development would require a reduction or elimination of the ad valorem tax on buildings and other improvements. The untaxing of improvements may be thought of as producing an unburdening effect.

The four above-mentioned effects provide the keys to a dynamic ad valorem tax policy designed to stimulate economic growth and development. Just how dynamic and stimulating the tax policy is depends upon the extent to which taxes are increased on land values and decreased on building values. Maximum stimulus requires taxing the full economic rent of land and eliminating the tax on buildings. The manner in which the four tax-policy effects lead to economic growth can be analyzed in micro- and macro-economic terms.

Micro-Economic Aspects of Taxing Land and Building Values

The Effect of Taxing Land

The advantage of the capitalization effect on economic development is that it reduces financial obstacles to the acquisition of land by a potential developer and releases his funds for additional investment in improvements. This financial gain arises because any additional tax burden on land values is capitalized into lower land values and prices, even though it leaves unaltered the total cost of land as a factor of production.

At first glance the capitalization effect merely seems to assure that a tax on land values is neutral as to cost and therefore cannot hinder the better use of land or a larger investment of capital improvements in land. The capitalization effect, however, has a corollary—a conversion effect. The latter provides to many investors the financial advantage of converting part of the capital value of land into an annual tax. This conversion is the equivalent of a perpetual loan provided automatically and immediately to new investors in land for financing part of their acquisition costs. The alternatives for financing land acquisition would be a temporary loan at best for the prime borrower, or, what is more likely, the time-consuming saving of relatively scarce equity funds.

The micro-economic dynamics of the holding-cost effect operates largely on land that is vacant or at a level of use that is too low to generate enough income (actual or implicit) to cover taxes. The holding cost of nonproductive land is a drain on the cash stock of owners, an effect that will spur them to improve their land in order to raise its level of use and net income to offset the tax burden. The size of the tax burden reflects the value of land based on its potential use. The strongest incentives to raise land use are on sites where the differences between the economic potential and the actual use are the greatest, because it is on these sites that the tax burden of holding land is the greatest. Since the tax liability recurs annually, the total burden accumulates if the making of improvements in land use is delayed. Thus, the owners of vacant land are stimulated to develop their land. On some improved land, buildings will be remodeled, rehabilitated, and conserved to raise or maintain land use and income. On land with improvements that are obsolete or too dilapidated to rehabilitate, structures will be razed and the sites redeveloped.

Land that cannot be developed very soon will be sold because of the holding costs. The price of such land will fall to levels at which prompt development can occur. Speculation in holding land out of use will be more costly and less profitable. Land will not often be purchased unless prompt development is intended and feasible. All of these effects will tend to lessen urban sprawl, which has been recognized as a highly inefficient manner of horizontal urban expansion.

The fixed-cost effect of taxing land values refers to the fact that the tax burden to the owner of a given site is unrelated to the value of the specific improvements on that site. The market and assessed values of a site are determined as though the site were vacant and are based on the site's locational advantages and disadvantages. In planning the development of any site the owner will be aware that with a larger investment in improvements his average tax (land) costs per dollar of investment in improvements will fall. The fixed-cost effect may be stated as follows: the average land-tax costs per unit of improvements on a site varies inversely with the total volume of improvements. The owner of a site is greatly encouraged to achieve maximum feasible levels of improvements on income-producing projects. Moreover, income-producing property can be further improved and modified without incurring added tax burdens.

Owners of sites for single-family residences will be encouraged by the fixed-cost effect to build larger or higher-quality houses since they know that their taxes will not be higher because of greater housing outlays. Owners of older houses will be free to conserve, remodel, and renovate their structures without inviting what appears to be a tax penalty for being responsible and civic-minded citizens.

Investment in land for speculation will be less attractive and will be dampened somewhat, especially in urban-fringe areas. Therefore, according to Neutze, taxing land values will probably reduce large-scale developments of both single- and multiple-family housing in urban-fringe areas. Redevelopment of central-urban areas will be encouraged rather than new development in suburban areas. Moreover, this redevelopment will involve investment in multiple-family dwelling units, whereas the foregone development in suburban areas would be largely single-family houses.

The Effect of Taxing Buildings

Taxing buildings and other improvements adds to their total net costs. The latter includes not only the actual or implicit interest on the investment, but also the ad valorem taxes paid as well. The tax increases costs in proportion to the value of investment on improvements. It follows that taxing improvements is not neutral but is biased against investments for a more intensive use of land and favors those uses of land that require few improvements. The tax produces a burdening effect. Increased costs cause lower investment returns and the capacity of land to absorb profitable investment funds to erect building facilities. Newly constructed buildings are limited in size, quality of material, and style, all of which reflect a lower total investment. Remodeling, restoration, and rehabilitation of buildings are inhibited. Building accommodations, whether offices or dwellings, with the style and quality that people demand are built in increasing numbers in suburbs to take advantage of lower taxes on improvements.

The taxing of buildings reduces high-density development in central-urban areas as well as the overall total volume of investment in buildings, according to Neutze. Suburban land development is encouraged as the land-users there enjoy subsidized communication, transportation, and utility services for housing. Investment in and the construction of apartment buildings is reduced compared to single-family housing. Investment and construction of apartments in central-urban areas are penalized most of all with a tax on buildings.

Conversely, reducing the ad valorem tax on improvements will eliminate the bias against greater investment in improvements and those land uses that require large improvements. A reduction in the annual cost of improvements will increase the efficiency of capital in developing the use of land and its capacity to absorb investments in improvements profitably. It will also raise investment in improvements and result in a more intensive use of land, particularly in central-urban areas.

The Combined Effects of Taxing Land Values and Untaxing Buildings

Since, according to Heilbrun, various kinds of taxes affect adversely, although in differing degrees, the elements of housing quality, it follows that the untaxing of buildings would raise housing quality, which includes building investment, the level of maintenance, and the level of operating outlays. The logical solution is to untax buildings completely. On the other hand, the taxing of land values is without any harmful effect on the elements of housing quality. As a matter of fact, as we have previously seen, incentives would be provided by taxing land values.

Grey regards the taxing of land values and the untaxing of buildings, as well as certain federal income tax reforms, as of great importance in achieving many ojectives of urban renewal. These include clearance of land of dilapidated structures, redevelopment with new buildings or other improvements, and the rehabilitation, reconditioning, and remodeling of existing structures. Furthermore, the values of property adjacent to project areas increase and benefit both the owners and the community at large because of the enlarged tax base. A special feature of urban renewal by means of untaxing buildings and taxing land lies in the fact that it utilizes the market system and private enterprise and does not require direct government intervention.

Macro-Economic Aspects of Taxing Land and Untaxing Buildings

The Effects of Taxing Land

The macro-economic effects of taxing land values can readily be determined by applying the capitalization, holding-cost, and fixed-cost effects of the tax. The application of these effects is the key to developing a more comprehensive understanding of how taxing land values affects the economic system as a whole.

The short-run increase in land transactions that will follow the introduction of a land value tax will raise the demand for money for that purpose. In the long run, however, the capitalization effect will lower the transactions demand for money to below what it was when the tax was first levied. The speculative demand for money (liquidity preference) will tend to remain unchanged as the holding-cost and capitalization effects operate in opposite directions (that is, in terms of the speculative demand for money). The net result will be to reduce the money-equilibrium curve, or, in other words, to permit money market equilibrium at lower rates of interest.

The fixed-cost effect will raise the marginal efficiency of capital and move the commodity-equilibrium (IS) curve upward and to the right; planned savings will equal investment at higher interest rates and higher levels of national income. It is probable that the shift in the commodity-equilibrium curve will more than offset the shift in the money-equilibrium curve and will produce an upward pressure on interest rates and a pronounced increase in national output and income.

The Opposite Effects of Taxing and Untaxing Buildings

The ad valorem tax on buildings reduces the marginal efficiency of capital (the profitability of investment in buildings). This will push downward the commodity-equilibrium curve, indicating that planned investment and savings will be in equilibrium at lower interest rates, or, alternatively, planned investment and savings will fall if interest rates do not decline. The reduction in building investments will lower the transactions demand for money, which in turn will shift downward the money-equilibrium curve. The money market will be in equilibrium at lower interest rates.

The combined effects of the above shifts due to taxing buildings will exert the twin pressures of lower interest rates as well as a reduced gross national product and national income. If, however, the policy of taxing buildings is reversed (that is, if building taxes are eliminated), the opposite results will be produced: the gross national product and national income as well as interest rates will tend to rise.

It appears that the overall macro effects of the (more or less uniform) American property tax are similar to that of taxing buildings. This is not surprising considering the fact that out of the total value of property which serves as the tax base, the aggregate assessed value of improvements is several times that of land. According to Stockfisch, the property tax lowers the marginal efficiency of capital, causing the level of investment spending to fall, and through the multiplier process consumption spending will fall, as will total income.

The Combined Effects of Taxing Land Values and Untaxing Buildings

Having observed how the taxing of land values and the untaxing of building values each affect money equilibrium and the equilibrium of savings and investment (in terms of the interest rate and gross national product), we can determine the effects of implementing both tax policies simultaneously. It seems fairly certain that there will be a net increase in the transactions demand for money both in the short and long run. This will force upward the interest rates in the money market. Several changes in the speculative demand for money seem to neutralize one another and any likely effect on interest rates in the money market.

Both taxing land and untaxing buildings will reinforce each other to cause a pronounced rise in the marginal efficiency of capital (investment in buildings). A strong shift in the commodity-equilibrium curve can be expected so that planned savings and investment will be in equilibrium at higher interest rates and larger gross national product and national income. The rise in interest rates caused by shifts in both the money and commodity markets will produce a slight dampening effect on the rise in national output (GNP) and income.

The combined effect of increasing taxes on land and reducing taxes on buildings is to raise aggregate demand in the economy. The magnitude of the rise in overall demand for goods and services will be several times the rise in building investment because of the multiplier effect. An increase in aggregate demand tends to be accompanied by a general price rise.

Increased investment, however, will increase the aggregate supply of building facilities and consumer goods (the latter due to the multiplier effect). The net effect will be to cancel out (or at least to minimize) any change in the general price level. But the increase in both aggregate supply and demand will reinforce each other to increase national output (GNP), income, and employment. Clearly, these land and building tax policies will have a positive influence in promoting economic development.

Lessons Provided by the Case Studies

Empirical evidence as to the effect of land and building taxes on economic development is a precious commodity, for it alone can provide a confirmation or negation of tax-policy theories. Since the thesis of this volume is that economic development is promoted by stressing the taxation of land rather than buildings, it is important to find out where land value taxation is being applied and what, if anything, has been learned by these experiences.

The Practical Determination of Land Value Assessments

An important lesson that has been learned is that the determination of land value assessments is administratively feasible. Assessors find little difficulty in assessing property at full value and separating land from building value in Australia and New Zealand. Undoubtedly, this can be attributed to the high level of professional training and qualifying standards for assessors, which results in very high professional competence in assessment. Administrative feasibility of determining land values for taxing purposes has also been demonstrated in Jamaica. In fact, in all three countries, assessors conclude that it is easier to assess land values alone than to assess both land and buildings separately or as a real estate package. Furthermore, it is claimed that site values are easier to assess (as in Jamaica) than are unimproved capital values of land (as in Australia and New Zealand).

The use of aerial photography to assist with the assessment of land has been found helpful in both Jamaica and Chile. This technique is very useful to the assessor in identifying property to ensure complete listing and in studying soils in order to estimate the best potential use of land. Additionally, in Jamaica it has been found that the use of aerial photographic maps with proper fiscal procedures can replace the far more costly and time-consuming legal cadaster.

The Land Value Tax Base

One of the basic questions raised has been the precise nature of the tax base that would be utilized. Several important lessons have been learned on this subject. The first is that a capital-value base is preferable to an annual-value base, considering the various advantages and disadvantages. Secondly, while the unimproved capital value of land as used in Australia and New Zealand is theoretically sound and administratively practical, it nevertheless creates more administrative problems than the market (site) value base, which is used in Jamaica, Trinidad, and Barbados. This basis of land valuation includes invisible improvements in (not on) land and embraces land fill, grading, clearing, and so on. These improvements become part of the land when they are made and should be assumed as integral with the land, at least for practical assessment purposes.

Special Land Assessments

The attempt to tax land value increments arising out of public improvements is known as a "special assessment" in the United States, a "betterment" tax in England, and a "valorization" tax in Colombia. These taxes are similar in that they are levied at the time public improvements are made in order to help defray their costs in part or entirely.

The valorization tax as practiced in Colombia has drawn both professional and popular support, which is in contrast to how special assessments have fared in recent years in the United States. Several factors account for Colombia's apparent success with its valorization tax. Apparently, public improvements are carefully planned with the participation and cooperation of benefiting property owners. Freedom from fixed formulas in tax burden assignments, careful costing of projects, extensive publicity of projects, prompt construction of projects, and prompt collection of all valorization taxes while the project is being built—all of these procedures are part of the success formula. These certainly merit consideration for use in the United States.

The Equity Question

The very fact that the various governments (in the cases cited in this volume) have adopted some form of special taxation of land indicates a general belief as to their equity in terms of expected benefits. An exceptionally strong case can be made on behalf of the justice of taxing natural resources and socially created values. It appears that there is considerable popular support for the various land tax policies, which leads one to believe that most persons feel that they are fair. Undoubtedly, some property owners feel otherwise, for it is hardly likely that any tax could generate unanimous support.

Whether a tax is regarded as equitable depends upon the direct or indirect benefits that the taxpayer receives from that tax as well as his opportunity to avoid the harmful (or more harmful) effects of an alternative tax. This raises the related question of the taxpayer's *awareness* of these benefits, especially the indirect benefits, and the disadvantages that he is avoiding by not being subjected to some other tax. Since equity is a subjective matter, the equity of any tax is dependent upon the taxpayer's understanding of the tax. Understanding the equitability of a tax, then, requires an awareness of its advantages and disadvantages, as well as those of its alternative tax or taxes.

Can Land and Building Taxes Be Differentiated Sufficiently to Provide Strong Incentives for Development?

The case studies in this volume leave little doubt that land taxes can be raised enough to provide a strong incentive for development where the taxpayer is fully aware of the benefits he receives. This appears to be the case with the valorization tax to finance public improvements in Colombia, and the land value tax to finance irrigation improvements in California. In both experiences there seems to be not only incentive to develop the public projects (being financed out of the tax), but also private development projects that are directly or only indirectly related to the public improvement.

In Australia and New Zealand, where land tax revenues are used for general purposes, the taxpayer is unable to see a clear benefit unless his improvements-to-land-value ratio is above average. This may produce uncertainty in the minds of the majority of property owners as to how far land value taxation should be carried. Strong support exists to the point of permitting the untaxing of buildings. There is, however, hesitation in taxing land more heavily in order that other taxes may be replaced. It may be that the relative advantages and disadvantages of these alternatives have not been studied, discussed, and publicized.

Effect on Economic Development

The key question that must be asked about the empirical studies described in this volume is whether raising the tax burden on land and lowering the tax burden on improvements will, indeed, stimulate economic development. As noted above, this seems quite definitely to be the case with the valorization tax in Colombia and the land value irrigation tax in California.

In both these cases the tax proceeds are earmarked for specific public improvements and the chain of cause and effect is clear and unbroken. This advantage in analyzing the results of a tax is not available when land value tax revenues are placed in a general fund for the benefit of the entire tax jurisdiction and it becomes necessary to measure the change, if any, in the flow of private resources into the land-taxing area compared with surrounding or other comparable area. The complexity of such comparisons along with appropriate discounting of many key variables (other than land value taxes) makes it difficult to attribute with absolute certainty a given amount of economic development to the factor of land value taxes.

It is the judgment of persons close to the land-taxing experience in Australia and New Zealand that the tax assists in promoting the development of land or its sale. This would imply a greater investment in buildings as well as less land speculation and a more compact and efficient type of urban development. Statistical proof, however, is not presented to support these judgments based on observation.

Topics for Further Study

It is hoped that this volume has raised the interest of the reader in the ad valorem taxes on land and buildings. A major objective has been to assist in the clarification and understanding of these taxes and thereby to provide a more rational basis for the formulation of tax policies. These two very different taxes have been forced by historical events to live as Siamese twins in the form of the real estate tax. A general conclusion of this volume is that the nineteenth-century tradition of treating land and building taxes uniformly in the United States does not stand up to economic analysis in terms of furthering economic development.

The examination of land and building taxes has concentrated purposely on their effect on economic development. Such concentration seemed to promise a greater likelihood of achieving a better understanding of the subject. Most extant studies treat ad valorem land and building taxes quite superficially. Even so, the work represented in this volume by no means exhausts all aspects of the topic.

What is still needed are many more empirical studies that show the effect of land and building taxes on economic development. Few opportunities to make such studies exist in this country, since both taxes are normally applied uniformly in terms of law and more or less uniformly in practice. Perhaps the development and use of new research methods may make it possible to extract significant effects from changes in real estate taxes where land-assessment ratios differ from building-assessment ratios despite legal uniformity requirements.

Tax policy is arrived at after weighing a variety of factors in addition to the effect on economic development. These factors include adequacy of yield, equity, administrative advantages and disadvantages, as well as political feasibility. There is no doubt but that the ad valorem tax on land and buildings needs to be analyzed and researched further in terms of these tax-policy objectives. Each of these subjects raises a multiplicity of questions that require careful, comprehensive, and systematic study.

Heilbun and others have doubts whether taxing land values alone can yield revenues comparable with those derived from taxing both land and buildings. The answer to these doubts can only be found in answering other questions such as: What effect will the untaxing of buildings have on the size of the land value base? What is the basis for determining the value of land (that is, market value or use value)? Is the valuation of land in terms of market value given primacy in the assessment process, or are cost and engineering processes given first consideration in determining building values? The assessing basis will affect the size of the land value tax base. If the base is large enough, tax rates need not rise too high.

It is somewhat ironical that questions on the valuation and assessment of land and buildings still demand consideration, in light of the generous amount of attention they have received in the past. Most of the study and writing on the subject, however, has been carried out by unqualified or biased researchers. Political pressures, the underfinancing of assessment administration, and insufficient concern by highly qualified assessors and economists have held back progress in assessing, especially when applied to land values. Political pressures have produced many changes in taxing land and buildings under the guise of advancing equity or fairness. It is to be hoped that further economic research and analysis can bring fresh and objective understanding of the issues involved in assessing both land and building taxes.

The answer to the question of the administrative feasibility of taxing land values and untaxing building values lies essentially in the ability of assessors to establish land values that reflect fair (and preferably full) market values on land already occupied by buildings. While our case studies show that assessing land value has been established as feasible in Australia, New Zealand, and Jamaica, special problems of assessment might be encountered in the United States and elsewhere. If so, they need to be identified and practical solutions must be found. While this question deserves full and satisfactory treatment in another study, it can be said that if current recommendations as set forth by Engelbert and others for improving the qualifications of assessors and the accuracy of assessments were carried out in the United States, it would seem that the question of administrative feasibility of untaxing buildings and taxing land values alone would be essentially answered, and in the affirmative.

Despite the probability or possibility that the land value base will expand or can be expanded, the untaxing of buildings may very well require a tax rate on land values alone that is considerably higher than customary property tax rates. At that point one must ask the question of how high tax rates on land values can go before they are to be considered unreasonable. The answer will lie essentially in terms of the equity and economic effect of the tax changes.

Thus, there is a need for greater clarification and better understanding of a variety of considerations pertaining to the equity of taxing land and buildings. Particular attention must be given to the question of whether net equity is enlarged if land assumes a larger tax burden. The comparative equity of taxing land and nonland property must be examined. Furthermore, taxing land values must be compared with alternative taxes in terms of equity. Lastly, questions of short-run and long-run equity arise in connection with any transition to taxing land values more heavily and building values less heavily. Throughout this analysis the interests of various parties, such as consumers (including tenants) and investors, besides the taxpaying landlords, must be considered. Once these interests are identified and evaluated many uncertainties about the equity of taxing land values should disappear.

Index

Aaron, Henry J., 230n

Abatement: of taxes, 72–73, 77–78, 79, 173

Abrams, Charles, 82n, 90n

Accessibility: definitions of, 116n; influence on land use of, 116–17; importance to dwellers of, 117–18

Adams, Frank, 144n

Adelaide, Australia, 172, 183

Advisory Commission on Intergovernmental Relations, 103n, 111, 167, 229n

Agency for International Development, 201n, 204, 239n

Allocation, of resources. *See* Asset-earnings taxes; Corporate income tax; General property tax; Land value tax; Taxes

Alonso, William, 206n

Alta Irrigation District, 142

American Institute of Real Estate Appraisers, 164

Anderson, Martin, 84n

Annexation of land: as a tax strategy, 108

Apartments. *See* Housing, multiple-family

Arvin, California, 142

Assessed annual value: defined, 162. *See* Taxes

Assessment: of fringe land, 103; ratios of, to true land value, 105–6; and property taxation, 107; effect of, on metropolitan areas, 110–11. *See also* Asset-earnings taxes; Cadaster; General property tax; Land value tax

—in Australia and New Zealand: and self-assessment, 154–55; administration of, 162–67, 293, 294, 295, 296, 297

—in Chile: by photo-interpretation and soil classification, 133, 195–96, 293; affected by inflation, 194; fixing unit land values for, 196–98; and urban property, 198–99

—in Colombia: 202, 214

Asset-earnings taxes: described, 49–56; effects on investment incentive, 58–60, 62; capitalization effects of, 60–62; effect on income, 62; "shifting" of, 62. *See also* Corporate income tax; General property tax

Atkinson, H. G., 66n

Auckland, Australia, 161, 170, 172, 178

Australia, 248, 269, 296, 297; significance of, for American study, 147–48; homeownership in, 148; intergovernmental relations in, 148–49; user charges in, 150; property taxes in, 150, 152, 248, 269; local–government revenues in, 150–52; bases of local tax rates in, 158–62; improved and unimproved capital value in, 158–62; administration of assessment, 162–67, 293; state valuation system in, 165; sales ratio studies in, 166; allocations of value between land and building in, 166–67; local rating systems and land use in, 167–72; rating system and urban pattern in, 172–75; building codes in, 175–76; slums in, 175–80; Housing Trust of South Australia in, 176; public construction of housing in, 176; social programs in, 176; rent control in, 179; "native" view on rating methods in, 180–84; General Council for Rating Reform in, 184

—land value taxation in: advantages to metropolitan communities of, 114; administration of, 131–33, 162–67,

—land value taxation in (*continued*) 180–81, 184–85; effect of, on land-use pattern, 132–33; introduction of, 153–58; impact of, on large rural landowners, 155–56; as a revenue producer, 156; rates for, 158–62, 167–72, 172–75; exemptions and abatements from, 173–75, 185, 186; criticism of, 180–84; advocates of change in, 184; evaluation of, 184–86; political objectives of, 185; social by–products of, 186

Barbados, 162, 294
Barranquilla, Colombia, 226, 226n
Beck, Morris, 126n
Beckwith, P. W., 239n
Benefit-cost ratios, 207
Benefit taxation, 233–34, 235
Best, Wallace H., 100n
Betterment taxes, 134. *See also* Valorization tax
Bird, Frederick L., 14n, 106n
Bird, Richard M., 201n, 230n
Blank, David M., 64n
Bloom, Max R., 93n
Bloomberg Commission, 243
Bogotá, Colombia: valorization tax in, 215, 216, 222–25, 229, 234, 237
Bolivia, 188n
Bollens, John C., 139n
Borrero, Hernán, 225n
Boulding, Kenneth E., 86n
Boyd, William J. D., 106n
Brisbane, Australia, 184
Brown, Harry Gunnison, 11, 94n
Brown, James R., 244n
Buildings, 17–18, 21, 65, 76, 276n; level of land use and, 22–24. *See also* Housing; Improvements; Incentives
—ad valorem taxes on: effect of tax on investment in buildings, 17, 21–22; effects of exemption from, 24–32, 36–44, 44–47; effect on buildings, 57; effect according to orthodox theory, 58
—codes for: to protect base and taxation, 107; in Australia, 175–76

Cadaster, 180, 229, 248, 249, 273, 293

Cali, Colombia, 203, 213, 215, 216; operation of valorization tax in, 225–26, 225n
California: farm land assessment in, 103; State Water Resources Board in, 110; irrigation districts in, 131, 140–45; public district legislation in, 137–40; Wright Act of, 140, 142–44, 145
Canberra, Australia, 172
Capital gains, 87–88, 117
—tax: 88, 93, 95, 191, 235. *See also* Land value tax
Capitalization effect: of asset-earnings taxes, 61–62
—of taxing land values: 25–26, 27, 28–30; on demand for money, 38, 39; on the commodity market, 38, 278, 282, 287, 291; and asset-earnings taxes, 60–62
Capitalization rate, 60–62
Caracas, Venezuela, 227n
Cardona H., Dr. Carlos, 211n
Cauca Valley Corporation (Colombia), 213, 227
Cecil, William J., 197n
Central business district, 110–11, 119
Chang, Wilfred S., 239n, 244n, 245n, 250, 250n, 251n, 269–70, 277
Chile, 133–34; reassessment by photo-interpretation and soil classification in, 133, 195–96, 293; structure of taxation in, 187–88; income tax in, 189–91; wealth tax in, 191–92; taxes on inheritances, gifts, and other transfers in, 192; incentives of taxation in, 192–93; taxation of agricultural property in, 193–95; real estate taxation in, 193–99; land revaluation in, 196–98; reassessment of urban property in, 198–99
Christchurch, New Zealand, 178
Clarendon, Jamaica, 249
Clark, Clifford D., 14n
Colombia, valorization tax of: importance of, 134, 202–3, 294, 295, 296; in urban areas, 203–7; in rural areas, 207; effects on investment and saving of, 207–8; incentive effects of, 208–10; administration of, 210; history and development of, 211–13; revenue

Colombia, valorization tax of (*continued*)
importance of, 213–17; in Medellín, 217–22; in Bogotá, 222–25; in other Colombian areas, 225–28; on the basis of benefit, 233–34; appraisal of, 233–36; exemptions of, 234; earmarking of revenues under, 234–35; relation to other taxes on property, 235–36; effects on income distribution of, 236; role in economic development of, 236–37
Commodity market, 38, 39, 42, 291
Commonwealth Institute of Valuers, Australia, 164
Community Services District Law (California), 138
Consumer-burden doctrine, 57–58
Copes, John, 239n, 244n, 249, 251, 252, 256, 267, 269, 272, 272n
Corporate income tax, 56. See also Income tax
Cost–value relationships, 20–22
Coughlin, Robert E., 106n
Credit, 33–34, 123–24. See also Valorization tax
Crouch, Winston W., 102n
Currie, Lauchlin, 204n, 226

Davalos R., Carlos, 228n
Davis, Otto A., 119n
Demand: elasticity of, for future dollars, 60, 76–77; effect on housing investment, 125–27. See also Land
Demolition costs, 122
Dinerman, Beatrice, 102n
Dinuba, California, 142
Discount rates, 123–24
Districts: creation of, to protect base and taxation, 107–8; irrigation, in California, 137, 138, 139, 140–45; California legislation for and types of, 137–40; definition of, 138; organization of, in California, 138–40. See also California
Dominguez, Oscar, 197n
Double taxation, 12, 15

Earmarking of revenues: in Colombia, 234–35
Ecker–Racz, L. L., 70n, 246n, 248, 269

Eckstein, Otto, 207n
Economic rent. See Rent
Economic surplus. See Rent
Ecuador, 134; valorization tax in, 228–30
Edgeworth, F. Y., 11
Elizabeth, Australia, 177
Employment, 36, 57, 62
Engelbert, Ernest A., 100n
Equipment, replacement of, 64–68
Equity: of land value taxation, 79, 103, 294–95, 298; of the general property tax, 109, 110–11, 112; in Jamaica, 135, 248–49, 253–57, 272. See also Assessment; Exemptions; General property tax; Land value tax
Exemptions, 12, 13, 14, 15; effect of, on land use, 106; in Chile, 133–34, 191, 192–93, 200; use of, in Australia and New Zealand, 173–75, 184; in Colombia, 216n; in Jamaica, 276–77, 283–85. See also Incentives

Falk, Karl L., 84n
Fefferman, Hilbert, 81n
Fernandez C., Alberto, 211n
Fiscal residuum, 236
Fitch, Lyle C., 114n
Fixed–cost effect: of the land value tax, 25, 27, 38, 42, 46, 287, 289, 291
Fixed-cost taxes: in Chile, 199–200
Foard, Ashley A., 81n
Fragmentation: metropolitan, 103, 112, 258
Frailey, L. E., 66n
Friedly, Philip H., 93n
Fringe land. See Land
Froomkin, Joseph, 243n

Gaffney, M. Mason, 110n, 121, 122n, 123n, 241n, 275, 281n
Garcés, Carlos, 191n
García-Huidobro, Jorge, 196n
General property tax: problems and criticisms of, 11–15, 44–45, 55–56, 99–101, 109–12, 146; rates of, 12, 122–23; exemptions under, 14; history of, 14–15; basic components of, 15–24; shifting and shiftability of, 21–22, 58, 125; time persistence of,

General property tax (*continued*)
26; compared to other taxes, 34–36, 49, 54, 64; and assessment, 106–7; administrative strategies for, 107–9; deductibility of, 112; and irrigation, 131; in Jamaica, 134–35; for financing capital improvements, 201–2; and other real property taxes, 236; progressivity of, 264n. *See also* Asset–earnings taxes; Australia; New Zealand; Taxes

—effects of, 17–24; on incentive and production, 12–13; on economic development, 24–30; micro-economic aspects, 24–36, 44–46; on aggregate value and the average price of land, 30–32; on a given site, 32; on resource allocation, 32–34; macro-economic aspects, 36–44, 46–47; on aggregate supply and demand, 42–44; on investment and employment, 49–56, 62; on metropolitan development, 109–12; on local government, 111–12; long-run, 119–27; on speculation, 120–23; on distribution of landownership, 123–25; on the intensity of land use, 125–27; on transportation, 126–27

—and land use, 22–24, 97–99, 110; and the quality of urban rental housing, 69–73; and investment in housing, 73–78; in metropolitan areas, 109–12; and multiple-family housing, 115; intensity of, 125–27

—reform of, 14–15; to improve housing quality, 63; political strategies for, 104–9; in metropolitan areas, 112–13

George, Henry, 85n, 87n, 95, 96, 122, 153, 155, 173, 180, 184, 186; economics and theories of, 85–89

Goldschmidt, Walter R., 142n, 143

Goldsmith, Raymond W., 54, 56n

Government. *See* Local government

Greer, Scott, 82n, 83n

Grey, Arthur L., Jr., 93n

Griffith, Peter, 187n

Grigsby, William G., 64, 64n

Groberg, Robert P., 84n

Groves, Harold M., 14n, 231n, 235n

Hagen, Everett, 217n

Haislop, E. G., 198n

Hallmuth, William F., Jr., 98n

Hanover, Jamaica, 250

Harberger, Arnold, 55n

Harriss, C. Lowell, 227n

Hawaii, 147

Heilbrun, James, 67n, 75n, 241n, 247

Henley, Albert T., 140n

Hicks, J. R., 242n, 244, 244n, 263, 264, 264n, 274, 282, 282n, 283n, 284, 285, 285n

Hicks, U. K., 242n, 244, 244n, 252n, 263, 264, 264n, 269n, 270n, 271n, 274, 276n, 277, 282, 282n, 283n, 284, 285, 285n

Highest and best use. *See* Land value taxation

Hipgrave, C. C. H., 247

Hirschman, Albert O., 202n

Hobson, J. A., 87, 87n

Hofmeister, Ralph, 226n

Holding–cost effect, 25, 26, 27, 32, 33, 36, 46; of the land value tax, 95, 123, 279, 287, 289, 291

Holl, James P., 170n

Holland, Daniel M., 70n, 123n, 208n

House and Home (magazine), 111–12, 112n

Housing, 54, 63–64; markets, 91n; single–family, 117, *passim;* in Australia and New Zealand, 175–80

—acts: 80, 82, 82n, 83n

—multiple–family: timing of apartment construction, 115–19; effect of adjacent land on, 117–18; speculation in land for, 118, 119; effects of property taxation on, 119–28; and speculation, 120–23; and the distribution of landownership, 123–25; and the intensity of land use, 125–27

—quality: and urban–housing policies and problems, 63–64; and rental housing, 64–69; operating effects of real estate taxes on, 69–73; and tax abatement, 72–73, 77–78, 79; investment effects of real estate taxes on, 73–78; and tax shifting, 75–76; and "moving" of buildings, 76–78

Howard, Ebenezer, 94, 94n

Hulse, F. E., 105*n*
Hutchins, Wells A., 140*n*
Hutt, Australia, 170

Implicit income: in Chile, 190
Improved capital value: defined, 158
Improvements, 57, 125; differentiation from land and personalty, 15–24; effects of untaxing, 24–47; in Australia and New Zealand, 158–62; defined, for Jamaica, 245–46. *See also* Buildings
Incentives: affected by capitalization rate and taxation, 92–93; in Chile, 133–34, 192–93, 200; in Colombia, 208–10. *See also* Asset–earnings taxes; Buildings; Corporate income tax; Exemptions; General property tax; Housing, quality; Investment; Land; Land value tax
Income effect, 58, 208–9, 209*n*, 275, 279, 281
Income tax, 34, 49, 56, 91, 272; and deductions, 112, 261, 264–65, 267; in Chile, 133, 188, 189–91
Incorporation: as a tax strategy, 108–9
Industrial location: effect of taxes on, 103. *See also* General property tax; Land value tax; Taxes
Inheritance and gift taxation: in Chile, 192
Institute of Valuers (New Zealand), 164
Intangibles: taxation of, 12, 15, 73
Inter-American Development Bank, 196, 204
Interest rate, 36, 38, 59, 59–60
International Association of Assessing Officers, 164
International Bank for Reconstruction and Development, 204, 243
Investment: incentive effects of asset–earnings taxes, 58–60; and the capitalization effects of asset–earnings taxes, 60–62; and tax abatement, 72–73, 77–78, 79; effects of real estate taxes on decisions for, 73–78; and tax shifting, 75–76; and "moving" of buildings, 76–78; incentives due to Colombian valorization tax, 208–9.

Investment (*continued*)
See also Asset–earnings taxes; Buildings; General property tax; Housing; Improvements; Land value tax
Irrigation District Act. *See* Wright Act
Irrigation District Law (1887), 138
Isard, Walter E., 106*n*

Jacobs, Jane, 91, 91*n*
Jacobsen, Alfred, 72*n*
Jamaica, 134–35, 162, 174, 239–43, 293, 294, 297; history of property tax in, 243–44; definition of the tax base in, 245–49; valuation procedures in, 249–53; relief from taxation in, 253–57; legislated tax rates in, 257–61; illustrative tax cases for, 261–63; tax progressivity in, 263–68; revenue problems in, 268–70; service rate charges in, 270–73; conclusions about taxation in, 273–77; and general unimproved value taxation, 278–86
Jenson, Jens Peter, 100*n*
Jurisdictions, overlapping, 100–101, 111, 112

Kaldor, Nicholas, 208*n*
Kass, Stephen L., 230*n*
Keiper, Joseph S., 14*n*
Keynes, J. M.: investment theory, 59–60
Kingston, Jamaica, 243, 250
Knight, Frank H., 60, 60*n*
Krzyzaniak, Marian, 55*n*, 58*n*
Kurnow, Ernest, 14*n*

Lagos, Ricardo, 195*n*
Land: characteristics of, 13, 14, 15–24, 44, 45; supply of, 13–14, 16, 17–20, 26, 42–44; value of, 14, 16, 20–22, 27, 32, 45, 121, 122, 206–7; and site improvements, 17; economic inducements for, 17–18; ratchet effect on supply of, 18–20; cost of development of, 20–21; and tax shifting, 21–22; level of use of, 22–24; definition and rights of, 86; residual technique, 89; land-use objectives for, 104–5; undertaxation of, 111; and time-indivisibility, 116; ripening of, 117;

Land (*continued*)

imperfect market for, 118 ; marginal, 118 ; ownership of, 123–25 ; substitution effect of, 209 ; as an inflation hedge, 242. *See also* Asset–earnings taxes ; General property tax ; Land value tax ; Taxes

—pattern of use of, 22–24, 97–99 ; effects of financial strategies on, 105–7 ; in metropolitan areas, 109–12 ; and timing of construction, 115–19 ; and indivisibility, 116 ; intensity of, 125–27 ; in Australia and New Zealand, 132–33, 167–72, 172–75 ; effects of valorization tax on, 208 ; effect of land value tax on, 209 ; and land value tax in Jamaica, 262, 264

Land value tax : nonshiftability of, 21–22, 24, 123–24 ; capitalization effect of, 21–22, 25, 120–22, 278, 282 ; rates of, 35–36, 158–62, 167–75, 180–84, 257–68 ; politics of, 97–98 ; to finance irrigation, 131 ; in Chile, 193–95 ; compared with valorization tax, 205–7 ; limitations on more intensive land use, 209 ; income effect of, 209, 279, 281 ; price effect of, 279, 281. *See also* Australia ; General property tax ; New Zealand ; Unimproved land value tax

—administration of : in Australia and New Zealand, 132, 162–67, 185 ; in Jamaica, 135, 272, 273

—advantages or benefits of, 16–17, 21, 23, 27, 31, 87, 114, 135 ; in stimulating development, 24–30, 114, 136 ; and increase in investment and employment, 24–31, 36–44, 46–47 ; to landowners on a given site, 32 ; and more efficient resource allocation, 32–34 ; neutrality of, 33, 45–46, 71 ; in Australia and New Zealand, 182, 183, 184, 186 ; in Jamaica, 273–76 ; and conversion effects, 288. *See also* Land value tax ; Urban sprawl

—criticism of, 78, 79 ; in Jamaica, 135, 275–76 ; in Australia and New Zealand, 181–82, 184, 186

—effects of on : use of land and investment in buildings, 24–30, 36 ; acquisi-

—effects of on (*continued*)
tion costs, 25 ; credit market, 25, 33–34 ; capacity to invest, 27, 36 ; urban renewal, 27–30, 89–96 ; aggregate value and average price of land, 30–32 ; site value, 32 ; efficiency of resource allocation, 32–34 ; interest rates, 33–34 ; tax yield, 34–36 ; base for, 35–36 ; rate, 35–36 ; marginal efficiency of capital, 36–38 *passim,* 46 ; employment, 36–44 *passim,* 46, 47 ; money-equilibrium and commodity-equilibrium curves, 38, 39, 42, 46, 291 ; aggregate supply and demand, 42–44 ; development, 45, 272, 295–96 ; house–operating outlays, 71 ; slums, 91–92, 125, 175–80 ; historical edifices, 92 ; real estate prices, 93 ; forcing idle land into use, 93–94, 114 ; holding costs, 95, 120, 123, 279 ; income from speculation, 120–21 ; speculation, 120–23, 127 ; large–scale developers, 122, 127 ; the distribution of landownership, 123–25 ; multiple–family housing, 125 ; the intensity of land use, 125–27 ; roads, 126–27 ; investment in land, 127 ; land-use pattern in Australia and New Zealand, 132 ; size of farms in California, 143–44 ; large rural landowners in Australia and New Zealand, 155–56 ; property in Australia and New Zealand, 182 ; development rate of fringe communities in Australia and New Zealand, 183–84 ; investment in farms in Chile, 200 ; credit rationing, 280 ; risk, 285–86

—effects of, on untaxing improvements : micro–economic, 24–36, 44–46, 288–91 ; macro–economic, 36–44, 46–47, 291–93

—in Australia and New Zealand : in Thebarton, 93–94 ; introduction of, 153–58 ; bases of local rates for, 158–62, 167–72 ; and administration of assessment, 162–67 ; and slums, 175–80 ; political objectives of, 184–85

—in Jamaica : history of, 243–49 ; valuation procedures under, 249–53 ;

—in Jamaica (*continued*)
and hardship and relief, 253–57; rates of, 257–68; and progressivity, 263–68; problems of, 268–73; evaluation of, 273–77

Leapfrog development, 110. *See also* General property tax; Land value tax; Urban sprawl

Lerner, Abba P., 87, 87n

Lessinger, Jack, 91n

Lewis, W. A., 243n

Lin, Sein, 244n

Liquidity preference, 36, 39, 59, 291

Local government, 111–12, *passim. See also* Politics of taxation

Los Angeles County Flood Control Act (1915), 138

McKeever, J. Ross, 98, 98n

MacPherson, John, 240n

Macro economics, of taxing land and untaxing buildings, 36–44, 46–47, 291–93

Maisel, Sherman J., 64n, 265, 265n

Malvern, Australia, 172

Manchester, Jamaica, 249

Manning, Harry, 147n

Manvell, Allen D., 107n

Maori (New Zealand), 178–79

Marginal efficiency of capital, 36, 38, 59, 60

Marginal land. *See* Land

Marginal utility of money, 124

Margolis, Julius, 99n, 103n

Marris, Peter, 83n

Marshall, Alfred, 11, 13n, 16n, 21n, 87, 87n

Martin, Alison M., 243n

Martin, R. F., 87n

Martinez, Dr. Guillermo, 211n

Medellín, Colombia, 203–37 *passim;* valorization in, 217–22, 229, 231, 233, 234, 237

Melbourne, Australia, 182, 183

Metropolitan fragmentation, 103, 112

Mexico, 134, 231n

Mexico City, Mexico: valorization tax in, 230–33

Micro economics, of taxing land and

Micro economics (*continued*)
untaxing buildings, 24–36, 44–46, 288–91

Mill [John S.], 60

Minneapolis, Minnesota: neighborhood assessments in, 213n

Modesto Irrigation District (California), 143

Money market, 39–44 *passim,* 46

Montego Bay, Jamaica, 250

Mora R., Rafael, 211n

Morton, Walter A., 22n

Multiple–family housing. *See* Housing, multiple–family

Multiplier effect, 44, 47, 59, 93

Municipal Utility District Act (California), 138

Municipal water districts (California), 138

Murray, J. F. N., 147n, 180n, 244, 244n, 248, 270, 271, 277, 284

Musgrave, Richard A., 33n, 58n, 73n

National wealth. *See* Wealth

Needleman, Lionel, 64n

Netzer, Dick, 54, 57n, 63n, 73n, 208n, 235n, 237n, 241n

Neutrality: of taxation, 32–33, 45–46, 208; lack of, in asset-earnings taxation, 55–56; of Chile's income tax, 190; of Colombian valorization tax, 236

New South Wales, Australia, 170, 184, 256; rent control in, 179–80

New Zealand, 248, 269, 296, 297; significance of, for American study, 147–48; homeownership in, 148; intergovernmental relations in, 148–49; property taxes in, 150, 152; local-government revenues in, 150–52; bases of local rates in, 158–62; improved and unimproved capital value in, 158–62; sales ratio studies in, 166; allocations of value between land and building in, 166–67; slums in, 175–80; building codes in, 175–76; public construction of housing in, 176; social programs in, 176

—Institute of Valuers, 64

—land value taxation in: administra-

—land value taxation in (*continued*)
tion of, 131–33, 162–67, 180–81,
184–85, 293; effect of, on land–use
pattern, 132–33; introduction of,
153–58; impact of, on large rural
landowners, 155–56; as a revenue
producer, 157; rates of, 167–72,
172–75, 180–84; exemptions and
abatements from, 173–75, 185, 186;
criticism of, 180–84; advocates of
change in, 184; evaluation of, 184–
86; social by-products of, 186
Nonhuman productive agents, 49
Nowak, Norman, 187n

Oldman, Oliver, 230n
Open space: effect on apartment loca-
tion, 118
Organization of American States, 133,
195, 196
Osborne v. *the Commonwealth of Aus-
tralia,* 155–56
Overlapping taxation. *See* Jurisdictions

Parish rate: in Jamaica, 257, 258–61
Pechman, Joseph A., 190n
Personal wealth tax. *See* Wealth tax
Peru, 188n
Photography: use of, in Chilean land
assessment, 133, 195–96, 293
Pierson, N. G., 11
Pigou, A. C., 16n
Pistono, José L., 195n
Pittsburgh plan, 79
Politics of taxation, 97–99; political
standards for, 99–101; and taxpay-
ing groups, 101–4; strategies of, in
metropolitan areas, 104–9; financial
strategies of, 105–7; administrative
strategies of, 107–9
Portland, Jamaica, 249
Posada, Jeanne de, 227n
Posada F., Antonio J., 227n
Prahran, Australia, 172
Price effect: of the land value tax, 275,
278–79, 280, 281
Price indexes, 56–57n
Progressivity: of taxes, 132, 135, 153,
155, 181–82, 189, 191, 199, 236;
in Jamaica, 257, 258, 259, 263–68
Property tax. *See* General property tax

Public Utility District Act (California),
138
Puerto Rico, 249
Pyle, David, 239n

Quasi-rents. *See* Rent
Queensland, Australia, 167, 184

Rapkin, Chester, 64n
Ratchet effect. *See* Land
Rate illusion, 268, 268n
Rates: in Australia and New Zealand,
158–62, 167–72, 172–75
Rawson, Mary, 98, 98n
Real estate, 74, 88, 243. *See also* Build-
ings; Improvements; Land
—tax: effects on operating decisions,
69–73; effects on investment de-
cisions, 73–78; recommendations for,
78–79. *See also* General property tax
Redevelopment: definition of, 81; of
"grey areas," 119. *See* Buildings;
General property tax; Housing; In-
centives; Land value tax; Urban re-
newal
Reform, of taxes, 112–14. *See* Taxes
Regressivity, of general property tax, 12
Rehabilitation. *See* Housing
Remodeling. *See* Housing
Rent, 13, 21, 30–32, 34, 35, 49, 56, 65,
85, 87. *See also* Housing; Rent con-
trol
Rental housing. *See* Housing
Rent control: in New South Wales,
179–80; in Mexico City, 232
Replacement, of equipment, 66–67. *See
also* Equipment; Housing; Investment
Restrepo T., Alvaro, 211n
Restrepo U., Jorge, 211n
Rhoads, William G., 201n
Rhodes, Benjamin Franklin, Jr., 143n
Ricardo, David, 13, 18, 60
Robinson, Herbert W., 65n
Robinson, Joan, 13n
Rowlands, David T., 98, 98n

Sacks, Seymour, 98n
St. Andrew, Jamaica, 250
St. Ann, Jamaica, 249, 258, 273n
St. Catherine, Jamaica, 249, 258, 259,
273n

St. Elizabeth, Jamaica, 249
St. James, Jamaica, 250
St. Mary, Jamaica, 249
St. Thomas, Jamaica, 249
Sales ratio studies: in Australia and New Zealand, 166
San Francisco, California, 110
Santa Clara County, California, 95
Schwartz, Eli, 110n
Seligman, Edwin R. A., 11, 93, 120n
Seltzer, Lawrence H., 88n
Service rate: in Jamaica, 257, 271
Shapiro, Harvey, 13n
Shoup, Carl S., 73n, 227n, 241n, 274n
Silverman, Leon, 104n
Simon, Herbert A., 11n, 73, 73n, 122–23, 123n
Single-family housing: mentioned passim. See Housing
Site value, 246n
—tax: defined, 161; mentioned passim. See Land value tax
Slums: and taxation, 91–92, 125; in Australia and New Zealand, 175–80
Smith, Wallace F., 64n
Snyder, J. Herbert, 95n
Social programs: in Australia and New Zealand, 176
Special assessment tax, 134, 152, 294. See also Valorization tax
Special improvement levy, 228. See also Valorization tax
Speculation: in land, 110, 116, 117, 118, 119, 266; and property taxation, 120–23; and the valorization tax, 210n; in developing countries, 242. See also General property tax
Spillover benefits, 92–93, 117, 122
Sporn, Arthur D., 99n
Squatting, 153
Stanislaus County Weekly News, 143
Stockfisch, J. A., 55n
Storm, William B., 100n
Substitution effect, 209
Supply. See Land
Sydney, Australia, 179, 183, 269

Tangible personalty, 15, 17, 21, 23, 54, 73, 74
Tasmania, Australia, 170
Taxes: on intangibles, 15; burden of,

Taxes (continued)
57, 73; shifting of, 58, 62, 73–76, 123, 125; abatement of, 72–73, 77–78, 79, 173; reforms for, 79; on special assessments, 92–93, 150; on improvements, 125–26, 128, 289–90; on improved capital value, 158; on unimproved capital value, 158–61; rates of, 158–62, 167–72, 172–75; on assessed annual value, 162; transfer, 166, 192; in personam, 210, 229; base of, 246–47, 287. See also Asset–earnings taxes; General property tax; Income effect; Income tax; Land value tax; Price effect; Transportation; Valorization tax
—effect on: resource allocation, 57, 85–86; operating decisions, 69–73; investment decisions, 73–78; land use, 98; industrial location, 103. See also Neutrality
Tenure, 199
Thebarton, Australia, 93–94
Time-preference theory of interest, 59–60
Tolls, water: in California, 141
Townsend, Roswell G., 98n
Transactions demand for money, 36–44 passim, 46, 291, 292
Transfer taxes: in Australia and New Zealand, 166; in Chile, 192. See also Taxes
Transportation: affected by taxes, 126–27, 206–7
TRED conference, 63n, 77n
Trelawny, Jamaica, 249
Trinidad, 162, 269, 294
Turvey, Ralph, 23n, 222n, 282, 282n

Ullrich, Kurt, 195n
Unburdening effect of exempting improvements, 25, 27–28, 30–31, 34, 42, 287
Uniformity rule of taxation, 14
Unimproved land value tax. See Land value tax
—in Jamaica: transition to, 240–41; advantages of, for developing countries, 241–42; history of, 243–44; definition of base for, 245–49; feasibility of, 247–48; valuation proce-

—in Jamaica (*continued*)
dures for, 249–53; hardship and relief under, 253–57; rates and rate schedules for, 257–68; deductible from income tax, 261, 264, 265, 267; effect on land use, 262–63, 264; and progressivity, 263–68; and revenue problems, 268–70; and growth of tax base, 269; and the costs of development, 270–73; administrative simplifications made in, 273; evaluation of, 273–77; and economic development, 273–82; and tax exemptions, 282–85

United Kingdom, 162

Urban decay: and general property tax, 110–11. *See also* Slums; Urban renewal

Urbanization: in developing countries, 201, 204n

Urban land: market for, 118. *See* Land

Urban renewal, 119, 290–91; definition of, 81; history of, in United States, 81–83; and economic processes, 84–85; and Georgian economics, 85–89; application of land value taxation to, 89–96; and spillover benefits, 92–93; multiplier effect on, 93. *See also* Buildings; Housing; Incentives; General property tax; Land value tax; Urban decay

Urban sprawl, 94–95, 289. *See also* General property tax; Land value tax

Valorization tax: explanation of, 134; and special assessments, 134; theory of, 203–10; in Ecuador, 228–30; in Mexico City, 230–33
—in Colombia, 134, 294, 295, 296; importance of, 201–3; in urban areas, 203–7; in rural areas, 207; effects on investment and savings of, 207–8; incentive effects of, 208–10; effect on land use of, 209; substitution effect of, 209; administration of, 210; advantages of, 210; history and development of, 211–13; and local autonomy, 212; revenue importance of, 213–17; in Medellín, 217–22; in Bogotá, 222–25; in other Colombian

—in Colombia (*continued*)
areas, 225–28; on the basis of benefit, 233–34; appraisal of, 233–36; exemptions of, 234; earmarking of revenues under, 234–35; relation to other taxes on property, 235–36; effects on income distribution of, 236; role in economic development, 236–37

Valuation procedures: in Jamaica, 249–53. *See also* Assessment; General property tax; Land value tax

Value, 71–72. *See* Assessed annual value; Improved capital value; Land value tax; Site value tax; Taxes; Unimproved capital value
—of land. *See* Land

Valuer general, 163–64, 166, 182, 186, 249; qualifications for, 164–65

Veblen effect, 209n

Velez U., Juan, 211n

Venezuela, 274, 274n

Vernon, Raymond, 98n

Vickrey, William S., 127n

Victoria, Australia, 167, 182, 184

Wald, Haskell P., 207n

Walker, Mabel, 93n

Walker, W. P., 105n

Wealth, 49. *See also* Asset-earnings taxes
—tax: in Chile, 188–93

Wehrly, Max S., 98, 98n

Wellington, New Zealand, 178

Wert, James E., 110n

Westmoreland, Jamaica, 249

Whinston, Andrew B., 119n

White, William L., 239n

Wilson, James Q., 84n

Windfall gains, 241

Wingo, Lowdon, Jr., 115n, 206n

Winnick, Louis, 64, 64n, 77–78

Wiseman, J., 268, 268n

Wood, Robert C., 105n

Woodruff, A. M., 70n, 244n, 246n, 248, 269

Wright Act (1887), 140, 141, 145; effects of irrigation development under, 142–44

Zoning, 107, 200, 223, 275